THE WORK OF CULTURE

THE LEWIS HENRY MORGAN LECTURES / 1982

presented at
The University of Rochester
Rochester, New York

GANANATH
OBEYESEKERE

THE WORK OF CULTURE

SYMBOLIC TRANSFORMATION IN PSYCHOANALYSIS AND ANTHROPOLOGY

THE UNIVERSITY OF CHICAGO PRESS
Chicago and London

Gananath Obeyesekere is professor of anthropology at Princeton University.

The University of Chicago Press, Chicago 60637
The University of Chicago Press, Ltd., London

Printed in the United States of America
99 98 97 96 95 94 93 92 91 90 54321

Library of Congress Cataloging in Publication Data

Obeyesekere, Gananath.
The work of culture : symbolic transformation in psychoanalysis and anthropology / Gananath Obeyesekere.
p. cm. — (The Lewis Henry Morgan lectures ; 1982)
Includes bibliographical references.
1. Psychoanalysis and culture—Sri Lanka. 2. Symbolism (Psychology)—Case studies. 3. Buddhism—Psychology—Case studies. 4. Hinduism—Psychology—Case studies. 5. Sinhalese—Psychology—Case studies. I. Title. II. Series.
BF175.4.C84024 1990 90-10904
306—dc20 CIP
ISBN 0-226-61598-7 (cloth)
ISBN 0-226-61995-5 (pbk.)

♾ The paper used in this publication meets the minimum requirements of the American National Standard for Information Sciences—Permanence of Paper for Printed Library Materials, ANSI Z39.48–1984.

For Mel and Audrey Spiro
to celebrate
a friendship of the long run

CONTENTS

FOREWORD

Professor Obeyesekere delivered the 1982 Lewis Henry Morgan Lectures at the University of Rochester on March 16, 18, 23 and 25, with the title "Psychoanalytic Anthropology and Some Problems of Interpretation." The individual Lectures were, (1) After "Medusa's Hair": Progression and Regression in Personal Symbols; (2) Dromena and Cathartic Rituals: Regression and Progression in Collective Representations; (3) The Impact of Psychoanalysis on Anthropological Inquiry: Prospect and Retrospect; and (4) The Positivist Tradition in Psychoanalytic Anthropology: A Critique.

These original Lectures provided a highly condensed overview of his full set of arguments, which the present volume develops at length. Much that is here was presaged in two of Professor Obeyesekere's earlier books, *Medusa's Hair* and *The Cult of the Goddess Pattini.* Correlatively, these lectures hark back to those volumes, but do not require a knowledge of them on the part of a reader. Thus we are offered a masterly presentation that is a theoretically oriented study, the third volume in a trilogy, and simultaneously a work richly rewarding in its own terms.

Professor Obeyesekere undertakes to establish connections between culture and individuals' motivations, constructing his lectures from a daunting array of Sri Lankan materials set in relation to Freud, much anthropological work, and key philosophers. He argues for a particular kind of psychoanalytic anthropology, and for a revival of generalization in anthropology.

Despite its complexity and subtlety, this is a book which is accessible to individuals only tangentially concerned with psychoanalytic anthropology. For professionals in the field, and for other anthropologists as well, it will serve to define and bring into clear focus many issues of importance.

In addition to being a major contribution, this book will stimulate discussion and debate, as did Professor Obeyesekere's Lectures and seminars during his stay in Rochester. Those who heard and talked with him then will, recalling their own experiences, look forward to the lively and stimulating exchanges this book will evoke.

Alfred Harris, Editor
The Lewis Henry Morgan Lectures

ACKNOWLEDGMENTS

The Work of Culture was in the process of creation from 1982 to the present day, and during this period I have been in debt to many people for their comments, criticisms, and encouragement. I take this opportunity to thank my friend R. A. L. H. Gunawardana for information on Sri Lankan history, and Senake Bandaranayake and his dedicated students and assistants, for facilitating my research in Sigiriya. Tissa Kumara, my field assistant, became an indispensable resource for Sinhala literature, and also assisted me in collecting folk texts from the villages in and around Sigiriya. I am especially grateful to James Boon and Robert LeVine for reading the completed manuscript and making suggestions for its improvement, and to the two readers for the Press, whose criticisms also helped me to reorganize an overlong original manuscript to its present (still somewhat overlong!) size. My wife, Ranjini and my friend Ernestine McHugh read the manuscript in meticulous detail, and their critical gaze prevented horrendous lapses in style, usage, and argumentative rigor. Others who provided encouragement, inspiration, or helped me in tracking down references are Julie Taylor, Diane Eells, Nicholas Gier, Ray Fogelson, Stan Mumford, Mark Whitaker, H. L. Seneviratne, James Brow, and Richard Gombrich. I also recollect fondly the warmth and generous hospitality extended to my wife and me by Grace and Al Harris, and my other colleagues at the University of Rochester, when I went there to deliver the Lewis Henry Morgan Lectures in March 1982. Then there are those "invisible presences," ancestral heroes like Bakhtin and Foucault, who never directly appear in the text but are there nevertheless.

I owe a special debt to Pauline Caulk, research secretary of the Anthropology Department at Princeton for typing endless versions of this work from handwritten notes. She was in her quiet and unobtrusive fashion also an editor of sorts. The manuscript of this book was completed in the fall of 1988 but, for a variety of reasons, publication was inordinately delayed. Consequently, I am very grateful to the University of Chicago Press for expediting publication.

Among my contemporaries, several scholars have influenced me deeply. When I first went as a graduate student with a background in literature to the University of Washington in 1956, I knew a little bit about Freud. I had been fascinated by the Oedipal theory, the importance of sexuality in human life, and the whole idea of unconscious motivation. It seemed to make sense of my own psychic conflicts and of what I saw beneath the facade of gentility that governed the lives of close kinsmen in closed families. Most of us born and raised in South Asia know what most anthropologists who worked there do not recognize; inside intimate family arenas go on a hidden form of existence where violence (however covert or symbolic), sexual preoccupation and anxiety, and the play of power are omnipresent. This is the stuff for a future autobiographical ethnography, but suffice it here to say that it was Melville Jacobs who in 1956, in his course on "Culture and Personality," inspired me to read Freud further, and take medical-school courses in psychiatry given by a great teacher, Gert Heilbrunn. Subsequently, Melford E. Spiro joined the University of Washington; I have learned more psychoanalytic anthropology from Mel than from anyone else. Psychoanalytic anthropology was never, however, my exclusive preoccupation. My first book was *Land Tenure in Village Ceylon: A Sociological and Historical Study*, a revision of my Ph.D. thesis. Indirectly, that book also was a study of roots, of the kind of village society into which I was born, and which I left at age four, to study in private schools in Colombo. On the theoretical level, however, that book had nothing to do with psychoanalysis. As the title suggests, it was inspired by British social anthropology, especially the work of Edmund Leach. I continue to retain that sociological interest: there is no way that deep motivation can be studied outside of the frame of social institutions and of culture and history. In the present work I have defined my position in relation to both Spiro and Leach: I have rejected Spiro's view of psychoanalysis as a natural science for a hermeneutical, Diltheyan view of the nature of the human sciences, including psychoanalysis. I have rejected Leach's structuralism in favor of a more subject- and content-oriented stand. Ever since I knew him in 1964 in Cambridge, Leach has been a powerful intellectual stimulus for me. I am saddened by his recent death, for he was a man who possessed an intellectual honesty and a refreshing iconoclasm that never became nihilistic or destructive. In a review of Geertz's *Works and Lives* that appeared posthumously in the *American Ethnologist* of February 1989, his voice reaches us as fresh, clear, and undogmatic as ever:

> An ethnographic monograph has much more in common with an historical novel than with any kind of scientific treatise.

As anthropologists we need to come to terms with the now well-recognized fact that in a novel the personalities of the characters are derived from aspects of the personality of the author. How could it be otherwise? The only ego that I know at first hand is my own. When Malinowski writes about Trobriand Islanders he is writing about himself; when Evans-Pritchard writes about the Nuer he is writing about himself. Any other sort of description turns the characters of ethnographic monographs into clockwork dummies.

PREFACE

Studying Culture and Deep Motivation

This book is a product of considerable rethinking of the Lewis Henry Morgan lectures I delivered at the University of Rochester in March 1982.[1] One thrust of the original Morgan lectures was to make a plea for a hermeneutical reorientation of Freud for cultural anthropology. Hermeneutics is no longer a novelty and is now part of the anthropological lexicon. Parallel with the concern with hermeneutics was another epistemological thrust of the 1982 lectures, namely, a critique of "the positivist tradition in psychoanalytic anthropology"—the title of an entire lecture. This was a detailed examination of the work of Kardiner and those inspired by him. I have deleted this lecture entirely because I doubt this critique is all that important or relevant to social and cultural anthropologists, who are my primary audience here.[2]

However, in order to study the relation between culture and deep motivation it is necessary, I believe, to move away from Kardiner's "pathological model" of culture. Hence, some part of my original criticisms of Kardiner are relevant, and I shall address them here. Kardiner, in converting psychoanalysis into a positivist sociology, not only eliminated the importance of subjective perceptions, accidental occurrences, and psychic realities central to Freud's thought, but also analyzed symbolic forms on the model or analogy of psychopathology. This was a wrong move, that alienated cultural anthropologists. Yet it is difficult to escape from this model, insofar as psychoanalysis itself is concerned with pathology, even though Freud himself consistently blurred the distinction between the normal and the abnormal. Freud thought of culture as a product of psychic discontent, if not of pathology, but he did express concern about the dangers of viewing social groups on the pathological model.

> I would not say that an attempt of this kind to carry psychoanalysis over to the cultural community was absurd or bound to be fruitless. But we should have to be very cautious

> and not forget that, after all, we are only dealing with analogies and that it is dangerous, not only with men but also with concepts, to tear them apart from the sphere in which they have originated and evolved.[3]

He made further qualifications and then, as if directly anticipating Kardiner, added that "in spite of these [qualifications], we might expect that one day someone will venture to embark upon a pathology of cultural communities."[4]

The question is, how does one escape from this model, while using a theory that fundamentally concerns itself with the pathological? This is where Ricoeur's path-breaking book, *Freud and Philosophy,* helped.[5] It not only produced a hermeneutical reading of Freud, but also suggested a way of breaking out of the pathological model for the study of art, literature, and culture. Freudianism, Ricoeur argues, essentially deals with the archaic substrate of a symbolic form in a regressive movement. Yet implicit in Freud's theory of sublimation is the *progressive* transformation of infantile and archaic motivations into art, religion, and public culture. Progression and regression are dialectical movements that may be found in such elemental expressions as dreams and fantasy, and in more complex ways in numinous religious symbols.

Ricoeur's thesis has a double virtue. It retains the Freudian concern with "deep motivation," but disentangles it from individual pathology. On the other hand, it is implicitly critical of a naive anthropologism which refuses to recognize that symbolic forms might at some level deal with basic human problems of the sort that Freud highlighted: Oedipal conflicts, incest, castration, and other terrors originating in infancy and childhood. For Ricoeur, *Hamlet* is not a drama *about* the Oedipus complex; the protagonist's Oedipal motivations are the basis for creating a poetic drama on profound aporias of human existence.[6]

The anthropological hostility to Freud, especially in England and the United States, is much deeper than a simple resentment against the pathological model of culture. It is based on the assumption of a radical hiatus between public and private, the operative ideology of modern industrial man. Anthropologists carry this ideological stance to other cultures, even though they might recognize that this distinction does not hold elsewhere, at least in such a radical fashion. It is the "demystification of the world" in the modern West that has produced this condition where fantasy must remain private, rarely yielding to transformation into public culture. The private world of fantasy is shut off, closeted as it were, from public culture.

Yet there are, after all, life worlds in which people talk about their dreams; and other people readily interpret them. This is but one conduit between the public and the private, between fantasy and culture. In South Asia, it is not the absence of private worlds that is at issue, but rather the movement back and forth between private and public. In this situation, the manner in which deep motivation gets transformed at every level into symbolic forms that in turn influence the structuralization of the unconscious, emerges as a significant problem for cultural anthropology. Concomitantly the strategy of analysis must also shift to the individual as the maker of symbolic forms. In consequence, case study becomes significant for psychoethnography as it is for psychoanalysis.

"The work of culture" is the process whereby symbolic forms existing on the cultural level get created and recreated through the minds of people. It deals with the formation and transformation of symbolic forms, but it is not a transformation without a subject as in conventional structural analysis. Furthermore the work of culture is not confined to deep motivation in the Freudian sense. While the symbolic transformation of the images of the unconscious into public culture is the main focus of these lectures, I do not confine myself to this exclusive domain. For example, in lecture two I show how the Gaṇeśa "family myth," itself a transformation of Oedipal motivations in the Hindu family, can produce a historical dialectic or "debate" which in turn yields alternative myth versions that have nothing to do with the deep motivations that instigated the original myth. In this case "debate" is the work of culture that produces a certain type of symbolic transformation in history.

The present Morgan lectures resemble the original set only in spirit, not in substance. Not only did I delete one lecture, but I have also rearranged the lectures and added much that is new. I have retained the format of four lectures, but each lecture is really a composite of several lectures, or a highly expanded version of a single lecture, delivered at various universities during 1982–1986. Lectures 1 and 2 of the original Morgan lectures are now fused into the first lecture of the book. Lectures 2 and 3 are new, though inspired by the original Morgan lectures. Most of the original lecture 4 is retained in the present lecture 4, but is supplemented with extra material. Given these circumstances, this book has no single theme. The idea of "the work of culture" helps unify it, but only as a leitmotif. There are many themes, many voices. Thus, ethnographically speaking, the book has a central concern with Sri Lanka and South Asia, Buddhism and Hinduism. The first lecture deals with "ritual," the second with "myth," and the third with "history," while the last probes into the methodological and theoretical problems pertaining to the deep motivational analysis of these arbitrarily and falsely defined substantive domains. Oedipal problems appear as a pervasive theme in all four lectures, and everywhere is the master argument with the master himself.

In this situation, I think it useful to appraise the reader very briefly of my argument with Freud spelled out in this book.

For me the critical breakthrough in Freud is *The Interpretation of Dreams* (1900) along with the great case studies that employed the "first topography" of the systems unconscious, preconscious, and consciousness.[7] This first topography contains concepts and ideas that are not too tied to European thought and hence could be employed to study cultures that place a premium on unconscious processes. I limit psychoanalysis in cultural anthropology to understanding the interrelationship between deep motivation and culture. Consequently a great deal of ego psychology is not relevant for my purpose.

I also think that the structural theory or the second topography of ego-id-superego is at best of limited value in the study of other cultures, since it locks us into a compartmentalist view of the mind and into the very Cartesianism that Freud initially broke away from.

If this is the case, self-theories such as Kohut's aggravate the latent Cartesianism and align psychoanalysis with English language games in which the reflexive prefix "self" abounds.[8] I emphasize "English" since this may not be the case even in other European languages. The French analyst Pontalis asks whether the concept of "self" can be exported elsewhere even though the French language has an equivalent in *soi.*[9] I agree; "self" theories, whether Kohut's or Mead's, must result in too radical an appropriation of other minds into Anglo-American language games and life-forms.

My concern with language games and forms of life connects with Wittgenstein, who is an important philosophical presence in this book. But I borrow only those ideas of Wittgenstein that I think are relevant to opening up the Freud texts for cultural anthropology. Hence, "family resemblance" is my way of escape both from a universalist view of Freudian propositions and from a positivist view of the comparative method. Thus, an important argument in the book is that the Western Oedipus complex is but one form of life among many others that exhibit "family resemblances" within or across cultures. This is admittedly a clear departure from Freud, but I justify it from my reading of both Freud and texts from Buddhism and Hinduism. I believe this liberates us from a straightjacket of a single universalist Oedipus complex into a more humane and richer view of other life worlds. However, I do not know whether the "fiction" I have created is any truer than Freud's.

Once one doubts the usefulness of the second topography and the universalist Oedipus, one can question other basic Freudian frameworks such as the theory of the instincts and the mechanistic language games in which that theory is embodied. Yet, in spite of my criticism of the drive theory, I go on to justify the Freudian metapsychology, in terms of its nomological structure, as the type of metatheory useful for cultural anthropology. I do this in the fourth lecture, where I engage in a critical reading of key Freudian texts.

This last lecture posed special difficulties regarding what I could say about Freud and cultural anthropology. The topic is so vast that some limiting formula was required—hence my idea of the three intersubjective realms the psychoanalyst and anthropologist must be involved in. To borrow a metaphor from Sophocles' *Oedipus,* the "three intersubjectivities" are the crossroads where the cultural anthropologist must meet Freud if he is to undertake any kind of serious psychoethnography. First, there are those intersubjective relationships bound by common values prevailing in the group that he studies. To study this realm of intersubjective relationships, the ethnographer must use himself as a tool. But he is not a tool; thus a second thrust of my inquiry in the last lecture is whether psychoanalysis can throw light on the subject-object relationship that prevails in this "second intersubjectivity." Third, the anthropologist is involved in a variety of other audiences with whom he must communicate by virtue of his profession as ethnographer and theorist. Most significant in this third intersubjective realm is communication with his colleagues, without which there can be no real expansion of knowledge. Hence the question: What kind of theory is helpful for studying the first and second intersubjectivities that simultaneously permits me to engage in a dialogue with my colleagues and beyond that reach into the world of contemporary culture?

The fourth lecture is, to use a Buddhist metaphor, "against the current" in several ways. It is against the kind of positivist science of the sort that Grünbaum advocates; yet it does make a plea for a special, though limited, kind of generalizing strategy for the human sciences that goes against the current climate of particularism and radical deconstruction. It makes a case for a Weberian stance that permits a thinker to achieve a theoretical mastery of the world through the use of increasingly abstract concepts or, to use the terms employed in this book, through metatheories and metalanguages that are not yet artificial languages divorced from ordinary speech.[10] It recognizes a need for evidence and validation but not for falsification in a strict Popperian sense, and certainly not for experimental and statistical verification.

The last lecture assumes that as thinkers, and as ordinary human beings, we have an ontological propensity to argue on political and social issues on the basis of the adequacy of evidence; even postmodernists generalize all the time about life and the world the moment they escape the specific context-bound and politically circumscribed arena from which their specialized discourses emanate. Some of us may even unwittingly descend into occasional abstract philosophizing on issues of existential significance. A critical examination of particularizing discourses, formal or informal, shows that they contain implicit generalizing assumptions. The very notion of cultural relativism is an ontological conception of man and culture that does not exist, as far as I know, in philosophical traditions outside the West. This recognition does not imply that I ignore the uncertainty regarding knowledge in any firm sense; I only object to the inference made from particularizing discourses in recent thought that denies all generalized understanding or interpretation on the basis of some generalized conception about the impossibility of such an understanding!

Theory, as I use the term in this book, provides a body of concepts ("metalanguage") to understand human life and culture. It employs ethnographic description and evidence with a willingness to justify and validate one's assertions empirically. In my view ethnography involves an existential or ontological quest on the part of the author. Consequently ethnographic understanding possesses an inner affinity with literature and philosophy but is similar to neither. This assumption is closer to the hermeneutical thought of scholars such as Dilthey, Max Weber, and Ricoeur than to very recent postmodern thought. My critical reexamination of the Freudian metatheory is to make a tentative attempt to fuse particularity and thick description with a more generalizing and conceptual framing of issues pertaining to human life and existence. Such issues are rooted in our time and place and are in fact meaningless if they are not; yet they may transcend them, too, in a variety of ways, though it is not possible for us historically determined creatures to determine this as we write about these issues.

The questions that I have raised above in respect to psychoanalysis have posed for me a major difficulty, namely, that almost anything one can say about Freud has been said already by someone, somewhere. Thus many of the specific issues that I raise in this book have been addressed by others, for example, by Lacan or Kohut or Pontalis or Winnicott or Erikson or Jacobson or Fairbairn or Bettelheim or Klein (Melanie) or Klein (George) or Schafer or the French (non-Lacanians), and all sorts of historians, feminists, literary critics, and occasionally an anthropologist. So what else is new? Perhaps nothing: maybe the only originality I can profess is to claim that I have selectively put together the various critiques and revisions of Freud that now lie scattered, into another vision for studying South Asian and other cultures. I also did not arrive at this vision through an argument with Freud's disciples, followers, and critics, but rather through a confrontation with the master himself. In doing this (I have been told) I will probably please none and anger some; diplomacy, however, is best left to other professionals.

While my own attitude to Freud is influenced by contemporary hermeneutics, critical theory, and postmodern thought, I resist applying any of these labels to myself. Yet if there is anything that recent thought has taught me, it is the idea that a text is not sacrosanct, and its reading is not fixed. Great social thinkers like Marx, Freud, and Weber spoke with many voices. To limit Freud's thought to a positivist, or a hermeneutical, or any other mold, is to silence these voices. I try to resurrect a "multiple Freud" in such a way as to produce eventually a version or reading of Freud that I think is useful for the study of symbolic forms in the cultures of South Asia that I am familiar with. Another thinker, in another time and place, might want to produce other readings. I think it a mistake to search for an essential Freud, as Lacan does, even as he breaks away from Freud.

A recent attempt to channel Freud in another essentialist and "authoritarian" direction is Grünbaum's *The Foundations of Psychoanalysis.*[11] Since I do not deal with this influential thesis in any of the four lectures, let me briefly consider it here. Grünbaum's argument is that Freud was a self-conscious natural scientist formulating his ideas very much in the spirit of contemporary physics. If so, he should be judged by criteria of falsification prevalent in the natural sciences, and Grünbaum adds that psychoanalysis fails miserably on this score. I think this is a caricature of Freud, who was too complex a person and too radical a thinker to fit into Grünbaum's narrow mold.

Not only is Grünbaum irrelevant to my project, but his criticism of hermeneutics is also, I believe, wide of the mark. He thinks Ricoeur misunderstood or misinterpreted Freud, whereas Ricoeur states clearly that his is a deliberate reinterpretation, or an appropriation of Freud. Grünbaum proceeds with a gratuitously insulting and intemperate attack on fellow scholars Habermas and Ricoeur, in a language peppered with castration metaphors—"ideological surgery," "amputation," "mutilation," "emasculation" are some of his favorite words. He denounces Ricoeur and Habermas for engaging in a "denunciation" of natural science:[12] something neither of them does. Furthermore, Grünbaum thinks he has demolished hermeneutics by his critique of Habermas and Ricoeur: but surely, even if Grünbaum's criticisms are valid, his thesis only proves that Habermas's and Ricoeur's interpretations of Freud's work were wrong, and not that hermeneutics per se is wrong. The fact that Grünbaum shows that, contrary to Habermas and Ricoeur, Freud is a self-conscious positivist, has nothing to do with the validity of hermeneutics as an approach to the human sciences. To do this Grünbaum must tackle some of the *philosophical* premises and assumptions of hermeneutics. These are quite varied and even disparate, but general agreement is possible on some issues, namely, on the nature of the subject-object relationship; the problems that arise when one studies subjects who have ideas similar to that of the investigator; the difficulty of operationalizing symbolic forms characterized intrinsically by a surplus of meaning, which operationalism is not; the idea of the hermeneutic circle. Grünbaum speaks of a "hermeneutical construal"—but there is no such thing. Like the equally dirty word "positivism," hermeneutics is no single or simple thing, though we have to use this word, as we have to use the word "positivism" in order to argue a position or present a case. Modern hermeneutics is essentially a post-nineteenth-century phenomenon that contains many viewpoints that have not yet been formalized into a credo like that of the Vienna school of logical positivism. Hermeneutical thinkers are, however, agreed that the simplistic transposition of natural science models and methods to the human sciences is wrong. Grünbaum sidesteps this issue by arguing that, contrary to Habermas and Ricoeur, psychoanalysis is a natural science—as if that mattered for the central problems of method (or lack thereof) in the human sciences that hermeneutics concerns itself with.

The most disquieting aspect of Grünbaum's work is his uncompromising dogmatism. It is as if he is not willing to recognize that knowledge can exist outside of the "scientific" enterprise. Hermeneutics, it is well known, sprang from biblical interpretation, but modern hermeneutics is not anchored to any form of faith. It is a method of open inquiry and also a method for opening fields of inquiry that seem to defy, or poorly fit, natural science explanations or models. Paradoxically, however, Grünbaum's own scientific philosophy expresses a closed mind. He insists that psychoanalysis must "rely on modes of inquiry that were refined from time honored canons of causal inference pioneered by Francis Bacon and James Stuart Mill."[13] The primary meaning of "canon," according to the Oxford dictionary, is "a rule, decree or law of the church"; and though this word has been extended to cover similar rules in science and literary criticism, it still carries an aura of sanctity. While for Grünbaum scientific methods are based on "time honored canons," the very discipline that emerged from biblical exegesis questions the applicability of time-honored methodological canons to the human sciences. Since the world is full of such paradoxes I think it appropriate to end this reflection by juxtaposing the *scientific philosopher's* reification of "time honored canons of causal inference" with the open voice of a *religious teacher,* the Buddha.

> Yes, Kālāmas, it is right for you to doubt, it is right for you to waver. In a doubtful matter, wavering has arisen. Come, O Kālāmas, do not accept anything on mere hearsay. Do not accept anything by mere tradition. Do not accept anything on account of rumors. Do not accept anything just because it accords with your scriptures. Do not accept anything by mere supposition. Do not accept anything by mere inference. Do not accept anything by merely considering the appearances. Do not accept anything merely because it seems acceptable.[14]

LECTURE ONE

◐

Representation and Symbol Formation in a Psychoanalytic Anthropology

1

Unfreezing the Text, Releasing the Narrative

In my book *Medusa's Hair,* I made the following observation: "There is no terminal point to my interviews, since the lives of my informants haven't ended. This essay perforce must be open-ended."[1] I shall start these Morgan lectures with something that happened to a major informant of mine soon after that book was written, something that triggered a series of reflections regarding the theory of personal symbols I advanced there. As an anthropologist my thoughts are conditioned by the data that I deal with, as the data themselves are conditioned by my abstractions. Unlike mathematicians, logicians, and other purveyors of purely abstract thought, anthropologists use their data to think with. My recent thinking about the data of anthropology has been very much influenced by the work of hermeneutical philosophers from Dilthey to Ricoeur who have rejected the various brands of positivist thought in the human sciences. This in turn has forced me to reflect on the positivist and empiricist traditions in psychoanalytic anthropology. In this lecture (and in others that follow) I shall try to communicate to you the impact of my rereading of Ricoeur's path-breaking book *Freud and Philosophy.*[2] As I was rereading Ricoeur, for the *n*th time, things were also happening to my informant Tuan Sahid Abdin, and Ricoeur and Abdin in turn forced me to revise, or rather to add a new dimension to, my theory of personal symbols.

So let me now come to Abdin's problems. Those of you who have read *Medusa's Hair* will recall that Abdin is a forty-four-year-old Muslim ecstatic who, regularly every year, at the annual festival for this god in July-August, hangs himself on hooks suspended from a scaffold erected on a cart, in abject surrender to Skanda, the great Hindu-Buddhist god, the son of Śiva himself. This act, which he repeats year after year, is due to a vow that he made in 1961 when, as a private in the army, he was accused of having participated in a coup planned by his superior officers against the government. Abdin was incarcerated in a cell with a Sinhala-Buddhist, Corporal X; one day the two of them made vows to Skanda to perform *pūjā*s in his honor if they were acquitted. Corporal X said that he would give the god a coconut sapling, a token of a life, his own life, in gratitude to the god, while Abd˙ made an entirely different vow: he would hang on hooks every year during the annual festivities for the god at Kataragama. Here were two people in the identical plight making radically different vows, and both were acquitted! The god will accept a coconut or a dangerous penance, a tray of fruit or a vow to walk on hot coals. What is given to the god is not the god's wish but the devotee's own deep motivation.

In my book I related Abdin's drastic vow to the terror he felt about his father. Abdin's father had two wives, one barren and the other excessively fertile. Abdin was given to the first, barren wife, Reyanthumma, who brought him up from infancy. When Abdin was four, the co-wives quarrelled and Reyanthumma left the household and lived alone with Abdin. For many years Abdin thought that his mater was also his genetrix. Abdin had little contact with his father, but when he did the consequences were traumatic for him.

1. About two years after his mother left the household, Abdin had a frightening encounter with his father. One day he played truant from school with a "younger brother." While they were loafing in the streets they saw an old man pull a handcart along the road. The two boys held the cart from behind, not allowing the old man to pull his cart. His father happened to see this; he picked up a stick and hit Abdin and squeezed his ear hard until it hurt badly. "He hit me twice, hard, with the stick on my thigh; he said he'd kill me if I did this kind of thing again and played truant from school." Abdin was frightened by his father's threat.

2. When Abdin was about twelve, his father saw him gamble at cards with some neighborhood kids. His father was in a coffee shop and summoned Abdin there. Abdin refused and went to a neighboring house. Abdin's father went there, got hold of him, and asked him to hold out his hand and swear he'd never gamble again. Then he took a knife and hit Abdin on the wrist with it. The cut was not very deep, but bled badly. The lady of the house took Abdin to a Malay doctor who stitched his wound. She told the doctor that Abdin had cut his hand with a broken glass.

In my book I interpreted Abdin's penance in terms of his deep motivation, especially his fear of his father. In prison Abdin was in a desperate situation: his life itself was at stake. He therefore sought the help of a powerful god, but the vow indicated abject surrender to the god, self-abnegation, and then punishing himself to please the deity and obtain his help. The cultural ideology governing this act is that of filial piety. The son surrenders to the father who then forgives him even though he has done wrong. In fulfilling his vow he is performing a public act in a special arena and simultaneously abreacting events from his past. He is repeating an earlier act of being beaten by the father, but this time he punishes himself, repeating the earlier experiences but reversing them. Yet on the other hand it is the god who is punishing him, perhaps for evil parricidal thoughts Abdin may have had when his father threatened to kill him. His father first beat him when he was mischievously trying to stop an old man from pulling his car. Now Abdin recaptures that experience when he draws the cart in surrender to another powerful father figure, the stern lord of Kataragama. Underlying all of these motivations may be other earlier and equally traumatic events in Abdin's relationship with his father in the first four years of childhood, but of these we know nothing. The father who makes the adult Abdin bow his head in fear could not possibly have been a benevolent figure to the child Abdin.

I wish to add a further comment on my earlier account: the only job that Abdin is capable of doing with any measure of regularity is that of a knife sharpener! The mode of practicing this profession once again capitalizes on the early trauma. His grinding stone and other implements of his profession are mounted on a cart which he pushes around in the upper- and middle-class neighborhoods of the city.

When Abdin joined the army in 1958 he needed a birth certificate, and Reyanthumma, his mother, told him to get it from his father. This he did. He also learned that his biological mother was his father's second wife, posing new problems of identity to an already confused youth. During his imprisonment his father visited him several times, and after his release he reestablished contacts with his father and his second mother. Around 1970 Abdin, with his present wife (his third) and his daughter, moved to a house across from his father's. About this time he started to perform a special ritual of countersorcery, the salient features of which I shall briefly present now.

The ritual starts at 6:00 P.M. in one of the rooms of the patient's house. An image of the goddess Kālī made out of flour and turmeric is lying on the floor, smothered in flowers and fruits. Incense sticks are burning by her side. The image is dressed in red cloth (*sāri*); the goddess is depicted in her terrifying form, her tongue protruding and painted red (depicting blood), her two canines (made with garlic) also protruding. An offering of largely red flowers and fruit is placed before her. The patient is lying on a mat beside the goddess. Other inmates of the house are in the back of the room or clustered around the doorway. Abdin's assistant, Albert, is also present with a small drum slung from his shoulder. At about 6:10 P.M. Abdin, wearing a red cloth like the goddess herself, sits on the floor before the offering. At a certain point in the ritual Abdin utters an invocation to Kālī. "Īśvarī, *ammā,* I now call you Issakeyi, Adiye, the very bad Nīli, I call you *ammā,* I call you the burning fire, the one who did terrible things in the cemetery . . . who controls the cemetery and performs black vengeance magic (*pali*), Oṃ Kālī, I call you bloody (*uthirai*) Mahā Kālī, I call you mother, *ammā,* who takes a blood sacrifice. . . ." When Kālī is mentioned Abdin begins to stutter. He now refers to her constantly as *ammā* (mamma), and also as Bhagavatī from Malayalam country. He spreads out his hands, as if pleading, "*Ammā,* here is an innocent child. *Caranam* (refuge), *caranam, ammā* please banish all my forests (i.e., troubles) my mother forgive my bad tongue (bad words), *ammā, ammā* Malayalam Bhagavatī *ammā* Īśvarī, *caranam, caranam,* I call you, *ammā* ruler of the land of Malayalam, the one with the thousand eyes, Īśvarī, *ammā* protect this poor child . . . *ammā* this innocent child. . . ."

Soon he chants, in his wonderful polyglot, again staring at the image and catching his breath several times as he chants. He sobs as his body starts to shake. Meanwhile his assistant fogs the room with thick incense. Abdin is seated before the image of the goddess, his body shaking, while his assistant sings and plays the drum. He faces the image, staring at the goddess, trembling. Still staring at the goddess's lolling tongue, Abdin protrudes his own tongue and cuts it in a few places. Blood oozes from the weals and stains his chin. He now asks for a torch—a stick wrapped in cloth at the end and dipped in coconut oil. Abdin takes the lighted torch and holds it against his chest. He then hits himself on the face mercilessly with the palm of his other hand. Then he burns his chest with the torch once more. He now holds the torch over the patient's head and incenses it. In the other hand he has a knife. The time now is 6:45 P.M. Abdin once more slashes his tongue, more so than on the previous occasion. Blood oozes profusely from his wounded mouth and spreads all over his chest. Now Abdin's bloody tongue lolls out just like that of the goddess. He then places the torch over the patient's head in a gesture of blessing, puts the burning end of the torch in his mouth, and shouts again (but not in pain). Abdin repeats twice again the "torch-eating" act. He now stares intently at the goddess, holding a lime in one hand and the knife over the patient's head, and after touching the patient's head with the lime, he cuts it. Prior to cutting the lime, he points the knife at the deity and hoots. Seven limes are cut in the same fashion. Someone brings a coconut; he incenses it; its fumes engulf his face. He beckons to the patient and makes a long prophecy. After this, the patient holds the coconut, then returns it to Abdin, who balances it precariously on his palm and places some ash on it. Meanwhile Albert is singing in the background. Abdin starts to prophesy again; after this he smashes the coconut on the cement floor. He tells the patient that his troubles will soon be over: ". . . if you do not think I am Kālī, think that it is someone who eats a dead body . . . hear, there, *caranam.*" Then he starts crying in uttermost agony, "*Ammā, ammā,* beat me and control me, *caranam ammā, ammā*"; his body bent forward, crouched, hands over head, "*ammā, ammā,*" he wails and collapses.

After a brief interval he repeats this action and in addition takes a coconut and hits his head with it till the nut breaks. He constantly catches his breath like an asthmatic patient. The ritual ends with his spraying ash on the goddess. Soon he utters another prophecy; then he shouts as if in great pain—*ammā, ammā* (mother, mother)—his body twitches spasmodically. His two hands seem knotted together; he shouts to the drummer to release him; the drums stop, and Abdin sprawls on the floor in a faint.

If hanging on hooks has its ontogenetic roots in Abdin's relationship with his father, tongue cutting has to do with his identification with the goddess based on a prior infantile identification with the mother. Appropriately, in the first he is hung on skewers but does not bleed; in the second he bleeds profusely. Perhaps the personal symbol that ties the two ritual enactments is head bashing, which he practices in both—as castration vis-à-vis his father and renouncing his maleness vis-à-vis his mother. In the second ritual he catches his breath; he pleads with the mother. The mother in the infantile consciousness is both good and bad; in the Kālī ritual the evil, castrating image of the mother is predominant, as Carstairs has noted also for his North Indian village.[3] In other Kālī rituals that he performs he shouts obscenities at the goddess: "When I perform sorcery rituals I scold her. I call her *vēsi* (prostitute), *bälli* (bitch); and then she is good and I obtain her love." Again: "If you invoke her with love she'll not possess you. You must insult her. I am also afraid of her. She eats corpses and drinks blood. . . . I must scold her." In everyday reality Abdin loves his mother; in the ritual, the darker aspect of that relationship is acted out.

It should be noted that he performed this ritual for the first time when he moved to a house across from his father's and reestablished a relationship with his biological mother. It was a time when his puzzlement over his identity would have posed problems of meaning for him. To add to these problems was his psychogenic impotence, which I think was based on his identification with his mother, such that all intercourse with women was for him tantamount to incest. He now resolves his confusions of identity by affirming his true being; he symbolically castrates himself, menstruates through his mouth, renounces his male identity, and unequivocally, if only temporarily, becomes his own mother, as he also becomes, on another level, the goddess Kālī helping those afflicted with the malevolent effects of sorcery.

When an anthropologist writes an ethnography he freezes the events of his narrative in time. But unlike in fiction or in other forms of literary narrative, the closure of the ethnographic world is merely a necessity of one's trade. Life continues to go on in the world one has of necessity shut out. To ask what happened to Stephen Daedalus after the last line in *Ulysses* is as absurd as asking, in naive fashion, how many children had Lady Macbeth. But it is not absurd to ask what goes on in the field the anthropologist has vacated, for the empirical life world knows no closure. Therefore let me consider Abdin's life after I had, admittedly very reluctantly, closed the book on him with *Medusa's Hair*.

Subsequent events in fact confirmed my hypotheses regarding Abdin's relationship with his father. Abdin's father had been bedridden for some time, having suffered from a stroke; he died in June 1979. His mater, Reyanthumma, had died a few months earlier, and I had paid for their funeral expenses. In August 1979 Abdin and I planned to visit Kataragama for the annual festival; but Abdin refused to come! For the first time since 1961 he missed the festival, and failed to hang himself on hooks on the scaffold in the cart in surrender to the god. Given my previous interpretation of Abdin's case history the conclusion was irresistible: the death of the father seemed to remove the infantile terror he had for him during his life; concomitantly he seemed to lose his fear of the god, at least sufficiently enough for him to forego the vow he had made seventeen years ago. His action was most unusual. The god of Kataragama is held in fear and awe by most people; to renege on a vow is unthinkable without permission from the god himself and a host of ameliorative ritual activities. Yet Abdin did so, seemingly without hesitation. However, his action seems too good to be true, since the terror of the father cannot easily be removed by his death, for it is something implanted in the infantile consciousness. And Abdin clearly felt guilt for his action since soon afterwards he went to a *local* shrine for the god in the city of Colombo and hung on hooks there!

In November of that year Abdin suffered a further mishap. I received a letter addressed to me in the United States from my lawyer in Sri Lanka to say that Abdin had collapsed while he was pushing his cart which contained the paraphernalia of his trade as knife sharpener. He was taken to the hospital, and the doctors diagnosed his illness as a stroke that had rendered his left side paralyzed. Physicians in Sri Lanka, as in the West, were ignorant of the possible psychogenic causation of "paralysis" and simply diagnosed his disease as a stroke. I wrote back to my lawyer and urged him to help Abdin with his medical expenses, but I also stated that I did not think it was a stroke at all but probably a case of conversion hysteria, or hysterical paralysis. I felt that the "stroke" was too much of a coincidence, since his father also suffered from one which left his left side paralyzed. I also asked my field assistant to visit him. He found Abdin in the same wheelchair used by his father. Knowing Abdin as well as I did I felt that he was suffering from guilt over the death of his father and of course the guilt from having broken the vow to another father, the divine father at Kataragama. I felt that he was performing a different kind of penance, a penance acted out on the level of symptom rather than symbol. When I came back to Sri Lanka in the summer of 1980 I met Abdin once again. He was a pathetic figure, unshaven, dressed in filthy clothes. He dragged his feet, and walked with great difficulty because of his "paralyzed" left side. He was full of self-pity and was very pleased to see me, for I was, in the special transference situation that obtained in our fieldwork relationship, the good father, a providential figure that helped him out in his life's travail.

I will not get into the details of what transpired during our reunion; suffice it to say that Abdin felt that his paralysis was due to sorcery practiced by envious neighbors, and perhaps he would feel better if he went to Kataragama for this year's festival and performed *pūjā*s for the god. I encouraged him in this; he went to Kataragama a few days prior to the festival and made special offerings to the god and stayed on for the whole duration of the festival. He hung on hooks on the scaffold attached to a cart, and on several occasions he dragged the cart on hooks attached to his back from one end of the festival premises to the other. In addition (to my dismay) he got his young daughter also to hang on hooks. By the end of the festival he could walk reasonably well, and by the time I left for the United States, in late September, he was completely normal. In December 1986, when I was revising this account, he was still without symptoms (though he had other physical problems).

How then did Abdin's recent problems, in conjunction with my reading of Ricoeur, affect my theory of personal symbols and, let me add, my view of the nature of psychological symbols in general? Abdin was engaged in a cultural performance when he was hanging on hooks and cutting his tongue: his actions were perfectly intelligible on the cultural level to members of his society. Yet these were performances practiced by the very few (sometimes not more than five or six persons) in the special arena of Kataragama. Arena culture—the culture that operates in an exclusively marked physical area—though not operative for most members of a society, is recognized by them as legitimate. In this case Abdin was abreacting his infantile past and using the pregiven cultural symbol system to express and bring some order to and control over his psychic conflicts. Yet there were features of Abdin's life that seemed different from my studies of other ecstatics.

In his most recent experiences Abdin reverted to the level of symptom from the level of symbol: he desisted from practicing his penance and suffered instead from a "conversion hysteria." When he resumed his penance, the hysterical symptoms disappeared. Abdin has a serious problem on his hands: he no longer wants to hang on hooks but he must! In 1981 he adopted an acceptable compromise: he went to the festival, made his obeisance to the deity with an offering, *but did not hang on hooks.* He went again in 1982 and 1983 but hung on hooks only once. Since then he has gone to Kataragama regularly but has only rarely hung on hooks.

Abdin's experience led me to reflect once again on the nature of the personal symbols he employs: they have a repetitive character and possess a compulsive motivation for him. In other words these symbols operate very much like neurotic symptoms and fit Freud's neat characterization of neurotic behavior as "repetition compulsion" owing to the "return of the repressed." Furthermore, even his penances entail body mutilation, bringing them, on the gross phenomenological level at least, close to the symptom. It is certainly possible to express notions of mutilation and castration in a totally indirect symbolic idiom radically different from actual acts of mutilation. I believe that symbolic formation can occur on various levels and in various degrees of remove from psychic origins. The symbolic idiom in Abdin's case is phenomenologically close to its counterparts in symptom formation; they share common features so that under certain conditions of psychic stress, symbol can revert to symptom and vice versa.

In my original analysis of Abdin's case I pointed out that he was not successful as a ritual specialist and interpreted his lack of success in sociocultural terms. He was a Javanese Muslim practicing a Hindu craft frowned upon by the mosque authorities as well as by the elites of the Muslim-Javanese society of Colombo. I also noted that he could not even hold a secular job consistently, except that of knife sharpener, which he has sporadically held and now seems to have practiced successfully for the last several years. I would now like to postulate an added psychological reason for his lack of focus, an inability to function consistently even as a part-time priest: he has not exorcised his own past, the pressures of his infantile history have not been resolved through the symbol system, and they continue to exercise control over his everyday existence.

Not so with many other ecstatic priests and priestesses whom I have studied over the years. Let me present you with a brief ideal typical sketch of the manner in which personal symbols are employed by the priestesses in my earlier study. In all of the cases, and in many more in my unpublished field notes, there is one major symbolic sequence—the individual suffers a spirit attack, she withers away and becomes skin and bone, she experiences terrifying visions, her body shakes as she becomes possessed, she runs away from home and acts very much like the demon within her. I have interpreted this dark night of the soul type of experience as a product of primary guilt and expiation. In all of these cases the patients had a common antecedent history: a betrayal of a loved one. A woman elopes and runs away from home; the parent of the loving kinsman dies; the woman cannot attend the funeral. Guilt; the dead relative becomes a vengeful spirit and attacks the living. Admittedly this betrayal is not a childhood one, but the later event was in turn based on earlier childhood loves, hates, and betrayals. The possessing spirit now punishes the patient for betrayal. The patient in turn suffers pain of mind and body and gradually overcomes this dark experience through a kind of penance and expiation. After the expiation of guilt the attacking, hostile ancestor takes on a benevolent and loving form and becomes a guardian spirit of the patient. The patient herself ultimately triumphs over privation, guilt, and loss and becomes a priestess. Her possession was initially demonic: it is now converted into a divine propensity and legitimated as such by the gods themselves. She has also effected a role transformation: she has given up her earlier mundane roles and role relationships and has become a priestess helping others in misfortune. She renounces ordinary domesticity and her ordinary sexuality for a devotional-erotic relationship with a divinity. She lives in grim physical surroundings in the slums of the city, but this everyday physical and social reality is of little consequence, for the true reality is her spiritual experiences with the gods in such ecstatic states as visions and trances. Once again the drama of the patient is a subjective and an objective one at the same time: deep motivations are being canalized and objectified in a culturally constituted symbol system.

This interpretation also holds good for a food that many ascetics typically consume during this period of the dark night—crushed margosa leaves mixed with milk. Margosa leaves are extremely bitter. Thus the patient consumes "bitter milk," a punishment for the betrayal of a loved one. Moreover margosa leaves are applied by mothers on their nipples to wean children. Hence it is a symbol that sends taproots into the archaic past; it is the bitter milk associated with rejection. On the cultural level this food indicates the ecstatic's ascetic disdain for everyday food; it is also, one may add, on the medical level, a cooling food to calm the heat of demonic possession and attack.

Now consider the use of personal symbols in the ideal typical case of the priestess, in contrast to Abdin's. There is clearly repetition, a repetition of an archaic episode: but not repetition compulsion, or an obsessive-compulsive performance. The patient drinks bitter milk during her dark night, but this act is not repeated in the compulsive manner of Abdin's. The spirit of a dead relative attacks her, and she suffers terribly; but this act is not repeated either, but *overcome*. Furthermore, and this is most important, unlike in Abdin's case, the transcendence of the act (the fact that it is not repeated) does not result in the emergence of a symptom, for the experience of the dark night of spirit attack has helped the priestess to exorcise her demons and with them the terror of the past.

A symbol and a symptom contain both motive and meaning, but whereas a symptom is under the domination of motive, a symbol is under the rule of meaning. This distinction between motive and meaning is purely provisional, for I plan to muddy it later. When I say that Abdin's symbol system is close to symptom formation, I imply that it is fully dominated by the archaic motivations of childhood, rather than by a surplus of meaning. The meaning of Abdin's personal symbols tends to be shallow. In symptoms and in the regressive symbols employed by Abdin, there is overdetermination of motive but underdetermination of meaning. Concomitantly the individual who uses them possesses little reflexivity; when reflection occurs it hovers around the infantile motivations as in psychoanalytic free associations. Hence Freud could use terms such as "rationalization" to conceptualize such phenomena. Overdetermination by meaning helps transcend the domination by motive, as the case studies of my female ascetics indicate.

In spite of these qualifications, there are clear examples of repetitive behavior in the priestess. For example, the initial attack enacted a painful possession by a demon: the possession is repeated, but now it is a joyous possession by a divinity. The act of repetition of the past is a transformation and transcendence of that past, whereas Abdin's symbol system is closer to the archaic terrors of childhood. Finally, if Abdin's symbolic actions entail body mutilation and other acts that are closer to parallel acts in psychological symptoms, not so with the priestess. It would be meaningless to see her signs of possession as hysteria: the "hysterical syndrome" has been totally transformed into a spiritual experience.

I would like to develop this theme further since it is the subject of considerable debate in psychological anthropology. Lewis Langness has described a related but not identical phenomenon in New Guinea and has labelled this "hysterical psychosis."[4] This term is completely inapplicable to our cases: for what occurs here is not a psychosis but a spiritual experience. Others would see the basic syndrome here as *hysteria,* but given cultural and religious interpretation, or existing as a "culture-bound syndrome." This again is misleading, for the cultural/religious embodiment of the "hysterical syndrome" is central to its etiology and prognosis: the hysterical symptoms cannot be isolated from their religious definition. Moreover the term hysteria does not occur as a clinical entity in this society: it is a disease that occurred in the context of Victorian culture. To transfer this notion to the context of Sri Lankan society is as meaningless as the reverse procedure. It is very likely that a hypothetical Sri Lankan who had observed a hysterical female in Victorian Europe would probably state that hers was a case of "spirit possession," for this is the only category term in the culture that could embrace the overt behavioral signs of "hysteria." This, of course, would be ridiculous; but then we must also see that the reverse process might be equally ridiculous. On the behavioral level I can isolate a set of symptoms, label it hysteria, and then find that these symptoms are universally present in human populations. But I can as easily do it with almost any disease. It is a common epidemiological fallacy to equate the universality of a set of symptoms with the universality of a disease.[5]

One can escape from this common fallacy of epidemiology only to become a victim of the "culturological fallacy" and say that the "hysterical syndrome" is essentially noncomparable to other forms which exhibit similar behavioral manifestations, as indeed do the several forms of spirit possession. Insofar as they are culturally contextualized, one might say that they are incapable of comparison. However, in my own analysis of Abdin's later symptoms I found the term hysteria useful, even though Abdin does not use it; he sees his illness as "paralysis" caused by sorcerers. I postpone the problem of comparison for a later lecture, but I believe that a certain level of comparison and nomothetic understanding is possible in anthropological interpretation. For example, in contemporary bourgeois society in Sri Lanka you can have women having fainting spells and bodily symptoms, as well as private beliefs ("kissing will cause pregnancy") which are identical with Freud's hysterical syndrome. In village society, in general, this would not occur except as spirit attack or a related cultural phenomenon. Western doctors, and nowadays even Ayurvedic physicians, have taken over the term "hysteria" to designate the former.

I think it reasonable to say that Abdin's relapse into "paralysis" is a case of "hysteria" and comparable with its counterparts in Victorian society. Not so, however, with Abdin's symbol system. While this symbol system (hook hanging, tongue cutting) shares features with hysterical symptom formation (repetition compulsion, return of the repressed), it is still not of the same class. Thus it would be naive to say that since Abdin suffered from a hysterical paralysis and shed it later by reverting to symbol, both are cases of hysteria. They are not; they exhibit different levels of remove from psychic origins. Nevertheless Abdin moves in a regressive direction as he acts out his symbol system, whereas the priestess does the reverse. Yet Abdin's symbol system, however rooted in archaic motivations, has the *potential* for transformation in a more progressive direction, away from psychic origins (even though Abdin is himself incapable of so manipulating it). Symptomatic manifestations, especially those confined to the body, possess little range of variation or capacity for continual displacements, or substitutive flexibility; consequently they may exhibit near identity cross-culturally. On the other hand, symbolic expressions of deep motivations show greater variation and freedom of maneuver and can only exhibit ontological affinities, family resemblances, or polythetic similarities across cultures. It is nevertheless true to say that symbolic forms show different degrees of remove from psychic origins with Abdin's far closer to them than that of the priestess.

Thus my position: even if hysteria and the cases of divine possession among our priestesses are qualitatively different phenomena, it may well be that certain forms of hysteria and possession may possess common antecedent conditions pertaining to erotic and hostile relationships with significant others in infancy and early childhood. The necessary conditions for spirit attack as well as hysteria may be possible of specification, and a general theory of "hysterical psychosis" may be constructed on this basis. But such a nomological theory would be a very limited one. Weber saw this very clearly when he stated:

> Let us assume we have succeeded by means of psychology or otherwise in analyzing all the observed and imaginable relationships of social phenomena into some ultimate elementary classification of them and then formulated rigorously exact laws covering their behavior. What would be the significance of these results for our knowledge of the *historically* given culture or any individual phase thereof, such as capitalism, in its development and cultural significance?[6]

To get back to our case studies—what our priestess illustrates is that a frightening threat from childhood is overcome; Abdin also attempts to do so, and his is clearly the use of a personal symbol, but one still rooted in the terrors of childhood. In one of Ricoeur's best discussions he reexamines a famous case study of Freud's in which a threatening reality, a negativity as he calls it, gets resolved by being metamorphosed into a new symbolic form. In *Beyond the Pleasure Principle,* Freud deals with the case of a young boy of eighteen months who invented a game to cope with absence and loss. The child was by acceptable standards a "good boy" who did not trouble his parents at night and never used to cry when his mother left him for a few hours, even though greatly attached to her. Yet he had a disconcerting habit of taking small objects, throwing them away from him into a corner or under the bed, and then uttering a long "o-o-o-o" followed by an expression of interest and satisfaction. Both Freud and the mother agreed that the interjection meant the German word *fort* (gone). To quote Freud:

> I eventually realized that it was a game and that the only use he made of any of his toys was to play "gone" with them. One day I made an observation which confirmed my view. The child had a wooden reel with a piece of string tied around it. It never occurred to him to pull it along the floor behind him,

> for instance, and play at its being a carriage. What he did was to hold the reel by the string and very skillfully throw it over the edge of his curtained cot, so that it disappeared into it, at the same time uttering his expressive "o-o-o-o". He then pulled his reel out of the cot again by the string and hailed its reappearance with a joyful "da" ("there"). This then, was the complete game—disappearance and return. As a rule one only witnessed its first act, which was repeated untiringly as a game in itself, though there is no doubt that the greater pleasure was attached to the second act.[7]

Ricoeur comments on this case very much in the spirit of Freud's own interpretation:

> Let us return to the intriguing example of the child's *fort-da* play. This game of making the mother symbolically disappear and reappear consists, no doubt, in the repetition of an affective renunciation; but unlike the dreams that occur in traumatic neuroses the play repetition is not a forced or obsessive one. To play with absence is to dominate it and to engage in active behavior toward the lost object as lost.[8]

Would not play, asks Ricoeur, in itself an appeal to symbols, "consist in one's mastery over the negative, over absence and loss?"[9] He continues:

> The work of art is also a *fort-da*, a disappearance of the archaic object as fantasy and its reappearance as a cultural object.[10]

The reality created by our ecstatic priestesses is "the work of culture" which parallels the work of art. The notion of "work" is as central to the Freudian analysis of representation as is labor for Marx's analysis of political economy. It is an act of creativity, a transformation of "negativity." Consider what has gone on in the priestesses I discuss. A lost archaic object, a dead kinsman, has been recreated as a special type of divinity on the idealized *parental* model: a guardian spirit, and also one who assists the priestess in her spiritual quest by acting as a mediator between herself and the gods. The symbol of "bitter milk" is the repetition of a primal episode. But it is more; it is a repentance, a plea for forgiveness and an expiation of the past. And so with the other acts of repetition; the traumas of childhood are, almost in a literal sense, acted out in play, in the play of ritual.

What major conclusion can one draw from the differing uses of personal symbols in the two cases, Abdin's and the priestess's? I noted earlier that for Ricoeur Freudianism is essentially a *theory of regression:* the psychoanalytic analysis of symbols, and of culture in general, deals with the ontogenetic substrate of the symbol. Thus god the father is nothing but the father of infancy projected into the cosmos. Ricoeur points out another movement, never explicitly formulated in psychoanalysis, but implicit in the theory of sublimation—that of *progression,* a term initially used by Freud himself in *The Interpretation of Dreams.*[11] A progressive movement of unconscious thought involves the transformation of the archaic motivations of childhood into symbols that look forward to the resolution of conflict and beyond that into the nature of the sacred or numinous. This double movement of symbols permits the theoretical reconciliation of the Freudian hermeneutic as illusion which has to be deciphered in terms of archaic motivations, with the phenomenology of religion of Leenhardt, Eliade, and others, for whom the symbol must be deciphered as a "revelation of the sacred." The latter, needless to say, is also close to Jung. Ricoeur points out that even in the ideal type of regressive symbols, that of dreams, there is often a progressive movement away from the archaic motivations of the individual to their eventual resolution.[12]

What is the significance of this distinction for the anthropologist interested in the interpretation of symbols, especially psychological symbols? The theological or phenomenological problem of the numinous or sacred is not the issue; but rather the notion that human beings may express the ontological problems of existence and being through systems of multiple meaning or symbols. Early social science theories seemed to denigrate this aspect of religion as in Durkheim's colorless definition of the sacred. Durkheim's formulation was an explicit attempt to debunk nineteenth-century historians of religion such as Max Müller who defined religion as the attempt "to utter the unutterable" or "a longing after the infinite." Durkheim quite rightly pointed out the limitations of this view since religion often dealt with everyday practical reality, with such things as increase, fertility, and the well-being of social groups.[13] But in doing so he swung in the opposite direction, ignoring the fact that certain classes of symbols may attempt to represent that which cannot be easily described in the language of everyday discourse. The Durkheimian trend has been reversed in the movement of social anthropology from function to meaning hesitantly begun by Evans-Pritchard, and boldly developed by Victor Turner and others influenced by phenomenology and hermeneutics. This must force us to ground our analysis in the tradition of thought that stems from Weber, rather than from Durkheim, since it was Weber who, following the German traditions of *verstehen,* emphasized culture as the imposition of meaning on phenomenal nature and human experience, based on a species-conditioned drive towards meaning. I cannot take up this theme here except to say that the reconciliation of a theory of symbols as illusion with a phenomenology of religion is perfectly possible in terms of the tradition of the sociology of Weber even if Weber did not explicitly concern himself with "deep motivation."

Unfortunately the reconciliation of cultural meaning with motivation was not possible in Freudian thought and in the tradition of psychoanalytic anthropology influenced by it. *Beyond the Pleasure Principle* is a key text that *we* could use for this purpose. While this work upsets some crucial Freudian notions such as the wish-fulfillment theory of dreams and the significance of the pleasure principle in human life, it did not introduce any real change in Freud's theory of religion. Freud could now see creativity in the fantasy life of children that he did not see in his earlier study of Little Hans, but he does not carry this insight into adult religion and ritual. Indeed he becomes more hostile to religion in his later work. In *The Future of an Illusion,* written in 1927, he sees religion as an illusion as Durkheim also did; that is, there is a reality out there, but people do not understand its true nature. But two years later when he started on *Civilization and its Discontents,* in many ways a far-reaching work, he castigates religion as a "delusion," parallel to psychotic hallucination in paranoia. "The religions of mankind must be classed among the mass delusions of this kind. No one, needless to say, who shares a delusion ever recognizes it as such."[14] In *Moses and Monotheism* (1938), his last major work, he sees a parallelism between the development of a neurosis and the historical evolution of religion.

A neurosis, Freud says, runs ideally in several stages: early trauma → defence → latency → outbreak of neurosis → partial return of the repressed material.[15] This is exactly isomorphic with the kind of prehistory he sketched in *Totem and Taboo* (1913) and reaffirmed in *Moses and Monotheism* (1938).

> From then on [i.e., from the time of *Totem and Taboo*] I have never doubted that religious phenomena are only to be understood on the pattern of the individual neurotic symptoms familiar to us—as the return of long since forgotten important events in the primeval history of the

> human family—and that they have to thank precisely this origin for their compulsive character and that, accordingly, they are effective on human beings by force of the historical truth of their content.[16]

Thus the neurotic repetition compulsion in religion has phylogenetic continuity (*Totem and Taboo*), ontogenetic continuity (*The Future of an Illusion*), and historical continuity (*Moses and Monotheism*).

The psychoanalytic anthropology of Kardiner, Whiting, Devereux, and others made little change in this basic orientation. All of these writers have a theory of cultural forms as defense, parallel to the defense mechanisms of the ego. Thus you have notions like "projective systems" (Kardiner), "systems of psychological security" (Whiting), "culturally constituted defenses" (Spiro), and more recently in Epstein's work the notion of symbol systems as defenses.[17] That symbol systems may act as "defenses" is indubitable; but these writers also postulate that, insofar as an isomorphism exists between personal and cultural defenses, so a similar isomorphism exists between symbol and symptom. For the most part the primary thrust of the analysis is on the regressive nature of the symbol system, rather than on its forward-looking prospective or progressive character. By contrast our case studies show that both processes are operative at every level of symbol formation, from dream symbolism to the complex symbols of the sacred and the numinous, and that they operate at different degrees of remove or closeness to archaic motivations of childhood. These degrees of remove cannot be prestated theoretically, but must be demonstrated contextually and historically through case studies.

Getting back to the case studies, it seems clear that Abdin's history is different from that of the ideal typical priestess. Both use preexisting symbol systems to give expression to deep motivations; but these personal symbols operate, as all symbols do, on different degrees of symbolic remove from archaic motivations. Abdin's set of personal symbols sends taproots into his infantile motivations; the symbols do not help to overcome his troubled past, but *repeat* that past through periodic catharses. The neurotic phenomenon of compulsive repetition and obsession still operates through the symbol system. In the case of the priestess the initial symbolic performance is never repeated; she overcomes her infantile terrors; and the symbols permit her to move away prospectively from these sources of motivation to another reality which she has defined for herself—a joyous existence and comportment with the gods. I failed to see this distinction in *Medusa's Hair* where I treated personal symbols as qualitatively identical, though clearly distinct from symptoms, instead of varying as all symbols do in terms of their remove from the infantile past. I saw a difference between Abdin and the priestess, but related these to sociocultural problems of role taking and adaptation. These sociocultural problems are important but subordinated to the psychological dialectic of regression-progression, or to use my own language, to the problems of symbolic remove. Nevertheless the cultural background of the person is crucial in assessing the *potential* for the "progressive" development of the symbol.

Abdin, it must be recalled, is a Javanese Muslim practicing a Hindu cult; the priestess is a Buddhist also practicing a Hindu cult. Being Muslim and being Buddhist both impose formal limits on the progressive development of the symbol. Consequently culture is not something outside of motivation but integral to it. I cannot develop this theme here, but let me state it rather baldly. As a Muslim, it is difficult but not impossible for Abdin to practice his Hindu cult, since the slum society in which he lives tolerates a considerable religious eclecticism. But no one in his community really believes that the goddess Kālī and other Hindu deities have any say over larger ethical interests, for these as well as problems of ultimate reality—salvation—are defined in Islamic terms. Abdin, though a good Hindu, also considers himself a good Muslim and often goes to the mosque. Thus it is virtually impossible for Abdin to treat the goddess Kālī as *śakti,* the principle that animates the universe, and to universalize her as *the* Mother. To do so would be to move away from his culture, renounce his religion, and free himself from his childhood religious enculturation. If Abdin had lived in Java, the home of his ancestors, he might have had greater freedom of maneuver.

For the Buddhist priestess the practice of the Hindu cult poses much less of a problem. Buddhism has always integrated Hindu deities into its fold, but classically these deities had to do with material interests—health, illness, welfare—rather than salvation, which was unequivocally defined in Buddhist terms. Thus Buddhism provides considerable freedom of symbolic maneuver to the priestess: she can interact with deities, love them, have visions of them, and draw in a variety of Hindu ideas from yoga and *śakti.* But once again there is a limit imposed on maneuverability: it would be impossible for a priestess to affirm Kālī as *the* Mother without renouncing her Buddhist identity; and none in my sample do this. The moment one moves into Hinduism proper these constraints are off, but others,

Hindu ones, set limits on symbolic maneuver. Consider the case of the great Hindu mystic, Ramakrishna, who, like Abdin, was possessed by Kālī and constantly saw her in his visions. Ramakrishna's Hinduism permits the progressive development of the personal symbol to a greater degree than in the previous two cases. To Ramakrishna his own mother is mother Kālī who is *the* Mother and the guiding principle of cosmic creativity. Through Kālī, Ramakrishna has achieved trance and knowledge of a radically different order from the others, and he can progress to the heart of a specifically Hindu reality that is essentially salvific.[18]

Let me end this part of my discussion of the regression-progression dynamic with a comment on the nature of reflexivity in the manipulation of personal symbols. George Devereux says that the ethnic symbols (personal symbols in our usage) may provide adjustment but not introspective self-awareness or "curative insight."[19] True insight can occur only in the analytic session. I suppose that most psychoanalytic anthropologists will take this position. But this poses an embarrassing historical and cultural problem, for then one has to assume that prior to the invention of psychoanalysis all of us went our muddled ways in the abysmal dark of ignorance, except for a few gifted poets and artists who intuitively grasped the reality of unconscious motivation. This simply will not do, and one has to recognize in psychoanalysis a specific type of reflexivity—that of *rational* self-reflection, itself a product of a modern universe demystified of the magical and religious worldview. The early work of Habermas helps us to put the problem of psychoanalytic self-reflexivity in proper perspective.

Habermas says that the patient suffering from a neurosis speaks a "privatized language" and is cut off from everyday communication.

> The object domain of depth hermeneutics comprises all the places where, owing to internal disturbances, the text of our everyday language games [is] interrupted by incomprehensible symbols. These symbols cannot be understood because they do not obey the grammatical rules of ordinary language, norms of action, and culturally learned patterns of expression. . . . Freud uses the term "symptom" to cover such deviant symbol formations, which he studies in the dream as an exemplar. . . . They restrict the flexibility margin of speech and communicative action. They can depreciate the reality content of perceptions and thought processes, unbalance the emotional economy, ritualize behavior, and

> immediately impair bodily functions. Symptoms can be regarded as the result of a compromise between repressed wishes of infantile origin and socially imposed prohibitions of wish fulfillment. That is why they mainly display both elements, although in varying quantities. For they have the character of substitute formations for a denied gratification, and also express the sanction with which the defensive agency threatens the unconscious wish. Finally symptoms are signs of a specific self-alienation of the subject who has them.[20]

The neurotic, says Habermas, cannot communicate his privatized thoughts. This privatized language has to be interpreted by the analyst so that the patient's self-communication is restored and the privatized language becomes transformed into ordinary language. "The analyst instructs the patient in reading his own texts, which he himself has mutilated and distorted, and in translating symbols from a mode of expression deformed as a private language into a mode of expression of public communication."[21]

Ricoeur makes a similar point: the psychoanalytic session makes possible a special self-reflection and a restoration of meaning. Freud, it is true, dethrones the Cartesian primacy of consciousness; but the goal of the psychoanalytic therapy is to restore self-consciousness by translating unconscious thought into the language of consciousness. This is the meaning of Freud's famous statement: where id was, there shall ego be.[22]

This is clearly not the detour adopted by the Abdins, the priestesses, and the Ramakrishnas of our discussion. Symptoms can exist in Hindu-Buddhist neurotics also as privatized modes of expression, but in our sample of ecstatics symptom has been translated into symbol. The symbol is both personal *and* cultural, and insofar as this is the case it provides a basis for self-reflection (the personal dimension) as well as for communication with others (the cultural dimension). Personal symbols are like the technical discourse employed in psychoanalytic therapy in one regard: they constitute a mediate language existing between the privatized language of symptoms and the ordinary language of everyday communication. But unlike psychoanalytic discourse, personal symbols do not constitute a rationalized theoretical language linking patient and doctor. They are public symbols that permit the expression of the unconscious thoughts of the individual; but since they make sense to others, they also permit communication with others in the language of everyday discourse. This double hermeneutic of personal symbols is integral to their nature, a double thrust of personal self-reflection and public communication.

Nevertheless the nature of reflexiveness and self-awareness varies on the dimension of symbolic remove. On looking back on my field notes I saw very little reflexivity in Abdin; he was too much rooted in the conflicts of infancy to stand outside of them and reflect on the nature of his experiences. By contrast reflexivity and existential anxiety appeared constantly in my interviews with the priestesses on several levels.

The spirit attack itself was preceded by a deep dissatisfaction with ordinary living. All of my informants have suffered from severe domestic troubles (such as a bullying or adulterous husband) that made them reflect on the emptiness of their lives and, inspired by Buddhist and Hindu ideas, ruminate on the fleeting and transient nature of existence, its essential impermanence. In other words ordinary Buddhist ideas, available in the cultural repertoire, permitted them to reflect on their own existential condition. This is of course one function of culture viewed as a system of meanings: it permits Everyman to reflect on the nature of experience, but this is especially so for introspective individuals.

The movement away from domesticity could occur in several directions. One is a Buddhist direction into monastic existence or, for these women, as Buddhist lay virtuosos or as nuns. The other is a Hindu direction in an adoration of the gods. Sometimes there is considerable indeterminacy as to which way to turn; in all my cases they ultimately turned in the Hindu direction.

The spirit attack was a decisive event. The end result of the spirit attack was a triumph of the will: the evil spirit is converted into a benevolent guardian who acts as communicant with the gods. Once in touch with this reality the priestess is in communication with the gods on the one hand and with various types of follow religious virtuosos on the other. Some specialists have formal discussion sessions, while for others discussion is largely in informal settings. None of this appears in the case of Abdin: his religious beliefs are shallow, and his cosmological knowledge is of the barest.

However, the moment one switches to great Hindu virtuosos such as Ramakrishna or Vivekananda the leeway for reflexivity is enormous; reflexivity and self-knowledge are linked with the knowledge of the cosmos itself and the quest for salvation.

The upshot of this discussion is to bring us back to Devereux's problem: it is not so much the absence of reflexivity and self-awareness in the case of religious specialists and its presence in psychoanalysis. Rather reflexivity itself is based on a cultural idiom; indeed it can *only* occur as a cultural idiom. The insight that emerges in psychoanalysis is but one form, as much a product of culture as the idioms of self-awareness of ecstatics. This does not mean that some idioms are not less or more conducive to reflection than others, but this cannot be judged a priori on the presumed superiority of the psychoanalytic session.

2

Dromena and Cathartic Rituals: Regression and Progression in Collective Representations

Personal symbols, I show in *Medusa's Hair* and in the cases discussed in the previous section, are cultural symbols that are related to individual motivation and make sense only in relation to the life history of the individual. They help us abolish the false distinction between public and private symbols. Personal symbols are public and private at the same time, so to speak. They provide the individual with option, choice, and the leeway for manipulation. Hook hanging is, for example, recognized by the people at large as part of the legitimate "arena culture" at Kataragama; yet only a very few, such as Abdin, practice it. Margosa mixed with milk is recognized by people as good medicine, but it is consumed only by those who crave the bitter milk of appeasement. These are cultural symbols developed through time for the objectification of the psychological problems of the individual, but they cannot be significantly related to group motivation. If a plurality of Sri Lankans hung on hooks, got possessed by vengeful ancestors, wore matted locks, the society as we know it now would change beyond recognition. Indeed it is doubtful whether a plurality of individuals could in fact undertake these performances. The deep motivations of these individuals are "recognized" by the society, and it has provided cultural symbols to give expression to the problems that beset them—problems of guilt, alienation, betrayal, and despair. In urban Western society these deep motivations might well receive expression in symptom formation, but here symptoms are transformed into symbols that give existential meaning to the motivations that instigated them and provide an avenue for self-reflection, communication with others, and in exceptional cases, for a radical transformation of one's being.

Collective representations that are the subject of this section are of a qualitatively different order. One can have group rituals, processional events, collective acts of worship that have significance for realms of human activity and thought but have little or no bearing on unconscious motivation. But insofar as collective representations encompass different domains, they may also give expression, in a variety of ways, to the deep motivations that beset a plurality of individuals in a society, as for example, psychic problems arising from relations with parents and significant others, themselves conditioned by the nature of socialization under the governance of specific familial structures and values. They do not constitute a global phenomenon and cannot therefore be seen as constituting a modal, or a group, or a basic personality structure. While they are cultural defenses or projective systems in Kardiner's sense, they are something more: they are publicly presented in ritual dramas, processions, and other performance genres. The audience at best identifies with the action; at worst they ignore it and go to sleep. The symbol is not and cannot be integrated into the life history of the individual. In a collective representation the narrative or drama or procession has a preconstructed form that cannot easily be changed by the individual. Indeed the individual is a special kind of participant; the major actors are professional personnel such as priests and other ritual specialists. But, as T. S. Eliot said, it is a mistake to see the ritual on the model of the theatre, since the theatre is a secular form that calls for the "willing suspension of disbelief," whereas without "belief" there cannot be any authentic ritual.[23] Belief is neither a reflex of the secondary process nor an epiphenomenon of the social structure.

Eliot's distinction between drama and the Eucharist is central to my argument: it is belief—more specifically, the quality of the belief—that constitutes at least one major difference between varieties of symbolic forms. The person who sees *Hamlet* or *Oedipus* on a modern stage is in a sense outside the performance physically: in a psychic sense less so, but his is still a willing suspension of disbelief. He goes out of the theatre, enriched no doubt, into a world which cannot easily articulate that experience with the shared culture or worldview of his group. Not so with a hypothetical Athenian of Sophocles' time, or a Sinhala watching the modern version of a traditional myth on the Sri Lankan stage. In both the experience of the drama is consonant, at some level, with the larger tradition from which it is derived, and this larger tradition exists coterminously as an active part of the culture and historical consciousness of the audience. The stage play is articulated to the ongoing life world of the individual and the operative cultural tradition. This articulation becomes less and less clear as one moves from tragic drama to such modern externalized expressive forms as novels, cinema, and television irrespective of the complexity and richness of their symbolic content.

Till very recently most Sri Lankan villagers believed in the truth of the myths of Pattini. But "belief" is not uniform in the passion or the commitment it evokes. It is certainly the case that the Eucharist for a Catholic is radically different than for a Protestant, but the *quality* of the belief itself is variable in degree and intensity even among Catholics. The quality of the belief is often dependent on the relationship between an individual's private experiences and the symbolic form he is engaged in. A person with an unresolved Oedipal conflict with his father might be more moved or emotionally torn when he witnesses *Oedipus* or *Hamlet* on stage than the "average citizen." Thus the existence of personal experience that is isomorphic with the externalized form is enough to evoke pity and terror, but if this is conjoined with "belief" the experience can be both personal and cultural at the same time. "Belief" is not necessarily religious belief, though this is the focus of this lecture.

"Belief" is central to the authenticity of the experience, as it is to the public legitimation of that experience. This is in sharp contrast to the Western intellectualist notion that "true belief" is private; that public expression of belief is conformism; and that idols must be broken for authenticity to emerge. This might well be true of modern bourgeois culture, but Western anthropologists make a mistake when they transfer this bias to the study of symbolic forms such as ritual drama or spirit possession which are then analyzed on the model of the theatre, or of a "performance," or as a phenomenon pertaining to the domain of aesthetics. All of the latter are present in both, but they cannot be segregated from the truth value of the experience, its reality as "belief" shared by a plurality of people. Even in small-scale societies nowadays people question, more than they ever did previously, the authenticity of the belief and the authenticity of the experience. It is when this kind of questioning occurs that one tries to search for a *more* authentic experience and a greater authenticity of belief.

If personal symbols are articulated to a life history, collective representations, of whatever form, are tied to the experience and historical and social consciousness of the people at large. Even when a collective representation mobilizes or utilizes motivations significant to a plurality of individuals, there is a sense in which it is profoundly social. On the one hand there is community participation at various levels, and this culminates in the presence of people at the performance. On the other, the anxieties and deep motivations of the group are externalized and presented in dramatic form. This externalization permits the individual to view what is within himself as a cosmic drama outside of him, as if he is not in it. One cannot expect in these circumstances the kind of radical personality transformation that I highlighted in the previous case studies and in *Medusa's Hair.* Quite the contrary, one *shares* the experiences with others, and it is in this sharing of one's anxiety that one achieves elation or consolation. It is impossible for others to share Abdin's experiences: people react to them with fear, awe, disgust. So is it with the performances of the priestesses. It is the *kind* of sharing that I shall discuss in this section. I shall show that collective representations also vary in relation to the degree of symbolic remove from archaic motivations, or to put it in Ricoeur's terms, they also exhibit the dialectical interplay of progression and regression.

In this section I deal with two types of rituals and the myths associated with them.[24] The first type is a solemn, stately ritual which enacts the myths of the goddess Pattini, specifically the death of the goddess's consort and his resurrection by her as *mater dolorosa.* I then describe a series of vulgar rituals which parody this solemn performance. I borrow a term from ancient Greek mystery religion and call the solemn and numinous performances *dromena:* things performed. In a dromenon the psychological problems of the group are brought under fine ego and cognitive controls. Dromena also embody cultural, religious, and philosophical values; they are not direct representations or isomorphic parallels of the psychological problems of the group. It is as if these psychological problems were symbolized many times over and brought in line with higher cultural values and given idealistic representation. By contrast, rituals that parody the numinous give a more direct expression to the anxieties that dominate the people. In the former type there is an overdetermination of meaning that radically transforms and transcends the motivations that lie at the base of the performance. In the latter there is an overdetermination of motives, and the meanings, though rich, can be related directly to the instigating motives. I label such rituals "catharses": the symbolization here is more forthright and easier to unravel. That which is camouflaged in the dromenon is laid bare in the cathartic rituals. Thus dromena are characterized by controlled behavior and seriousness, catharses by acting out behavior and often, but not always, by levity. If a dromenon is engaged in a progressive movement away from the sources of infantile conflict and anxiety, the cathartic ritual moves in a regressive direction.

Killing and the Resurrection

The goddess Pattini is the Sri Lankan exemplar of wifely devotion, fidelity, and chastity. Though depicted as ideal wife in myth, she is generally addressed as mother in rituals. The myths and rituals associated with this goddess are embodied in thirty-five ritual texts, most of which are sung or enacted in collective postharvest rituals traditionally performed in the western and southern parts of the country. I shall briefly present the central myths of this goddess followed by their psychoanalytic interpretation. Then I describe a central dromenon, a ritual known as the "killing and resurrection," followed by its parody in several cathartic enactments. I then show how identical or similar psychological motivations are expressed in radically different movements of remove from psychic origins.

According to our texts, the goddess Pattini was incarnated in the human world to destroy the might of the evil king of Pāṇḍi (Pandya) who was possessed of a third eye in the middle of his forehead and considered himself to be a god on earth. One myth recounts her "birth" in the human world. A golden mango appeared in a tree in the orchard of the king of Pāṇḍi; the king wished to bring it down, but all attempts failed. Ultimately the king of the gods, Sakra, descended from heaven in the guise of a humpbacked beggar and said he could bring the mango down. The king and courtiers were amused, but they gave him permission. Sakra wielded his bow and shot at the mango, and it fell down to earth. The king looked up in wonderment; some juice from the stem fell on his middle eye, which was blinded. Frightened, the king placed the mango in a golden casket and floated it down the river Kāveri (*kāviri*). It was recovered way downstream by a merchant prince and his wife who were bathing there. They took the casket home, and lo, after seven days they found an infant girl, whom they adopted as their daughter. The myth of the goddess's "birth" in the mango is enacted in a ritual drama known as the "shooting of the mango."

At age sixteen Pattini was given in marriage to a merchant prince, Pālanga. But before they could consummate the marriage, Pālanga fell in love with a courtesan, Mādēvi. The fickle Pālanga left his legitimate spouse and lived with Mādēvi, on whom he squandered his wealth. Ultimately he became destitute and returned to Pattini, who suggested that he sell her precious anklet and recover his fortunes. It should be emphasized that though Pālanga came back to Pattini, he did not have intercourse with her. She remained a virgin, unsullied and pure and also "barren"; by contrast, Pālanga has a daughter by the courtesan, Mādēvi. Sinhala people are fully aware of the contrast. Pattini is totally pure, unsullied by sexuality; she was conceived in a golden mango to ensure that this goddess, like the Buddha himself, is untainted by the womb's impurities.

The third part of the myth of the goddess deals with the departure of the pair to Madurai, the capital city of the king of Pānḍi, to sell the anklet and recover their fortunes. The texts describe the vicissitudes of the journey in graphic detail. Pālanga leaves Pattini in the outskirts of the city of Madurai at a village of cowherders and goes into the street of goldsmiths. The cowherders are milk givers; they symbolically form the ideal community of devotees, whereas the goldsmiths are viewed as cheats and usurers and are symbolically viewed as the community antipathetic to the goddess. Pālanga shows the anklet to the goldsmith; the cunning goldsmith pretends friendship and asks Pālanga to wait while he goes on an errand. The goldsmith goes to the king and tells him that he has found the thief who had stolen the anklet of his chief queen. The king's "torturers" bring Pālanga before the king; Pālanga protests his innocence. Even the queen says that it is not her anklet, but the goldsmith persuades the king that the queen must have been infatuated with the thief. The king orders Pālanga to be taken to the execution grounds, where he is tortured and killed by the king's executioner.

Meanwhile Pattini has forebodings of disaster, and she decides to go in search of her husband. Accompanied by her servant, Kālī, she departs for Madurai. On her way she meets with several adventures, the most notable being her confrontation with, and subjugation of, the goddess of pestilence, Vaduru Mālā. Ultimately she discovers her husband's mutilated body under the shade of the margosa tree. She wails piteously in some of the most poignant ritual poetry in Sinhala.

She invokes the power of her chastity and resurrects Pālanga from the dead, and he ascends to heaven. Now she goes to the palace and confronts the king and accuses him of injustice. She shows that her anklet had rubies, while the queen's had pearls. In her wrath she tears off her left breast, flings it and it burns the city of Madurai. Only the good are spared, including the queen, whereas the king and the whole street of goldsmiths are destroyed. The cowherders plead with her to desist; she agrees, calms the fire and produces rain, and then ascends to heaven to join her husband.

The last part of the myth is enacted as a ritual drama, an impressive and awe-inspiring dromenon entitled "killing and resurrection," that I saw twenty-five years ago. I cannot describe it here except to state that the priest of the cult dresses as the goddess Pattini; he wears female clothes and, what is both striking and unusual, a tiara on his head and seven veils of different colors, not, however, covering his face but falling at the back like the headdress of a Catholic nun. The goddess is accompanied by Kālī, her servant, dressed as a Sinhala housemaid! Several of the dramatic sequences are especially impressive. In one, the executioner enters the ritual arena wearing a demon mask while the drums beat the notes for summoning demons. He circles around Pālanga lying prostrate on the floor, whips out a knife, puts his hand under Pālanga's sarong, and pulls out his bowels—rags dyed in red ingeniously placed in Pālanga's belly beforehand. Then he hacks him to death and leaves the ritual arena as suddenly as he had entered. Another moving sequence is the goddess weeping and wailing over the dead body of her husband, singing songs asking him to wake. The destruction of Madurai was not enacted in the two ritual dramas I saw in 1956, but it is possible that it was performed in an earlier historical period.

Let me initially examine one major theme of the myths outlined above—that of the virgin goddess, the fickle husband, and the courtesan. This theme is expressed not only in the ritual texts but also in popular narratives and folktales. I shall first analyze this theme in classical Freudian terms and then show how the Freudian analysis of symptom is incorporated into the symbolic structure of the myth and ritual.

The problem of the virgin and the harlot was dealt with by Freud in two brilliant essays on the psychology of love.[25] I cannot go into the details of his argument, but Freud referred to a widespread psychological problem in some male patients of his period, namely, an inability to choose an object of love unless the woman is already attached and also unless she is sexually discredited. One choice for people of this sort is the harlot who, in conscious thought, is the very opposite of the mother who is considered pure, indeed virginal. In the second paper, Freud relates this dichotomy of tenderness and sensuality to a problem of sexual impotence, even when nothing is physically wrong with the sexual organs. Freud argues that the reason for this peculiarity is that the sexual object is unconsciously associated with a mother or a sister and comes under the governance of the incest taboo. Hence the refusal of the sex organ to perform the sexual act, since intercourse is tantamount to incest.

If the fixation on incestuous objects has been less severe, psychosexual development may result in milder forms of impotence. In these cases the sensual feeling is sufficiently strong to be expressed in sexual relationships with others, but it is devoid of tenderness. Consequently, Freud says, a restriction is imposed on object choice.

> The sensual feeling that has remained active seeks only objects evoking no reminder of the incestuous persons forbidden to it; the impression made by someone who seems deserving of high estimate leads, not to a sensual excitation, but to feelings of tenderness which remain erotically ineffectual. The erotic life of such people remains dissociated, divided between two channels, the same two that are personified in art as heavenly or earthly (or animal) love. *Where such men love they have no desire and where they desire they cannot love.*[26]

How do these people resolve their dilemmas? They lower the sexual object in their own estimation. "As soon as the sexual object fulfills the condition of being degraded, sensual feeling can have free play, considerable sexual capacity and a high degree of pleasure can be developed."[27] There is a polarity of feeling here, tenderness and affection being exclusively reserved for the incestuous objects and others who represent them (e.g., the wife), while sensuality is reserved for the sexual object (e.g., the mistress). Now Freud can link up this discussion with the theme of the previous paper. "The motives behind the phantasies mentioned in the preceding paper, by which boys degrade the mother to the level of the prostitute, now become intelligible. They represent efforts to bridge the gulf between two currents of erotic feeling, at least in phantasy: by degrading her, to win the mother as an object of sexual desires."[28]

I agree with Ricoeur that some of the most numinous myths and rituals rest at base on archaic motives and their immediate ideational representations in fantasy life. The Freudian analysis helps us to isolate a psychological problem in Sri Lankan culture. In South Asia, the strength of the mother-child bond is the most powerful conceivable, and its strength is hardly mitigated in adult life. In this lecture I cannot detail the sociological and cultural evidence but can only affirm that this situation could indeed foster an incestuous attachment on the mother, though it is impossible to specify this in frequency terms. Sudhir Kakar, the Indian psychoanalyst, has noted this preoccupation in Hindu India and, in agreement with Freud, he also notes the consequences of this incestuous fixation—widespread prevalence of sexual guilt, feelings of inadequacy, and fears of impotence.[29] In Sri Lanka, as in Hindu India, as elsewhere, the incestuous feelings for the mother must result in fears of castration as a punishment for incestuous wishes, either by oneself or by another. In Sri Lanka, castration anxiety caused by incestuous feelings may be complicated by the father who can be strong and loving.[30] The psychological consequences of a strong father role in the context of mother fixation is the fear of the father as the castrating agent.

As a result of castration anxiety caused by incestuous wishes, one would expect, on the psychological level, a great deal of anxiety regarding one's sexual potency. I shall label this, for purposes of convenience, "impotence anxiety." Impotence anxiety does not mean that actual psychogenic impotence is common; only that the *fears* of impotence are extraordinarily widespread in the society. As evident from Freud's analysis what is empirically expectable would not be total psychogenic impotence but rather concern with one's sense of sexual adequacy. Impotence anxiety is reinforced by the cultural mores that define sexuality as a necessary but lower form of human activity. I am not concerned with the incidence of sexual inadequacy but rather with the more widespread, almost universal, *anxiety* regarding one's potency, irrespective of whether such anxiety has an objective basis in actual sexual inadequacy. In contemporary Sri Lankan society, as in India as Kakar demonstrates, there are many psychic representatives that indicate this underlying anxiety, as, for example, preoccupation with aphrodisiacs and medical prescriptions for curing impotence and premature ejaculation, and the tying of talismans prior to the wedding night.[31]

From the point of view of contemporary psychoanalytical anthropology, one can view the myth of the goddess Pattini *on one level* as a "projective system," or an expression of the complex that Freud delineated, and a mode of coping with it. At the core of the myth is the symbolism of the triangular relationship of wife cum mother, the fickle husband, and the harlot. But the myth is something more: it presents the Sinhala view of the ideal wife and of course the conflicts that arise from her sexual inapproachability. Furthermore, the motivations are encompassed in a narrative dealing with a variety of topics central to the traditional society, and these meanings have nothing to do with the core psychological conflict. Let me mention one such theme: that of the unjust king who emulates the gods and neglects the ideals of just kingship and the plight of ordinary people. The goddess rectifies this injustice by tearing out her breast and destroying the evil king: the breast indicates the passionate, the maternal, and the angry human reaction against the ossified and pretentious justice of the king's court. The manifest level of the myth is not a rationalization and a secondary elaboration of the psychological core; it is intrinsic to the values of the society and is locked into its history and traditions. Yet at the same time the power of the myth lies in its embodying the infantile or archaic motivations at the base of the myth.

Idealization is the psychological movement that transforms the object, Freud said; whereas sublimation entails the transformation of the drive.[32] Idealization is best seen in the transformation of the harlot figure into Mādēvi of the myth. According to psychoanalytic theory one should expect a degraded sexual object in the harlot figure. But in fact the harlot figure is also idealized and treated as the polar opposite of the virgin goddess; she is desirable, loving, and faithful to the fickle Pālanga in her own way. Mādēvi is no harlot; she is a courtesan, descended from Urvasi, the divine dancer in Indra's heaven. Ritual songs as well as popular secular poetry describe her beauty, her accomplishment in the sixty-four arts, and her extraordinary skill in dancing, in lavish detail. Nevertheless the myths of Mādēvi, the courtesan, are never enacted in village rituals; they are also only rarely sung there. The reason is not difficult to seek: the myths and rituals of the goddess embody the values of village society, whereas the harlot figure, though desirable and idealized, violates its central values. Thus village ritual affirms the goddess myths and, for the most part, omits to sing or perform the courtesan myth, even though the latter is part of the larger corpus of ritual texts of the Pattini cult. Though neglected in village ritual, versions of the courtesan myth were popular with the people in the form of ballad literature.

However, this identical theme of the harlot-type figure is enacted in the collective rituals of the great pilgrimage center in Kataragama in southeast Sri Lanka, in the magnificent public dromenon of the god Skanda's union with his mistress, Valli Ammā. This great processional event is a historically developed substitute for the texts of the courtesan Mādēvi's relationship with Pālanga. At the pilgrimage center of Kataragama village values are temporarily suspended. For example, caste norms are not observed, and some people propitiate the god for blatantly immoral purposes. Here there is a public celebration of the "nuptials" of the god who had left his legitimate wife Dēvasēna, the daughter of Indra, the king of the gods, for Valli Ammā, the daughter of aboriginal hunters, a woman of the wilds. Both the Pattini rituals and the Skanda rituals deal with a similar triangular relationship, but with a significant difference in emphasis. In the former, Pālanga, the fickle husband, leaves his erstwhile loving mistress and goes back repentant to his wife, and the focus of the rituals is on the importance of the final domestic reconciliation. In the Skanda myth, the god leaves his wife and comes to Kataragama to live permanently in erotic communion with his mistress. Both aspects of the triangular relationship are idealized and performed in two different settings. The celebration of the god's relationships with his mistress is a reification in symbolic form of a powerful desire (wish fulfillment) that has a great deal of attraction to Sinhala males, but insofar as it flouts conventional values, it must be celebrated *outside* the village, at the central pilgrimage place at Kataragama. (I think the myths and rituals of Skanda have a great deal of significance for females also, but I shall not deal with this in the present lecture.) Let me present the myths and rituals that express the former relationship.

The god Skanda left his home in India after he became angry with his mother over her preferential treatment of his older brother Gaṇeśa. I shall discuss this cluster of familial relationships in detail in lecture two. These myths in any case are not well known to the generality of Sinhalas. Most Sinhala myths take over at the point when Skanda lands in Sri Lanka and comes to Kataragama. There he saw Valli Ammā (Mother Valli), a beautiful young girl adopted by the aboriginal hunters. She was picking flowers, and he approached her playing his flute (like another erotic deity, Kṛiṣṇa). Gods can take many shapes, and so he confronted her in the guise of an old man, still playing his flute. He told Valli: "You are very beautiful. I desire you greatly. Will you marry me?" She said, "Chi! I am not going to marry an old man like you." Said he, "If so I will die," to which she responded: "I couldn't care less." Skanda was sick of life because Valli was so beautiful and she wouldn't have him. But Gaṇeśa saw this with his divine eye and thought of making up with his brother. He appeared as a wild elephant before Valli. She was terrified and asked Skanda to save her. He said, "I will, if you marry me." She agreed, but meanwhile the elephant had run into the forest. Then the god revealed himself to her in his handsome form as Murugan, and she was happy. However, when she told this to her father, he was angry and locked her up in a cave. But Skanda broke open the cave, and ultimately her father agreed to give her to him. The festival at Kataragama is the commemoration of these "nuptials."

Let me interpret what I think Skanda represents as against Gaṇeśa. Gaṇeśa, I shall show in lecture two, is castrated and impotent, a Pālanga *in extremis,* while Skanda is virile and potent. However, the public celebration of his potency is not with his wife but rather with his mistress, Valli Ammā. According to Sinhala beliefs, Skanda left his legitimate spouse Dēvasēna, daughter of god Indra, for Valli, who is "the secret woman" (*horagäni*), i.e., the mistress. Valli is a wild plant; she is the forest creeper, the wild woman. Skanda's virility is manifest not in his relationship with his legitimate wife, but with his mistress. Note that this is identical with a key theme of the Pattini rituals—that of the fickle husband's relation with his mistress. At Kataragama, the great pilgrimage center in the jungles of southeastern Sri Lanka, the Skanda–Valli Ammā relationship is enacted in colorful detail.

The public ritual conducted in Kataragama is one of the fascinating cases in cross-cultural ethnology where an illicit and immoral relationship, from the standpoint of the people themselves, is celebrated joyously without a trace of criticism. If the village ritual idealizes the wife, this central ritual idealizes the mistress. This is symbolically recognized in iconography where Valli is on the propitious right side of the god while Dēvasēna, the wife, is on his left. Every evening for a period of fifteen days the god is ceremoniously conducted in a magnificent procession to the shrine of Valli Ammā, his mistress, located a few hundred yards away, at the end of the "street." It is also interesting to note that the procession bypasses the shrine of Dēvasēna, his legitimate spouse, without acknowledging her presence.

The secret, furtive nature of the journey is expressed in several symbolic sequences. For example, when the procession nears the shrine of Valli Ammā, the torches held by attendants are lowered, and the god enters the mistress' chamber in this "dim light." During this whole procession men and women display an extraordinary religious devotion. Hindu women and men follow the caparisoned elephant carrying the god, singing hymns on Murugan, the handsome one.

Some weep, and others are absorbed in worship, while all shout, "Harō! Harā!" which is hallelujah for Skanda. Few are consciously aware of the fact that they are publicly celebrating an act which violates some of the most central and cherished moral norms of their society.

The god Skanda, we noted, is virile with respect to his mistress, but the reverse must hold with respect to his wife. This aspect of the Skanda myth is not enacted in Sri Lanka, since it is the parallel myth of Pālanga and Pattini that is dominant there.[33] In the Sinhala case one would expect Pālanga's relation with his wife-mother to produce several psychological consequences: one, a concern with sexual inadequacy (impotence anxiety), and the other, a fear of castration for incestuous thoughts. Yet none of these expectable themes appear, except in specially disguised and virtually unrecognizable form in the myths. But what was disguised in the ritual emerged in the "myth associations" of the priests. When I asked ritual specialists why Pālanga did not have sexual intercourse with his wife, Pattini, since this was his legitimate right, the answer invariably was this: Pālanga failed to have intercourse because he was impotent. The blank space in the myth is supplied by informants, but it should be noted that the ritual refuses to deal with this psychological theme.

It is tempting to see in the fickle Pālanga a castrated figure like the god Attis of ancient Western Asian myth. In Sinhala myths Pālanga is presented in the husband role as weak, vacillating, incapable of "executive autonomy" in contrast to the strong character of both his wife and his mistress. In one symbolic sequence the theme of castration seems to be enacted again in a totally oblique manner. I refer to the sequence where the executioner, in the guise of a demon, kills Pālanga and then thrusts his knife under Pālanga's sarong and draws out his bowels. It is possible to see this as a displaced castration episode. Shulman quotes a South Indian myth which suggests that disembowelling equals castration. Here, the goddess Ankalamman requested her male devotee to prove his worth and fidelity to the goddess; the devotee then disembowelled himself and put on female clothes.[34]

I now refer to three other symbol sets which seem to imply the notion of Pālanga as a "castrated" person.

1. The first relates to Pattini's reaction to her husband's death, which is a primitive one (in the psychological sense) of *lex talionis.* It is also wildly out of proportion to the provocation, for she destroys a whole city and many of its inhabitants with her breast: I do to them a hundredfold what they did to me. If her reaction is one of talion, then

it would be plausible to infer that the object she used to destroy Madurai (i.e., her breast) is also based on a psychologically motivated talion reaction: my husband is castrated, and I now castrate myself by tearing off my breast. Regarding breast tearing as castration symbolism, Flugel says:

> There is one way in which it is possible to carry out a fairly satisfactory (displaced) castration of the female . . . that is, by cutting off the breast. The breasts constitute an outstanding and vulnerable part of the female reproductive anatomy, corresponding in these two respects to the penis of the male. We know, moreover, that the penis and the breast are often unconsciously identified and that the breast is already for other reasons frequently associated with the earlier development of the castration complex.[35]

August Starcke and Nolan D. C. Lewis present case material that fully substantiates the view that breast equals penis.[36] Both Flugel and Starcke also point out that the breast-equals-penis symbolism is overdetermined by the infantile rage felt by the child owing to the weaning trauma.[37] I might add that as far as the South Asian material is concerned the breast-equals-penis idea is a *male* fantasy.

The data from South Asian myth seems to confirm this equation. Let me present evidence from the myth of Vijaya, the founder of the Sinhala race, which suggests this symbolism is a valid one. According to most versions of the myth, Kuvēni the demoness had three breasts. The middle breast fell off when she met Vijaya, her future lover and husband, i.e., she doesn't need the fantasized "penis-breast" (middle breast) since she has the real one! A similar belief is recorded by Whitehead for Mīnakṣi of Madurai. Mīnakṣi was a warrior-woman, an anomalous being, who refused to marry anyone (i.e., she was a kind of male), and she also had a third breast (substitute for the penis). But when she met her future husband Śiva the middle breast withered away and she dropped her weapons; that is, she became a normal woman.[38] Shulman quotes other cases where the breast-equals-penis equation seems to hold.[39] In the Pattini myth itself it is said that Pattini's breast will be restored when she meets her husband in heaven.

It will be a mistake, however, to see breast tearing solely as symbolic castration for, as I said earlier, the dromenon is governed by an overdetermination of meaning. The breast is the seat of nurturance; in the narrative this is thrown out, and the goddess can assume her wrathful mode. Her compassion is restored, according to some myths, when the community of cowherders rub butter, a cooling substance, on her burning breast. The whole myth is inextricably linked with the theme of kingly and divine justice.

2. The peasant enactment of Pālanga *mutilans et moriens* finds a striking parallel in the superb sculpture of the grieving Pattini and her dead consort by Sri Lanka's most gifted contemporary sculptor, which I have reproduced in my book on this goddess.[40] No traditional artist could have produced anything like it, since the formalism of Sinhala painting and sculpture inhibited the expression of deep psychological motives. But since the modern sculptor does not suffer from the constraints of tradition he can express in his art the hidden psychological significance of the image of the mutilated husband. It is not unlikely that the modern artist was influenced by Michelangelo's *Pietà,* yet the total effect of the sculpture is different, a unique and powerful rendering of the Sinhala dilemma as expressed in ritual drama. In the *Pietà* the Virgin Mary is *dolorosa,* yet composed, even serene in her grief, with the dead, limp Jesus in her arms. By contrast Pattini is contorted with agony, her left breast gouged out, her left hand over the head in the typical Sinhala gesture of despair. Unlike Jesus whose body is intact, Pālanga's body is mutilated, his right leg cut off at the knee and the left at the ankle; his genitals are missing and replaced in the sculpture with long and deep gashes. But the castration theme is fully disguised and has to be extricated, somewhat painfully, by the analyst! The ritual drama does not require it; the drama, as far as this theme is concerned, is far removed, if not *disconnected,* from the sources of motivation.

3. Yalman noted as I did that Pālanga is often called Pālanga Terunnānse, "the monk Pālanga," by ritual performers.[41] On the manifest level this is absurd, since he is not a monk, nor does he act like one. Moreover celibacy, the hallmark of the monk, isn't exactly one of Pālanga's virtues! But on a deeper unconscious level of signification, the monk by virtue of his shaven head is a "castrated person." It is this level of signification that is tapped in the designation of Pālanga as *terunnānse.* Some performers were aware of its anomaly and substituted the term *gurunnānse* (teacher, exorcist), but this makes little sense on either manifest or latent levels.

If motivations such as impotence anxiety and castration are disconnected from the ritual, why is it necessary to deal with them in a psychoanalytic anthropology? I suggest there are good reasons for this. The basic theme of the fickle husband and his relationship with his two spouses (the wild and the tame) has deep motivational roots, and the power of the narrative derives from them, as the power of *Hamlet* or *Oedipus Rex* derives from the poetic drama that encompasses the powerful human motivations of the Oedipus complex. In our mythic enactment the overt themes of righteousness and justice are expressed through a special type of narrative that sends taproots into the unconscious motivations and deep anxieties of Sinhalas. But while the narrative is a progressive development of a set of psychic motives, the specific expectable motives (i.e., castration and impotence anxiety) are not directly dealt with in the drama, since they are not germane to its profound and consciously recognized themes. Yet they do appear in the symbolism of the ritual drama, as my discussion of disembowelling, breast tearing, and other examples shows. Here, unlike the foundational relationship of the fickle husband to his spouses, the expectable symptomatic reactions are totally disguised in symbolic action governed by the overdetermination of meaning. Nevertheless, the power of some of these symbols comes from the hidden motive. When disguise and disconnection occur a psychoanalytic anthropology must become a kind of historical philology inciting us to practice a historical (genetic) etymology of the symbol to extract its hidden power.

The grand ritual drama of the "killing and resurrection" is out of vogue today. I saw several performances in the period 1956–1961. Even at that time, ritual specialists were afraid to perform it for fear of *vas,* meaning "ritual danger." They were especially afraid of two sequences: the killing of Pālanga and that of Pattini tearing off her breast. Everyone felt that a slight mistake or inadvertent error might result in the actual death of the person who acts the role of Pālanga and dire consequences for the priest dressed as Pattini, especially blindness or impotence. In fact one senior priest interpreted his infertility as a consequence of *vas* from acting the goddess role. It is interesting that the priests implicitly connected blindness and impotence. These myth associations seem to lend credence to our interpretation that impotence anxiety is represented in disguise in the enactment. I could never be certain, though, whether the nonperformance of this ritual drama was the fear of ritual danger (*vas*) or whether this fear was a rationalization for the nonperformance of the ritual (owing to its length, difficulty of mustering resources, etc.) or both. Either way most performers even in 1956–1961 substituted for the numinous ritual several vulgar and obscene dramas that showed little manifest or thematic linkage with the myths and rituals of the goddess. In parts of the southern province, they enacted the comic rituals of Bam̆bura or Hātabam̆bura; in the Western and Sabaragamuva provinces, a comic drama known as "the killing of Rāma" (*rāma märīma*). Let me consider the significance of these cathartic rituals for the theme of this lecture.

The Bam̆bura Rituals

The first Bam̆bura ritual commences when two priests enter the arena to the beat of drums. Each wears a long white beard trailing down to the naked belly, a set of large false teeth made of mother-of-pearl with two tusks protruding at the ends, a large "false" nose, and a pair of huge bulging (phallic) eyes. The head is covered with a black turban. This grotesque apparition wonderfully captures the gross carnality and lasciviousness of the *senex-amans.* They dance in the arena shouting, clutching at their stomachs, their dancing bells jingling. Then they start singing and introducing themselves in song—the songs are not so much sung as shouted and laced with peals of raucous laughter. After further dancing and horseplay one priest leaves the arena. An attendant places a chair in mid-arena and sits on it.

Bam̆bura dances around the chair for a few minutes, and then he gets to work on the poor follow seated. He dances up to the attendant, throws a white cloth over the man as the barber does, steps back in a dance to survey his work, then sharpens a razor (a strip of banana bark) in superb comic mime, makes "soap suds" with a brush (another piece of banana bark), and brushes the man's face. He steps back to survey his work, dances for a while in the arena, snatches a piece of decorative banana bark from an altar, sharpens this "razor" again, and once again "shaves" his victim—from his face down to the armpits, then to the chest and stops at the stomach. Next he shaves the victim from the feet upwards and stops self-consciously above the knees. Then he trims his victim's beard in the same marvelous mime with two thin strips of banana bark. Now he moves the white cloth and uses it as a towel to wipe the attendant's face. This done, he replaces the cloth, steps back, dances in the arena rubbing the palms of his hands together with talcum powder as the village barbers do, then goes up to the attendant and "powders" his face and massages it. He dances in the arena once more, comes back with a "cup of oil" (a cupped leaf), and rubs the attendant's head. Finally he "combs" his hair, removes the cloth, fans him with it. Then he hauls the man out of the chair, embraces him, and dances with him in mid-arena to the embarrassment of his victim. What is impressive is that all the while he performs sodomous and homosexual pranks with his victim. While shaving he faces his victim and thrusts his body forward and backward. While "oiling" the head he commits a sodomous mime. He attempts to fool around with the genitals of the victim. Unlike in the other two dramas to be discussed below, the audience reacts to the antics of Bam̆bura of the *shaving* ritual with hesitant, almost anxious laughter.

The second Bam̆bura ritual, known as *Shooting of the Gun,* is again performed by the priest dressed as Bam̆bura. It is generally performed at about 4:30 A.M. when the audience is feeling drowsy—a marvelous comic antidote for sleep. The essential features of the drama are described below.

Bam̆bura: Well, friend, I've come.
Drummer: You've come?
Bam̆bura: Ha! Ha! Friend, I've come, friend, friend. . . .
Drummer: Then it's time to shoot. . . .
Bam̆bura: Ha, friend, I've come to the *nara* [human] world from the *nari* [fox] world.

The word *nari* (fox) is a mistake, and the drummer corrects him, but at the same time the word has a peculiar appropriateness, since the Bam̆bura does come from a smelly underworld, like the fox.

Bam̆bura: . . . that woman is pestering—ah, friend . . . she says she hasn't eaten for a long time . . . and so she gave me . . .
Drummer: What did she give you?
Bam̆bura: A cigar.

Again he confuses his words—he mutilates the words *cigar* and *cigarette* and makes them rhyme with *gun.*

Drummer: No, a gun.
Bam̆bura: Ah, friend, where is that?

While talking, Bam̆bura struts up and down the arena floor. He now sits in front of the gun made of banana bark with his legs stretched apart. Bam̆bura tells the drummer that his wife, the demoness Sācāpiri, had given him this gun to come to the human world to make a kill.

Bam̆bura: So I brought this thing along [pointing to the "gun"], but I don't know how to use it. . . .
Drummer: Have you brought it? . . . You'd better take it up.

Bam̆bura looks around him and pretends not to have seen the "gun"; instead he slowly takes his hand up along his thigh and rests it below his abdomen. More ribald comment soon establishes the connection between the gun and the penis. For example, he looks for the flintlock in the same manner, and the drummer of course corrects him and shows him the "gun."

Bam̆bura: Ah, friend, is this my one?
Drummer: Smell it and you'll find out!

In the same manner he looks for the ramrod which the drummer says is found at the end of the *kan̆da* (trunk, thigh, barrel). Then once more the drummer has to show him the real "gun" lying on the floor. He takes it and tries to pull out the ramrod—pushing his hand up and down in a masturbatory gesture—but finds the ramrod encrusted with rust through long disuse. No wonder he hasn't "shot" for quite a time and is now impatient to make a kill, he says. The ramrod does come out at last, but the drummer has further work for him. He asks Bam̆bura to tie a few rags round the ramrod and clean the barrel. This he proceeds to do with the same obscene gestures, by cupping the end of the "barrel" with one hand and continually poking the barrel with the finger of the other hand, imitating intercourse. Gunpowder is rammed in with similar gestures, and then he is asked to put in two bullets.

Bam̆bura: Bullets? Never heard of them. What are they like?
Drummer: Round balls.
Bam̆bura: Ah, now I remember.

He puts his hand under his buttocks and exclaims: "I've got two, but if I use them up how could I do any more shooting?" But the drummer corrects him, and Bam̆bura puts the bullets in with obscene gestures.

Drummer: Now you will have . . . to pull the trigger.
Bam̆bura: How is that done?

And so it goes on, obscenity piled upon obscenity. Finally Bam̆bura has the gun all ready to shoot and tells the drummer: "Do something quickly as the gun is about to go off!" The matter is taken care of when a man, taking the role of the quarry, lies on a mat. Bam̆bura places the gun below his abdomen, a huge extended penis, and struts up and down the arena. Finally he sees the quarry, jumps on him, thrusts the gun between his legs, and falls down in a pretended faint. He wakes up and exclaims that the gun is broken. He then goes looking for the missing parts.

On the face of it there seems no commonsense reason why a ritual depicting a shaving episode and one dealing with a gun should find a place in the ritual cycles of the Pattini cult. The mime of shaving is not a caste ritual of barbers; indeed no such caste existed in Buddhist Sri Lanka. We know that there is a deity called Bam̆bura among the aboriginal hunters (*Väddas*) of Sri Lanka, but if the present ritual had its roots in a Vädda fertility cult, it is no longer so. It is impossible, then, to see this ritual as having some conscious purpose or end, unlike other rituals of the Pattini cult. Furthermore, as far as informants were concerned, there was a total and complete inability to "explain" the ritual, whereas they could at least state the overt purpose of other rituals. Asked why it is performed, priests simply asserted that it has always been performed in that manner and that it *must* be performed in order to banish misfortune. Following a suggestion by Victor Turner we ought to at least inquire whether a ritual dealing with unconscious primary process material might not provide a block in native exegesis.[42]

What is going on in these two wonderfully obscene ritual dramas? Let me reiterate the very obvious and important fact that these two farces (and the one that follows) are self-consciously recognized as substitutes for the dromenon or numinous resurrection drama. And yet the one has no substantive or thematic connection with the other. A connection is supposed to exist between the two types of performances, yet in fact no connection can be seen on the surface. I suggest that we go beneath the surface and see the two types in a dialectical relationship with each other. The numinous and the obscene dramas have at base similar motives, but the former moves in a progressive direction that encompasses archaic motives in a larger universe of meaning, while the latter moves regressively, tapping the audience's unconscious anxieties. The symbolization is direct and powerful: castration anxiety is represented in the shaving ritual (the symbol of the razor) and impotence fears in the shooting ritual (the gun symbol). Homosexual sodomy is also acted out in the shaving ritual, though this is not the main motive that is being expressed therein, as I have shown in my longer work.

The demon Bam̆bura is an old person, i.e., sexless, "castrated," incapable of functioning sexually. Bam̆bura also is sexually incompetent with his wife, who says that "she hasn't eaten for a long time." In the shaving ritual he depicts the communal fears of castration anxiety, through shaving, which is a form of symbolic castration. Moreover, all parts of the body are shaved, except the genital area which is deliberately and self-consciously left out. It is as if powerful motives that are held in constraint in the numinous drama are being expressed directly in the obscene ritual. Yet, in the shaving ritual, the funny old man is not so funny—he wields the razor, and he is the castrating father. In the gun ritual, impotence anxieties are bared; fears regarding potency are expressed in the preoccupation with preparing the gun for shooting, the idea that the gun is about to fire before reaching the quarry, and so forth. Castration fears and the painful, violent nature of intercourse are expressed in the very choice of the symbol—the gun—which breaks into pieces after the shooting is over, and Baṁbura has to go look for the missing parts.

In my previous detailed description and analysis of this comic drama, I stated that the symbolization process here is strictly parallel to that of dreams insofar as they are not incorporated into a higher-level cognitive scheme. I now think this is a mistake, and I was a victim of my own language game in describing these rituals as "cathartic." This term is a heuristically convenient one, but no more than this. The fact that these rituals send taproots into deep motivations—that they exhibit a regressive movement and provide catharses—does not mean that they are isomorphic with dreams. Quite the contrary, since the work of culture has transformed fantasy material into comedy. The dramas are *ludicrous* because they are constituted of the ludic—an adult game of *fort-da* whereby people handle anxieties through shared humor and objectification in external action.[43] These humorous dramas provide myth models for people to deal with their anxieties and also with other, more consciously recognized, social problems through satire and comedy. Insofar as these are social forms and communal actions, they permit Sri Lankan men to "talk" about their anxieties, not in common everyday discourse, but in the indirect yet personal language of symbols articulated into ritual dramas.

It is therefore a pity that the relentless encroachment of bourgeois values has, along with other social forces, tended to erode comic dramas, not only in the rituals described here, but in exorcistic rituals and in folk theatre. Even when I first saw these rituals in the late fifties the chief priest had sometimes to make a speech to the audience to apologize for the vulgarities that custom compelled them to perform. In 1986, as I was engaged in writing up this lecture for publication, I met a priest I knew from earlier times. He told me that now, when they perform a rare or occasional cycle of rituals for Pattini, only the "shaving ritual" is enacted; the shooting of the gun is too vulgar to be tolerated by present audiences. In this instance it is very clear that the demise of the drama is caused by the influx of bourgeois values into village society rather than the demise of the motives precipitating symbolic formation. These motives will continue to exist, but they will be expressed through personal defenses and also perhaps in socially disruptive ways. There is no connection between the "causes" that led to the formation of the drama and the historical causes that led to its decline.

The Killing of Rāma

The killing of Rāma deals with a Tamil merchant from India who comes to Sri Lanka to sell his wares. His servant Rāma steals some of his goods and runs away, but the merchant manages to get him back by magic. He then tortures Rāma and cuts him up, but the Sinhala people are not pleased. They tell him to resurrect Rāma. The merchant asks Rāma to awake by the command of his mother, mother-in-law, and sundry kinsmen; but of course this does not resurrect Rāma. The verses sung here are a superb comic parody of Pattini asking her consort to arise from the dead. Ultimately the merchant asks various gods to resurrect Rāma, but only when he invokes Pattini does Rāma awake.

I shall not discuss the rich comedy of this play except to mention the central act of the killing of Rāma. Since this ritual is a substitution for the "killing and resurrection," we can legitimately infer that the mutilation, death, and resurrection of Rāma is a parody of the mutilation, death, and resurrection of Pālanga. Yet since Rāma is not Pālanga but only a substitute for him, the actors not only cut his body up and disembowel him, as they did with Pālanga, but, unlike in Pālanga's case, they conclude the mutilation of Rāma by humorously and self-consciously chopping off his penis!

There is no need to repeat the previous argument here except to say that the ritual performers have substituted the vulgar drama for the numinous. It is possible that they have taken an extant secular drama and converted it to suit their purposes here; or they might have created this drama de novo. In any case I think that there was a strong imperative in traditional Sinhala culture to represent anxiety as comedy to the extent of substituting the ludicrous for the numinous, or changing the whole tone of a preexisting numinous or serious performance into a comic one. This is the subject that I shall now explore.

"Distortion" in the Work of Culture

In the previous sections I discussed the substitution of one form for the other, the cathartic rituals in place of the dromena. In the ritual drama that I shall now discuss a different process has occurred. A serious ritual or dromenon has been converted into a vulgar comic drama under the impetus of the comic imperative in Sri Lankan culture and, of course, by the need to objectify in communal drama the kind of motivations and anxieties discussed earlier. These kinds of motivations have resulted in a radical change in the direction of the myth from a progressive into a regressive mode and a *distortion* in the form of the presentation.

Distortion, a basic process in the dream work, also operates in the work of culture, but with an important difference. In the dream work, distortion is the work of the censor (superego); in the present case where a serious text is converted into a comic one, distortion is part of the work of culture.

The ritual that I shall now discuss is called "the shooting of the mango" (*aṁba vidamana*). I have seen several versions of this text in the manuscripts of ritual specialists. The myth, I noted earlier, deals with several past births of the goddess Pattini culminating in her final conception in a golden mango in the orchard of the king of Pāṇḍi (Pandya). The king is informed of this, and he asks the people to shoot it, but none succeed until the king of the gods, Sakra (Indra), disguised as an old man, shoots it. The juice from the mango blinds the king's middle eye, the symbol of his divine power and arrogance. The frightened monarch places the mango in a golden casket and floats it down the river Kāvēri (kāviri). A merchant prince and his wife bathing in the lower reaches find the casket and take it home; after seven days a female infant is "born" of the mango. It is she who will later marry Pālanga and get deified as the goddess Pattini.

Reading the myth one is hard put to see anything comic in it. From internal evidence it is also clear that the myth is meant to be enacted—but in serious, not comic fashion. While it is true that no ritual drama is a literal enactment of a myth, this one almost totally ignores the content of the myth it is supposed to enact! The underlying deep motivations result in the distortion of the content and the direction of the myth. Some performers say that they are scared to enact the blinding of the king's middle eye for fear of ritual danger. In this case, the explanation is at best only partly true, for the rest of the ritual could be enacted; moreover there are ritual techniques for indirectly or symbolically enacting episodes that deal with blinding. The ritual drama then largely ignores the serious content and purposes of the myth and focuses on a specific episode therein—the arrival of god Sakra disguised as an old beggar who comes down to earth to shoot the wondrous mango. The myth text describes Sakra as a humpbacked old man; the ritual drama transforms him into one with a "humped front," that is, possessed of a huge lump below his abdomen, a pair of enlarged testicles. He comes hobbling into the arena, wearing an old-man mask, clutching his lump, and engages in a comic dialogue with the priests, the drummer, and sundry members of the audience. Let me quote a few excerpts from this drama.

Sakra: Grandson (*munuburē*)! (Sakra exclaims and moans. He feigns great pain, holds his "lump" below the abdomen, and collapses on the floor.)

Members of the audience, in feigned solicitude, ask concernedly: Oh, grandpa (*muttē*).

Assistant Priest: Muttē, it certainly looks as if you are in great "pain" (*amāru* pain, trouble). I'll send you a helper (*ādārakāraya*).

Sakra now falls on the floor, holding his "lump." Laughter and loud comments from the audience.

Sakra: Grandson, *ammā* (mother) is going past my groin (*älapata*).

Priest: Not *ammā* (mother)—you mean *ämma* (rheumatism).

Sakra: Yes, yes it is *ammā* (mother), you're right.

Priest: Ämma!

Sakra: All right, *ämma.* Alas, Grandson, I have the "big disease" (*mahaleḍa*). (A pun; *mahaleḍa,* literally "big disease," referred traditionally to small pox, but here it refers to the size of the "lump.")

Priest: (continuing the pun) That is infectious; we cannot have you anywhere here—we'll send you to the hospital.

Drummer: Now try to sit down properly grandpa, sit properly.

Sakra tries to sit properly, but the "lump" gets in his way.

Drummer: Grandpa has a dangerous disease, I think.

Sakra: Grandson! I have a "big" (*loku,* large, big, serious) illness.

Drummer: What is the nature of your illness?

Sakra: It is like—like a ball (he shouts out the last phrase, *bōle vageyi*).

Drummer: Jam-bōle? (large citrus known as *jambōle*) Or *rubber-bōle* ("rubber ball")?

Members of audience: Bälun bōle de? ("Is it a balloon ball?")

Sakra utters a volley of gibberish.

> *Drummer:* The disease you've got is not at all good.
> *Sakra:* I've got the *bōle leḍa* ("disease of the balls").
> *Drummer: Jambōle?* (large citrus)
> *Priest:* Here! if you can't tell us plainly what it is, write it down for us, will you?

Kids in the audience come close to him, and Sakra shouts, "Children, don't come here saying huk! huk! (fuck, fuck)." Sakra goes on holding his "lump" and shouting in agony.

> *Drummer:* I'll tell you how to get this cured quickly.
> *Sakra:* What remedy do you suggest, grandson?
> *Drummer:* I'll get an Ayurvedic doctor who'll pierce it (*vidinavā*).
> *Sakra:* (anxiously) Pierce it?
> *Drummer:* Yes, he has *kaṭu* (thorns, sharp surgical instruments) to incise it.

The incising of the testicles by an actor dressed as an Ayurvedic physician occurs with a great deal of vulgar humor. The drama concludes with Sakra recounting his life with his spouse. His spouse has had a visitor who comes smelling of perfume. Sakra thinks this is a *preta,* an ancestral spirit; but this *preta* smokes cigarettes and leaves the stubs for Sakra as an oblation! Sakra says his wife is very nice looking and kind to him; she gives him knocks on the head all the time. "Such love," says the drummer. The audience also constantly butts in with ribald comment and laughs at Sakra, the sexually incompetent husband and cuckold.

The amazing feature of this ritual drama is that it virtually ignores the myth it is supposed to enact. The ritual is extremely humorous, and everyone seems to enjoy it because no one truly identifies with Sakra, the hump-fronted old man. Castration anxieties are expressed in this manner, but the person who suffers is the old man—the father—rather than the son. If in reality castration anxiety is the fear deriving from the threatening father, this is reversed in the ritual: it is a talion reaction in which the castrating father becomes the ridiculous, laughable castrated person, no longer a source of threat to the son.

When the central theme of the drama—the myth of the goddess' birth—is ignored and an obscene feature is introduced, might we not assume that it is due to important motivational concerns that demand psychological expression? A commonsense explanation will not do. For example, Sakra appears in Buddhist *jātaka* folklore as a humpbacked old man, but the "humped front" is a Sinhala innovation specific to the ritual. The physiological model for the presentation of god Sakra is that of a person suffering from filaria of the testicles, but it is unlikely that the Sinhalas are so obsessed with the occurrence of this rare disease, or with the commoner and less dramatic case of hydrocele, that they have to depict it in their rituals. The syndrome of a person suffering from enlarged testicles is an expression of the more powerful unconscious motives of castration and impotence anxiety discussed earlier. These motivations are expressed in the ritual drama by a distortion of the serious into the comic and the creation of a set of regressive symbolizations: the large size of the genitals, as in the Baṁbura rituals; the striking, almost blatant, expression of castration where the testicles are pricked with pointed instruments accompanied by expressions of pain by Sakra; sex as painful and presented as if it were psychologically associated with castration anxiety; Sakra himself presented as a sexually inadequate person receiving knocks from his wife who cuckolds him with her paramour; and degradations of the mother as, for example, when Sakra confuses the rheumatism of the groin with his mother going past his groin.

The Limits of Cultural Elaboration

In my work on the goddess Pattini, I used the terms "dromenon" or "ideal representation" to describe the serious drama and "catharsis" to describe the vulgar, using catharsis in the sense of "acting out" rather than the Aristotelean idea of the purgation of pity and terror. On reading Ricoeur I found that these terms seemed to echo his view of the processes of symbolic formation as progressive and regressive. I am not fully satisfied with these terms, but I think they will at least help us organize the Sri Lankan data.

In both types the mythic tradition is not a direct reflex of unconscious primary process material, as in symptoms; but they exhibit different degrees of symbolic remove from the sources of motivation. Conventional psychoanalytic anthropology would see both types of symbolic structures as defense systems and symptomatic representations of archaic motivations. But clearly in the dromenon these motivations have been worked and reworked in the minds of men and brought in line with the philosophically profound aspects of the culture. Thus it is not only Pattini who is idealized: Valli Ammā and Mādēvi are also idealized in their own way, as sensually and erotically desirable images, representing a thoroughgoing transformation of the infantile image of the degraded mother-harlot into another picture of the divine. What is striking about the Sinhala situation is that the unrealizable goal of searching for the two mothers is resolved in the symbolic plane of myth and religion: the idealized Oedipal mothers are the goddess Pattini and Valli Ammā. Contrast this situation with Western romanticism where one tries to divinize the spouse, an ultimately unrealizable quest, for no flesh and blood human can measure up to the ideal. In Sinhala culture idealization can hold full sway untrammelled by the realities of mundane experience.

On the other hand the myth model of the two mothers, though based on fantasy, itself influences the fantasy and helps perpetuate it in the consciousness of people. Not only fantasy though; for while no woman can match the ideal figures of Pattini and Mādēvi, or Dēvasēna and Valli, they can influence the way men choose their wives or their mistresses. Myth model, fantasy, and reality are involved in a causally interlocking circular network of cognitive operations that reinforce one another.

In reflecting on the ecstatic priests and priestesses I noted that culture imposes limits on the development of the personal symbols. These are limits imposed on the creators or makers of the symbols. In collective representations also similar imposition of limits occurs, limits on the interpretation the myth or symbol system can achieve in the discourse of a plurality of people living in a particular society. The pageant of Skanda and Valli as a collective representation is the same for Buddhists and Hindus assembled at Kataragama. But its interpretation is not. For the Buddhists the significance of the ritual relates to the idealization of the god's illicit love affair with his mistress. It can hardly go beyond this. But in philosophical and speculative Hinduism, there can be a greater proliferation of meaning. In Hindu *bhakti* thought as expounded in texts such as the *Bhagavata Purāna,* adulterous love (*pārakīya*) ideally represented in Kṛiṣṇa and the *gōpi*s (milkmaids) is so intense and passionate an experience that it could serve as model for the individual's devotion to god, since that too is a love that should ignore all conventional restraints.[44]

The austere presence of the Buddha prevents a parallel process happening in Sinhala culture. The Buddhist religion suffuses the domain of the sacred and defines its outer boundaries. Pattini cannot become a Hindu *śakti* or a manifestation of Pārvati, or having anything to do with salvation or human redemption. Salvation lies in the Buddha word and nowhere else. Pattini in Sinhala society can develop only in terms of the limits imposed by Buddhism: she is an exemplar of Buddhist piety and will in ages to come achieve Buddhahood herself. When a passionate Buddhist devotee spills over the boundaries imposed by Buddhism he must pull back; or practice a private esotericism; or become a socially recognized crank or eccentric; or become a member of a small semisecret religious enclave or cult group; or what is rare, if not impossible, become a formal convert to Hinduism. The philosophical interpretation of the ritual, however, does not cancel the psychological ones. Quite the contrary: the Valli-Skanda relationship, for example, has erotic meaning and deep motivational significance over and above the meanings imposed by the philosophically sophisticated. Shulman has noted this very neatly in respect of the profoundly abstract symbolism that South Indian Śaiva Siddhānta philosophy imposes on Dēvasēna and Valli. "According to Śaiva Siddhānta, Tĕyvyāṉai (Dēvasēna) symbolises the *kriyā śakti* (Tamil, *kriyācatti,* 'the power of works or motivations'), while Valli embodies the *icchāśakti* (Tamil, *iccacātti,* 'the power of desire'). Even on the level of abstract symbolism, Valli is connected with the human experience of desire (*icchā*)."[45] I might add that it is "the human experience of desire" that will have primary significance for most people unacquainted with Śaiva Siddhānta. All of these reinforce my analytical strategy in which I explore the psychoetymology of the representation to unravel its deeper meanings.

❸

Symbolic Remove and the Work of Culture

In this section I shall spell out the implications of the previous ethnographic presentations for a psychoanalytic anthropology. Thus far we have only made one major point taken from Ricoeur: that of the dialectic of progression and regression. This notion implied a criticism of psychoanalytic anthropology which tended to treat cultural phenomena as direct reflexes of unconscious or deep motivations, or as defense systems where philosophical and cosmological notions are subsidiary products of the secondary process. Here I shall develop these arguments further in order to show the limits as well as the exciting possibilities for a psychoanalytic anthropology geared to the study of symbol systems.

Let me start off with a practical reason why psychoanalysis is useful for the study of symbol systems in South Asia. In Southern Asia we are dealing with societies that have already dethroned consciousness in preference to realities which are achievable through states of trance where "unconscious thought" (using this term advisedly) prevails. The philosophical significance of psychoanalysis for Western society, as Ricoeur points out, is precisely this dethroning of consciousness which Freud along with Marx and Nietzsche achieved.[46] The Cartesian notion of consciousness, central to Western science and philosophy, lost its primacy since consciousness could be "false." But the existence of unconscious processes implied an important paradox; they are by definition inaccessible and also manifest as nonlingual forms of communication, a privatized communication as Habermas put it. Consequently psychoanalysis is both a tool or technique for reaching that which is normally inaccessible (free association and psychoanalytic therapy) and a theory that provides a set of rules for interpreting these processes. It is in the latter sense, as providing rules for interpretation, that Ricoeur says psychoanalysis is a hermeneutical system or, as Habermas puts it, a mode of "general interpretation," as contrasted with a purely phenomenological "being in the world" description of reality.[47]

To shift our argument to South Asia, we have a situation where consciousness lacks primacy to begin with. If so, one could argue that unconscious processes have a greater saliency in those societies, and perhaps psychoanalysis is equally if not more relevant there. No one doubts that the kind of unconscious processes that South Asian philosophers and practical meditators dealt with were related to their own views of the world and life. But for some striking instances to be discussed later, South Asians did not develop anything like a psychoanalysis. This would be *our* task, living in *our* own times to find out whether the psychoanalytic theory, if not the therapy, is applicable to other societies. It is as ridiculous to argue, as anthropologists often do on prima facie grounds, that since psychoanalysis developed in the West, it is inapplicable elsewhere, as it is to argue that since Buddhist meditation developed in India it is inapplicable to the West. Buddhist meditation, like other systems of thought developed in India, has moved in the course of its history to a large part of the then-known ancient world. So why should it not, with appropriate changes and modifications, be applicable elsewhere? Anthropologists in particular have a naive notion that a system of thought, if developed in one culture (especially in the West), is inapplicable elsewhere. Or if it is applicable, it is due to some *other* reason and not due to the intrinsic value of the ideas. Thus even a discerning scholar like Shweder thinks that psychoanalysis is popular because it is part of a wider theory found in folk psychobiologies of Ancient Greece, among Zoroastrians, Orthodox Jews, and New Guinea Highlanders.[48] But even if he is right, the question of an ontological affinity with other forms of life is not the issue. Rather, does psychoanalysis as a nomological system help us to understand and explain Western man, and also, can its rules be manipulated with sufficient flexibility to understand man in South Asia and man in general?

Right through human history intellectuals, be they scientists, philosophers, or religious thinkers like the Buddha, thought that their speculations, though generated in a particular social milieu, could nevertheless transcend and embrace larger worlds. Unhappily anthropologists, and recent thinkers like Foucault, while noting the rootedness of thought in the framework of history and culture, have made the fallacious inference that nomological thought lacked the ability to transcend time, place, culture, and the trap of history. Even deconstruction is an activity that can transcend itself insofar as it can mobilize scholars from different backgrounds to enter into a common agreement as to its validity as an intellectual operation. The difficulty in the way of knowledge—its embeddedness in accepted conventions, its frame in history, its domination by vested interests—only illustrates the poignancy and finitude of our search for what it is to be cultural and human, and not the impossibility or incapacity for cultural and historical transcendence. It is one thing to reject the naive belief in Method and of a universally and logically integrated body of laws of man and society, but it is another to affirm the vision of an ontology of being human and cultural that can be anchored in, and also transcend to a greater or lesser degree, its rootedness in history and time.

As a starting point of my discussion of the relationship between symbols and deep motivations I dealt with two movements of meanings in relation to the sources of motivation—that of progression and regression, which in turn may appear separately in different symbolic forms or dialectically within the same form, or also dialectically in two forms that make sense in terms of contrast. It is time to develop this important insight of Paul Ricoeur into a vocabulary that might make sense for a psychoanalytic anthropology. The fundamental problem of a psychoanalytic anthropology is the manner in which the archaic motivations of childhood are transformed into symbolic forms, whether they be personal symbols, myth, or collective representations. The basic model for this is already set by Freud in *The*

Interpretation of Dreams. To start off let me ignore Freud's own naive theory of universal symbols which he incorporated into the later editions of the dream book. Here, influenced by his brilliant and erratic student Wilhelm Stekel, he developed the idea that some symbols resisted the dream work and could be interpreted in universal terms almost in the manner of Jung's archetypes. Context was not crucial for such universals as pillars, planes, snakes, cows and climbing stairs.[49]

It may well be that human experience focuses on certain types of images more than others—for example, nurturance could be expressed in milk-yielding animals, milk trees and milk-producing people (shepherds)—but context, as anthropologists have pointed out, is central to their full understanding in both dream and culture. Thus it is not that these images escape the dream work; their contextualization is part of the dream work. And it is difficult to believe that these symbols cannot acquire, either in the individual or in certain cultural contexts, different or even contrary meanings, and that the *processes* by which these meanings get formed are not intelligible in terms of such mechanisms of the dream work as displacement, condensation, and so forth.

Having rejected Freud's theory of universal symbols one can now consider the enormous significance of his dream theory. In it Freud traces the manifest dream regressively into its archaic roots in unconscious infantile motivations; then from these motivations he moves forward, progressively, to construct the rules by which the dream thoughts (the deep motivations) get transformed into the manifest dream. These rules are the dream work, wonderfully illustrated in chapter 6 of the dream book. These discoveries, though revolutionary in significance, are based on a circular logic: from the manifest dream (the ideational representation of a motive) to its genesis in deep motivations; then from the deep motivations back to the manifest dream, but now enriched with the understanding of the rules (the dream work) that transforms motives into images. Freud did not realize that this circular logic was forced by the nature of the subject matter, rather than based on the rules of inference formulated by philosophers.

Unconscious motivations cannot be seen, but must be inferred from their representation in an idea ("ideational representative"); but these motives are real and linked in a chain of indeterminate causal significance to the representation. The "causal chain" linking in complex ways the motive with the representation was once again not based on the philosopher's logic of necessary and/or sufficient conditions; it could be better understood as the dream *work,* or to use another vocabulary, as the rules by which the motivations of childhood get transformed into the images of the manifest dream. These rules cannot be mechanically applied, and they have no predictive significance whatever. They have to be used as part of an interpretive process whereby one begins to understand the significance of a dream in the life history of an individual.

Paul Ricoeur noted that in this scheme the dream is a text. Freud himself recognized this and viewed interpretation as the deciphering of a text, or the replacement of one (unintelligible) text with another.[50] But Freud did not fully consider the nature of the dream text since he did not have the benefit of contemporary experimental research on dreaming. The experimenter's invention of the dream is *not* the dream as we know it. No human culture ever knew of REM states, and consequently, the dream for all of us was not the dream that was dreamt, but the dream that was reported. It was therefore a text. The manner of reporting could vary according to the values of a society, as, for example, whether people thought dreams had prognosticative meaning or not, whether they were analogous to narrative, and so forth. The dream as dreamt may well lack form, but the dream text generally has it; and in some dreams, particularly in cultures where narrative is significant for living, both the dreamt dream and the text may have greater form than, let us say, in the United States. Freud then dealt with the reported dream, or the dream text, and the rules that produced this text.

The dream work constitutes the rules that produce the manifest dream from the dream thoughts (deep motivations); these rules deal with the transformation of complex motives into dream images (or dream symbols if one doesn't confuse "symbols" with Freud's discussion of representation through symbols). Thus Freud's theory is essentially one of symbol or image formation, albeit confined to the dream as a symbolic set. But dreams are not culture, though they may be the stuff from which some types of cultural forms are psychogenetically derived. Culture is a symbolic order far removed cognitively, ontologically, and ontically from dreams. A psychoanalytic study of cultural forms must move from the dream work to more complex processes that can help us comprehend these more complex forms. One must move from the work of dreams into what, following Freud himself, I call *the work of culture.*[51]

In the dream work Freud dealt with some of the fundamental rules or principles of symbolic transformation—condensation, displacement, representation by its opposite, projection, and so forth. These rules of the dream work are basic and apply to the work of culture also, and some, such as condensation, representation by its opposite, and projection, are more important than others. If dreams according to Freud lack the logic of causality, syntax, and temporal sequence—not so with cultural forms, which have all of them. The work of culture assumes much of the dream work but develops in a more complex direction, since it deals with the more complex processes whereby unconscious motives are transformed into cultural symbols that deal with our adult lives in the vigilance of daylight, not in the poorly guarded dream time of the night. Even the basic mechanisms of the dream work are, in the work of culture, subject to a higher level of cognitive ordering. Further, if the dream work is basic to the work of culture, the latter might also help understand the former. Why so? Because, in the first place, culture influences dreams (and vice versa) and, secondly, because Freud simply did not believe that dreams could have creative and cognitively complex components.

Ideally one should be able to formulate the rules of the work of culture in the manner of the dream work. But this may in fact not be possible, and perhaps one should be content with the following:

1. A descriptive account of the manner in which deep motivation gets transformed into public culture;
2. A tentative formulation of the rules of the work of culture in broad areas of life, as for example in *Medusa's Hair* where I talk of such things as subjectification and objectification;[52]
3. A more rigorous formulation of rules in specific types of symbolic forms, such as spirit possession.

In this work I can only highlight the issue as a priority for research in the development of psychoanalytic anthropology and concern myself with a few basic principles that underlie the work of culture.

If psychoanalysis focussed on the overdetermination of motive, one must, in a psychoanalytic anthropology, balance this with the overdetermination of meaning (i.e., polysemy). Thus overdetermination as I use it, and I think this is not a departure from Freud, refers to either the multiple motives that go to make a symbolic form, or the multiple meanings in a symbolic form or sequence that are determined by a variety of motives; or combinations of both. For example, the Bam̆bura drama is a symbolic sequence, rich in meanings of a special sort (puns, malapropisms, spoonerisms) that are in turn overdetermined by the motives of impotence and castration anxiety, among others. Nevertheless the meanings of this ritual move towards the motives, or are intrinsically associated with them, whereas what we call the dromenon (or ideal representation, or the numinous ritual) draws on the motivational sources to develop a system of meanings that move away, in a progressive direction, from these archaic motivations of childhood. In my reworking of Ricoeur I prefer to describe these phenomena as *levels of symbolic remove* from deep motivations, and symbolic remove in turn produces different *levels of symbolization,* some closer to, some more distant from the motivations that initially (psychogenetically) triggered the symbolic formation. I use levels of symbolic remove because *all* cultural symbols are *removed* from their motivational springs, unlike, let us say, a hysterical paralysis or an obsessive compulsive neurosis that is, more or less, a direct precipitate of the motive. For example, Freud has a classic study of the obsessional neurosis of a woman who wanted to arrange her tablecloth in a certain way, so that she might purposelessly ring the bell for the maid. This obsessive action was related directly to the traumatic experience with her sexually incompetent husband on her wedding night and her fear that the ink stains she placed on the sheet would not fool the maid.[53] But even in this case, unlike a body symptom, there is symbolic elaboration, though the "symbol" is directly related to the underlying anxiety. Though I retain a distinction between symptom and symbol for analytical purposes, there are situations where it is not possible to draw a fine line between them. The idea of symbolic remove and levels of symbolization resolves this difficulty by recognizing that some symbolic forms are closer to, or isomorphic with, symptoms while others are far removed from them; whereas for Freud, as well as for those anthropologists who deal with cultural defenses and projective systems, there was indeed an isomorphism, if not a simple replication, of symbol and symptom.

The idea of symbolic remove is, in my analysis, fundamental to the work of culture and is in turn based on a principle that Freud noted with respect to dreams—the infinite substitutability of symbols (ultimately related perhaps to man's neurological makeup). If, however, the rules of the dream work are operative in the work of culture, then one might argue that the rules of the work of culture might also be operative in the former. Let me spell out two reasons for this assertion. First, symbolic remove is anchored to the more basic principle of substitutability, especially where substitutability is important as in dreams. Second, since dreams are influenced by culture, basic principles that influence culture might also be expected to influence dreams. I shall soon demonstrate the validity of both these assertions.

In this section I can only argue the case for the notion of degrees of symbolic remove; the metatheoretical formulation of this problem must await further study and research. If I were to list the key problem in psychoanalytic anthropology, it is this and not the problem of normal and abnormal, which George Devereux thinks is central to this field.[54] The idea of degrees of symbolic remove has considerable importance for the interpretation of cultures and for the comparative method, and therefore I shall spell it out further.

I noted that "symbolic remove" is based on the psychoanalytic idea that symbols in principle, if not always in practice, show infinite substitutability. Related to this idea is another principle of the work of culture that psychoanalysis has not, and could not, consider seriously since it would threaten the isomorphism between symbol and symptom. And that is the principle of disconnection of the symbol from the sources of motivation. Substitution implies that symbol *X* related to motive *Y* can be replaced by symbols *A, B* or *C . . . n. A, B, C* are all "isomorphic replacements" of *X,* related to motive *Y* in identical or similar manner.[55] "Disconnection" questions the postulated isomorphism and suggests that *A, B, C . . . n* might exhibit degrees of symbolic remove from *Y* and might eventually lose its connection with *Y.* Freud identified this process in the dream book when he used Nietzsche's phrase "transvaluation of all psychical values" or "psychical transvaluation of the material," though he did not develop this idea very far.[56] In *New Introductory Lectures,* however, he came close to the idea of symbolic remove in his discussion of dream symbolism.[57] Admittedly, total disconnection is rare, but one can make a reasonable case that the more the symbol is removed from the sources of motivation the more it gets the attribute of arbitrariness, thus approximating the Saussurean idea of the arbitrary relation between signifier and signified.

Let me illustrate this process on the very basic level from a textbook case on dream imagery. The case is from Brenner's well-known *An Elementary Textbook of Psychoanalysis,* where he discusses the constant displacement and substitution of one dream by another, though the motivation for the dream (the dream thoughts) remains unchanged.[58] Assume, says Brenner, that the dreamer is a woman and that the crucial part of the latent dream derives from the Oedipal period of childhood and has to do with sex relations with her father. How is this represented in the manifest dream?

a. There could be a dream based on an appropriate fantasy from the oedipal stage of her life. Thus, in the dream *the dreamer and her father are fighting with each other, but, however, she experiences in the dream a feeling of sexual excitement.* But if the censor opposes this as being too close to the sources of motivation, you can have dream 'b' where the sexual excitement is debarred from consciousness.
b. She *dreams of fighting with her father.* But if this is also close to the original fantasy and provokes guilt or anxiety, you could have another substitute where the image of the father is deleted and you have 'c'.
c. The dreamer is *fighting with someone else—for example, her son.* But the image of fighting itself may be too close to the original fantasy and could therefore be replaced by another physical activity.
d. The dreamer is *dancing with her son.* But even this may be too disturbing, and you could then have the following substitution which eliminates the dreamer herself from the dream.
e. *A strange woman appears with a boy (who is the dreamer's son) in a room with a polished floor.*

Substitution can go on and on in this manner. To quote Brenner: "The example is not intended to imply that, in a particular dream, manifest content 'A' is tried first, then, if the ego will not tolerate 'A,' 'B' is substituted; if not 'B' then 'C'; and so forth. On the contrary, depending on the balance of forces between the defenses and the latent dream element, either 'A' or 'B' or 'C' will appear in the manifest dream."[59] Brenner, however, does not deal with the parallel process whereby these displacements and substitutions might result in a progressive *distancing* and ultimate *disconnection* of the dream from the sources of motivation, as a result of the "psychical transvaluation of the material." There are levels or degrees of symbolic remove here; the last dream has distanced itself from the Oedipal motive, whereas the first is locked into it. It is possible for an analyst to show its psycho-etymology in the Oedipal motive through free associations, as much as I showed the motive for castration in the "killing and resurrection" ritual. But the retrospective tracking of the dream has little to do with the ongoing meaning of the dream in the dreamer's deep motivation. The first and the last dream are qualitatively different. To go back to our terminology they exhibit, on the very basic and elemental level, different levels of symbolic formation. The last dream is like the game of *fort-da:* a disturbing dream thought is converted through play into an acceptable dream. It is doubtful whether "wish fulfillment" in the Freudian sense in fact occurs here: the dream certainly preserves sleep by producing a fantasy, but this fantasy is only peripherally, if at all, connected with the disturbing archaic motivations that initially instigated the dream work. The function of the dream has been to disconnect the dream text from the motive.

The preceding argument has considerable implications for the psychoanalytic study of society and culture. What I have said of the dream text is also true of cultural symbols: inasmuch as the degree of symbolic remove occurs in two types of ritual such as a dromenon and a catharsis within a single cultural tradition, as in Sri Lanka, one must grant the possibility that this may *not* occur in other cultural traditions. To put it differently, in Sri Lanka we noted the existence of both dromena and cathartic rituals, but surely it is possible for a society to have either dromena or cathartic rituals, or none, or combinations thereof. If within a single society you could have some symbol systems closer to the sources of infantile motivation than others, then it is also possible that some societies may utilize one propensity as against the other, or neither propensity and consequently remain relatively indifferent to symbolic elaboration in either direction. Thus cross-culturally you could have four ideal typical symbolic orientations:

1. The full utilization of both regression and progression entailing degrees of symbolic remove from archaic motivations. This is true of Sri Lanka.
2. The utilization of progressive or prospective symbols at the expense of regression. This is true of special groups in South Asia such as Brahmins. For example, in Sri Lankan ritual there is plenty of prescribed obscenity, but this is simply nonexistent in Brahmanic ritual. Moreover the power of the Brahmanic model is such that even non-Brahmanic ritual also tends to lack extreme obscenity (though of course clowning occurs in other contexts). Or take the case of the *lingam,* the phallic representation of Śiva. In mythology Śiva tries to rape the wives of ascetics, and they, enraged, chop off his penis, which then is transformed into the *lingam.*[60] Thus it is clear that psychoetymologically speaking the *lingam* is Śiva's penis. But when it is represented iconographically in Śaivite

temples it ceases to be a penis symbol, but represents instead god himself. The iconographic representation of the Śiva *lingam* is far removed, but not disconnected, from its psychogenetic source as a penis symbol.

3. The utilization of regression where the symbolic system is close to motivational sources. This is true of a society like that of the Sambia of New Guinea described by Gilbert Herdt.[61] There sometimes occurs an occasional parallelism between Sambia and India (or Sri Lanka). In both cultures there is a belief in semen loss and in semen-fostering foods or medical ingredients. But in Sambia there is a greater elaboration of these ideas in terms of deep motivations. Thus during male puberty rites the initiate must commit homosexual fellatio with his elders. This action results in the direct ingestion of the semen. In India direct semen ingestion occurs only in the rare idiosyncratic case. Sometimes raw eggs might be substituted as a semen-fostering substance; or more symbolically removed is *ghee* (clarified butter), an ingredient used in cooking and in medical prescriptions. Sambia ingestion of semen in homosexual fellatio, along with similar rites at puberty, directly tap deep motivations, whereas the Indian ones progressively move away from them. In all of these cases of psychological symbols, signifier and signified are metonymically or analogically, and not arbitrarily, linked. Arbitrariness tends to occur only in the extremities of symbolic remove.
4. The utilization of cultural symbolization is minimal, as in modern Protestantism and perhaps traditional societies like the Manus, or the Baining of New Guinea, an extreme case.[62] In the former the whole historical tradition and the institutions it later developed were hostile to the development of cultural symbolization.

Since I have an aversion for typologies, let me deconstruct this one and highlight a major problem in cross-cultural anthropology, namely, the symbolic potential of human beings everywhere, as a consequence of their neurophysiological nature, may be identical, but the utilization of that potential in existent human societies in respect of their symbol systems must show considerable variation and cross-cultural differences, some societies being more prone to symbolic elaboration while others are not, some permitting symbolic elaboration in special areas of social life while others, like Hindu India, permit the extreme proliferation of cultural symbolization in practically every domain of species existence. Everywhere there are probably institutions that foster, inhibit, or hinder the development of religious symbol systems.

The symbolic potential of a society is also probably linked to problems of reflexivity, awareness, or self-consciousness. Thus regressive symbolization may encourage abreaction and catharsis, whereas progressive symbolization may tend to encourage intellectual and philosophical reflection depending, as I stated earlier, on the limits imposed by the historical tradition of a group.[63] Symbol systems everywhere are articulated to what Weberians call "problems of meaning."

The position adopted here does not, I believe, entail a radical cultural relativism, but it does make problematic cross-cultural comparison and experimental procedures adopted in the anthropological study of symbols. Let me highlight this problem in relation to the "positivist" tradition in psychological anthropology of Kardiner, Whiting, and others.

In terms of the preceding argument, I can demonstrate that the conventional cross-cultural method and cross-cultural tests of causal hypotheses pertaining to symbols are for the most part meaningless. Thus the hypothesis that if you have X, a certain motive, you would also have Y, a certain cultural symbol causally associated with it, is impossible to test on a random sample for the simple fact that Y may show degrees of symbolic elaboration ranging from the absence of Y in some societies to its fullest symbolic elaboration in others. Furthermore the notion of substitutability of symbols implies that where X is related to Y in one society, X would be related to a substitute symbol Z in another society, rendering predictions either dubious or outright impossible. Third, the notion of disconnection implies that a postulated correlation between X and Y may not be a true casual relation insofar as Y has become disconnected from X, through the processes described earlier. Finally, while X may exist, Y may not since the motive may not have its symbolic counterpart in the society simply because Y may occur as a symptom on the individual level rather than as a symbol on the cultural level. The assumptions underlying conventional tests of hypotheses in psychological anthropology are that symbolic capacity is equivalent in all human societies and that this capacity must be uniformly manifest in cultural symbol systems everywhere.[64]

The lack of symbolic equivalence, the tolerance or lack thereof for cultural symbolization, has theoretical significance of the highest importance. That is, what are the conditions that permit the toleration of cultural symbolization, for example, in societies of South and Southeast Asia such as Sri Lanka, India, Indonesia?

I can only sketch the outlines of the problem here, for this complex question must be the subject of future research.

Consider the structural model of the id, superego, and ego as it was developed by Freud. In this model there is a barrier that separates the id and the primary processes located there from surfacing into consciousness, and this barrier is maintained through repression, a product of the action of both ego and superego. Distorted representations of unconscious motives appear through disguises as dreams, symptoms, slips of the tongue, and so forth. Consequently there is a block in public communication of the problem that afflicts the individual. In the societies of South Asia this model cannot be duplicated: the meaning of the barrier is different here. Primary process material from the id can move across the barrier the moment it is expressed in cultural symbols; id processes which are expressed as fantasy in the West can be transformed into culture, and, in such cases, they obviate the necessity for fantasy. Freud himself implicitly recognized this in his brief aside on the psychology of the mystic. "It is easy to imagine, too, that certain mystics may succeed in upsetting the normal relations between the different regions of the mind, so that, for instance, perception may be able to grasp happenings in the depths of the ego and in the id which were otherwise inaccessible to it."[65] If so, it is not all that difficult to imagine a culture, where mysticism has high value, effecting a blurring of the barrier separating consciousness and unconscious or ego, id, and superego and treating this as perfectly acceptable.

The replacement of symptoms and fantasies with symbols which permit movement across the barrier does not tell us much about the social and psychological conditions that foster this development. One thing is clear though: unconscious ideas, themselves unacceptable to consciousness, can obviously become acceptable to the conscience or to the superego when they are transformed into public culture. Unlike dreams, there is no censor at work. But this does not answer how these symbols came into being and continue to be created and recreated in the societies of South and Southeast Asia and how they have managed to pass through the barrier in the first place.

It seems to me that the kinds of societies I am talking about must tolerate fantasy coming into open consciousness. In addition to ideological reasons that I dealt with earlier there are also socioeconomic reasons parallel to the ideological. Following a suggestion of Marcuse, this must reverse the situation of Western industrial society (at least until recently) where the "performance principle" operates and there is a low premium on leisure. In the West the barriers among ego, id, and superego are strong; unconscious thoughts exist as *fleurs du mal*, as fantasies denigrated by the reality-oriented ego that is in turn a product of an achievement-oriented society. Marcuse says that while the infant is born polymorphously perverse, the performance principle (the dominant form of the reality principle in the West) channels these impulses into genitality and legitimate sexuality in monogamous marriage. At the base of this lies an extremely punitive superego with guilt entrenched as a powerful motive.[66] Now it is very likely that a different reality orientation occurs in South Asia. I shall develop this theme later but shall stress for now the fact that these societies place a much greater premium on leisure and less on the "performance principle" in Marcuse's sense. Concomitant with this there is a greater tolerance of fantasy and of the primary process in general. It is this tolerance that permits the transformation of fantasy into culture, the constant invention, creation, and re-creation of personal and collective symbols that permeate the life of the individual and the society.

In addition to this societal dimension, there may be, as Kakar suggests, a personality dimension that accounts for the fluidity of the barrier separating the three structural components of the mind.[67] In his perceptive study of Hindu personality and culture, Kakar argues that the contours of ego development are, in Hindu India, radically different from those in the West. He says, rightly, that the center of the child is the mother and notes the powerful symbiotic tie that binds this relationship. Mothers in India accede to their children's wishes rather than control them, so that there is no real detachment of the self from the mother in early childhood. This detachment comes later than in the West, and even when it does "the mental processes characteristic of the symbiosis of infancy play a relatively greater role" even in the personality of the adult Hindu. Consequently the boundaries between ego and id are not firm; id processes are permitted entry into the ego. In addition one might add that superego organization is different, with guilt less integrated into the structure of the conscious and shame playing a larger role than in the West. Kakar concludes:

> The projection of one's own emotions onto others, the tendency to see natural and human "objects" predominantly

> as extensions of oneself, the belief in spirits animating the world outside and the shuttling back and forth between secondary and primary process modes are common features of daily intercourse.[68]

In this situation reality becomes "inner oriented" and consonant with the ideological predisposition of the society. The true reality is not the phenomenal external world of economic want and scarcity or the political and social realm but the set of meanings, symbols, and cultural values that were originally created and concurrently mediated through unconscious and preconscious processes. The ordinary ego-oriented reality is *māya,* "illusion." Kakar perceptively observes:

> The distinctions between reality and *maya,* between *vidya* and *avidya*—true and false consciousness—illustrate a fundamental difference between Hindu and Western world images. . . . The maintenance of ego boundaries—between "inside" and "outside" and between "I" and "others"—and the sensory experiences and social relations based on these separations, is the stuff of reality in Western thought and yet *maya* to the Hindus. The optimal discrimination of this reality of separatedness, expressed in terms of heightened ego functions such as reality sense, reality testing and adaptation to reality, is the stated goal of Western psychotherapies, but of paltry importance in the Hindu ways of liberation.[69]

For Buddhists also this everyday world of reality is *māya,* "illusion," whose true nature must be seen and overcome. By contrast the propensity of Freudianism, based on Western conceptions, is to see social life as the reality and religion as the illusion. Central to the societies that we are dealing with here is a special mode of reality orientation that necessitates a further revision of the Freudian notions of the pleasure principle and the reality principle. As is well known, the pleasure principle is the propensity of the organism to maximize pleasure and reduce pain and achieve a constancy of the excitations. The pleasure principle has its origins in the primary process; eventually it must come to terms with and become subordinated to the reality principle or the sociopolitical order in which we live, itself based on economic want or scarcity or Ananke. Thus as far as everyday existence goes the pleasure principle must adopt a "detour or roundabout road to satisfaction." By contrast, given its primacy in the unconscious life, the pleasure principle rules supreme over fantasy and dream.

The reality principle, in the Freudian scheme, is contrasted with the pleasure principle that dominates the primary processes. Freud developed the notion of "psychic reality" in contrast to material reality and rightly insisted that it is the former that is determinative of the neurosis. However, he did not extend the idea of psychic reality to the realm of the reality principle, because, I think, the culture in which he operated had already defined the external sociopolitical and economic world as the real world. For the societies that I am talking about the world of everyday living (where reality operates) may also be influenced by, or constituted of, a "psychic reality." The everyday world is culturally defined in Hallowell's sense, since according to him, physical reality does not exist in any significant perceptual sense.[70] If so the real world is constituted of the subjectively perceived set of objectively defined cultural meanings. The world of ghosts and spirits is as real as that of markets, though real in different qualitative ways that can be ethnographically described. Needless to say, this redefinition of what constitutes the external world does not include all of "psychic reality," as for example, the paranoid's delusions. The latter are psychically real for the paranoid but lack consensual validation through intersubjective understanding—the real touchstone of reality. Since Freudians do not consider the culturally defined (psychic) reality as real, one is faced, in psychoanalytic anthropology, with a barrage of meaningless discussions relating to this problem. For example, consider a recent (and continuing) argument inflicted on the academic community regarding the shaman (if there is such a creature). Is the shaman psychotic? Or is he schizophrenic? Does he suffer from vitamin deficiency or excess calcium?[71] All these bypass the obvious answer, namely that in a given cultural definition of reality you can have psychotic or nonpsychotic shamans. The idea of the psychotic shaman is implicitly based on the definition of reality in its Western economic and empiricist sense.

Though the external world is culturally defined, it is naive to assume that all its segments or domains are of the same qualitative order, or that individuals orient to the different domains in identical fashion. Ordinary people in South and Southeast Asia know that the world of scarcity is of a qualitatively different realm from that of spirits and that they must relate to these domains in different ways. Kakar's assertion regarding the nature of Hindu reality does not imply that the average Hindu has subordinated the workaday world of *māya* for a different reality: it is clear that he must live and cope with the world of everyday want and scarcity and, for the most part, that is how he lives. Yet he recognizes that there is also a different reality;

hence his "fascination and respect for the occult and its practitioners."[72] Furthermore, he can, if he wants to, move away from this mundane reality to the other reality; and the institutional orders of South Asia provide ample scope for this movement. Thus, most people, most of the time, orient themselves to the socio-political-economic order, or the reality principle, in Freudian terms. While this is indeed the case, the recognition of a truer reality, in principle open to all, renders the key psychiatric notions of "reality testing," "adaptation to reality," and "reality sense" completely problematic and incapable of grasping the uniqueness and complexity of the South Asian scene. Let me illustrate this further by getting back to my case studies of ecstatics in *Medusa's Hair* and in the first part of this lecture.

Consider the average person who must cope with reality in its Freudian sense. If his reality testing is impaired it may mean one of two things: he may be "abnormal" in the Western sense of the term, as in the psychoses; or it may mean that he has rejected the mundane reality for the supramundane. When the second alternative occurs, it is meaningless to talk of "abnormality" in Devereux's sense, for one has ceased to be an average person living in the mundane world. In the case of our ecstatics, since they have given primacy to the divine world, their testing of reality must occur in respect to that world, not in relation to the world of economic want and scarcity. They act "irrationally" in terms of the average expectable behavior of others in the same environment. Some have deliberately given up their jobs; others have courted bankruptcy; others have deliberately given away their wealth; and everyone has refused to give primacy to the economic imperative.

Ecstatics tend to see what is ordinary for the average person in an extraordinary light. For example, an ecstatic priest may make the following statement: "Yesterday I saw an old man dressed in white who came up to me and smiled. . . . That was the god himself," whereas the average person would simply say "I saw an old man" or "an old beggar" or "a mendicant." But if the ecstatic's behavior is not the average one, it is certainly not "abnormal" in its psychopathic sense, for there is no loss of reality here; ordinary reality or *māya* has been subordinated to the deeper reality that dominates his life. His behavior is not irrational for at least two reasons. First, the ecstatic is acting in terms of the supramundane reality that he has constructed for himself; second, the average citizen does not see the behavior of the ecstatic as "abnormal," only different from his, but intelligible according to the central values of the culture that *both* share. In other words, reality testing occurs within the same "cultural frame." It is only when one moves out of this frame into an incomprehensible one, as for example in paranoia, that there inevitably occur problems of miscommunication and radical alienation.

The ecstatics in my sample do not move out of the cultural frame. The psychotic shuns reality because it is disturbing; he tends to withdraw from it into his idiosyncratic personal world; we say that his capacity for reality testing is impaired. Initially you have a similar phenomenon among our ecstatics; they turn away from the ordinary world of family and domestic and social responsibility because it has become unbearable and they can tolerate it no longer. There is a temporary breakdown, a withdrawal from a painful mundane reality into a terrifying inner world inhabited by demonic powers. Yet after their struggle with these powers, what have they done? They have, through the *work of culture* which parallels the dream work, recreated and moved into another level of reality that makes life not only bearable but transfigured and meaningful, and what is most interesting, utterly pleasurable—at least for most of them and for some of the time. It is this new level of reality that is now the crucial one: the mundane world where the Freudian reality testing takes place is left behind entirely or subordinated to the new reality. Yet what is striking about this new reality is that, unlike the mundane reality, it is in conformity with the pleasure principle. The virtuoso who undergoes trance—either possession trance or contemplation as in *samādhi*—does so at the service of the ego; it is not regression, however, but progression. In spirit *attack* the priestess is overwhelmed by outside forces; after recovery she acts with autonomy to bring about divine possession. The same dynamic occurs in *yoga* and Buddhist *samādhi*. They are all pleasurable activities; those who suffer pain, like Abdin, have not achieved this state fully or cannot. That the pleasure principle should operate here is not surprising since these spiritual realities are attuned to the primary process and were *originally* (I stress this word) created or recreated out of these processes; and it is in the primary process that the pleasure principle exercises its domination. Yet if in the primary process a simple hedonistic drive reduction model of pleasure operates, not so in its transformation in the new reality of higher levels of symbolization that ecstatics have created, an independent reality different from both the primary process of the unconscious and the secondary process of the world of everyday consciousness and the reality principle. In this process of symbolic remove the Freudian notion of idealization and sublimation prevails; it is here that symbols prospectively and progressively move away from the sources of motivation to the realm of the sacred or the numinous.

LECTURE TWO

Oedipus: The Paradigm and its Hindu Rebirth

1

Relativizing the Oedipus Complex: The Trobriand Case

The anthropological debate on Oedipus commenced with Malinowski's thesis that the Oedipus complex did not exist in the Trobriands in its classic form and that its place was taken by a matrilineal complex in which the hostility of the male is directed to the mother's brother while the sister becomes the incestuous object. Concomitantly, the son develops few ambivalent feelings towards the father while his sexual feelings towards the mother get extinguished naturally in the course of time. For Malinowski, as for many anthropologists and for psychoanalysts like Fromm, the centrality of the Oedipus complex lies in the structure of authority in the family, rather than in its sexual interrelationships; consequently the Oedipus complex, according to this influential exegesis, varies with the type of family structure, especially in relation to the allocation of authority.

Using Malinowski's own data, Spiro argued that the Oedipus complex in its classic Freudian form is central to the Trobriand family.[1] The key element in Spiro's thesis is that there is enough evidence to show the intensity of the mother-child bond and its intrinsic erotic component and, further, the irrefutable evidence that in the first five years of childhood, when the Oedipus complex is formed and resolved, the Trobriand son lives with his father and mother and siblings in a single household. The mother's brother, a key figure in matrilineal systems, is never physically present in the life of his sister's family during this formative period. He begins to wield his avuncupotestal authority in relation to his nephew only in early and sometimes late adolescence.

Let me begin my reevaluation of both Spiro's and Malinowski's theses by reflecting on Freud's own view that the Oedipus complex is based entirely on the erotic nature of the son's tie with the mother and the sexual jealousy he has for the father, all of this reinforced, if not caused, by the witnessing of the primal scene. The trouble with the sexual thesis, as with Malinowski's authority thesis, is the implication that these motives—sex and domination—that are analytically separated by the scholar exist as disaggregated entities in reality, or in the consciousness of the child. Freud himself was not all that clear even in his early work regarding the empirical reality of separate drives, as for example words such as "anal-sadistic" suggest. But when one goes beyond the early work to *Beyond the Pleasure Principle,* Freud could argue that a whole series of drives and needs could be subsumed under a larger interdependent cluster—the life instincts or Eros—and these as a totality can act on a person, guiding his actions in a certain direction. Another set of drives—the death instincts or Thanatos—act in a reverse direction, such that man's life as a totality is affected by the dialectical relationship between these two reified dualities. One implication of this latter view of Freud is that drives cannot be neatly disaggregated, and they may "fuse" with one another. In *Civilization and Its Discontents,* he says:

> The two kinds of instincts seldom—perhaps never—appear in isolation from each other, but are alloyed with each other in varying and very different proportions, and so become unrecognizable in our judgment.[2]

This argument can now be transferred to the context of childhood. In infancy the child comes under the love, domination, and protection of its parents. As Freud himself recognized, in the earliest oral stage the child is connected to the mother in terms of food, care, and nurture. But this contact produces in the child erotic feelings toward the mother, and these erotic feelings are also diffuse and unrelated to a specific bodily organ. Thus at the very earliest stage feelings pertaining to dependency and sexuality are all involved in the mother-child relationship. Nor can domination be excluded from this relationship since it exists in relation to both child care (nurture) and sexuality and these in turn may provoke aggressive feelings toward the mother. It is therefore not likely that drives like sex, aggression, and dependency exist in empirical reality and in the child's consciousness or unconscious as disaggregated entities.

Can one also avoid the issue of authority in the structuring of Oedipal relationships? In an overwhelming number of societies, authority is formally vested in males. In socialization, particularly in late childhood during the period of the resolution of the Oedipus complex, this authority is exercised by the father. If so, can the child's perception of the father as a sexual rival be disaggregated from his authoritarian role? The very idea of castration anxiety, so intimately connected to the formation and stabilization of the Oedipus complex, implies the child's perception of the father as exercising punitive authority over his sexuality. Consequently it is not likely that the child can separate in his own consciousness his sexual hatred for the father as his mother's lover from his role as the authority figure in the family. If this is correct, then the *degree* of authority exercised by the father is relevant to the Oedipus complex.

If drives were pure and analytically differentiated in the consciousness of the child as they are in the psychologist's laboratory, one would expect the ideational representation of the drives to reflect this purity. Sexuality, nurturance, domination, and so forth are not simply engendered in the child's body; they are primarily products of his social relationships in the family, not only with his mother and father but also with his siblings, as Freud makes very clear in *Group Psychology and the Analysis of the Ego*.

> In the individual's mental life someone else is invariably involved, as a model, as an object, as a helper, as an opponent; and so from the very first individual psychology, in this extended but entirely justifiable sense of the word, is at the same time social psychology as well.
>
> The relations of an individual to his parents and to his brothers and sisters, to the object of his love, and to his physician—in fact all the relations which have hitherto been the chief subject of psychoanalytic research—may claim to be social phenomena.[3]

The infant's polymorphous perverse sexuality is not a reflex of his biological nature; it arises from his social relationships with his mother. Even this can be complicated in many human societies where, with the birth of another child, the caretaking role is transferred to a female sibling, in which case it is inevitable that the sibling, in addition to being sibling, also becomes a surrogate mother. In other words, not only are there no such things as differentiated drives in the phenomenology of early childhood, but what we call drives are products of, or influenced by, interpersonal relations within the family. As my simple case of a sibling surrogate implies, these interpersonal relationships are not confined to the triangular relationships among mother, father, and child as the classic Freudian theory seems to state.

The argument regarding the physical absence of the mother's brother in the Trobriand households is also not convincing to me. Is it necessary for the mother's brother to be physically present in his sister's household for the sister's son to have a negative image of him as an authority figure? Consider the role of the Sri Lankan mother's brother who, as in many patrilineally oriented societies, is almost the opposite of the Trobriand. In Sri Lanka, the mother instills in the child a fondness for the mother's brother as a potential source of emotional support for her son. It is not necessary for the mother's brother to be physically present in the household to create this image. Indeed in some cases it is not even necessary for the sister's son to have actually seen him. Thus, for example, in early adolescence when the son fears an Oedipal confrontation with his father, he might run away from home—in which case he goes to his mother's brother or to another relative in a similar structural position. I suspect similar patterns exist elsewhere, as, for example, the grandfather role in the American family. It is therefore likely that the same principle, in reverse, holds for the mother's brother in the Trobriand family. The mother's brother is probably made into an authoritarian and fearful person to the sister's son in the socialization of the latter by his parents. To put it differently, the physical absence of the mother's brother in the early family life of the Trobriand child does not deny the "psychic reality" of his presence. This is probably something that Malinowski could not understand: he recorded fear of the sister's son for the mother's brother but could not substantiate it with empirical information. For me, it would indeed be surprising that if the mother's brother were a crucial figure in Trobriand matrilineal society, he would not be socialized in Trobriand consciousness in early childhood, irrespective of his physical presence. After all, gods, demons, bogeymen are not physically present entities in the domestic household; yet they are everywhere socialized in the individual consciousness *as if* they were physically present. In the West, a divorced parent may acquire a similar significance in the child's mind by being socialized by one parent to perceive the other as evil. The child need not have seen the divorced parent for him to form a representation of that parent in his consciousness. So is it with the black, the Jew, the alien.

While Malinowski naively substituted domination for eroticism, he rightly emphasized the significance of Trobrianders' social structure to their Oedipus complex. The Trobriand avunculate is intrinsically a part of their matrilineal social structure with its locus of authority centered on the maternal uncle. In this sociological context, the young Trobriander must himself become a mother's brother to his sister's children and the wielder of avuncupotestal authority over them. To take this role he *must* identify with the mother's brother. Thus Trobriand inevitably poses a special problem for the *resolution* of the Oedipus complex; the son must renounce identification with his father for a sociologically and psychologically necessary identification with the mother's brother. He must also introject the matriarchal values on which the whole continuity of Trobriand society depends. If introjection and identification are to be effective they must occur in childhood. In other words the very nature of Trobriand matrilineal organization requires the presence of the mother's brother as a member of the child's *circle* of family relationships centering on the "Oedipus" complex. He then, like the mother, father, and sister, must be represented as an object in the boy's fantasy life and represented again in varying degrees of symbolic remove in Trobriand myth. There is consequently a different form of the Oedipus complex in Trobriand culture: one might as well call this form, which bears a striking family relationship (no pun intended) to the Western form, the matrilineal complex, or the matrilineal Oedipus. In this matrilineal complex, in my view, there are four crucial relationships in the son's circle of Oedipal kin: father, mother, sister, and mother's brother. Within this group, it might well be that the child's relation to the sister and mother's brother is the set that is significant for the formation of neuroses in Trobriand. Since the Trobriand identification with the loving father must be renounced for an identification with the hated mother's brother, this must surely be a psychologically difficult task. If in Western families the child's fantasy is to beget a child from his mother, in Trobriand, given the fact that it is the sister who produces the children for his lineage, he might well develop the fantasy to have her bear his children.[4] There is no nuclear Oedipus complex of which the Trobriand is a variation; there are several, possibly finite, forms of the complex showing family resemblances to one another. One might even want to recognize the likelihood of different forms of the Oedipus complex within a single group, especially in complex societies, a problem that I will now begin to explore.

2

Further Steps in Relativization: The Indian Oedipus Revisited

In an exceptionally important essay, "The Indian Oedipus," Ramanujan helps us relativize further the Freudian Oedipus complex.[5] Ramanujan's thesis is that the Greek form of the complex is very scarce in India, but though the Indian cases show real substantive difference from the Western, they exhibit identity on the level of structure. I find the structural argument misleading, since it once again binds us into a universal Oedipus, which is contradicted by Ramanujan's own plea for placing the Oedipus complex in the context of varying familial relationships in different cultures. The family drama in the Indian household, according to him, is quite different from the Western, and consequently a different representation of the Oedipus complex occurs there.

He begins his paper with a startling story related by a half-blind old woman in a village in North Karnataka.

> A girl is born with a curse on her head that she would marry her own son and beget a son by him. As soon as she hears of the curse, she willfully vows she'd try and escape it: she secludes herself in a dense forest, eating only fruit, forswearing all male company. But when she attains puberty, as fate would have it, she eats a mango from a tree under which a passing king has urinated. The mango impregnates her; bewildered, she gives birth to a male child; she wraps him in a piece of her sari and throws him in a nearby stream. The child is picked up by the king of the next kingdom, and he grows up to be a handsome young adventurous prince. He comes hunting in the self-same jungle, and the cursed woman falls in love with the stranger, telling herself she is not in danger any more as she has no son alive. She marries him and bears a child. According to custom, the father's swaddling clothes are preserved and brought out for the newborn son. The woman recognizes at once the piece of sari with which she had swaddled her first son, now her husband, and understands that her fate had really caught up with her. She awaits till everyone is asleep, and sings a lullaby to her newborn baby:
>
> Sleep
> O son
> O grandson
> O brother to my husband
> sleep O sleep
> sleep well
>
> and hangs herself by the rafter with her sari twisted to a rope.[6]

In this text "it is the mother, the Jocasta figure, who is accursed, tries to escape her fate, and when finally trammeled in it, it is she who makes the discovery and punishes herself with death."[7] Once again, says Ramanujan, the structure is the same as the Greek but the narrative point of view is exactly in reverse. Though a tragic Jocasta-type figure emerges in the preceding story, not so with the many variations around the key elements of the myth: the prophecy, the nature of impregnation with all sorts of bodily exuviae through different body apertures, the lullaby, and the conclusion. In some there is humor (the absurdity of it all!); in others the protagonists accept their fate and live happily ever after. All these tales have been told by elderly women; it expresses their point of view ranging from the tragic to the ludicrous. One must also not assume that one version excludes another: it is possible for the same person or the same village to relate different versions of the same myth. The parody can coexist with the tragic vision, as it does in Shakespearean tragedy in the voice of the Fool.

The power of the mother-son tie has been noted by almost everyone familiar with Hindu society. The dependency of the son on the mother and the erotic ties that bind them together are not only significant in childhood but, as I showed in the previous lecture, continue into adulthood.[8] In many versions the father is excluded from the relationship.

> There is a recurrent motif in folktales in South India and elsewhere (Motif J. 21.2): A father returns from a long exile or journey and enters his bedroom to find a strange young man sleeping next to his wife. He draws his sword to kill them both, when either his waking wife or a remembered precept ("Don't act when angry") stays his hand. The young man is really his son grown to *manhood during his long absence but still sleeping innocently in* the same bed as his dear mother.[9]

In an earlier version of his paper, Ramanujan noted the virtual absence of parricide in the Indian Oedipus; rather the brunt of literally hundreds of myths and folktales are focussed on the killing of the son by the father.[10] Once again owing to a radical overvaluation of blood relations, to use Lévi-Strauss' phrase, there is a reversed aggression from father to son, the opposite of the Greek model.[11] In all of these myths, the son is killed, maimed, castrated (symbolically or actually) by the father. The myth that paradigmatically expresses the

Hindu Oedipus is that of Gaṇeśa, to be discussed later. In the triangular relationship expressed in that myth, the son has no chance. Bad enough to be pampered by the mother; worse to suffer the father's anger and sexual jealousy that brooks little compromise, at least initially.

In another cluster of myths, dealt with at great length by Goldman, the father's sexuality and power of domination are both emphasized.[12] In the ideal-typical myth, that of Yayāti found in the *Mahābhāratha,* the father asks his several sons to give up their sexuality for his (the father's) own lost potency. The elder sons refuse, and they are banished, killed, or castrated, while the youngest willingly agrees. In these myths, the unquestioning subservience of the son to the father's patripotestal authority is as significant as sexuality. The sons must not only unquestionably yield to the father's authority, but they must also renounce their own sexuality. Transgression and disobedience must result in the frightening and irrational wrath of the father. Goldman quotes a wonderful myth from the *Ramāyana* where the king of the gods, Indra, seduces the wife of the Brahmin sage, Gautama. Indra noted Gautama's absence from his ashram and took the sage's physical form to have intercourse with the latter's wife, Ahalyā. Ahalyā sees through the disguise but, smitten by love for the god, she agrees. But after making love Indra is frightened, possessed of an almost childlike fear of the sage (a father figure in Indian thought), and slinks away, "terrified of Gautama." When at last he meets the sage, Indra stands with his face lowered. The sage knows what has happened and curses the god: "Fool! Since you, taking my appearance, have done this forbidden thing, you shall be deprived of your testicles." And of course Indra's balls fall to the ground![13]

When Ramanujan first wrote on the Indian Oedipus in 1972, Goldman responded with his impressive and scholarly article showing that, contrary to Ramanujan, the Hindu epics contained references to the "positive" Oedipus complex of the West, in addition of course to the typical Indian form. In summarizing the data from the epics, Goldman showed that there are three basic versions of the Oedipal conflict.

1. The "positive" Oedipus complex where the son kills his father. However, there is only one case in the epic literature where the actual son kills his own father—that of Arjuna and Babhruvāhana, to be discussed later. In others a son or surrogate son attacks a father figure, but there are only about three of these in the epic literature.[14] One of the most famous is where Arjuna kills Bhīsma; Bhīsma, however, is

not Arjuna's father but a kind of grandfather to him as head of the clan of the Bhāratas.[15]

2. The second is a much more common, yet disguised, version of the positive Oedipus complex. Here a character in the epic launches an attack on a surrogate father (or mother)—such as a *guru,* an elder brother, or a Brahmin. In Indian languages the terms for *guru* and father are interchangeable, so that Goldman's thesis could be borne out. But the other cases are more problematic. It may well be that the hatred for the elder brother is a displacement from the father, but insofar as the elder brother is a kind of father substitute in the Hindu joint family, he may well be an independently significant member of the child's circle of infantile objects. And how does one disentangle caste resentment of Brahmins from the Oedipal conflict, since the former seems as intrinsic to Hindu culture as the latter? In some cases Goldman sensitively disentangles the Oedipal elements by tracing in the epics the past history or sequel of the displaced Oedipal conflicts; and he shows that the paternal, filial, or maternal relationships displaced in one version reappear in the historical prologue or epilogue. But in other places it is impossible to disentangle the Oedipal conflict from other conflicts endemic to the society.

3. The last type is where the heroic son anticipates and avoids the Oedipal conflict with the father "by submitting to the father's will and in effect castrating himself."[16] These heroes are never punished, but are instead rewarded by their fathers. If we transfer this idea to the myths of filicide noted by Ramanujan we can formulate a tentative (yet unprovable) conclusion. If the son who emasculates himself and yields to the father is *not* punished, then the son who is punished is one who fails to yield. Gaṇeśa, for example, is too attached to the mother to yield pliantly to the father: he must therefore be decapitated and rendered ugly, and made subservient to the father's will. The third type discussed by Goldman is similar to the "typical" Indian Oedipus discussed by Ramanujan. Both types of sons are defeated by the father and in this sense stand opposed to the Western model. Goldman takes exception to Ramanujan's thesis that only third type myths are found in India but agrees with Ramanujan that the latter is the dominant Hindu form. "The legends of the third type, or to be more precise, the heroes of these legends occupy a special place in the hearts of Hindu India. These heroes are by no means the only ones worthy of the title 'Indian Oedipus,' but they are without doubt representative of an oedipal type the culture strongly favors."[17]

The fact of the matter is that Goldman is hard put to find myths in the epic literature that unequivocally parallel the Greek model, even in respect of the father-son relationship. There is only one story—that of Babhruvāhana and Arjuna—"the only unambiguous example of parricide that I can find in the Sanskrit epic literature."[18] In this story that appears at the end of the *Mahābhāratha,* Arjuna, the great hero of the epic, wanders all over the territory with the sacrificial horse of his elder brother, the just Yudhiṣṭhira. The custom is that the territory into which the horse wanders must submit to the king who is to make the sacrifice, or offer battle to those who escort it. The horse eventually enters the realm of Manipur ruled by Babhruvāhana, Arjuna's own son. Now Babhruvāhana must either surrender (a cowardly act) or fight his own father (an ethically horrendous act). Babhruvāhana decides on the former and respectfully approaches his father. But Arjuna is enraged at this pitiful display of filial piety and affection! He unleashes a torrent of verbal abuse at his son as a coward and a violator of kingly ethics. But even so Babhruvāhana cannot act hostilely towards his father until he is urged to do so by the serpent princess Ulūpī, a stepmother to him in kinship terms (and psychically a mother). The father and son fight, and the son scores the first shot. Arjuna is seriously injured and appears to be dead, but he regains consciousness and praises his son for his heroism. The battle then recommences, and Babhruvāhana finally shoots his father in the heart and kills him. Babhruvāhana is stricken with guilt and proposes to expiate it by living for twelve years clothed with his father's skin and begging for alms, using his father's skull as begging bowl. But none of this is necessary, for Ulūpī tells him that nothing can kill his father. She revives Arjuna with the restorative snake jewel she possesses, and son, father, and father's wife are all happily reconciled.[19]

While it is perhaps true that the "parricide and the horror of it are hardly concealed" in the Babhruvāhana myth, it is also the case that the father does not in fact die. Goldman says:

> Most notable is the great effort expended on the attempt to deny the significance and even the existence of its central event, Babhruvāhana's murder of his father. The son is represented as entertaining no hostility for the father. He fights him only as an act of filial devotion to his father and "mother." Finally, in a welter of confused and even contradictory rationalization we are told that (1) the battle was staged to please the father, (2) the murder was arranged to save the father from hell, (3) the father killed himself, and

> finally, (4) the father was not killed at all, the whole affair being nothing but a conjurer's trick.[20]

If this is the one case of the positive Oedipus complex, it still remains quite remote from the Greek. This one case, and other disguised ones, are hardly enough evidence to formulate an "Indian Oedipus" on the Western model. Goldman insightfully notes:

> What these stories show, however, is that in almost every case in which this struggle is worked out between a son and his actual father in the Sanskrit epic literature it is the latter who succeeds. Actual sons are, if good sons, passive to the point of self-destruction and are rewarded for their passivity and subservience. If they are bad they are passively disobedient and are degraded as punishment for their sins. The latter case, moreover, exists largely to serve as a contrast to the former. In neither case are they actually aggressive to their father, nor do they ever gain unimpeded access to the goals of maturity, independence and the free expression of sexuality.[21]

The family relations that underlie the reversed Oedipus complex in India, then, have two conspicuous features. The first, already noted, is the erotic-nurturant bond that binds mother and son. These myths recount the mother's erotic seduction of her son or her sexual relationship with him. Once again eroticism is compounded by a key feature of Hindu family relationship—the domination of the mother. In the reversed relationship between the father and son there is a different form of domination, the patripotestal authority of the father and the unquestioning loyalty of the son. Failure in yielding to the father results in social degradation, emasculation, death, or mutilation.

The father-son relationship in the Indian situation seems to be the very opposite of that in the Trobriand. The role of the father is parallel to that of the mother's brother in Trobriand; each is related to a certain type of authority structure in the family. Unlike the maternal uncle of Trobriand the Hindu father is a live presence. His authority is part of the Hindu patriarchal joint family, as much as the mother's brother in the matriarchal system. Furthermore, the Hindu father-son relationship is governed by religious norms, as for example the view that the son is necessary for the performance of the funeral rites for the father. The idea is also widespread that the father may be reborn as the son, even though it contradicts any ethically based view of karma. The religious sanction given to filial piety is absent in Trobriand; there the mother's brother could be symbolically slain. Not so in Hindu India. The myths recounted in Ramanujan's and Goldman's essays are not just Indian Oedipal myths but also edifying tales that are related in a variety of contexts and act as myth models for both emulation and warning. The Hindu son of the epics has little chance of killing the father; it is the father, jealous of his rival's erotic attachment to the mother, who slays the son. Not in all myths is the son totally passive; in popular Gaṇeśa myths, both folk and classical, the son tries to assert himself, but he is inevitably worsted in the confrontation with the father.

In the context of Hindu familial relationships, can one reasonably speak of a universal Oedipus complex—the Greek model—that then, through various symbolic mechanisms (especially displacements), is expressed in the kind of mythic representations presented earlier? Goldman follows the classic Freudian argument that there is everywhere a positive Oedipus complex and that the Hindu is but a transformation of it. But the Hindu son is in fact born into a family system where these relationships are pregiven. If so it is meaningless to speak of a set of infantile relationships paralleling the Western model, since no such relationships exist (except in unusual and individual cases). Thus the Oedipus complex in the Indian family must be structured in terms of these pregiven relationships, rather than in terms of a nonexistent Western model. The Greek Oedipus can hardly exist in the Hindu joint family; even if he does exist in an individual example he rarely survives as a mythic representation.

If this line of reasoning is correct then the whole development of the Indian Oedipus complex, as a psychic structure, and not just as a myth model, must take a different form from the Western one. It needs Indian psychoanalysts to deal with this problem through case studies. However, I shall present one likely Indian Oedipal problem, based on its own family relationships—the psychosexual problems that arise out of the son's symbiotic tie with the mother.

Talcott Parsons argued that in the Western family the universally operative mother-son ties must be eventually terminated. The father must yank the son out of the erotic dependency with the mother, thereby acting both as father and as the representative of the larger society.[22] Parsons also universalized this model but did not recognize that this was not only uniquely Western, but also had a socioeconomic dimension in Western individualism and capitalism. It is the nuclear family structure, and the individualistic work ethic based on capitalism, that makes the father the agent of the society in the family. He helps the son to break loose from the erotic dependency on the mother and pitchforks him into the competitive world outside. This socioeconomic background of the contemporary Western Oedipus complex does not obtain in India—at least until recently. The focus is on the welfare of the patrilineal joint family and the larger institutions of the society—caste and the political order—that together conspire to suppress individualism (if not individuality) in the interests of the collectivity. Kakar, following Erikson, has labelled these internalized norms as the "communal conscience."[23] In this situation, the unity of the joint family, as I pointed out in the previous section, rests on two axes of control—the affective ties binding the individual to his family through the nurturant and erotic dependency of the son on the mother continuing into adulthood; and the patripotestal authority of the father, the repository of the religiously based values of the Hindu family and larger society. Thus the emotional relationships in the family are linked to the suppression of individualism, the unity of the joint family and larger supra-individual structures such as caste, and the religious values on which these are grounded.

Unlike the Western model, the son cannot affirm his separation and individuation from either parent because of the nature of the emotional ties involved and the socioeconomic forces that reciprocally feed into those ties. One might therefore guess that both neuroses as well as the resolution of the complex must have a reality intrinsic to the Indian pattern. In neuroses one must expect symbiotic ties to the mother, which cannot be individually or symbolically controlled or sublimated, to produce a variety of psychological problems, as, for example, sexual impotence and inadequacy. But these are in turn reinforced, or exacerbated, in the relationship with the father. The anthropologist can do little to document these, which belong to the field of clinical psychoanalysis, but he can help reformulate the Oedipus complex and the neuroses that might result from the child's relationship with his parents in specifically Indian terms. Above all the anthropologist, with his concern for cultural values, might provide some insights regarding the *resolution* of the Indian Oedipus complex. Here also we can take a hint from the Western model of Oedipus which in Freudian thought mythicized the childhood fantasy. In this, the son marries the mother and overthrows the father and replaces him psychologically in the affections of the mother and displaces him sociologically by usurping the paternal role. In Hindu myth the son is erotically dominated by the mother and is under the father's authoritarian rule. How then can he assume his father's role, at age five or thereabouts, identify with him and replace him and become the bearer of his father's values and the values of the society? One of the most powerful myth models, so powerful that one can label it paradigmatic of the Indian Oedipal conflict and its resolution, provides us with the answer. The son must submit to the father; by submission the son has the father's love and forgiveness (for attachment to the mother?). *Identification through submission* might even capitalize on a homosexual and a phylogenetic propensity; this is the dominant Hindu form of Oedipal resolution, rather than identification through the dethronement (metaphorically "killing") of the father. It is a mechanism of defense specific to Hindu society, permitting the son to introject the parental value system and simultaneously resolve the Oedipal crisis. He duplicates the father, instead of replacing him. This is the psychological counterpart to the popular Hindu belief that the father can be reborn as the son's son and the son might once have been the father.

Attempts by the son to possess the mother and usurp the father's role are totally nonnormative and reprehensible: any thought of this will result in direct and fearful reprisal from the father, as in the myth of Indra's emasculation or the decapitation of Gaṇeśa by Śiva. The Western Oedipal reaction is a rare alternative; the only other way of affirming one's autonomy *over* and above the father's value system is by a radical avoidance of the father, or by a total rejection of the parental values by becoming an outcaste and introjecting a totally new value system. Running away from home is in fact a well-known, if not normatively sanctioned, code of conduct. Though scholars have focussed only on one form of this—ascetic renunciation—this is by no means the adolescent (or later adult) reaction to the unbearable presence, psychic and physical, of the father. Other alternatives are less well known in the literature: joining semicaste or guild organizations of criminals, or homosexual groups like Hinjras, or deliberately joining outcaste groups. Further possibilities also exist: joining the military, or monastic orders like Jainas and Tantrics that accept youthful recruits, or Hindu groups like Lingayats that have a relatively open policy of recruitment, and I am sure many other alternatives not documented by scholars.

Freud and the Indian Oedipus: An Imaginary Journey

It was *The Ego and the Id*, published in 1923, that fully developed the second topography of the ego, superego, and id.[24] This important work contains one of the simplest and clearest statements of the Oedipus complex as far as the male child is concerned.

> In its simplified form the case of the male child may be described as follows: At a very early age the little boy develops an object-cathexis for his mother, which originally related to the mother's breast and is the prototype of an object choice on the anaclitic model; the boy deals with his father by identifying himself with him. For a time these two relationships proceed side by side, until the boy's sexual wishes in regard to his mother become more intense and his father is perceived as an obstacle to them; from this the Oedipus complex originates. His identification with his father then takes an hostile coloring and changes into a wish to get rid of his father in order to take his place with his mother. Henceforth his relation to his father is ambivalent; it seems as if the ambivalence inherent in the identification from the beginning had become manifest. An ambivalent attitude to the father and an object-relation of a solely affectionate kind to his mother make up the content of the simple positive Oedipus complex in a boy.
>
> Along with the demolition of the Oedipus complex, the boy's object-cathexis of his mother must be given up. Its place may be filled by one of two things: *either an identification with his mother or an intensification of his identification with his father. We are accustomed to regard the latter outcome as the more normal;* it permits the affectionate relation to the mother to be in a measure retained. In this way the dissolution of the Oedipus complex would consolidate the masculinity in the boy's character.[25]

In this very important statement Freud recognizes that identification with the mother might well be one form of the resolution of the Oedipus complex. It does not seem too radical to suggest that the identification with the father and the consolidation of masculinity is the one Freud was "accustomed to" because it was the personally and culturally operative and acceptable form. But imagine Freud working with Indian patients and confronted with myths dealing with filicide and symbiosis with the mother. In these circumstances Freud would most likely have made the inference that Indians were "accustomed to" an Oedipal identification with the mother in the resolution of their complex. He might even have considered submission to the father as a reasonable Indian form. Freud, however, was barely acquainted with

Hinduism. He was only aware of the fact that, even in Western culture, identification with the mother was a possible scenario. For Freud this alternative pattern of identification was due to constitutional bisexuality: "the relative strength of the masculine and feminine sexual dispositions is what determines whether the outcome of the Oedipus situation shall be an identification with the father or with the mother."[26] Reverse identification, however, does not occur solely in respect of the mother. He says that "the simple Oedipus complex" quoted earlier is good enough for "practical purposes," but constitutional bisexuality produces in addition "an effeminate feminine attitude to the father and a corresponding jealousy and hostility to the mother."[27] The Oedipus complex is much more complex than the simple triangular relationship where the son hates the father and loves the mother!

One might of course argue that the preceding account pertains to the resolution of the Oedipus complex and not the complex itself—if one can make this somewhat artificial distinction. But the matter isn't all that simple, as is evident in the development of Freud's argument. "It may even be that the ambivalence displayed in the relations to the parents should be attributed entirely to bisexuality and that it is not, as I have represented above, developed out of identification in consequence of rivalry."[28] If constitutional bisexuality could channel the way identification and the Oedipal feelings of ambivalence to parents develop, is it then not reasonable to suggest that in another time or place, cultural conditions could as easily affect or aggravate the direction of identification and ambivalence?

Now let our fantasy transgress normal bounds and imagine Freud, not in Vienna, but in Delhi as an Indian doctor working with Hindu neurotics. There is no Sophoclean myth here; instead there is the Gaṇeśa myth, to be discussed soon, and related ones discussed earlier. The Greek myth, owing to its absence, would be irrelevant for Freud. Hindu patients, he would note, have wish-fulfillment dreams of submitting to the father and marrying a mother figure. There might be rare cases of father killing, but more normative and frequent are the many dreams, expressed in many guises, of the son being worsted (killed, castrated) by the father. What interpretive choice would Freud have had? Is it likely that he would have independently formulated, and foisted on the Indians, the Greek model of the Oedipus complex in the face of a different body of data? I think not. He would have had little choice but to formulate the positive form of the Indian "Oedipus" complex in terms of the Indian clinical and mythological data, i.e., in terms of identification with the mother and submission to the father. He would also have noted that this situation would result in the male developing feminine characteristics—enhanced of course by constitutional bisexuality!

Freud, however, never retracted his view of the triangular nature of the Oedipus complex. Yet this did not exhaust erotic attraction among family members. In his 1922 paper on jealousy, paranoia, and homosexuality he speaks of the normal jealousy that "originates in the Oedipus or brother-sister complexes of the first sexual period."[29] Here he clearly recognizes the existence of both Oedipal and sibling complexes—another way of saying that empirically *all* familial kin are erotically desired. In addition to this Freud noted the power of homosexual fantasies among familial members, especially in his great case studies.[30] In 1931, he recognized the importance of homosexuality in girls in their phallic stage.[31] This contained "active wishful impulses" towards the mother, but he was not sure whether it had a sexual aim—a somewhat strange statement since Freud says on the previous page, in relation to the *passive* impulses of the phallic stage, that girls "regularly accuse their mothers of seducing them."[32] And as for the pre-Oedipal stage in both boys and girls, he could say: "We have as yet no clear understanding of these processes, with which we have only just become acquainted."[33]

In *The Ego and the Id,* Freud noted that the female Oedipus complex was the exact parallel of the male.[34] But in 1931, in his paper on female sexuality, he thought otherwise—once again illustrating the sense of doubt regarding even the fundamental principles that underlie the Oedipus complex and expressing the need for constant vision and revision. Here Freud initially admits that there is little doubt regarding the male Oedipus complex. But "with the small girl it is different. Her first object, too, was her mother. How does she find her way to her father? How, when, and why does she detach himself from her mother?"[35] Again doubt: "The way in which these two tasks are connected with each other is not yet clear to us."[36]

In this paper he talks of the "many women who have a strong attachment to their father" and yet may not be neurotic.[37] This is based on a strong pre-Oedipal attachment to the mother "in a very rich and many-sided manner" and could last up to even four years.[38] Insofar as this phase permits all sorts of fixations and repressions to develop, he asks whether it forces us to "retract the universality of the thesis that the Oedipus complex is the nucleus of the neuroses."[39] Freud reassures us; there is no need for this. "On the one hand, we can extend the content of the Oedipus complex to include all of the child's relation to both parents; or, on the other, we can take due account of our new findings by saying that the female only reaches the normal positive Oedipus situation after she has surmounted a period before it that is governed by the negative complex."[40]

These important new findings in respect of female sexuality were for Freud momentous ones, analogous to the discovery of the Minoan-Mycenian civilization as a precursor of the Greek. Here also he tried to salvage the female Oedipus complex by postulating positive and negative phases—but their chronological order is reversed in the psychosexual development of the sexes. In women, the negative complex precedes the positive; in men it is the other way around. "We have, after all, long given up any expectation of a neat parallelism between male and female sexual development."[41]

It is clear that female sexuality was a troublesome problem for Freud, not only owing to its intrinsic difficulty but also because it rendered problematic the whole issue of Oedipal relationships. Regarding the manner in which girls respond to the threat of castration and the prohibition on masturbation, he says: "In truth, it is hardly possible to give a description which has general validity. We find the most different reactions in different individuals, and in the same individual contrary attitudes exist side by side."[42]

Though Freud tried to solve these difficulties, and the others listed earlier, by postulating constitutional bisexuality and the two phases of the Oedipus complex, one can also read this paper as a kind of unwitting deconstruction of the Oedipus complex. The idea of the negative complex discovered so late in his career effectively demolished any simplistic notion of the Oedipus complex. The Oedipal relationships now can be governed by love for the parent of the opposite sex and hate for the parent of the same sex (positive Oedipus complex); *and* it includes love for the parent of the same sex and hatred for the parent of the opposite sex (the negative complex). Add homosexuality and the sibling complex and what we have is, in my phrase, an "erotically desirable circle of familial kin."[43] Within this circle each culture (or some cultures) isolate in their fantasy lives a group of kin that are significant for the neuroses. These are the "Oedipal" kin; and the complex that emerges in the psychosexual development of the child is the "Oedipus complex." This complex can be represented at different degrees of remove in culturally significant Oedipal *myths.* Neither myth nor complex is universal in the sense of exhibiting an invariant pattern or structure; but they might exhibit "family resemblances."

❸

Universalizing the Oedipus Complex: Argument with Wittgenstein

In this section I enter into a dialogue with the "edifying thinker," Wittgenstein, who, for many anthropologists, is the arch exponent of relativism.[44] In *Philosophical Investigations,* Wittgenstein says: ". . . one human being can be a complete enigma to another. We learn this when we come into a strange country with entirely strange traditions; and, what is more, even given a mastery of the country's language. We do not *understand* the people."[45] In *Zettel* he talks of a hypothetical strange culture where "life would run on differently" and where they would have "essentially different concepts."[46] While we cannot dismiss these insights, history must teach us not to fall into the same kind of trap that we did with positivist methodology. Methodology or the Wittgenstein antimethodologism is a raft for crossing the river but not for getting a hold of it—if I may rephrase a quotation from a Buddhist text.

I choose to start with Wittgenstein because like Marx, Freud, Nietzsche, and Heidegger he was an "edifying thinker"; yet he was the least given to asking questions of ontological import. His strategy was essentially deconstructionist; he questioned and ridiculed philosophies that were concerned with the foundations of knowledge. Gier rightly says that Wittgenstein rejected any semblance of a phenomenological life world common to man and serving as an ontological anchorage for different forms of life. According to him "cultural and linguistic differences are so great that forms of life and language games diversify rather than unify."[47] Is there any place for speaking about man and society in general terms for a person who could say, "If a lion could talk, we could not understand him"?[48]

Let me start with Wittgenstein's strongly polemical review of Frazer's *The Golden Bough.*[49] Wittgenstein inveighs against Frazer's view that the religious and magical ideas of primitive people were mistakes. "Was Augustine mistaken then when he called on God on every page of the Confessions"; or a Buddhist mistaken in believing in his religion? "But *none* of them was making a mistake except where he was putting forward a theory."[50] We cannot, as Frazer does, explain one system of beliefs in terms of another; "we can *describe* and say human life is like that."[51]

> In other words, one can begin a book on anthropology in this way: when we watch the life and behavior of men all over the earth we see that apart from what one might call animal activities, taking food etc etc, men also carry out actions that bear a peculiar character and might be called ritualistic.
>
> But then it is nonsense if we go from there on to say that the characteristic feature of *these* actions is that they spring from the wrong ideas of the physics of things.[52]

It is clear that Wittgenstein is affirming that cultural beliefs are forms of life that have their own inner coherence and integrity and, when seen in context, are no more irrational than European beliefs. There is an implicit relativism here. What one can do is describe these forms of life, not "explain" them. To explain them as Frazer does is to "make this practice plausible to people who think as he does."[53] Implied in this account is that any anchorage of these beliefs in a panhuman ontological base is impossible. It is this latter idea that I must now question.

Wittgenstein says, "I must plunge again and again into the waters of doubt."[54] The question I must ask is, does he ever reach the muddy bottom?

There are two places where he seems to touch ground, though not very firmly.

> That a man's shadow, which looks like a man, or that his mirror image, or that rain, thunderstorms, the phases of the moon, the change of seasons, the likenesses and differences of animals to one another and to human beings, the phenomenon of death, of birth and of sexual life, in short everything a man perceives year in, year out around him, connected together in any variety of ways—that all this should play a part in his thinking (his philosophy) and his practices, is obvious, or in other words this is what we really know and find interesting.[55]

This is a catalogue of things that has influenced man's thinking, but it does come perilously close to a general view of man—the things that he perceives "year in and year out," and the stuff which he uses to construct his world. Wittgenstein goes on to say that Frazer's primitive man does not try to "explain"—"a stupid superstition of our time." What Wittgenstein does not realize is that this "stupid superstition" is itself a *human* characteristic—Frazer's savages explain their social practices, and so forth, as we do, but they use different idioms, such as etiological myths, for the purpose. At other times they attribute causality to events, and it is rare, contrary to Wittgenstein, that "in magical healing one *indicates* to an illness that it should leave the patient."[56] Explanation itself is ontological; it is the "stupid superstition" of human beings.

I think there is a giveaway statement in "Remarks," where he touches the muddy bottom—or does he clutch at a straw?

> There is one conviction that underlies [or is taken for granted in] the hypothesis about the origin of, say, the Beltane festival; namely festivals of this kind are not so to speak haphazard inventions of one man but need an infinitely broader basis if they are to persist. If I tried to invent a festival it would very soon die out or else be so modified that it corresponded to *a general inclination in people.*[57]

What I find interesting in Wittgenstein is that he too could not avoid hinting at an ontological substrate from which "forms of life" emerge. We all know the famous phrase "family resemblances"; forms of life are not truly unique entities but may exhibit family resemblances. Language games are themselves part of a more inclusive form of life. This is what Wittgenstein probably meant when he said that the term "language game" is "meant to bring into prominence the fact that the speaking of language is part of an activity, or a form of life."[58] This emphasis on life and experience links him not only to the phenomenologists but also to thinkers like Freud and Nietzsche.

Forms of life are also not of the same type. Wittgenstein says there are "those forms of life which are primitive and those which arise out of them."[59] In *Philosophical Investigations* he can speak easily of the "common behavior of mankind."[60] But unlike Heidegger or Merleau Ponty, for whom a specific life-form is part of a larger human drama, Wittgenstein refuses to commit himself to any firm ontological anchorage for "forms of life." He recognizes, as commentators rightly point out, that forms of life are characteristically *human;* animals do not share these with man, but this does not commit him to an acceptance of any Archimedean point or foundation since that would, for him, violate the very basis of his deconstruction of post-Cartesian thought.[61] Nevertheless a sympathetic interpreter of Wittgenstein, Anthony Kenny, can state: "The datum on which language rests, the framework into which it fits, is given not by the structure of unchanging atoms, but by a shifting pattern of forms of life grafted on to a basic common human nature."[62] Wittgenstein himself says, very much in the spirit of Paul Ricoeur: "All great art has man's primitive drives as its groundbass. They are not the *melody* (as they are with Wagner, perhaps) but they are what gives the melody its power."[63] This basic common human nature is what Wittgenstein reluctantly, hesitantly, and with constant denials and equivocations seems to have taken for granted. It is the muddy bottom that lay beneath the swirling waters of doubt.

Wittgenstein was a master of doubt, but he was far from being a "master of suspicion." He was not only averse to erecting universal existentials on the phenomenological model, but he was also opposed to it. "Family resemblances" is as far as he went. There is an admirable lack of suspicion in his critique of Frazer; the killing of the divine king has to be taken in its own right, and it is as sensible as anything else anywhere. Or is it naivete? In his criticism of Freud's dream theory he wrote:

> Freud called this dream 'beautiful,' putting 'beautiful' in inverted commas. But *wasn't* the dream beautiful? I would say to the patient: "Do these associations make the dream not beautiful?" It was beautiful. Why shouldn't it be? I would say Freud cheated the patient.[64]

This criticism comes from a stylist who was a master of paradox and equivocation, who deconstructed conventional logic and insisted that the law of contradiction was *not* a law and that contradictions can have a rightful place in language games. Yet he could not accept that, in the grammar of the unconscious, one can have something that is both beautiful and not beautiful, that it can contain paradoxes, contradictions, and a lack of conventional logic and grammar—forms that Wittgenstein himself celebrated, in iconoclastic fashion, in his own work. Wittgenstein is acutely sympathetic to paradox, and paradox can exist in conventional "language games." But while he was fascinated with Freud and his work, he could not countenance the idea that the unconscious could be a form of life with its own language games, or rules of grammar. His objection, it seems to me, is a hangover from Cartesian thought. The objection *is* to unconscious motivation, for Wittgenstein's approach, as Thompson rightly says, "leaves everything as it is."[65] Thompson also notes that there is little critique in Wittgenstein. While he was deeply suspicious of the work of his own colleagues and predecessors (and his own *Tractatus*), he was uncritically accepting of "forms of life," particularly if they were outside of Western culture. One reason for this prejudice is laudable. He saw in Frazer a refusal to recognize the rationality of alien life-forms and lampooned his fatuous ethnocentrism.

> What narrowness of spiritual life we see in Frazer! And as a result: how impossible for him to understand a different way of life from the English one of his time! Frazer cannot imagine a priest who is not basically an English parson of our times with all his stupidity and feebleness.[66]

These alien life-forms, it is clear, helped him in his critique of Western thought and culture, but he could not see the rationale for the critique of forms of life per se irrespective of their cultural source. All he can do is to describe such forms of life, but he tells us very little as to how we can even do that. There is no critical theory in Wittgenstein; not even a notion analogous to Gadamer's "fusion of horizons." Even those who expanded on his thought, such as Peter Winch, cannot escape advocating a kind of descriptive formalism in social science.[67]

What has the preceding argument with Wittgenstein to do with the Oedipus complex and its mythic representations? I think the lesson is that we must, to understand the Oedipus complex, deal with its historicity and touch bottom, however muddy it may be, in order to comprehend the ontological anchorage of the myth and the complex.

Let me start out with my own strategy of interpretation, which is exactly how Freudians themselves interpret the complex (even though they may deny it). There is no straightforward line of argument from complex to myth; from the complex we discover a paradigmatic myth, and we use the myth to construct a paradigmatic complex. Freud initially observed the complex in his own life; then in very scattered form, in dreams; he saw its parallelism with the myth; the myth then helped him to formalize the complex; then back to the myth to legitimize the complex.[68] This mode of reasoning, as I see it, is the methodological dimension of the hermeneutic circle; a form of circular reasoning which builds up our understanding and then helps to give it form.

If one looks at Freud's formulations of the complex, everything *seems* clear-cut, but we know that this formulation is not only a product of circular reasoning but also is replicated in pure form in fantasy and myth only in the rare case. Almost every type of representation of the Oedipus complex (in dream, myth, history) is symbolically removed from the ideal type of the "pure" complex delineated by Freud. There is no way to directly translate motive into representation (or representation into the motive). I might want to kill my father and marry my mother, but I will not be permitted to dream this by the censor. Instead my father was killed in an accident, and I married the queen of Spain. Again, Little Hans's fantasy is not a simple expression of the complex, but a complicated representation of his relationship to his parents. Yet it is from representations such as life stories, and from dreams, that the simpler formulation is made that the child erotically desires the parent of the opposite sex (myth: to marry the parent) and hates the parent of the same sex (myth: to kill the parent). The complex is never seen; it is inferred from the representation; and though the representation does not directly express the complex, a clear-cut complex of unseen motives has been framed on the basis of the evidence of the seen representation. It is therefore legitimate to say that the inference of the complex on the basis of the representation (fantasy, myth) is false or at least partially in error; or as I would argue, the Oedipus complex is a "fictitious term" constructed on the basis of circular reasoning.

Social science concepts often have a "fictitious" character. Fiction is obviously not a falsehood, but a way of expressing a truth that cannot be expressed otherwise.[69] We can also counter one fiction by other "fictions," but we must also justify them in terms of an anchorage on first principles. If we radically question the nature of first principles, as Wittgenstein does, we must then resort to another, shakier ontological base—in man's human nature. But insofar as our knowledge of man's human nature is not very advanced, one can only do it in an exploratory manner by delineating a narrow segment of our human nature or species being that is related ontologically to the Oedipus complex and myth. It is then that we can begin to appreciate the significance of the Freudian fiction of the Oedipus complex and the necessity to substantiate or counter it with other fictions, derived as forms of life from the identical muddy bottom.

The segment of our human nature relevant to the Oedipus complex is the phylogenetically grounded human family, and thanks to the recent work of primate sociologists, we can sketch its significance for our problem. The outlines of the primate family constellation are well known.[70] Phylogenetically the primary family group is the mother and child; the infant's prolonged primate helplessness forces the mother into a caretaking role, so that the survival of the infant and the well-being of the mother are dependent on outside help. Hence the conditions are right for a male to attach himself to the primary matrisegment. The primate bond is complicated in human beings because the woman is released from her estrus cycle. She is sexually active, or can be, at any time; this has several implications for the mother-child bond. Primates in estrus are so dominated by sexuality that this single preoccupation can well result in the rejection of the infant. Not so with the human female, whose sexuality is evenly distributed; her caretaking role could also be continuously operative. She is also sexually active and could, in fact, respond erotically to the infant's stimulation. It has been argued that this form of life attracts a male who can be bonded sexually to the female, owing to her continuous sexual receptivity. I myself belief that this aspect of pair bonding has been grossly exaggerated by the present-day Western definitions of marriage and family life in terms of sexuality and the (initial) erotic bond between man and woman. What is crucial is not only the mutual sexual attractiveness, but also, in the human scheme of things, the sense of the helplessness of the infant and the empathy with the mother-child bond that evokes the pity, love, and sense of caring in the male. This aspect of familial bonding has been rightly stressed by Enlightenment thinkers like Rousseau.[71] These complex feelings are in turn made possible by the development of the human brain, at least in its present form. For without the capacity for complex symbolization that the brain, by its intrinsic nature, makes possible and necessary, there could not exist a human unconscious with its continual production of imagery and symbolic forms in dreams, fantasy, and myth. The rules of the dream work that Freud so wonderfully formulated could not exist without that human endowment. The kind of universal existentials noted by phenomenologists also develop initially in this situation. Wittgenstein was probably right when he said that *he* could imagine a primitive group without a sense of feeling of any kind, but I doubt he could find it in any existent community.[72]

The ontological ground of the Oedipus complex then is the existence of the powerful bond between mother and infant, and the family, nuclear or extended, in which a male (or males) care for the helpless infant, not just a caretaking role required for the survival of the human infant, but a *sense* of caring that is specifically human. Yet, one must emphasize, it is impossible to infer a universal (and uniform) Oedipus complex on the basis of a universal form of a human family life, as it is to infer a universal family model from a common human nature. Diverse grafts, exhibiting at best family resemblances, can be implanted on a universal human nature.

The situation sketched above is complicated by several conditions in human family life: (a) the existence of the incest taboo among family members, excluding the parental pair; (b) the sexuality that all members possess, including infants, stimulated by the diffuse affection, body contact, and care by the parents, and especially the mother; (c) the coexistence of complex feelings of pity, love, fear among the members that produces a fundamental feature of familial relations—ambivalence or multivalence; (d) the continual frustration that is implied in all these relationships, such as the impossibility of a sibling or parent being a love object and the moral difficulty of retaliation against those who dominate you.

Put in other words, given the existence of human family living, there is no way one can escape from ambivalence and the desirability of *all* intimate familial persons. The power of the mother-son bond, for example, is undisputed; but, insofar as the sibling is also a member of the family, why is it that it also cannot be an intrinsic object of erotic attachment? If the father is loved and feared, why not other intimate members in the circle of familial relations, like the mother's brother? And, as I said earlier, how is it possible to divorce one affect or drive or motive from the other in this context of intense, yet diffuse, emotional relationships, especially of power or domination and nurture? Freud rightly noted that in this kind of situation the individual has developed automatic techniques for coping with his complex emotions—the most significant being repression, followed by displacement and projection and the other mechanisms of defense.

A good case for questioning the simple triangular nature of the Oedipus complex was made by George Devereux, one of the most creative minds in psychoanalytic anthropology, in his notion of the complementary Oedipus complex first written in 1953.[73] In this important paper Devereux points out the cultural reasons in Freud's time that led him to neglect complexes that are complementary to the Oedipus complex; namely, the love, indeed actual seduction, by the parents of the son (and daughter). The deliberate "scotomization" of these complementary complexes is due to nineteenth-century authoritarian attitudes that foisted all responsibility for the Oedipus complex on the child, ignoring parental attitudes that stimulate the infant's Oedipal tendencies.[74] "The scotomization of the Laius and Jocasta complexes then led certain later writers to develop an elaborate, and unconvincing, theory of the phylogenetically determined infantile fantasy-life, which predicates that, regardless of how loving the father may be, the infant's instinctually determined and phylogenetically anchored fantasies will cause him to view even his kindly father as *primarily* a monster."[75] Then Devereux proceeds with a detailed analysis of non-Sophoclean versions of the Oedipus myth that underplay the heterosexual love of Oedipus for his mother, but instead deal with a *circle* of Oedipal relationships originating not from the son but from the mother and father. It is likely, he argued, that the Jocasta and Laius complexes reflected the Oedipal seduction from the parental point of view. In respect to Laius, sources emphasize his homosexual rape of a youth, Chrysipus, and a curse that for this reason Oedipus' own son will slay him. Consequently Laius refuses to have sex with Jocasta, but when drunk does so and produces Oedipus. According to one version, Laius and Oedipus fought each other because they were rivals for Chrysipus' love; therefore, their fight was a homosexually motivated encounter.[76] Devereux's psychological interpretation is that "Chrysipus is, in a sense, the representative of Oedipus' own passive homosexual characteristics, which were brought into being, or were at least aroused, by Laius' aggressive homosexual impulses towards his son."[77] In a continuation of his analysis Devereux says that after the quarrel Oedipus took his father's sword and belt. Undoing a woman's belt in Greek thought is preliminary to coitus, and by this symbolic gesture Oedipus turned the tables on his homosexual father by castrating (sword) and feminizing him (belt), and then of course marrying his mother. The striking features of all these myths is that they emphasize "the homosexual element in the causation of Laius' death and bring in incest with Jocasta more or less as an afterthought."[78] Devereux goes so far as to suggest that cohabitation with Jocasta must be viewed "primarily as a symbolically homosexual and only epiphenomenally as a heterosexual act."[79] Consequently, Laius' death, according to Devereux's sources, "was not primarily caused by Oedipus' own incestuous impulses, but by Laius' character."[80] Oedipus then was only partially motivated by the violent impulses of the normal Oedipus complex.

Devereux unfortunately did not fully recognize the radical implications of his findings. It is true that his findings are compatible with psychoanalytic theory but not with its specifically Oedipal theory.[81] If the Oedipus complex is not primarily phylogenetically determined, then the way is open for a variety of socially conditioned sexual motivations. Devereux himself notices the homosexual attraction between the parent and child of the same sex; also its mutuality. This is expectable in family relations and might be accentuated by cultural preoccupations like the Greek interest in homosexuality. But if the circle of relationships and the type of erotic relationships get widened in Devereux' treatment, it is only a step further to include crosscutting sibling relations into the picture. Devereux infers the existence of the complexes from the myth, and that is why he does not deal with sibling eroticism as part of the complex since these are not expressed in his selection of Greek Oedipal myths. The actual Oedipal circle must include the siblings; but the Greeks, unlike the Sinhalas, exclude it from their mythology. The mythological representation of the Oedipus complex then may express a society's concern with a segment of Oedipal relations which for them are culturally and historically significant, whereas the empirical Oedipal relations are far more complicated, embracing all the significant persons in the family. Thus a clear distinction must be now drawn among (a) an empirically existent circle of Oedipal relationships among significant family members, (b) the analyst's isolation of an Oedipus *complex,* and (c) the mythic representation of culturally significant Oedipal relationships.

What then is the Oedipus complex? To appreciate the implications of the distinctions we made earlier we must not assume that culture is extrinsic to motivation, or that motivation is precultural (though it may well be prelinguistic). Freud noted in his patients (and in himself) a set of Oedipal relations that were significant in the causation of neuroses. He thought all neuroses were implicated in it, a naive assertion. These patterns were culturally more significant than, let us say, sibling or homosexual eroticism for him and the society of his time. His mistake was to isolate this segment of Oedipal relations as the universally significant one and consequently to see the set of relations thus demarcated as a *theory* in the positivist sense, rather than an important *fiction,* with heuristic significance for clinical psychoanalysis. To put it differently: the fiction of the Oedipus complex is the isolation of a segment of the actual empirical circle of erotically desired kin that are "clinically significant"; the Oedipus myth is the isolation of a similar segment that is "culturally significant."

Freud's scientistic bias springs from his nineteenth-century views. Wittgenstein, who was an astute critic of Freud as often as he was an obtuse one, noted:

> Freud was influenced by the 19th century idea of dynamics—an idea which has influenced the whole treatment of psychology. He wanted to find some one explanation which would show what dreaming is. He wanted to find the *essence* of dreaming. And he would have rejected any suggestion that he might be partly right but not altogether so. If he was partly wrong, that would have meant for him that he was wrong altogether—that he had not really found the essence of dreaming.[82]

Anne Parsons, for example, working on her material from Naples, observed another set of significant Oedipal relations—another fiction;[83] and so did I in my brief reinterpretation of Trobriand. This fiction of a complex is historically and culturally conditioned, sometimes in the very complex ways that Devereux has noted for nineteenth-century Europe. Similarly, the Indian Oedipus is not a variant form of a universal complex: it *is* the segment of Oedipal relations that is culturally significant and also determinative of a great many neuroses. A myth then can be paradigmatic of the complex, for it is indeed likely that the set of significant relationships isolated by the analyst may also be the culturally significant one, and is consequently represented in myth. But on the other hand this might *not* be the case; it may well be that some cultures do not organize psychic conflicts in the family into a complex or a myth or both, in which case these conflicts can exist as more or less free-floating deep motivations that may or may not be represented in symbolic forms. Psychic conflicts engendered in childhood will, however, be relevant for the formation of both neuroses and fantasy which then have to be clinically or psychoethnographically investigated and described.

The preceding argument implies that the Freudian Oedipus complex is but one form of life constructed out of a circle of desire in the family. The Hindu Oedipus is another form showing family resemblance to the Western complex. Related forms may exist in other cultures, or as variants within the same culture. The idea of family resemblances also implies that some forms may be so symbolically removed from the Western one as to be virtually unrecognizable. And in the extreme case one must recognize the possibility of free-floating deep motivations that are not organized systematically into a "complex."

Thus the attempt to see the Oedipus complex that Freud constructed on the basis of his self-analysis as an invariant and universal life-form is extremely dubious. It is also restrictive and constricting of the imagination. Consider the problems that arise from the conventional ethnographic strategy of investigating the Freudian Oedipus in other cultures.

Insofar as the "Oedipus complex" is a technical term for an organized psychic structure that exists in the unconscious of Western parents and children, psychoethnography assumes an identical organized psychic structure in every known human society under the sun, in spite of variations in family structures, values, and modes of socialization. The psychoethnographic evidence for this improbable assumption comes mostly from myth and dream, rather than from clinical investigation. Nevertheless, rarely is the myth a direct representation of the complex, as I noted earlier. Yet if the ethnographer carries with him the theoretical assumption of a universal Freudian Oedipus complex he can see its existence everywhere in the distorted representations of myth and fantasy; hence the standard explanation for Oedipal variation as products of displacements, denials, reaction-formations, and other ego defenses. But the trouble with this formulation is that I could as easily say that the Freudian form is a displacement, etc., of the Hindu Oedipus and affirm that the Hindu Oedipus *is* the universal life-form. By the same evidence—myths and fantasies—I can also "prove" its universality as long as I use displacement, denial, reaction-formation as the logic of my explanation. This exercise, however, is a travesty of the Freudian insight from clinical studies: the formation and use of ego defenses must be *demonstrated* from the concrete case history. Unless anchored to the empirical data of case histories, the mechanisms of defense can be used to explain any deviation from any ideal typical form of the Oedipus complex that I might construct.

The problem can be restated differentially. It seems that Oedipal relations, insofar as they are manifest in representations, almost always appear in fragmented symbolic form. I noted earlier that it is rarely that a wish ("I want to marry my mother") is directly represented in dream and fantasy owing to the work of the censor (or superego) which distorts the representation. But fragmentation need not be the result of distortion alone: it could be the result of the context in which a particular Oedipal relation is activated. Take Ramanujan's assertion that there is no known case in Hindu history of patricide whereas filicide is well known. Here the historical and social context pertaining to succession and authority activates the infantile motive of domination; and the erotic motivation of incest so crucial to the Freudian complex is contextually irrelevant and hence submerged. That is, Hindu kings might kill their sons, but they do not marry their mothers, daughters, or sisters. The lived world of Hindu culture will not permit the latter unless disguised in a symbolic formation. By contrast *myths* that deal with family relations might activate the incest theme. Finally and most importantly, one must grant the possibility that an organized psychic structure such as the Oedipus complex might not exist at all in the unconscious of people in another culture, and consequently desired or hated kin might well be represented in myth and fantasy in an ad hoc manner. For example, in my hypothetical culture my love for my mother (or sister) and hatred for my father (or brother) may exist without being interconnected into an organized totality one calls a "complex." Consequently these free-ranging motivations might be separately represented (or even perhaps remain unrepresented) in culturally constituted symbolic forms, if not in fantasy. The usual explanation that persons in such societies have not successfully articulated or resolved their Oedipal conflicts is meaningless if the complex as an articulated entity does not exist in any form (as complex, myth, or fantasy) in that culture. The organization of psychic conflicts as well as their resolution or nonresolution must be examined in the context of a particular culture.

The segment of the psychic reality that I might want to isolate from the empirical circle of desire is also best characterized as a "fiction," rather than a law of human behavior. Thus one can, I think, talk of different Oedipus complexes as "fictions" existing in different cultures, though these fictions are probably limited and exhibit family resemblances to one another. Why so? Because of our common human nature or basic human behaviors or existential universals or our species being or whatever—a muddy bottom that even Wittgenstein, for all his relativism, was forced to recognize. The ground of this universal human nature is psychobiological: man as a kind of species possessed of a complex brain, relatively freed from the instincts, with a capacity for complex symbolization, especially in language and fantasy. One could add more and more to this psychobiological ground of our nature as research in psychology, neurology, and genetics develops. This is the area from which anthropologists borrow, not the area of their research.

Out of these assumptions of a common human nature, whose basic contours only are yet known, one must construct the social or human sciences, the *Geisteswissenschaften*. At one time, in the heyday of positivism, this was relatively easy: everyone lived in families, they married, they exploited nature and the environment, they had machinery to effect law and order—and so one could talk of universal institutions or domains like marriage and the family, political systems, economics, and so forth. But soon we recognized that this naive universalism, fostered by scientific philosophies and the power of sister disciplines, came into a radical confrontation with our experience as ethnographers. In the first place, we came up with that master idea, and now an assumption, that human beings construct their own symbolic worlds—what we called culture. Man may belong psychobiologically and neurologically to a single species, and the capacity for complex symbolization may be species determinate, but culture emancipates man from his human nature and gives him a peculiar capacity for speciation or dividing the world. This shift in perspective coincided with the massive attack on positivism by philosophers coming from different directions—from the tradition of German hermeneutics of Dilthey; American pragmatism, especially Dewey and Peirce; Wittgenstein and ordinary language philosophy; and the phenomenology of Heidegger. Influenced by these streams of thought we further began to bare our bleeding hearts and show the world how vulnerable we were. Not only are the cultural worlds constructed by man highly variable if not infinite, but we are not even sure whether we can construct an accurate representation of that world, for the nature of the anthropologists's situation, as an alien studying alien language games, forced him to realize the truth of the philosophers' radical questioning of subject-object relationships, and of truth and objectivity in the human sciences. We can now only *appropriate* the other, or fuse our horizon with the other, or carry on a conversation or dialogue with the other. But few of us have asked how boring this might become if anthropologists, some of whom aren't even witty, were to carry on a dialogue with the other! And what ghastly appropriations of the other would emerge when ordinary anthropologists try to assimilate the rich and often complex worlds of other cultures into the narrow, stultifying cultures of academia, whether in Peradeniya or Princeton.

But let me push away these troubling asides and get back to the nitty-gritty of our discipline. The work of contemporary philosophers fused with the horizon of our own experience in ethnographic fieldwork reinforced the stray opinions of earlier dissidents like Benedict, that cultures were relative and that ethnography was a genre of writing not all that removed from fiction. But how relative is relative? Relativism can be a near infinite regress. The richer the ethnographic data the more relative it becomes, extending even to the neighboring village or tribe (and one can only scoff at people who have the temerity to study complex and false entities like nations). One can grasp the whole it seems only in parts. Where the data are lacking or skimpy then it *is* possible to study the whole, as in Valeri's study of Hawaiian sacrifice or Geertz's Theatre State.[84] But who nowadays seriously think of fieldwork that encompasses the Hawaiian or Balinese nation? As far as positivism is concerned we might have thrown out the baby only to keep the bath water. The older generation of anthropologists could see "relativism" simply as a variation from something else such as a cultural universal or as data for concomitant variations for testing causal hypotheses. We now seem to have got stuck with relativism and descriptivism; there seems no natural place where we could draw the line, and there is little space available for nomological understanding.

The fundamental dilemma of cultural relativism can be explicated in the following manner. If each culture must be understood in its own terms, and if one cannot go beyond this, it must also mean that those other people (our informants) who create culture are also different from one another and from us. But this forces the relativist into an untenable position, for few will doubt that one can nevertheless talk to one's informant and seek his help in constructing an ethnography. If there is a marriage of minds here, how can I say that my informant's mind is as different from mine as is the very culture he (and others like him) creates? The very fact that my informant as a coparticipant in the creation of my ethnography implies that there is an affinity between us. Moreover, even more fundamentally, relativists tend to believe in culture as a symbolic system. But this belief implies a common *human* capacity to create symbolic forms. Thus eventually the relativist also must touch bottom, must also recognize some kind of a common human nature from which emerge different life-forms. But the moment one postulates a common human nature (or mind or qualities or existentials) the question of relativism itself becomes problematic. I noted earlier that it is false to infer common cultural forms or universal social institutions from a common human nature; yet surely it is even more fallacious to infer relativism from a common nature! The solution, it seems to me, lies in our recognition of family resemblances among various life-forms in the cross-cultural record.

This is where I think my argument with Wittgenstein is instructive. He, of all the edifying thinkers, seemed the most relativistic, yet he too was forced to anchor the different language games and forms of life in the ontological ground of a human nature. Family resemblances make sense because of a *family,* in the sense of a larger unity or ground that encompasses diverse life-forms. Naturally such a ground is an *assumption,* yet one based on our psychobiological knowledge of man. Nor can this ground be defined as a firm foundation, a bedrock of our Being. Our knowledge of man does not permit it, hence my metaphor of the muddy bottom. But there as a basis for building on firmer ground, as knowledge in human genetics and neurology and primate studies develops. Thus the biological ground of our being, which now is an assumption, is also the ontological foundation for developing a human science. In other words we must construct our understanding of being human and cultural on the basis of our assumptions of a human nature. And this buildup need not be fortuitous, for we can grasp the manner in which human association, family, and kinship ties might well be erected on a common base. The Oedipus complex illustrates how this task might proceed. We assume a common human nature—an assumption, not an axiom, since this must be justified by research in neurology, genetics, and primate sociology. This basic nature is itself the ground of a set of universal parameters that we tentatively construct—the existence of the mother-child as the basic familial unit; the phylogenetic conditions that lead to the attachment of a male (or males) to this unit; the infant's prolonged dependency and the ties this creates among family members; the conflicting emotions that develop in this family situation; and so forth. Through the developing research in a variety of disciplines, it is possible to construct the universal parameters of human family life, and it is against this kind of universalism that the different forms of life that one calls the Oedipus complex make sense. These forms exhibit "family resemblances" because they fold back into the parameters of human life and are intelligible in relation to them. The Oedipal forms of life—myth and complex—are fictions, I noted, because they are segments of the empirical reality we have isolated as significant to us. They permit us to talk of the *human* situation (the parameters) in different cultural settings (the fictions). The analytical strategy that suits this anthropology should, I think, contain a hesitant dialectic of deconstruction-reconstruction, a dialectic necessary for any research enterprise where there are no firm foundations, only a muddy bottom.

The idea of a human science is, in this view, not methodological, but existential, a continual ontological search. The dominant Anglo-American tradition of social science believes that true knowledge can be achieved by *method.* Hence epistemology is key to the social sciences, and ontology is to be shunned. I think the reverse is true: the human sciences (*Geisteswissenschaften*) are "ontological" in the broad sense of a concern with human existence. And any attempt to divorce ontology from epistemology cannot succeed but can only produce a shallow ontology. We have only a few philosophically well-developed ontologies in the human sciences, a good example being Cassirer's philosophy of symbolic forms or Heidegger's *Dasein.* Yet incipient or partially developed ontological assumptions underlie such notions as "forms of life," "species being," "cultural relativism," "economic man," "pleasure principle," and so forth. Our criticisms of our colleagues' works are very often based on our ontological beliefs about men, women, and society. These kinds of "prejudices" are inevitable, and desirable, as long as we recognize them for what they are. The advance of theory or knowledge in the *Geisteswissenschaften* entails a parallel advance in our knowledge of being cultural and human. This expanding ontological vision must then be self-consciously and explicitly recognized and used as a ground for a developing epistemology, and so the process must move back and forth from epistemology to ontology in a circular fashion. But any ontology we use to ground the human sciences must ultimately be based on "faith" since an ontology of even minimum significance must derive from a variety of sources, including the scholar's religious and cultural heritage; and any ontology that we employ can never be final since the very historicity of our being prevents that. Consequently any systematic ontology defies "scientific" validation, but it can be rescued from the underground where it now lies and be given explicit formulation.

4

The Indian Oedipus in Sri Lanka: Pulleyar and the Lord Buddha Revisited

The preceding discussions focussed on the theme that the Oedipus complex is not only culturally variable but that even within a single culture there might be several Oedipal models with one form dominant insofar as it is the most frequent form or reflective of the ideal cultural value configuration. I believe it wrong to assume a single Oedipus complex for Western cultures either, if the evidence of myth models is to be trusted. Thus Abraham's sacrifice of his submissive son is a possible model; so is the relationship among the divinities in the holy family, even if that myth model is symbolically removed from actual Oedipal motivations in the family. My approach not only opens up the Oedipus complex to the impact of cultural and societal conditions but also obviates the necessity to postulate an exact repetition of a particular type of Oedipus complex from one generation to another. For example: if there is a model of the authoritarian father who produces a submissive and gentle son, then it is possible that when the son becomes a father himself he might *continue* to be submissive and gentle. He can of course give up family relations as Jesus did, but if he becomes instead a weak or gentle father he can produce a son who then becomes capable of dethroning ("killing") the father. Thus one Oedipal model can be replaced by another in a matter of a generation or two.

I shall probe further this issue of a "multiple Oedipus" by examining the myth of Gaṇeśa, the popular god who straddles a large part of the South Asian universe. In terms of the logic of my analysis Gaṇeśa is obviously the dominant myth model for Hindus, whereas he is an alternative or subsidiary one for Buddhists. I shall also show that there are several such subsidiary models that are shared by both Hindus and Buddhists; yet they are not only strictly limited but also share strong family resemblances.

I shall expound my thesis of the multiple Oedipus through an argument with Edmund Leach, who wrote an essay on Gaṇeśa in 1962 entitled "Pulleyar and the Lord Buddha: An Aspect of Religious Syncretism in Ceylon."[85] This was reprinted with minor changes in the popular *Reader in Comparative Religion,* through its many editions, and consequently nurtured generations of anthropology students in United States universities.[86] In the introduction to the piece Lessa and Vogt state:

> Combining concrete ethnographic data with some insights from Lévi-Straussian structural analysis and Freudian psychoanalysis, Leach explores the function of mediating figures—those who share various attributes of logically opposed domains—in the syncretistic belief system of modern Ceylon. He emphasizes the effectiveness of the "totality of symbols" in resolving the seemingly universal problems of preservation of life and preparation for death. Leach is also able to show that relatively simple logical principles underlie the most seemingly complex religions.[87]

Given Leach's broad interests my own argument with him cannot be constrained by the Oedipal theme alone, but will concern other issues of significance for psychoethnography, such as the relation between structure and motivation, and the limitations of both structuralism and psychoanalysis when it comes to issues of historical change.

Gaṇeśa is the popular and widely revered Hindu god, the son of Śiva, who for many Hindus is God himself. In South India, but not in the North, he is called Pillaiyar or son (of Śiva), and the Sinhala of Nuvarakalāviya call him Pulleyar, obviously borrowed from the Tamil. Gaṇeśa is like Hermes, says Leach, a kind of trickster who, like the

Winnebago trickster, carries his phallus in a box. Like other tricksters his sexuality is in doubt. "It is part of my thesis that Ganesha's broken tusk is a phallic emblem and that its detachability denotes a certain ambivalence about Ganesha's sexual nature."[88] However, Leach says that in certain contexts Gaṇeśa may be virile and potent and in fact may have a female counterpart or *śakti*. The sexual qualities of Gaṇeśa are dependent on context and are the opposite of those attributed to the father (Śiva) and to his other brothers, Skanda and Aiyanar. "As Shiva varies so also Ganesha varies but in the inverse direction."[89]

Gaṇeśa is also worshiped by Sinhala-Buddhists in the Nuvarakalāviya District of Northern Sri Lanka just south of the region of Tamil-speaking Hindus. Here he is known as Pulleyar, the elephant lord of the forest. Aiyanar, his elder brother, is the guardian of the village and its reservoir. There is no cult of Śiva here nor of mother goddesses, but there is instead "a reverence for the Lord Buddha."[90] If in Hinduism Gaṇeśa and his mother and brothers are "simply appendages and aspects of Shiva," not so with the Sinhala Pulleyar and Aiyanar who lack specific parents. Instead these deities are feudal dependents of the supreme ascetic, the Lord Buddha. Leach does not ask the question why a supreme ascetic requires feudal dependents, but he poses another interesting one—"What happens to Shiva's son Ganesha when he is transferred to a Buddhist context as a servant of the Lord Buddha?"[91]

Before he tackles the Buddhist case Leach deals with the Hindu, which he finds substantively and structurally similar to the Christian. The major problem underlying both, and perhaps all religions, is that supreme power is vested in a great god, the origin and source of the sacred. The purpose of religious activity is to obtain benefit from this source, but direct approach to God is felt by participants to be dangerous. Hence religions invent mediators—saints, godlings, prophets, mediums—who can act as intermediaries between man and God.[92] In Catholicism, God the Father is powerful but remote whereas God the Son has become human and more accessible; equally accessible is the semidivine Virgin Mary. The latter two are mediators whose potency is derived from God himself. The Catholic saints are also of the same class but closer to the human end of the continuum. The Hindu pantheon shows a striking structural similarity, except for some slight substantive differences regarding the theme of sexuality.[93] Śiva and his *śakti* (female counterpart) are sexually active, whereas God the Son is sexually passive. If Gaṇeśa is castrated, Jesus is also asexual, often represented without genitalia or with infantile ones, and resembles his iconographic prototype, the eunuch deity Attis. The Virgin Mary is also ascetic and sexless. Hence Leach's conclusion: "Whereas Christ is a secondary and sexually inert manifestation of a sexually potent God the Father, Ganesha should be a secondary but sexually inert manifestation of a sexually potent Shiva. It is therefore to the physical and sexual characteristics of Ganesha that we must now turn our attention."[94]

These physical and sexual features are as follows: Gaṇeśa appears in iconography as an obese, effeminate male with an elephant head and flaccid trunk and one tusk only, and he rides a rat. His magical names ("single tusk," "elephant face," "pot belly," etc.) confirm his appearance. Above all he is a Janus-trickster facing both ways, a remover of obstacles, and one who both withdraws and bestows success as he also ignores and fulfills desires. Leach continue to describe other attributes of Gaṇeśa: He gets his way by ingenuity but not strength; he is the keeper of his father's (Śiva's) harem and thus a eunuch or sexually inadequate person; he is the guardian of the threshold and of all entrances and consequently addressed at the beginnings of enterprises of all sorts, as, for example, journeys, constructions, writing of books. The psychoanalytically minded, Leach says, would see him as a phallic creature like Priapos, and his head is "strikingly like the obscene little Greek pottery figurine which was the subject of one of Freud's observations. . . . And, as to the incongruous rat—well yes, a rat can penetrate even the smallest openings, like Rumpelstiltskin in the fairy tale."[95] Leach goes on to say that the myths of Gaṇeśa are pervaded by the themes of "castration, mother-love and sexual frustration", while the decapitation of his head by his father Śiva adds the Oedipal elements.[96] Leach quotes fourteen myths, but following structural fashion he neither contextualizes these myths in geographic or sociocultural settings, nor deals with the relative popularity or public appeal of these myths. The psychoanalytic themes are also not the crucial ones. Instead "in these stories the contrasts of male versus female and of sexuality versus asexuality are employed as binary pairs as to 'mediate a contradiction' in the manner which has been demonstrated for other materials by Lévi-Strauss."[97]

For present purposes I will deal only with Leach's treatment of two popular Hindu myths of Gaṇeśa; I refer the reader to Leach's article for the rest.

Myth of Gaṇeśa's birth

Shiva left home to go hunting. He took all his servants with him. Parvati wished to take a bath, but there was no one to guard the door so she made a guardian out of the dirt from her own body. Shiva, returning, was furious that he was prevented from entering his own house and struck off the head of the guardian, Ganesha. Parvati in turn was furious and ordered her husband to restore Ganesha to life. Shiva could not find the head so he replaced it with the head of an elephant which was the first animal that his servants happened to see when they went out into the forest. Thereafter Ganesha became the favorite son of Parvati and Shiva and is above all the guardian of entrances.[98]

Leach's structural summary of this myth is as follows:

Male sexuality (Shiva) is opposed to female sexuality (Parvati). Parvati creates a secondary male who separates Shiva and Parvati. Shiva destroys the secondary male and is reunited with Parvati. Ganesha is recreated deformed and unites Shiva and Parvati.[99]

Here is the second myth:

Myth of sibling rivalry and competition

There was a beautiful mango (*amba*) in the garden. Ganesha and his brother Kataragama (Skanda) both wanted the mango. They were told by their mother to race around the salt sea. Kataragama set off around the sea but Ganesha ran around a salt dish in the kitchen. Ganesha won the mango but Kataragama hit him and broke off his tusk.[100]

Leach provides this structural summary:

Two brothers (Skanda and Ganesha) are rivals for their mother's love. Skanda fails to achieve his objective through a display of virility. Ganesha achieves his ends by cunning but suffers mutilation at the hands of his rival.[101]

Now comes the overall structural interpretation of all the myths.

The themes throughout seem quite consistent. The male principle and the female principle stand opposed; a third principle (Ganesha), a kind of impersonalized sexuality,

> stands in the middle and serves both to unite and to separate. The combination male-plus-female is fertile but if the outcome is a secondary complete male, then jealousy will separate what was united. The alternative male-plus-male is sterile, and the two males will be jealous over the possession of women. The myth offers a "resolution" of the paradox. If male unites with female to produce a sterile offspring then the latter will serve as a mediation between the sexes instead of a source of hostility. The "man in the middle" must be either no sex at all or both sexes in alternation.[102]

Let me subject Leach's structural interpretation of the prototype myth of Gaṇeśa and related myths to a few criticisms.

Even if one agrees with Leach that the "complicated facts of Indian religion are . . . reducible to an elementary structural pattern," one wonders whether his analysis really teaches us anything new or profound about Indian religion or myth or sociocultural life.[103] This denudation of meaning must be overcome if structuralism is to achieve any significance, says Ricoeur. "I believe that if this were not the case structural analysis would be reduced to a sterile game, a divisive algebra, and even the myth would be bereaved of the function that Lévi-Strauss assigns it, that of making men aware of certain oppositions and of tending toward their progressive mediation. To eliminate this reference to the aporias of existence around which mythic thought gravitates would be to reduce the theory of myth to the necrology of the meaningless discourses of mankind."[104]

More specifically, consider Leach's view that the male and female principles stand opposed and that a third principle (Gaṇeśa), a kind of impersonalized sexuality, stand in the middle and serves both to unite and to separate. One is immediately struck by the denudation of myth here: those interesting and complex Indian deities are converted into "principles," and Gaṇeśa, the highly personal god whose extraordinary myths Leach himself quotes, though in summary form, is "a kind of impersonalized sexuality"!

Leach ignores Gaṇeśa's brother Skanda (and another brother, Aiyanar, according to some accounts), who shows exceptional signs of virility. Contrary to Leach, the situation is quite unlike the holy family of Catholicism where god has one son, Jesus, a castrated or asexual figure. In Hindu thought generally, and in the myths that Leach quotes, the Śiva-Gaṇeśa/Gaṇeśa-Pārvatī relationship is matched by

Gaṇeśa's relationship with his brother Skanda, and this in turn is based on sibling rivalry for the mother's love.[105]

Thus far Leach has dealt with the prototype figure of Gaṇeśa in Hindu India. The main thrust of his thesis is the transformation of this deity in the Nuvarakalāviya District of Buddhist Sri Lanka where he did fieldwork in 1954. Leach says that while villagers vaguely know that Pulleyar is the same as Pillaiyar (Gaṇeśa) of Hindu Tamils, they do not view him as a son of Śiva. He is a god in his own right, the lord of the forest. In Leach's village Pulleyar was simply represented: a small stone was placed under a large tree, and on this stone was painted an elephant's head.

In Hindu India, Śiva and Gaṇeśa are associated as father and son; the father, as was noted earlier, representing potency and the son mediation. But in Sri Lankan Sinhala conception Śiva is absent: the relationship is between the Buddha and Pulleyar. Leach argues that while substantively the relationships are different they are structurally the same. However, the Buddhist situation is complicated because the Buddha has an orthodox role of an enlightened being in the doctrinal tradition and a practical role as a god in peasant belief, while Pulleyar's role as mediator remains constant.

In the orthodox doctrinal conception, the Buddha is an enlightened human being, not a god. Consequently he is a mediator between Man and the Infinite, thus analogous to the Hindu Gaṇeśa, Christ, and other mediators. From this orthodox point of view "it is quite appropriate that the Buddha who mediates between death and the next life should have a counterpart who mediates between the previous life and birth. And it is appropriate that just as the cult of the Buddha lays stress on the ascetic, the sexless, the repudiation of emotion, the cult of his counterpart should be concerned with sex and fertility."[106] It may be necessary to have a mediator between the previous life and the present birth; unfortunately that which is structurally necessary is nowhere culturally practiced in Buddhist Sri Lanka, where baptismal rites are either very minimal or nonexistent. Thus one can flatly reject this aspect of Leach's discussion when he says: "Pulleyar is the *devata* [mediator] of birth, while the Buddha is the *devata* of death."[107]

The Buddha is a mediator in the orthodox doctrinal sense only, continues Leach. In popular thought he is "unquestionably the supreme God" and represents authority, not mediation.[108] "In these circumstances the role of mediator, that is, of a secondary deity who can 'fix things', which in orthodox theory should belong to the Buddha, is filled by a variety of godlings of the type I have labelled *devata* [mediator]."[109] In Nuvarakalāviya these mediators are Pulleyar and his elder brother Aiyanar. Leach goes on to describe the intermeshing of Buddhism with rituals for "godlings."

Buddhist rituals are many, but among the more important ones is Vesak, the celebration of the Buddha's birthday, which for Leach, but not for Sinhala Buddhists, is also New Year's Day! Another is *pirit* rituals where Buddhist texts are recited by monks (or laymen) on a variety of occasions, but especially at death. "The *pirit* type rituals of mortuary ceremonial are of special importance. These resemble both in form and function the Hindu rite of obsequies known as *śraddhā*. In *śraddhā* the heirs of the deceased provide food for kinsmen and Brahman priests; in mortuary *pirit* the heirs provide food for kinsmen and Buddhist monks."[110] The comment is too brief for us to figure out how these two are equivalent, since the Brahman ritual is an ancient ancestor cult whereas *pirit* texts and practice have no reference whatever to the dispatch of the dead soul to the realm of the ancestors. Yet the mortuary aspect of *pirit* is important for Leach, since this proves that the Buddha cult is "death-focussed" while the godlings cults are life-centered. I agree with Leach that Buddhism is much possessed by death, except his view that *pirit* is a mortuary ritual is simply wrong! *Pirit* is almost never recited at death, except very recently among bourgeois Buddhists in Colombo (but even they recite *pirit* at weddings also!). Even in Pul Eliya where Leach worked villagers I met denied that *pirit* was ever recited in their village as a mortuary rite. I think this is an exaggeration since there is no prohibition on the recital of *pirit* on such occasions, but it was clear that *pirit* is only rarely, if at all, performed on such occasions. It is possible, however, that Leach mistook *pirit* rituals for commemorating the dead (generally three months after death, and yearly thereafter) for mortuary rituals at death.[111]

In contrast with the death-focussed Buddhist rituals are the rituals for "godlings," especially the rituals for the new rice timed respectively during the period when the rice is green and during the commencement of harvest. "But apart from these occasions, Pulleyar, as distinct from the other *devata*, receives a great deal of special attention. It is Pulleyar who makes women and cattle pregnant, who assures bountiful crops, who gives success in hunting, who heals sick children."[112] The food given to Pulleyar is eaten by devotees; that offered the Buddha is thrown away since it is contaminated with death.

The Pulleyar priest is an ecstatic who acts as the mouthpiece of the deity himself; by contrast the Buddhist monk is sedate. The Pulleyar priest wears his hair long and dances violently, whereas the monk has a shaven head. The Buddhist monk bridges the gap between this world and the next "by moving himself halfway into the next world," whereas the Pulleyar priest is fully involved in the world.[113] Thus you have a binary antithesis, says Leach; Pulleyar is what the Buddha is not:[114]

Buddha cult	*Pulleyar cult*
concern of the elderly	concern of the young
asceticism	ecstasy
contemplation of death	preoccupation with fertility and sex
polluted food offerings	food offerings fit for children
OTHERWORLDLY	THIS-WORLDLY

Hence the Nuvarakalāviya Pulleyar differs significantly from his Hindu prototype Gaṇeśa. "Ganesha is seemingly an eunuch in contrast with his virile father Shiva, Nuvarakalāviya Pulleyar is sexually potent in contrast to the ascetic Buddha."[115] Yet overall the two cults are integrated into a larger religious system. One can now see that Pulleyar and the Lord Buddha are not only a structural reversal of the Hindu theme, but also of the Christian. "As between Christianity and the Sinhalese situation the contrast seems complete: God the Father is sexual—Jesus is sexless; Buddha is sexless—Pulleyar is sexual."[116] The argument is a powerful one: underlying the substantive variations of the three great religions is a stark, simple structural transformation based on a few basic concerns—that between life (this world) and death (the other world), and those mediating principles that help to bridge these irreconcilable extremes. No wonder then that among the Buddhists of Nuvarakalāviya Pulleyar is radically different from the Hindu prototype Gaṇeśa. Much as the castrated Gaṇeśa is the son of the virile Śiva, so the virile Pulleyar is the son of the castrated Buddha. Leach adds that no Nuvarakalāviya peasant would ever say this, but he thinks they are wrong "and this is in fact his status."[117] "Pulleyar, the son, becomes the essence of sexuality. Whereas Ganesha has only one tusk but carries the other in his hand, Pulleyar has both tusks intact; he is moreover the source of fertility in women, in crops and among animals."[118]

The Potent Pulleyar of Pul Eliya: Ethnographic Doubt

Leach's thesis that Pulleyar of Nuvarakalāviya is the opposite of the Buddha and also of his Indian counterpart does not fit in with the ethnographic evidence from elsewhere in Buddhist Sri Lanka where the myths of Pulleyar are very similar to the Indian.[119] I felt that Leach may have obtained atypical views of Pulleyar from a single informant or that his middle-class interpreter may have unwittingly distorted the information through what I have elsewhere called "interpreter effect."[120] To put my doubts at rest I visited Nuvarakalāviya briefly in the summer of 1983. I also obtained valuable information from James Brow and his field assistant, who were then engaged in fieldwork in Kukulāva, a Vädda village also in the Nuvarakalāviya District. Moreover nowadays large sculptures of Pulleyar are found in public places such as bus terminals in many parts of Nuvarakalāviya, and here also Pulleyar appears in his classic Hindu form with the broken tusk. The myths I collected from Nuvarakalāviya make it very clear that the common view of Pulleyar is exactly as he is perceived in most of Hindu India, though these myths are fewer in number and show less variation. Pulleyar *is* Gaṇeśa or Gaṇa Deviyo, which is also how he is called elsewhere in Buddhist Sri Lanka and occasionally in Nuvarakalāviya itself. Since Leach's whole structural thesis seems to rest on the sexuality of Pulleyar in contrast with the asexual Buddha, the new ethnographic evidence must force us to question that thesis. It also makes it possible to see Pulleyar in larger South Asian perspective, rather than as a deity narrowly located in one district in the North Central Province.

Let me present the Sinhala myths of Pulleyar followed by a psychoanalytic cum sociological analysis of these myths, since he is *par excellence* the Hindu Oedipus discussed in part two of this lecture. In Nuvarakalāviya, Pulleyar myths pertaining to his birth and beheading by the father are well known, as they are in the Western and Southern Provinces where I have done considerable fieldwork.[121] The Nuvarakalāviya version presented below is a rendering from an informant from Kukulāva. It is only slightly more detailed than the one told to me by the *kapurāla* (priest) of Pul Eliya.

> The goddess Umayanganā went to bathe in the river while her husband God Īśvara (Śiva) was attending the divine assembly (*deva samāgama*). Īśvara came back home on his royal

elephant and did not see his wife-goddess (*dēvinnānse*). So he went everywhere in search of her until he came to the river. There he saw his wife immersing and sporting in the river. When Īśvara went up to the riverbank he saw a prince near the "clothes house." A suspicion grew in his mind that this was her secret lover, and raising his sword, he struck at the prince's head. The noise startled the goddess, who looked up and saw that her child was missing. Instead there lay his fallen corpse. She came up to Īśvara and said: "If you do not give me back my child I will commit suicide by jumping into these waters." Then Īśvara asked her: "How did you get this prince?" She replied: "This is the child I created (miraculously)." Īśvara asked: "How can *you* create anyone?" She said she could, and Īśvara challenged her to come up to the bank and prove her point. Umayanganā came up, broke a blade of grass, and planted it after invoking the earth and sky. And lo! from that blade of grass emerged a young prince. Īśvara asked her to create another, and she repeated her former act. In this manner she created seven princes from seven blades of grass. When Īśvara saw this he (proudly) said, "My group (lit. mountain) of children," and grasped them together. However, one of these managed to escape from underneath Īśvara's armpit. Īśvara said: "Isn't this fellow a real Kaḍavaraya (one who broke away)?" He is the god Kaḍavara while the six who were lumped together formed one being—the god Skanda, or Kataragama. [It should be noted that Skanda is also called Kaňda Kumaru (mountain prince), since he emerged from the "mountain of princes."]

Īśvara meanwhile cut off the head of his royal elephant and planted it on Pulleyar. Then by the power of his fiery energy (*tejas*), the elephant's head grew on Pulleyar's shoulders and he got up. The broken head of the prince floated downstream and out of this emerged, the pond of *olu-manel* (*olu-manelvila; olu* is a white water-lily, and it also means "head"; *manel* is the blue lily). The body of the elephant which also fell into the river emerged as the golden crab or *svarṇa kakuluvā*.

Note that according to this myth Pulleyar was also created "miraculously" by Umayanganā, but none of my informants elaborated on this. However, Parker, writing in 1909, gives the following account he gathered from Indigollāva, a Sinhala village in the dry zone.

> At that time Basmasurā a was a servant of the god Īswara (Śiva): The goddess Umayanganā (Parvatī) was married to Īswara. While Basmasurā was employed under Umayanganā she went alone to the river to bathe . . . and pulled up a small quantity of *Singarael* (a plant) and created from it a prince, and instructed him to remain [and protect her]. She then entered the river. A tale bearer went and falsely told Īswara that Basmasurā had gone to watch the Goddess.[122]

The rest of the myth is as before, except Śiva's jealousy has a rational component in the myth quoted by Parker. Both versions are variations of the classic myth of Gaṇeśa's origins where he is created by Umā from her dirt and guards her bathhouse.[123] The Oedipal theme is very clear in all versions and has been noted by many modern commentators, including Leach.[124] There is the symbolic castration by the father and the substitution of the elephant head. While all Hindu deities are created out of nonbiological processes, most of these myths, classic as well as folk, state that Gaṇeśa was created by Umā alone and not by Śiva. The classic Sanskrit myth, also known by some Sinhalas, is even more powerful than the Nuvarakalāviya one. "Body dirt" comes closest to conventional birth in the impurities of the womb (but goddesses do not have such impurities). It is also part of her substance. The Sinhala version from Nuvarakalāviya amends this to give consistency to Umayanganā's miraculous powers—she creates *all* her children miraculously from a plant (or grass). All these myths, as Courtright puts it, give Gaṇeśa privileged access to his mother's nakedness.[125] This aspect of the relationship is recognized in Gaṇeśa's substitute elephant head with its phallic trunk, "a gross visible sign of his incestuous fixation."[126] The Oedipal theme with its denial of the father's role in creation (if not procreation) is paralleled by the theme of mother fixation. The father accepts the son as a member of the divine family only after Gaṇeśa's head has been decapitated (Gaṇeśa is castrated) and the (handsome) prince is disfigured and no longer a rival of the father. But the hostility of the father only pushes the son (as in actual Hindu families) closer to the mother, and the phallic trunk recognizes this fixation. That the trunk represents a phallus is clearly shown in a South Indian myth: "During Gaṇeśa's fight against Surapadma, each time he overcame a demon his

(Gaṇeśa's) mother gave birth to another—so he (Gaṇeśa) closed her *yoni* [vagina] with his trunk."[127]

In this myth, Gaṇeśa's trunk is flaccid and infertile, and he uses it to prevent birth rather than to engage in intercourse. Gaṇeśa is also the remover of obstacles, and his trunk can, like the elephant's, reach into remote recesses and hidden places; so can the rat he rides on. In the myth quoted above the hidden recess is his mother's vagina.

Let me come back to the Sri Lankan myths. The core theme is the Oedipal one, yet the Nuvarakalāviya version also employs the Pulleyar myth to account for the origin of the lily pond and the crab. More importantly, the myth introduces two other actors in the drama: Gaṇeśa's brother, the handsome six-headed god Skanda, and another brother Kaḍavara. Kaḍavara is not a true brother, since he escaped from under Śiva's arm (and from his protective tutelage). Elsewhere in Sri Lanka, the brother who escapes is Aiyanar. Both Aiyanar and Kaḍavara are *local* deities, while Skanda and Gaṇeśa are national deities, the former being one of the guardian gods of Sri Lanka. The myth incorporates a local deity into the national hierarchy by making him a brother of Skanda though not on a par with him.

Let me now consider the contrast between Skanda and Gaṇeśa. Skanda is what Gaṇeśa is not: Gaṇeśa lost his own princely head and was given an abnormal one, whereas Skanda has six heads instead of the normal single head. Skanda is handsome, while Pulleyar-Gaṇeśa is ugly; Gaṇeśa was what Skanda is, but Skanda does not have the privileged access to the mother that Gaṇeśa has. It is inevitable then that jealousy and hostility should develop between the brothers.

When then is the sociological background of these myths? I have dealt with this problem in *The Cult of the Goddess Pattini,* and I can only briefly summarize that complex argument.[128] I deal with *one* model of the Hindu joint family, where the woman is transferred from her family of orientation where she had love and succor to the husband's family, largely unknown to her prior to her marriage. The situation produces kinship alienation and affection starvation; the hostility of her mother-in-law is explicitly contrasted with the love of her own parents. This sociological situation produces an important psychological consequence. The woman projects her starved affective needs on the first-born male child, resulting in a symbiotic mother-child relationship. This relationship is beautifully expressed in the *Bhagavata Purāna* where Kriṣṇa is tied to a mortar by a string by his foster mother Yasoda, the nurturant supplier of milk (cowherdess). On the symbolic level, I pointed out that this is the umbilicus tied to the womb. Out of this sociological and psychological situation emerges one model of the Hindu Oedipus fixated on the mother and dependent on her and attached to her erotically. From the woman's point of view he is mama's dearest. This situation is repeated, but with diminished intensity, in respect of other children, so that both mother's love and the son's erotic attachment and dependency are less, but nevertheless there. Thus you have a second model of the Hindu Oedipus who is attached to the mother, but not totally, and who is jealous of his rival. I might add also that as the woman's status in the family increases, she can produce children who are even less fixated and can, symbolically or actually, move *out* of the joint family with its twin foci of solidarity and control—the affective dependency-fostering role of the mother and the authoritarian rule of the father.

The ideal typical model of the joint family I sketched does not exist in pure form anywhere though type approximations are common. Even when there are no joint families, as in Sri Lanka, much of what we say about the female role is applicable. Yet in these latter situations the first model of the son is not as common as in India, whereas the second and the third are. This third model of the Hindu Oedipus is represented in Kaḍavara-Aiyanar who is created by his mother and escapes from under the (authoritarian yet loving) arm of his father, but he is the rebel, and he goes his own way, never truly a part of the family (divine or human). It should now be obvious that Gaṇeśa-Pulleyar is model one, while Skanda-Kataragama embodies the second. The younger sons do not have to bear the brunt of patripotestal authority; nor are they crucial for the performance of the funeral rites for the father. The younger the son, the older the father and mother, and this means less patripotestal authority, less matrifocal love. All these models engendered in the socialization of the child in Hindu (and Buddhist) societies provide the basis for a variety of mythic elaborations in the religious traditions of Southern Asia. I have depicted the three sons of Śiva in terms of birth order. While this is a useful way of looking at Hindu family relations in general, one must not define birth order too rigidly. These three forms of the Hindu Oedipus can exist outside of strict birth order in individual families, since they are acceptable myth models in popular Hinduism.

The preceding analysis forces us to make an important qualification in Leach's analysis of the Gaṇeśa myths. Leach emphasizes the parallelism between the Hindu and Christian divine families. Yet it is clear that even on the formal level there is one key difference—in the Christian there is only one son (Jesus) but in the Hindu there are two

(Gaṇeśa and Skanda), not to mention the wayward rebel son of the Sinhala family. The relationship between the brothers and their relation to the parents are crucial to the Hindu-Buddhist myths. From the point of view of parent-child relationships there are also obvious differences between the South Asian and the Christian. Gaṇeśa and his father, Śiva, are always in conflict in most of the myths. It is clear that this is due to jealousy over Umā's love. Gaṇeśa is so attached to his mother that he must be near her, and this provokes the father's rage, and he becomes an easy target for the father. In this conflict Gaṇeśa has no chance, and he is always worsted in battle. By contrast Skanda has greater freedom; he is not as tied to the mother, and consequently he is more favored by the father. Note that the god is given his many heads as a result of the father's embrace. Most myths describe him as created by the father (not the mother) and modelled on him. Moreover he is strong and handsome, and therefore could, perhaps, displace the father, creating in turn the possibility of a Greek form of the Oedipal myth, rather than the typical Hindu form of the father killing or maiming the son.[129] From the son's point of view the very idea of hostility to the father violates the cherished norm of filial piety and can only activate anxiety and guilt. But these need not occur for a very good sociological reason embedded in some Southern Asian family structures—a father-son avoidance relationship, which Leach also notes for Pul Eliya. Skanda also should know from his brother's example what could happen in a confrontation with the father: Gaṇeśa the handsome becomes Gaṇeśa the ugly, and Skanda is also called Murugan, "the youthful." Skanda's structural position is such that he can avoid both father and mother and distance himself from his psychological conflict and possible physical conflict with his father. And then there is that freak Kaḍavara, who says "plague on both your houses": and runs away from it all. He also runs away from the main body of Gaṇeśa-Skanda myths to which I shall now return.

A well-known myth, noted also by Leach, is found in parts of the Sinhala low country and all over South India (but is not as popular in Nuvarakalāviya):

> The god Skanda came to Sri Lanka after having fallen out with his brother Gaṇeśa. This was how it occurred: A mango was floating down the stream, and Umā [Pārvatī], the mother, said that whoever rides around the universe first will get the mango. Skanda impulsively got on his golden peacock and went around the universe. But Gaṇeśa, who rode the rat, had

> more wisdom [cunning?]. He thought: "What could my mother have meant by this?" He then circumambulated his mother, then worshiped her and said, "I have gone round my universe." Since Gaṇeśa was right, his mother gave him the mango. Skanda was furious when he arrived and demanded the mango. But before he could get it Gaṇeśa bit the mango and broke one of his tusks.

We have here the continuity of the familiar familial symbolism. Umā, the mother, has a mango (a golden mango). In the previous lecture I noted that in Sri Lankan ritual traditions (and I suspect in Indian too) the mango is an explicit vaginal symbol. Umā's mango is the forbidden fruit for which the (jealous) brothers compete. She gives it to Gaṇeśa, who circles his mother, his true universe and the center of his life. This is very explicit in the myth. Psychologically it is Gaṇeśa who is incestuously fixated on his mother and also gets maternal favors (the mango). Moreover Gaṇeśa is potbellied. In South Asia, as elsewhere also, maternal love is often expressed in overfeeding, and consequently Gaṇeśa is the pampered son of Umā. A cruder peasant version of the myth says that Gaṇeśa circled the salt container in his mother's kitchen. The mother's salt container reminds me of the symbolism of James Joyce's dead sea: "the grey sunken cunt of the world." In all these myths Gaṇeśa's tusk breaks—he is symbolically castrated, for this is the consequence of incestuous wishes. And Skanda in fury, disgust, and despair flees from it all to Sri Lanka.

In the previous lecture I described at some length the myths that deal with Skanda's arrival at Kataragama and his amours with Valli, the adopted daughter of aboriginal hunters. Here let me reemphasize the differences in sexuality between Gaṇeśa and Skanda, based on different models of the South Asian son. Gaṇeśa can never marry (unless he flees to Nepal); he is castrated and impotent, and he cannot separate himself from his mother. But Skanda can; he leaves both mother and wife, and the festival at Kataragama celebrates his amours with his mistress, the wild woman of the forest, the child of aboriginal hunters. But while Skanda is virile, he can have pleasurable sex only with the wild woman, Valli. Skanda, in running away from his mother, has also run away from his wife, since it is likely that the wife (Dēvasēna, the daughter of Indra) is too close to the image of the mother. For women, Skanda is a powerful erotic figure in the family drama. We noted that he appears before Valli as an old man and later reveals his true handsome form. He represents the fantasy of the Oedipal father.

Myth Associations: Validation in Interpretation

For the purposes of this lecture I shall leave Skanda-Murugan aside and focus on Pulleyar, the subject of Leach's thesis. The Pulleyar myths quoted above are well known in South India, in the Hindu Jaffna District of Sri Lanka, among Sinhala Buddhists in the North Central Province of Sri Lanka, in parts of Uva Province, and at the pilgrimage center of Kataragama. In Sri Lanka, people are no longer familiar with these myths nowadays simply because myth traditions are breaking down. In the Nuvarakalāviya District, the myth pertaining to rivalry between the brothers is being forgotten and only few informants could relate it. James Brow, who did fieldwork in Kukulāva, tells me that his informants could relate it, and so did one young man I interviewed in Pul Eliya. Older informants in Pul Eliya could only make statements such as this typical one made by the priest (*kapurāla*) there: "Pulleyar used to live with his mother in the palace. As a child he once went to pick a mango and broke his tusk. He ran towards the mango, and fell down and broke it." The old priest of the neghboring Pulleyar shrine in Pūnāva also made a similar statement, which indicates that both Pul Eliya and Pūnāva folk once knew of the myth but they have either forgotten it, or they do not want to talk about it, or both, since forgetting is due to not wanting to talk about it.

One could, of course, argue that there is no evidence that the "forgotten" myth is a version of the prototype quoted earlier. While this may be the case, several informants, including two in Kukulāva who could quote the myth of Gaṇeśa's birth, had standard associations about Gaṇeśa's fixation on the mother—standard since similar views are held by Hindus in Tamil Jaffna (Sri Lanka) and in India. "Pulleyar-Gaṇeśa is a bachelor god because he refuses to marry any woman unless she is as beautiful as his mother. That is why he waits in road junctions and public places, at entrances to villages, at the embankments of reservoirs—he is looking out for a woman resembling his mother." Similar associations cluster around the special sweet known as *mōdagan* offered to Pulleyar (and Pulleyar alone). It is made of rice flour, coconut, sugar, and *mun* and shaped like a ball or a small bun. Etymologically *mōdagan* is derived from the ancient Sanskrit word *mōtaka* (sweetmeat), and similar foods are offered everywhere in India to Gaṇeśa since he is mama's pampered son. James Brow (pers. comm.) has this to say about Kukulāva notions of *mōdagan:* "Some villages make a pun with this, taking *mōdagan* as *mō* ('mother'), *de* (interrogative), *gan* (*ganne,* 'take,' 'fuck')." Thus "*mavu de ganne?*" ("Are you screwing your mother?"). Another view was that *mōdagan* was shaped like a breast, with the nipple included. Let me add there is not the remotest philological justification for the folk etymology of *mōdagan,* and it strains both sound and sense in Sinhala to convert it into "take your mother." Some do not even pretend to justify it etymologically. One educated Kukulāva informant said: "*Mōdagan geḍiya*—the rounded *mōdagan*—is like a lactating mother's breast. *Mōdagan* means screw your mother (*tope ammāgan*)." Note that the two myth associations—"screw your mother," "mother's lactating breast"—are not logically interrelated, in the sense that one pertains to incest and the other to fixation. Yet psychologically, it is clear that, even when the myth is not fully recalled, informant projections cluster around Gaṇeśa's mother fixation and infantilism, thus validating but not providing proof or scientific verification of the two hypotheses pertaining to incest and fixation.

The presence of myth associations indicates that the myth itself was well known but is being currently forgotten. If and when the sweet *mōdagan* ceases to be given as an offering, the myth associations will in all likelihood wither away.

More importantly, the myth associations seem to validate our interpretation of the Pulleyar myth since they cluster around the psychological themes discussed in this essay. For some anthropologists validation is simply the fit or the logical congruence of the interpretation. I think wherever possible we should go beyond that and adduce types of validation such as the one pertaining to myth associations about mother fixation found among people not familiar with psychoanalysis.

Back to Leach: Motivation and Structure

Leach is fully aware of the psychodynamics of the myth, but to him Gaṇeśa's structural significance (as mediator) is paramount. The basic myths of Pulleyar-Gaṇeśa primarily elucidate structural themes, and the Sri Lankan theme is the reverse of the Hindu-Indian: Pulleyar is the virile potent deity bringing about fertility while the

Buddha is the sexless bringer of salvation. Moreover, even if Pul Eliya folk do not recognize it, Pulleyar is the son of the Buddha. But the evidence presented above indicates that Pulleyar is in fact close to the Buddha in Leach's own terms—both are sexless, though in substantively and mythically different ways. But what about Leach's stated assertion that not only is Pulleyar virile, but he is also a giver of fertility, and his cult entails ecstatic shamanistic possession?

Leach's thesis assumes that a castrated, impotent deity cannot bring about fertility, assuming that the structural opposition is between sexlessness (infertility) and sexuality (fertility). The Indian case clearly shows that structural oppositions of this sort are also culturally rooted. In India virginal and barren mother goddesses can bring about fertility and rain, because virginity confers power, which then can bring about the common weal (or bring about its opposite). So is it with the ascetic, whose abstinence confers power that can be directed to a variety of ends. As for possession consider the ancient West Asian cult where the self-castrated deity Attis provokes his followers (the Galli) into ecstatic trances during which they castrate or slash themselves. So why not Gaṇeśa? In other words I am saying that there is no "natural symbolism" here that universally equates castration, sexlessness, bachelorhood with infertility, passivity, and so forth. Yet interesting enough Gaṇeśa-Pulleyar is *not* associated with possession cults and fertility rituals in Pul Eliya and elsewhere in Nuvarakalāviya. An old priest of the Pulleyar shrine in the nearby village of Pūnāva told me that he never gets into possession states when he propitiates Pulleyar but does so when possessed by other deities. The priest (*kapurāla*) at Pul Eliya made a similar statement, but added that the Pulleyar cult does not require a priest at all. In general Pul Eliyans go to the stone slab representing Pulleyar and make their own pleas, without the mediation of a priest. The priest added: "When we are in trouble we say Pulleyar *hāmuduruvō* (venerable), please help us. Pulleyar is very *sānta* (calm, peaceful). He helps us when we are ill and protects the village." Pulleyar is the protector of crops, especially from the ravages of wild elephants. There is no possession cult associated with Pulleyar, but the priest gets possessed in the communal rituals for two other village deities, Aiyanar and Ilandāri Deviyo.[130] The upshot of the preceding discussion is that while I believe that there is no intrinsic reason why the Pulleyar cult cannot be associated with possession trances, in fact this association is not found in Pul Eliya (contrary to Leach's assertion).

To resolve this problem let me consider the Indian meaning of sexuality, rather than its more universalistic structural significance. In Indian thought generally the fundamental relation is not between sexuality and fertility or, to put it in Leach's terms, the opposition between the passivity of castration and the potency of possession, but rather the opposition between sexuality and *knowledge* (unlike in Christianity where sexuality is linked with forms of worldly knowledge). The opposition between sexuality and knowledge is widespread, and therefore most religious virtuosos (who seek true knowledge) must abstain from sex (*brahmacārya*) and preserve semen. Sex is never viewed as evil or the cause of man's fall; it is associated with worldliness and world involvement, and consequently legitimate and acceptable. Thus Pulleyar in Pul Eliya is not a figure opposed to the Buddha in sexual terms, as Leach says, but *similar* to him. In fact the priest (*kapurāla*) of Pul Eliya often referred to Pulleyar as *hāmuduruvō* (venerable) which is the term employed for Buddhist monks. When I asked him why he addressed him thus, the priest corrected himself and said "deviyo" (god), but soon reverted to "hāmuduruvō"! Pulleyar is like the shaven-headed and symbolically castrated Buddhist monk. With one difference: if the Buddha (or his representative, the monk) is involved in otherworldly knowledge (salvation), Pulleyar is associated with wordly knowledge, so that children learning the alphabet have to propitiate him. There are two popular Sinhala texts known as *Gaṇa devi hälla* (Praise of god Gaṇeśa) and *Vadan kavi pota* (alphabet songbook) that ask this deity to bestow knowledge to the worshiper. In iconography he sometimes appears as an astrologer carrying a book under his arm. By contrast, the Buddha despises astrology as one of the "beastly arts" to be shunned by the true renouncer. The structural similarity and opposition between Pulleyar and the Lord Buddha can be schematically represented, thus:

Gaṇeśa-Pulleyar	*Buddha-Monk*
castrated (broken tusk)	castrated (shaven head)
intellect	intellect
peacefulness	peacefulness
secular learning	salvific knowledge
cunning-trickster	wisdom-saint
THIS-WORLDLY	OTHERWORLDLY

Beneath the structural similarity between Pulleyar and the Lord Buddha there lies a fundamental binary opposition. This opposition, as Leach pointed out and as any Sri Lankan knows, is between the this-worldly interest represented by Pulleyar (and all other gods in the pantheon) and the otherworldly orientation of the Buddha cult. But what about the role of mediators? I have already pointed out that it strains the ethnography to see Pulleyar as a deity of birth ("the son of the Buddha") connecting the other world to this one: no myth or myth association or ritual could bring this out. And while popular Buddhism may see the Buddha as a deity of sorts, it is, contrary to Leach, impossible for the Sinhalas to view the Buddha as a mediator (a *devatā* or "godling") without ceasing to be Buddhist. In Leach's structuralism the mediating function is performed by some personified entity or being like Pulleyar, but this simply does not occur in Buddhist culture. What then replaces the mediator? The answer is very clear, and it is completely surprising that Leach never mentions it—the karma theory. It is karma, the theory that an individual's good and bad actions determine his fate in the other world and his birth in this world. Karma is not a mediating principle between the two fundamental oppositions, this-worldly/otherworldly; it is a "flow concept" that embraces all of human existence and deliberately transcends all oppositions, distinctions and mediations.[131] It is no accident that in his essay Leach nowhere refers to karma. Karma is neither a binary term, nor a mediating construct; it flows through life, cuts through and renders fuzzy all binary distinctions, and binds man and every other being into an ethically determined cosmic order.

If Gaṇeśa is associated with the world he is by definition inferior to the Buddha, since secular knowledge is a lower form of thought. This is apparent in the substantive content of their respective mythologies: the Buddha leaves his wife and family in a total break with the world. Pulleyar is attached to his family by the emotional bond with the mother and the authoritarian rule of the father. Pulleyar, it should be noted, has only *one* tusk broken, and that partially; the monk's head is fully shaven. In both instances the castration symbolism implies not just the cutting off of sexuality, but also the acquisition of wisdom. Nevertheless the difference in symbolic castration (partial versus whole) indicates where the psychoanalytic interpretation breaks down. To say that both Pulleyar and the Buddha are symbolically castrated misses the important detail, that Pulleyar has one tusk intact. Pulleyar is analogous to the orthodox Brahmin priest who shaves his head but leaves one tuft unshaven and sticking out conspicuously as if to defy the symbolism of castration—a sprig of defiant hair sprouting from a barren pate. In both instances, the deep motivational meaning of the broken tusk or barren head is castration: the castration symbolism in turn has structural significance as wisdom. The latter is based on the former. Both motive and structure are interrelated in this manner in other symbols also. For example: the motivational significance of the elephant head is "fixation on the mother," especially the symbolism of the trunk; but the trunk is not erect, it is flaccid. It fits the character of Gaṇeśa-Pulleyar as it also fits the popular view that the elephant is the wisest of animals. But the body of the elephant is opposed to the head. When the elephant has an erection (an impressive sight, I can assure you), people humorously refer to the "elephant with five legs." Sexual prowess is associated with the elephant's feet (body), not with the head with its flaccid trunk. When the body of the elephant fell into the water, it became a golden crab. There seems to be no logical or substantive connection between a crab's and an elephant's body, *except in relation to their legs.* The crab is called *kakuluva,* "legged creature"; both the crab's and the elephant's bodies are connected through the multiplicity of the legs they possess. By contrast Gaṇeśa's original princely head becomes the pond of white and blue water lilies, symbols of purity in Buddhist thought. To conclude: as far as the Pulleyar myth is concerned there is no contradiction between motivation and structure. Quite the contrary, structure is built on motivation, rather than the other way around.

5

Change, History, and the Forgetting of Pulleyar

In the two villages of the Nuvarakalāviya District, the cult of Pulleyar is slowly fading, but more so in Pul Eliya than in Kukulāva. This is especially true of the older informants and children: in fact younger informants knew more about Pulleyar than did the old. Old people have little to do with Pulleyar anyhow since, as Leach says, they are now more oriented to the death-focussed religion of the Buddha. But children, who a few generations ago had to invoke Pulleyar when they read the alphabet, no longer have to do so, since he has been banished from the modern school curriculum. Children in Pul Eliya know Pulleyar, but they know little *about* him.

In discussing the forgetting of Pulleyar we must leave both the psychoanalytic and the structural realms and move into the historical. I do not think that the causes for the decline of the cult can be isolated as "variables"; instead they have to be placed in a specific historical context. Thus the major cause for the decline of the Pulleyar cult is the spread of a doctrinal and fundamentalist Buddhism all over Sri Lanka. When Leach worked in Pul Eliya in 1954 (and briefly in 1956), there was a Buddhist temple but there was no resident monk. Now there is a newer, fancier temple but still no resident monk. Leach wrote that Pul Eliya folk were hardly interested in doctrinal matters; when I visited the village in the summer of 1983 on a full moon day, at least a dozen old people were engaged in meditation and *dhamma* ("doctrinal") discussions. All children are taught Buddhism in school; they are not taught anything about the gods and the spirit cults. Buddhism introduces a form of rationalization inimical to the Pulleyar cult. One old and barely literate informant, to whom I posed the question of Pulleyar's birth, told me that he had forgotten most of it. "Seven were born in one queen's womb. Thereafter they got separated and one become Pulleyar and the other Kaḍavara." To this old man it is inconceivable that Pulleyar can emerge except out of normal birth processes, since the Buddha himself was born out of a womb, though undefiled by its impurities. Moreover the effect of Buddhism is to sever connections with Śiva (Īśvara) mythology since Śiva has no formal place in the Buddhist pantheon. Immediately below the Buddha are the four great guardian gods and other deities of the same class, followed by local gods such as Aiyanar, Ilandāri, Kaḍavara, and then by demons and evil spirits. In Leach's time, the crucial operative gods were the village gods in level three of the pantheon. When the new Buddhist temple was built Pul Eliyans installed, in addition to the Buddha, sculptures of two of the national guardians, Viṣṇu and Saman, and a painting of the third, Skanda, the brother of Pulleyar. This installation symbolically indicated the exercise of the sovereignty of the Buddha and the guardian gods over the life of the village and its local deities. Nowhere in the temple premises is there a shrine for Śiva (Īśvara). Thus Buddhist rationalization has another effect: it tends to sever Pulleyar's (and Skanda's) connection with the father, Śiva.

The contemporary situation also renders redundant several of Pulleyar's key roles in the local pantheon: as the protector of the village from wild animals (especially elephants), as one who ensures the prosperity of the crops and protection from illnesses, and as the deity of the alphabet. All of these have been eroded as a result of modern facilities—education, roads, fertilizers and pesticides, and the destruction of forests. But if "modernism" has eroded the field of influence of Pulleyar, it has *increased* the domain of the Buddha. What

I am suggesting here is that there as a complex political debate going on between Pulleyar and the Buddha in contemporary Sri Lankan culture, and Pulleyar is being worsted in this debate. This debate, however, is not a purely modern phenomenon, since Buddhism has carried on a historical debate with Hinduism on both popular and doctrinal levels, except that in our time Buddhist doctrinal values have been appropriated by ordinary people as never before. To sum up: Structuralism dechronologizes narrative. The idea of debate, or the hidden discourse that underlies myth variations, helps restore the historical dimension of myth.

Let me illustrate the kind of debate that occurred between Buddhism and Hinduism prior to the social changes in the late nineteenth century with reference to two popular texts on Gaṇeśa referred to earlier—*Gaṇa devi hälla* (Praise of god Gaṇeśa) and *vadan kavi pota* (lit., songbook on the learning of words). *Vadan kavi pota* is a book of verses for memorizing the alphabet, with a prose commentary on how to articulate each letter in physiological terms. At the end there are many stanzas invoking Gaṇeśa, including the kind of offerings to be given to him. Then there are praises to other gods followed by praises to King Narasin, which must be Narendrasinha reigning in Kandy in 1707–1739. Since that time, if not before, the "alphabet songbook" has been extremely popular.

What is striking about this text is that though there is detailed praise for Gaṇeśa, it has virtually no concrete mythological details. There are brief references to him being the son of Umā and Maheśvara, and one reference to his broken tusk which I quote below:

> With the intention of getting a mango
> Greedily he ran and broke his tusk(s)
> For sure I shall serve you and you alone
> Why don't you then give me wisdom?

It is this reference that the Pul Eliya informant slightly expanded when he said that Pulleyar lived with his mother in a palace and broke his tusk when he ran to pick a mango. The reason for the demythicization of Gaṇeśa is simple: the text was very likely composed by a Buddhist monk, or an educated layman, for a peasant audience, since in premodern times they were the teachers. The text begins with an invocation to the Buddha, the Dhamma (doctrine), and Sangha (monk order). This is, however, no formality: all mythological references that might bring in Śiva and Pārvatī (Umā) are eliminated and the tusk-breaking event rationalized as an accident that could have happened to any kid! This does not mean, however, that peasants accepted this version to the exclusion of others. Quite the contrary: this text is for learning the alphabet; other texts used in other contexts would have, I think, coexisted with this one. In contemporary editions the "alphabet songbook" is printed together with the "Praise of god Gaṇeśa," a short text of forty-nine verses asking Gaṇeśa to give the supplicant "intelligence and knowledge" (*nuvana*), written about a hundred years later. Here the birth of Gaṇeśa in Umā's womb is described, including Umā's pregnancy cravings and labor pains. Once again there is a debate with Hinduism, where it is impossible for Umā or any other major goddess to give birth to a child in the normal way. Though there are plenty of Buddhist myths of the same type, and Buddhism has a technical term—*opapātika*—for births outside normal processes, this text insists that Gaṇeśa was born in his mother's womb. Clearly the attempt is to cut down Umā, the wife and *śakti* of Śiva, to human proportions. The text makes sense in the context of Hindu-Buddhist debate. Yet at the end of the text there is the well-known reference to Skanda circling the ocean. This poses no problem since Skanda has been assimilated as a Buddhist guardian deity, subservient to the Buddha. The lines are as follows:

> Gaṇeśa the Lord and Mahasena (Skanda)
> With the lance in his right hand
> Because of the mango fruit that was promised
> Prince Skanda performed a miracle.
>
> Heeding the word of Umā, the lady
> He climbed the peacock vehicle
> In an instant he circled the Universe
> I bow my head and take refuge in him.

Several inferences could be drawn from this reference. It is clear that the Buddhist author of the text was familiar with some part of the Skanda mythology that was popular with ordinary folk. Yet neither this text nor the alphabet book makes the slightest reference to popular myths on Skanda's birth. We know from ritual texts, such as those of the Pattini cult dating from at least the sixteenth century, that ordinary folk had a variety of myths of the birth, the life, and the amours of Skanda, if not of Gaṇeśa. This proves that contradictory versions of a myth may coexist in the same time span as products of debates. Insofar as debate is an accompaniment of all myth, I would like to explore the connection between myth and debate in the next section of this lecture.

Debate and the Historicity of Charter

I start off with the truism that a text does not exist by itself; it is embodied in a context. Ever since Malinowski's classic study of myth as charter, anthropologists have placed myth in its sociological context. But the social placement of myth as charter and its social functions are not all there is to context. To go back to Malinowski's case one can argue that precisely because myth is charter it is going to provoke a debate between groups: those outsiders who deny the validity of the charter and those insiders who have to respond to the challenge. Further, myth not only provokes a debate by its very existence, but it also embodies the sedimentation of past debates, a dialogue if you will with the tradition's perception of its past. You see all of these processes at work in Malinowski's own study of myth. It is very clear from his account that the major Trobriand myth (the Laba'i myth) on autochthonous origins emerged as a consequence of debates, especially on rank and precedence.[132] One must also assume that when this "main myth" allocated relative rankings for the four major clans it also created the potential for further political argument and conflict. Malinowski himself recognized this, though he emphasized the aspect of myth as sociological charter, rather than as a debate that produced the myth-charter.

> One of the most interesting phenomena connected with traditional precedent and charter is the adjustment of myth and mythological principle to cases in which the very foundation of such mythology is flagrantly violated. This violation always takes place when the local claims of an autochthonous clan, i.e. a clan which has emerged on the spot, are overridden by an immigrant clan. Then a conflict of principles is created, for obviously the principle that land and authority belong to those who are literally born out of it does not leave room for any newcomers. . . . The result is that there come into existence a special class of mythological stories which justify and account for the anomalous state of affairs.[133]

Malinowski's charter is an ongoing debate, with historical roots in past debates, but he freezes the myth in time in accordance with the synchronic imperative guiding British social anthropology.

Not all myths are charters, though some that are primarily noncharter may have charters attached to them, as, for example, when the myth of Gaṇeśa's birth is attached to the origin of the crab and the lily pond. The variations of myth, on one level, express structural transformations as Lévi-Strauss and Leach argue but, on another level, they express argumentation and debate—in fact transformations are not independent of debate but are formed by it. Consider the debate that occurs with the very existence of the Pulleyar myth in Sri Lankan Buddhist culture. In Sri Lankan Buddhism I noted that the God Skanda is one of the guardian deities in a category immediately below the Buddha himself. In the Gaṇeśa origin myth both he and Gaṇeśa are sons of Śiva, and therefore Śiva, according to all South Asian hierarchical norms, must be above them. But the elevation of Śiva comes up against the Buddha who occupies that very position. Hence a peculiar debate must occur in Buddhist Sri Lanka that cannot occur in Hindu India in respect of the myth of Gaṇeśa's birth. Normally Buddhists can tolerate Śiva as long as he exists in myth, but is never part of ritual (and thereby of the pantheon). However, confrontation gets accelerated in times of Buddhist revival, whether such revival occurs nationally or in a specific village through the actions of local virtuosos. Yet when Buddhism becomes ossified and emotionally unrewarding, the Sri Lankan tradition gets an infusion from Hinduism, bringing Shaivite mythology once again—and we see this happening in present-day Kataragama. And so it goes on: confrontation, debate, reconciliation, debate, and provocations—all producing new myths, variations of myths, resurrection of old myths, myth associations and interpretations.

Every scholar knows what myth variations are; myth associations, however, of the sort discussed earlier are not well known. They refer to standardized views *about* the myth held by a collectivity. Myth interpretations are the more individual, generally intellectually generated reactions to the myth, such as my own reactions to Leach's version of the Pul Eliya myth of Gaṇeśa, resulting in this lecture. Since myth associations have received little anthropological attention, let me discuss them in relation to the Gaṇeśa myth.

Myth associations, like myth variations and interpretations, are products of debates. In the Pulleyar myths they are provoked by the psychological content of the myth, but myth associations cluster around any popular myth and help us to understand the myth, as dream associations help us understand the dream. In lecture one I dealt with a set of myth associations clustering around the Pattini myth. When I asked people why the goddess Pattini was a virgin many specialists responded that it was because her consort was impotent.

This is never stated in the myth: it is a popular myth association. So is it in the Pulleyar myth: the god cannot marry because he is waiting for a woman who resembles his mother. A myth association is quite different from myth; it has no "story"; it is the crystallization of past "debates." The myth associations of Pulleyar's mother fixation have been recorded from Maharashtra to South India and Sri Lanka. But they need not have this universalist character at all and may remain confined to a small region. Thus Sri Lankan informants of Nuvarakalāviya interpret *mōdagan* as "screw your mother," a standardized association provoked by the preceding myth association. I do not know whether this association holds elsewhere in South Asia.

The offering of *mōdagan* to Gaṇeśa as a ritual food must surely have been provoked by myth associations, and once this food is adopted it provokes a fresh set of associations, such as the ones just recounted. When the myth tends to be forgotten, this ritual food acts as a trigger releasing those associations and simultaneously provoking people to remember the myth. But *mōdagan,* unlike *sōma,* is not an immortal substance, and it too must yield to the process of Buddhist rationalization. Thus people in Pul Eliya give *mōdagan* to Gaṇeśa only "when we can make it," whereas the offering is standard practice in Kukulǟva.

What then do I mean by debate? Debate is the form of "hidden discourse" operative in history, rather than in deep motivation, and responsible for variations and symbolic transformations of myth. A myth is a cultural product that provokes people into an argument or a contentious discourse which then forces people to create alternative versions of the myth. The work of culture here is quite different from "symbolic remove." In symbolic remove, one is dealing with a series of symbolic forms that are psychogenetically related to an identifiable cluster of deep motivations. Not so with debate which often, but not always, has a rational discursive character. Debate can produce a myth version that is the very opposite of the one it is reacting against. The myth releases a discourse, but this can only be inferred from the various versions of a myth. Thus debate is the hidden discourse that the analyst must unravel as a rational aspect of the work of culture affecting symbolic transformations in myth and other kinds of narrative. As far as myth is concerned, debate both foreshadows myth and follows myth. A myth therefore is a sedimentation of past debates, and it precipitates new myths or myth variations. Not all myths have this character, though. For example, myths that are intimately tied to the ethnic identity of a group may resist debate, as do myths that constitute the axiomatic bases of a religious or political order. But no myth fully escapes debate. Seemingly noncontentious myths, it should be noted, are also not timeless, since radical changes in polity, religion, and identity do occur and can provoke new debates leading to a revision of the old myths or the formulation of new ones.

Thus we can say that always in principle, and often in fact, the existence of a myth of any significance is a provocation. Does this mean that for methodological purposes one has to isolate a prototype or key myth and deal with other myths as variations? The Sri Lankan case may suggest that one can have a prototypical myth of Gaṇeśa based on psychic conflicts in the family, since there are very few variations from this myth type. But I think this as a mistake. One should, for example, be able to take a Gaṇeśa myth from the philosophical corpus and treat the family myth as a variant, or vice versa; the myth one chooses depends on the investigator's choice of problem, not on the empirical existence of a key myth or prototype myth (though perhaps one could talk of a dominant or the most widespread form of a myth).

The Indian situation is especially conducive to debate and myth variation, since there are a multiplicity of social groups—castes, sects, denominations, religious orders, and all sorts of individual virtuosos—who will react to an existent myth from their own perspectives. A myth debate could arise out of personal anxiety, social position, philosophical orientation, and so on, or a combination of "reasons." I selectively discuss below some "reasons for" myth variations from the point of view of the Gaṇeśa-Pulleyar myth of Oedipal conflict and mother fixation. What I have deliberately oversimplified as reasons are complex social and historical processes that must, in any detailed study, be contextualized.

1. The Oedipal conflict in the Gaṇeśa-Pulleyar myth provokes debates regarding personal, ethical, and even philosophical issues. How could it possibly be that Śiva could kill his own son? In normal social life anywhere there are few things as horrendous as incest, patricide and filicide—the ingredients of both Greek and Indian Oedipal myths. Hence you have a variety of myths recorded by Courtright where Śiva does *not* in fact kill his son, one of the most popular myths being that of the inauspicious planetary deity Sani (Saturn) killing Gaṇeśa. The psychological mechanism of displacement has perhaps occured here. In some of the Sani myths Śiva is also involved indirectly for, as Courtright puts it, "it is his [Śiva's] touch which precipitates the decapitation."[134] These myths still hover around the

theme of son killing. But in other Sani myths full displacement has occurred, and Sani takes the blame entirely. This means that a new form of the Gaṇeśa myth which has little to do with the deep motivations underlying family relations has emerged; this myth now can take on a life of its own. Moreover it should be noted that these new myths and myth variations once created can exist conjointly within the same time span. In this situation, we cannot test hypotheses of an "if *X*, then *Y*" sort, because *Y* is not related to *X* through a concomitant variation, but through a debate which produces a variation *Y* which might have no substantive and thematic connection with the original myth, *X*. Contradictory myths coexist because they are variations produced by debates rather than the product of concomitant variations sought by anthropologists given to testing hypotheses.

2. Umā giving birth to Gaṇeśa provokes a debate with the patriarchal ideology, the "ancient Indian view that a father reproduces himself in his son, thereby saving himself from death by passing a remainder of himself to his offspring."[135]

> Śiva looked at Pārvatī, and whilst thinking how he could effect the wishes of the gods, from the splendor of his countenance there sprang into existence a youth shedding radiance all around, endowed with the qualities of Śiva, and evidently another Rudra, and captivating by his beauty all the female inhabitants of heaven. Umā, seeing his beauty, was excited with jealousy, and in her anger pronounced this curse: "Thou shalt not offend my sight with the form of a beautiful youth; and therefore assume an elephant's head and a large belly, and thus shall all thy beauties vanish."[136]

In several of these myths, however, a familiar theme reappears—once Śiva creates a beautiful youth, it provokes his wife's lust, and all sorts of consequences flow including the Oedipal conflict between father and son. Ergo: once again the myth pulls to and fro the family myth, hovering around the family myth, as if by a magnet, and also drawn away from it to another pole.

3. Gaṇeśa can provoke a variety of philosophical debates which may or may not have any thematic relevance to the myths about family relationships. One philosophical debate does, it seems to me, relate to this theme—the problem of *śakti,* the creative energy of the god embodied in his female consort. All major gods have *śakti,* so how is it that Gaṇeśa has no *śakti?* It is awfully hard for a castrated, mother-hankering deity to have a *śakti,* but if one were to give him *śakti,* what kind of

śakti could he have? Now you have a nice variant of the ocean-circling myth, noted by Shulman.[137] Here Gaṇeśa circles *both* his parents, and they, impressed by his wisdom, marry him to Siddhi and Buddhi, the daughters of Prajāpati, the Creator. This variant of the myth gives Gaṇeśa two *śaktis* and also denies the psychological and social conflicts in the divine family: harmonious and rounded family relations are emphasized. This again has its parallel in the actual Hindu joint family, where internal conflicts are endemic to the system but are often plastered over especially in relation to the outside world. The philosophical solution also remains purely formal: *Siddhi* means "knowledge" and *Buddhi* is "wisdom," so that the myth variant hovers around Gaṇeśa's intellectual rather than sexual attributes, whereas sexual potency is the basis for *śakti* in Hinduism. Courtright correctly points out that Siddhi and Buddhi remain at the level of abstractions quite removed from sexuality.[138] And Gaṇeśa still remains the god with the potbelly and broken tusk. However, when we move north into Nepal an interesting variant of the Gaṇeśa myth appears. Here in addition to the classic view of Gaṇeśa, fat and fond of *laḍḍu* or *motak* (Sinhala, *mōdagan*), there appears another Tantric-based version of Gaṇeśa and his consort(s). Gaṇeśa often appears in Tantric iconography with his female *śakti* sitting on his lap facing him and engaged in sexual union. Concomitantly, he is depicted with his tusks intact. Here both myth and iconography have taken a radically different turn from the dominant Indian and Sri Lankan myths. Freed from these constraints the Nepalese tradition can weave into the myth a whole set of philosophical and cosmological speculations based on Tantrism.

Where a new myth arises as a consequence of debate it can take on a totally independent existence. In this situation the new myth can carry on a variety of new debates on the new problems fostered by the new myth. This means that at least in Hindu society, Gaṇeśa is so popular that he permeates every aspect of life. Even if one were to focus on family relationships, the set of Oedipal myths is simply one of several, though very significant since they are both widespread and popular. It seems therefore that one cannot have an *explanation* of Gaṇeśa, since there are different Gaṇeśas, products of different debates. Only a segment of interrelated myths makes explanatory sense. I have, for methodological reasons, isolated initially a set of myths with the themes of mother fixation and reversed Oedipal conflict and then reflected on a sample of myths that might have arisen out of the debates provoked by this myth set. But other myths and myth sets must forever remain outside our interpretive net.

4. Individual debate based on personal anxiety, social position, intellectual or religious convictions, may produce idiosyncratic versions of the myths that, under proper sociocultural circumstances, can be accepted by the society. This is how I think the Pul Eliya myth "recorded" by Leach emerged through the mediation of his interpreter. These two have constructed a new form of the Gaṇeśa-Pulleyar myth, which might eventually get accepted by Sri Lankans (if others also invent similar ones). It has been accepted by anthropologists, however, as the Nuvarakalāviya myth of Gaṇeśa. I might hazard a guess as to how it happened. Leach's interpreter was a middle-class person who worked as a clerk in the government secretariat in this area. He was probably an outsider to the village and had little knowledge of local tradition and probably little sympathy for it. As long as he had to work on "social facts as things"—land tenure, inheritance, property rights—he had no problem. But myth and religion were different: a totally symbolic realm of multiple meanings, metaphors, and the juxtaposition of opposites. I think Leach's interpreter was like the old Pul Eliya informant who couldn't understand how anyone could be born outside of a womb, since after all even the Buddha couldn't escape this fate. And then there is all that peculiar stuff about mother love and broken tusks, and of course that mother-fucking sweetmeat. This is too much—and so Leach's interpreter invents a new myth: Pulleyar *is* a virile deity, his tusks *are* intact, he *is* associated with procreation and possession and he is (this is Leach's touch) the son of the Buddha. The new myth is a point by point reversal of the old. Leach's own contribution to the myth is determined by his structuralist presuppositions; so is his *acceptance* of his interpreter's inventions. But is that all there is to it?

I think the new myth of Pulleyar suited the emerging puritan Buddhism of Sri Lanka in 1954, and I would not be surprised if someone in Pul Eliya did relate to Leach's interpreter a Buddhicized form of the myth, though I doubt any Pul Eliyan could have produced the version so diametrically opposed to the older ones. But then a further problem emerges: if Obeyesekere did not write the present essay, consider what might have happened. A native middle-class Sinhala folklorist might well have noted Leach's myth of Pulleyar and included it in a prospective book on Gaṇeśa myths for a Sinhala audience as the Grimm brothers did for the West. Once a version appears in print Buddhists can surely accept it, as Europeans accepted the Grimms' tales with their sanitized emendations. But this speculation worries me a little bit: insofar as an interpretation, according to some hermeneutical thinkers, is a re-vision of the myth, I have some concern as to what will happen if my hypothetically real Sinhala folklorist confronts Obeyesekere's interpretation of poor Pulleyar in terms of castration, mother fixation, Oedipal conflict, sibling rivalry—not to mention the less technical language I have indulged in, in this lecture. What will he make of it? But I do not worry. I take consolation in the fact that it will be a long while before my Sinhala folklorist appears on the historical scene in Sri Lanka. But if . . . ?

The Buddhist Form of Life and the Emergence of the Father Killer

I shall cast aside the fragile doubts that assailed me in the previous section and proceed to trace the fate of Gaṇeśa and the third brother in the areas of Sri Lanka with a long and continuing Buddhist tradition. The second brother is nonproblematic. He is known everywhere in Sri Lanka, and the myth of his marriage to the wild woman is equally well known. Gaṇeśa is more problematic, for we noted that he loses in the historical contest between his myth and cult and that of the Buddha. Thus his cult was operative in the area traditionally known as the Vanni, now part of the North Central Province. These areas were, at the time of the British arrival, lodged close to the Tamil-speaking areas of the North and East and strongly influenced by Hindu values. Indeed it is likely that many communities which are Sinhala-Buddhists now might have been Hindu at one time, as many classified as Hindu now were once Buddhist. The Nuvarakalāviya District where Leach and Brow worked is even today fairly close to the Hindu culture of the north; and Parker, we noted, collected a Gaṇeśa myth of the same type somewhat to the south and east of Nuvarakalāviya. In all these areas even today Gaṇeśa images are omnipresent. Yalman recorded myths of the same type in Terutänne, a remote area in Uva.[139] Gaṇeśa, it seems to me, holds sway in areas that traditionally did not come under the full influence of Buddhist values, though they were nominally Buddhist. In the Western, Southern, and Sabaragamuwa Provinces, and in the region around Kandy, he was an important deity, but his cult was mostly confined to secular learning, especially the learning of the alphabet. But none of the practitioners I knew—exorcists and priests (*kapurāla*) of the god cults—possessed in their ritual texts the myths of Gaṇeśa found in the North Central Province. Some of these myths are well known to individuals, and they circulate fairly freely at Kataragama where Hindus and Buddhists from all over the country congregate, but public images or shrines for Gaṇeśa were rarely found in these regions (until recently).[140]

In my earlier discussion I noted the kind of rationalization that Buddhist values and contemporary social change have had on the Nuvarakalāviya cult of Pulleyar-Gaṇeśa. But the social changes discussed there are recent and had no application to the Gaṇeśa cult as it would have existed traditionally. I therefore suggest that Buddhist culture, in the institutions it creates, does not give preference to Gaṇeśa, and indeed prefers the second and third son to him. Skanda, the second son, straddles both worlds, at least the world of Sri Lankan Buddhism and South Indian popular Hinduism. The third son is a well-known type in South Asia as in the West and elsewhere too. He is the rebel, but in a passive sense. He is the forerunner of the hippie. He runs away from home and takes different forms in the societies and subcultures into which he is accepted. Thus Kaḍavara, "the one who broke away," is a god of low-caste Roḍiyas (untouchable beggars) in the dry zone of Sri Lanka and of Väddas, the aboriginal hunters of the proximate region. In the Southern and Western Provinces he does not appear as a brother of Skanda; this role is taken by Aiyanar, who is viewed as the older brother. Yet Aiyanar is never propitiated here, while Kaḍavara is. Kaḍavara has several forms, one as part demon and part god. He is placated at the Kataragama firewalk; in other rituals of this region he is both a single deity and a collectivity that constitutes part of Skanda's demonic retinue. The further away from Nuvarakalāviya, the more distant his connection with the Gaṇeśa or Skanda mythology.

In all these images of the son there is no win for him in his agonistic relationship to the father. The argument I shall develop in the next lecture is that while all three images are representations of the Oedipal conflict in actual families in Hindu and Buddhist societies of Southern Asia, there nevertheless exists a fundamental contrast between Hinduism and Buddhism in respect to the son. My thesis ("guess" is the better term) is that the images of the second and third sons are fairly widespread in Southern India and Sri Lanka whereas Gaṇeśa straddles the whole South Asian universe. Yet he becomes progressively diminished in importance in the more Buddhist areas, and another version of the son emerges on the center of the stage, overshadowing the others. I shall show in the next lecture that Buddhist Sri Lanka glorifies the son who kills the father, whereas Hindu India glorifies the son who submits. Buddhism unwittingly gives prominence to a parricidal Oedipus. If in Hindu culture there are several models of Oedipus with the son who submits to the father predominating, Buddhism by contrast unwittingly pushes a parricidal Oedipus into center stage. This contrast must force us to investigate the differential impact of Brahmanic and Buddhist values on the formation of the Oedipus complex and its mythic representations, the theme of my next lecture.

LECTURE THREE

The Parricide in Buddhist History

1

Myth Models of the Parricide: Oedipus in Sri Lanka

The great Sri Lankan historical chronicle, the *Mahāvaṃsa,* "the chronicle of the great dynasty," was written in *Pāli* in its present form in the sixth century A.D. from earlier versions that were "here too long drawn out and there too closely knit; and contained many repetitions."[1] These versions were in turn based on Sinhala records kept in local monasteries and contained, according to scholars, both popular mythical accounts as well as scrupulously recorded historical events. The *Mahāvaṃsa* is distinguished from chronicles written in India, owing to its strict sense of chronology, with the death or the *parinibbāṇa* of the Buddha ("the final passing into *nirvāṇa*") as the Archimedean point. The events preceding, for the most part genealogies that had little historical validity, take their place from this date; the events following also are traced in terms of the Buddha era. The earliest dates are historically suspect, but the chronology of kings from the reign of Davānampiyatissa (250–210 B.C.), when Buddhism was introduced and temple records maintained, shows considerable accuracy, according to historians. The *Mahāvaṃsa* is continued by other monk traditions (inaccurately known as the *Cūlavaṃsa*) up to the reign of Kirti Srī Rājasinha of Kandy (A.D.1741–1780). If considerable historically accurate information and a sense of chronology were reflected from the time of the introduction of Buddhism, not so with the earlier period. These early events are also expressed in the historical style of the chronicle, but they are of a popular and mythic character. These early mythic events, however, have considerable historical truth when examined sociologically: they depict the destiny of Buddhism with that of the dominant ethnic group, the Sinhala. Historians have shown that the events of the period were enormously complicated; but they were interpreted in the *Mahāvaṃsa,* by at least the sixth century, as a mythic charter, in Malinowski's sense, that gave historical unity to the identification of Buddhism with the Sinhala people.[2] The text's focus is clear: it deals with the dynasties of kings who were guardians of the religion and the nation of the Sinhalas. Needless to say the *Mahāvaṃsa* did not see the Sinhalas as a "race" in the vulgar modern sense of the term; they were a cultural group speaking the Sinhala language. Hindu Tamils from South India could easily become Sinhala through the adoption of the language and the religion, Buddhism.[3]

The first chapter of the *Mahāvaṃsa* deals with the visits of the Buddha to Sri Lanka. No serious historian accepts these as actual historical events, yet their cultural significance is enormous. The Buddha vanquishes demons and snake beings; the former he banishes to a distant isle, the *giridīpa,* while the latter are converted to Buddhism and live in their abode in Nāgadīpa, an island in the very north of Sri Lanka. In his three visits to the island the Buddha visited other sacred spots—Kälaniya and Mahiyangana—where his relics were later enshrined; and he placed his foot on the great peak of Samantakūṭa (Adam's Peak), still venerated by all Buddhists for its historic importance. In all these the Buddha acts as a kind of arch shaman or exorcist (a role he adopts in some contemporary ritual dramas of exorcism). Evil spirits have been banished or converted; the ground itself consecrated and made sacred by his presence symbolized in his sacred footprint. The way is clear for the coming of the founder of the Sinhalas, Vijaya, who arrived in Sri Lanka on the very day that the Buddha achieved his final "passing away," release, *nirvāṇa.*

The story of Vijaya is, however, not very Buddhist. According to the *Mahāvaṃsa,* the king of Bengal had a daughter at whose birth it was prophesied that she would marry a lion, the king of the beasts.[4] When she grew up, the princess, "desiring the joys of independent life," ran away from home by joining a caravan travelling to the Magadha (Bihar) country. A lion attacked the caravan as it was passing a forest but while everyone else fled helter-skelter, the princess followed the lion. The lion beheld her and fell in love with her. Remembering the prophecy, she "caressed him, stroking his limbs." "Roused to the fiercest passion by her touch," he took her to his cave, united with her and she eventually bore twins. The son had the feet and hands of a lion, and was named Sinhabāhu (lion limb) by his mother; the daughter was called Sinhasīvalī. When the son grew up, part lion but mostly human, he asked the mother about his strange father, and why he imprisoned them in the cave, shutting the cave door before he went out gathering food. The symbolism is one of exclusion, a marker that separates the matrisegment (mother and children) from the father. I think it recognizes, more powerfully than any myth from the Western repertoire, the psychogenetically primordial nature of the mother-child bond, indicating the continuity of a primordial symbiosis. The father, though a provider, is excluded on one level and yet included in another, familial level.

Age sixteen is the marriageable age according to Buddhist tradition, and Sinhabāhu is now ready to challenge the father as provider for his mother and sister. He opened the rock cave with his powerful lion arms and with his mother on the right shoulder and the sister on the left he ran away from home. The cave now is a womb symbol; three people emerge from it into another symbolic rebirth. The myth identifies the mother and the sister: but the superiority (and seniority) of the mother is recognized by Sinhabāhu carrying his mother on the right shoulder, the propitious side. They clothed themselves with branches of trees; this of course implies that they were naked in the cave and only partially clothed outside. The commander of the border village is the princess's mother's brother's son; when she told him who she was, he took her back to her father, the king of Vanga; he then married her, the ideal cross-cousin marriage that corrects the earlier "wrong marriage." Meanwhile the lion, no longer eating food owing to his unassuaged grief, ravaged the countryside. The son set out to kill him, but the mother stopped him. The third time, the son left without the mother's permission and accosted the lion. According to the *Mahāvaṃsa* account, and according to most versions, the son knows that he is going to kill his father. The father recognizes his son, but the arrows aimed by the son at the father's forehead are deflected owing to the power of the father's love for the son. But when the father senses his son's implacable hatred he is enraged; he loses his love for his son, and the latter's arrow, this time aimed at the body, kills him. The son now decapitates his father and heads back home!

The Sinhala *Rājāvaliya,* reflecting a more popular view, pathetically indicates the culpability of the son.

> The lion, on hearing his son's voice [was delighted] as if nectar had been poured into his ears [and] ran towards Prince Sinhabā. On seeing the lion, he [the prince] shot an arrow, but its point was turned and it fell to the ground: in like manner the second and third arrows fell off, their points being turned; but when he impelled the fourth arrow with both his hands, the royal lion thought within himself that it was intended to kill him, and being enraged glared on [his son] fiercely resolving to devour him. The arrow struck the lion on the forehead, and he fell to the ground. Then he called his son, and laying his head on his son's lap, asked him to say that he had spoken of both mother and daughter [ere dying], and died. Thereafter Prince Sinhabā cut off the lion's head and presented it to the king.[5]

We must note here a striking feature of the Sinhala Oedipal myth in contrast with, let us say, the Gaṇeśa myth discussed in the previous lecture. The father loves the son, but this love is not reciprocated. In the Sinhabāhu myth the son does to the father what the father does to the son in the Hindu: he not only kills the father but also symbolically castrates (decapitates) him. This feature of myth is based on, but not determined by, an important psychological (perhaps even neurological) feature of human species life. The child after age five or thereabouts suffers from at least a partial amnesia regarding his infantile life. He has little or no memory of the loving father whereas the father can nostalgically recollect that past.

To get back to our story: According to the *Mahāvaṃsa* version the old king had died seven days earlier, but the people, recognizing Sinhabāhu as the king's grandson, elected him king. Sinhabāhu accepted the kingship but then renounced it in favor of his mother and her husband (and cross cousin) and went with his sister, Sinhasīvalī, to found a new kingdom, Sinhapura ("the city of the lion"), in the very forest in which he was born. In other words he distances himself physically from his mother's husband (avoidance relationship) and settles down in a new kingdom after marrying his mother-surrogate, his sister.

It is obvious that the myth of Sinhabāhu is more than an Oedipal myth: it is also an etiological myth that explains the origin of the Sinhala people of Sri Lanka, the people of the lion. But it is also obvious that in order to explain the origin of the Sinhalas it is not necessary to have an Oedipal myth at all, since etiological myths are not intrinsically tied to parricide, bestiality, and incest. And it is out of these three moral violations, held in abhorrence by ordinary humans everywhere, that Vijaya, the eldest son of Sinhabāhu and Sinhasīvalī, sprang. Now bestiality is enough bad "blood," but parricide and incest are worse, except for one paradoxical feature. A wayward princess (royalty) cohabits with a lion (also royal beast); this union brings forth a man whose blood from his father's and mother's seminal fluids goes to form a composite creature. "Blood" is preserved through sibling incest. Thus Vijaya carries the purity of a special kind of royal blood, but also the taint of the history of unlawful sexuality and parricide, the latter a horrendous sin in Buddhism, for which there is almost no salvation. What kind of offspring would emerge from this terrible mixture of pure blood (royalty, lion) and impure blood (bestiality, parricide, and incest)? Vijaya, a rowdy and violent man "of evil conduct." So the father now rejects the son by shaving his head and sending him, along with his companions, to an unknown fate in a ship. Now let me anticipate what is to come: the ship on the waters employs the well-known symbolism of the watery rebirth. Vijaya (victory) and his evil followers are reborn in a new role and in a new land, Tambapanni (copper colored) or Sri Lanka with its dark copper-colored soil. Vijaya is ready to start a new life and found a new kingdom.

Before pursuing the adventures of Vijaya, let me say why I consider the Sinhabāhu myth the paradigmatic myth of the Sri Lankan Oedipus. Its sociological significance as the origin myth of the Sinhalas gives it special significance to them. In the previous lecture I pointed out that myths that centrally define the origin and ethnic identity of a group permit little debate, unless people face serious problems pertaining to their origin and identity as a consequence of historical vicissitudes. No such questioning of this myth has occurred throughout Sri Lanka's long history (except perhaps in contemporary times among very small groups). Since its initial mention in the *Dīpavaṃsa* (fourth century) and the *Mahāvaṃsa* (sixth century) many scholarly Pāli texts and popular Sinhala chronicles refer to it without much change. More vivid and poetic accounts of these are sung in village ritual. And the most popular play in modern Sri Lanka is "Sinhabāhu" by Ediriweera Sarachchandra, a beautiful and moving poetic drama based on the original myth. The basic variation in modern versions pertains to the only debatable point of the myth—how is it that the son knowingly killed his loving father, as the *Mahāvaṃsa* explicitly says he did. Thus the expected answer: the son did not know that the lion was his own father. From a commonsensical point of view this is absurd, since not much time had lapsed between the son's departure with his mother and sister and the depredations of the lion. Moreover, unless Sinhabāhu was stupid he should have at least known the significance of his mother asking him to desist. Nonrecognition of the father cannot make logical sense; it does make psychological sense. It is the operation of the mechanism of *denial* such that the son, unconsciously, fails to (or does not want to) make the connection between his own father and the lion terrifying the villagers on the borders.

The Sinhabāhu myth is striking for the absence of reference to remorse, or any ethical qualms, for father killing. It is in fact set in a pre-Buddhist, preethical stage of Sinhala history. This history then consists of two lines: one a Sinhala history that deals with the origin of the people of the lion; the other a Buddhist history that deals with the events leading to the introduction of Buddhism to Sri Lanka. The two lines converge in the reign of Devānampiyatissa (250–210 B.C.), a later descendant of Vijaya, who is converted by Mahinda, the missionary sent by the great King Asoka (by some accounts his son or brother). Thereafter Sinhala history is Buddhist history. However, if the preethical and pre-Buddhist myth of Sinhala origin begins with parricide, so does the Buddhist history. The *Mahāvaṃsa* traces the origins of the Moriyas (Maurya), the dynasty of Asoka, who introduces Buddhism to Sri Lanka. The account starts with the reign of Bimbisāra, friend and lay devotee of Buddha. Now this line also commences with a parricide when Ajātasattu, Bimbisāra's son, kills his aged father (at sixty-four by *Mahāvaṃsa* computation). There is, however, a striking difference in the two Oedipal myths: if the paradigmatic myth of Sinhabāhu ignores the problem of ethics, guilt, and responsibility, not so with the Ajātasattu myth. In other words, with Buddhism, parricide takes on ethical meaning and significance. This myth is not recounted in any detail in the *Mahāvaṃsa,* but is well known in Buddhist tradition since it is intrinsically linked to the Buddha legend. I recount below a popular version from the thirteenth-century Sinhala compendium of Buddhist stories known as the *Pūjāvaliya.* The story is quite long and I can only present a summary here, quoting part of the text when apposite.

> The daughter of the Kōsala king of Sāvatthi was given in marriage to Bimbisāra of Rajagaha. From the time she conceived Ajātasattu, the queen had an intense craving to drink the blood from the king's right shoulder. But she did not tell anyone about it and consequently became like a withered garland of flowers. The king, seeing her in this state, said: "By not telling me what you crave you are acting like my enemy." Eventually after much persuasion he knew she wanted his blood. "Your craving is a propitious one for me." Summoning his chief physician, he had his shoulder incised with a golden blade; mixing his blood with water, he gave her to drink it in a golden plate. Her cravings were now satisfied. Soothsayers who heard about this said: "The queen will give birth to a son who will hate his father, and the king will die because of him; he has a great store of merit, and though he will kill his father he will also reign over the capital city." The queen, hearing this, went to the palace garden and tried many time to abort the fetus, but owing to the prince's good karma ("power of his merit") no harm came to him. The king, noticing her going to the garden frequently, said, suspecting: "You do not know whether it's going to be a son or a daughter. The neighboring kings will say what you have done to the child and shame me. Henceforth desist from this action," and kept guards around her. The queen thought: "If it is a son I will kill him as soon as he is born." The king sensed those thoughts also and

persuaded the midwives to take the infant, as soon as he was born, away from the mother.

When the prince was two or three years old he was nicely decked out and shown to the queen. The queen, owing to the love for her son (lit.: because of "son-love"), erased from her mind all her previous thoughts and lovingly brought him up. She simply could not kill him. Because he emerged from his mother's womb unwanted and because of his enmity for his father he was named Ajātasattu (enemy before he was born). When he was sixteen his father, the king, made him prince regent (*yuva-raja,* subking).

Now enters into the story the Buddha's cross cousin, Devadatta, himself a monk, yet the Buddha's arch enemy from multitudinous past births. Devadatta wanted to enlist Ajātasattu's aid in his plan to oust the Buddha and kill him. Devadatta had miraculous powers obtained by Buddhist meditation. So he took the guise of an infant divinity (*ladaru divya kumarek*). Having created seven cobras, he wrapped four on his hands and feet as if they were bracelets, one on his head like a garland, and one on his neck, and draped one huge cobra over the right shoulder [like the sacred thread]. He then rose in the air and appeared before King Ajātasattu and frightened him. The cobras raised their separate heads and hissed, and the frightened king asked his people to save him from the *nāga rākṣa* (snake demon). The courtiers had goose pimples from fear. The king shivered with fear of being bitten by the cobras. But then a voice said "Fear not, O king, I am no demon, I come not to harm you but to win your heart (mind)." Devadatta then took his normal form as monk. Then like the two royal horses in the *Sutami Jataka* who kissed each other and sucked each other's lips, these two, who shared the same essence (*dhātu*), were soon pleased with each other.[6]

The text goes on to describe how Ajātasattu supported Devadatta by building a monastery for him and generously provided alms and requisites for him and his five hundred followers. All this wealth, says the author, was the cause of his downfall. But Devadatta, swollen with pride at his new fortune, thought: "The Buddha is king, and so will I be. In which way am I a lesser being than the Buddha?" With this thought, Devadatta lost the *dhyāna* powers (miracle making through higher stages of meditative trance) given to him by the Buddha. Undaunted he eventually went up to the Buddha and told him that kings have regents and commanders, so why shouldn't he. The World-Conquering-Buddha-Monarch-of-the-Dhamma should do the same, he said. "Make me the commander-in-chief of the Dhamma and give me charge of the order." It is rare for the Buddha to scold anyone, but here he calls Devadatta a fox and tells him that such positions do not exist in the order.

Devadatta now incites Ajātasattu to kill his father. "Follow my advice, go kill your father and take the kingdom, and I'll kill the Buddha and take over the kingdom of the Buddha." Then Ajātasattu tied a dagger to his thigh, hid in the palace, and waited shivering. The ministers caught him and, seeing the dagger, knew that he wanted to kill the king. One group conspired to kill him and Devadatta along with his monks; another thought it best to inform the king first. The latter prevailed. The king was wrathful against those who wanted to kill his son and gave gifts to the others. Summoning his son he asked, "Son, for what reason did you want to kill me?" and Ajātasattu replied, "For the desire (greed) of kingship." "My son, take the very kingdom that you desired so much." And kissing his son, and consoling him, he abdicated the kingdom in his favor.

But Devadatta incited Ajātasattu and told him that it was a trick, that his father would lull him into a sense of security and kill him in a few days. "What shall I do, Lord?" said Ajātasattu. "Don't babble, but kill your father straightaway." Ajātasattu: "I cannot kill my father with a weapon, so how should I kill him?" "Kill him by not giving him any rice (food) to eat."

So Ajātasattu put his father in prison and ordered that no one except his mother should have access to him. The queen carried rice on a gold plate against her lap (secretly) and the king lived by eating this. After seven or eight days Ajātasattu wondered how his father seemed alive and well and made inquiries and found out the truth. He ordered the guards that his mother should not be permitted to carry anything in her waist. Now she hid the rice in her hair, and in this manner the king lived for seven or eight days, till Ajātasattu found this out also and forbade the practice. She then hid the rice inside her golden slipper; but when this practice was discovered she rubbed her body with rice paste and asked Bimbisāra to lick it. When this was found out she went to the doorway [of the prison] in great distress and said: "King Bimbisāra, Lord, you did not want to kill him in infancy, you nurtured your own enemy." She asked for forgiveness for any wrong she might have done and told her husband that she would not be able to see him again. From that day onwards the king was without food.

But the king who had achieved *sotāpanna* (the first stage of *nirvāṇa*) could pace up and down in meditative concentration and do without food, such being the fruit of having achieved the path. Ajātasattu then ordered that the soles of his father's feet be cut up, having salt, lime, and oil inserted into them, and then be held over the fire so that the salt and oil would splutter. When the barbers came the king thought that the son had relented and sent them to shave him. The barbers told him the truth, and the king replied, "Do as your king bids you." The barbers asked the king's forgiveness. They split his feet and inserted the salt and held the king's feet over a sandalwood fire.

On the very day that the king, his father, died, Ajātasattu's son was born. Ajātasattu's courtiers brought two letters to him—one informing him of the death of the father and the other about the birth of the son. They decided to place the joyous epistle on his hand. Immediately the king's hair stood on end, so great was his joy. He thought of his own father's goodness. "When I was born my father must surely have felt this same love. Lads, go immediately and free my father." The ministers then placed the letter with the sorrowful news in his hands. He read it and was filled with a great sadness. He went weeping to the palace where his mother lived and said, "O noble mother, did my father also feel the same love on the day I was born?"

The mother wept loud and replied: "Son, you sinner! What am I to say? Once when you were a child you were crying because of a blister on your finger, and your father carried you to his hall of justice, and in the midst of his ministers he placed you on his lap. Seeing you cry in pain, your noble father, because of the enormous love he had for you, actually sucked out the pus from your blister." Then King Ajātasattu wailed and went forth to cremate his father.

The text then goes on to develop the parallel case of Devadatta, who wanted to kill the Buddha and take over the kingdom of the Buddha. This planned regicide is also a form of patricide, since Devadatta, being a monk is, in official Buddhist terminology, a son of the Buddha. Devadatta's attempts were obviously futile. His last attempt was to send a drunken elephant, Nālāgiri, to attack the Buddha, but the Buddha tamed him and wished that the elephant give up his animal speech for a human one. Nālāgiri then uttered the five precepts of Buddhism. (This event is well known and celebrated by Buddhists everywhere.) Those ministers who saw this triumph of the Buddha informed Ajātasattu and made him feel ashamed. Ajātasattu then stopped supporting Devadatta and his schismatic monks. The rest of the Devadatta story is continued from there till he is finally swallowed up by the earth and dragged into hell.

The day Devadatta was swallowed up by the earth there were great festivities in the city of Rajagaha. The citizens had decorated the city as if it were a heavenly one, and they wore festive clothes and sported like divinities. King Ajātasattu was seated with his ministers on his throne like moonlight shining on a silver pot. Why was he in his throne at this time? asks the text. In order to avoid sleep. Why is it that he wanted to avoid sleep? From the time he killed his father, the king, whenever he shut his eyes, it was as if his head was being hit by sledgehammers and his body was being cut up by a hundred and thousand weapons. When this happened he shouted loudly, shivered, and went to sleep. And since he could not confide in others for shame, he told people otherwise. But the fact was that from the time he killed the king, his father, he could not obtain sleep, he had no desire for sleep [since he wanted to avoid the horrible pains mentioned earlier]. And it was in order to avoid sleep that he told his courtiers: "The moon's radiance has brightened this night. . . . [T]o obtain some solace tell me whom shall we go see, which monk or brahmin can enlighten us."

Let me skip the next part of the tale. The upshot of the king's inquiry was the decision to see the Buddha himself. Ajātasattu was afraid to see the Buddha and wanted Jīvaka, the famous physician in Buddhist legend, to take him there so he could hide behind his back! Why did he want to see the Buddha? Because, says the text, of the crime of having killed his father who was a devotee of the Buddha and the harm he did to the Buddha by joining up with Devadatta. So if he went with Jīvaka he could hide behind him and see the Buddha.

The text then says: on that occasion my Lord the Buddha-King, seeing Ajātasattu come toward him, and sensing the latter's fear, projected his great compassion towards him so that Ajātasattu felt like a child being kept on the lap and feeling his hair being stroked. The Buddha sent from his body a large amount of Buddha-radiance to the king. But still the king would not come before the Buddha and instead procrastinated by pointing out the various structures constructed by Jīvaka in the mango grove and praising them. This was because of the great harm that he did the Buddha by joining with Devadatta. He held Jīvaka's hand. He asked Jīvaka, "Where is the Buddha, where is he?" though he knew him, having met him when his father was alive. He still dared not face the Buddha.

Ultimately at Jīvaka's urging he went up and saw the Buddha

and the *arahant* ("monks") and stood respectfully to one side. They looked serene like a forest of lotuses blooming in a windless place. That is, because of their discipline the monks were seated serene and quiet. The king was amazed that not one of these monks as much as raised his head to look at the impressive force that accompanied the king, but instead all were looking at the Buddha. The tranquility of these monks was like a pond without mud, thought the king, and he looked again and again at the monks with their calm qualities and restrained senses. He thought: may my son, Prince Udaya, also enjoy the freedom of similar serenity. This is a natural human wish, says the text. Whenever one sees a great victory, a noble form, or a fine quality one wishes that one's son be endowed with it.

My Lord, the Buddha, read the king's thoughts—that he is afraid to worship or to speak to me, unless I speak to him. With one word I shall dispel his fears and let forth words from my whole body as it were, with a resounding Brahma-sound. "Great king, like the rain that falls over a rock and collects in a hollow down below, the waters of love that sprang within you as a result of my dispensation have now gone toward your son, haven't they?"

On hearing these words, the king's whole being was full of joy. "I now know the limitless goodness of the Buddha, there is no one else who has betrayed the Buddha like I have; I have with my own hands killed his chief lay devotee, the king; I have listened to the words of Devadatta and encouraged him to kill the Buddha, and at Devadatta's instigation sent Nālāgiri to kill him; and at my urging Devadatta hurled a huge rock at the Buddha. . . . Yet a traitor though I am, the Buddha speaks only kind words to me, it is a great wonder. . . . Like a man exchanging coals for gold, I went to various useless teachers, leaving this treasure, this river . . . of compassion." Saying thus, the text continues, he spoke of the love he had for his own son, and like a man who leaving the burning sun has gone into a cool pond, he worshiped the Buddha again and again. If I were to worship the monks I would have to turn my back on the Buddha, he thought, and therefore instead of worshiping them he greeted them from afar with clasped hands, indicating his love for them.

The next part of the text deals with the various exhortations given by the Buddha to Ajātasattu culminating in the Buddha reciting the *Samaññaphala Sutta*—a well-known text extolling the fruits of renunciation. The king now dedicates both himself and also (symbolically) the wealth of the kingdom to the Buddha. He asks for the Buddha's forgiveness (*samāva*) and departs. After his departure the Buddha tells the monks that if the king had not committed the sin of parricide he would have even today achieved the state of *sotāpanna.* And the text continues: "That King Ajātasattu could not sleep day or night from the time he killed the king, his father; yet having heard the sermons of the Buddha he now could sleep peacefully."[7]

Let me briefly examine this extraordinary myth. Two stories run parallel to each other, both parricidal ones. That of Ajātasattu is a straight case of parricide. As far as the Devadatta story is concerned it should be remembered that when someone joins the order he severs his kinship ties and becomes a "son of the Buddha" (*Buddha putra*). Thus Devadatta's case is also a form of indirect parricide, or attempt at parricide, since everyone knows that the Buddha cannot be killed. The pity and horror come from the story of Ajātasattu; Devadatta is necessary to appreciate the full significance of Ajātasattu's act. The most powerful part of the myth is where Devadatta frightens Ajātasattu with his terrifying vision and then calms him by appearing in his own normal form as a monk. Since the infant coiled with snakes is the form taken by Devadatta, it is reasonable, I assume, to treat it as Devadatta's alter ego, his vicious and "evil persona," the dark, shadow side of his personality, as Jung would say. But it is more than that. It is the parricide's infantile persona that is presented in the story, the unusual image of an infant with cobras coiled all over him, unusual because, as far as I know, this demonic form does not occur anywhere else in Buddhist mythology. The apparition of the infant swathed with serpents that hiss at Ajātasattu represents the rage of the infant-parricide. It is not only Devadatta's parricidal unconscious, but also Ajātasattu's; perhaps an objectification of a more general Oedipal rage in us all. Freud said that dreams are thoughts transformed into images. By "thoughts" he meant dream thoughts or the deep motivations of childhood. But one can go a step further; in this narrative *images are converted* into thought, if by "thought" we now mean *logos.* The infant in this story is of the order of imagery of dreams and fantasy; but image is here given verbal representation and then articulated into a story. I think that the hissing cobras in this vision are also phallic objects, as is the dagger that Ajātasattu ties to his thigh, shivering, when he first attempts to kill his father. How different he is from the fearless (and conscienceless) Sinhabāhu!

As in the paradigmatic myth of Sinhabāhu, here also the son is evilly disposed toward the father, but the father loves the son and does not reciprocate with hate. Since the son wanted the throne, the father kisses him and abdicates in his favor, even though the son attempted to kill him. But the son feels no pity and orders the father killed in horrible fashion. Ajātasattu's attitude changes when *he* has a son and feels the power of "child-love," an intrinsic force, implies the text. But it is too late. Remorse. Hence the nightmares, the sledgehammer hitting his head, his body being cut up, and the inability to sleep, "sleep that knits up the ravelled sleeve of care." Neither in *Macbeth* nor here is the word "remorse," or a similar term, used to depict the mind of the protagonist, but the *idea* is present in both, if by remorse one means the "reaction after an act of aggression that has been carried out."[8] Now such ideas need not be identical; they need only exhibit "family resemblances" if one wants to carry out acts of comparison and acts of theoretical inquiry.

It is with remorse that Ajātasattu parts company with Sinhabāhu. There are two kinds of father killers in history and culture: those without remorse (or those who have suppressed or denied it) and those with remorse, guilt, and the wish to atone, the wish to be forgiven. The terrible questions that the Sinhabāhu myth raises are given ethical meaning in the explicitly Buddhist myth of Ajātasattu. It is with Buddhism that the father killer makes the pilgrimage to assuage his conscience.

In this pilgrimage Ajātasattu wants desperately to seek and see the Buddha; yet he prevaricates. Fear, says the text, fear from having incited Devadatta to kill the Buddha and the fear for having killed the king his father, a devotee of the Buddha. But a reading of the story in the light of our knowledge of deep motivation reveals much more—the Buddha is the father who could not be killed by Devadatta, Ajātasattu's friend and one who, according to the text, shared the same essence. He tries to seek the help of another lay devotee of the Buddha—Jīvaka, the healer—to go seek the Buddha. He is like a scared child, he must hide behind Jīvaka. The pomp, noise, and splendor of his royal retinue (described in detail in the text) must be contrasted with the stillness of the Buddha's monks. Ajātasattu's retinue become silent as they approach the residence of the Buddha. This stillness frightens him; he thinks someone must be trying to kill him. Guilt: the voices of his conscience playing games. He is cooled by the mighty compassion of the Buddha, the surrogate parent—as if he were stroking the head of a small child, a scared child. This cool compassion and the serenity of the monks who appear like lotuses in a still pond present the Buddhist picture of the conquest over desire or greed—the source of sorrow both in the world and in the mind of Ajātassattu. The Buddha is not a savior like Christ; he cannot forgive the deed, nor cancel the magnitude of Ajātasattu's crime. It is the compassion of the Buddha that seems to flow from his whole body, and his words, that calm Ajātasattu and permit him to sleep at last. The text then presents a specifically Buddhist way of "forgiveness." Ajātasattu asks for *samāva* or forgiveness; the idea, the wish for forgiveness is recognized explicitly in the "language game." But the Buddha does not give it—he cannot because it is not in his power to do so, since Buddhism is a form of life that has a radically different soteriology from Christianity. It may seem a paradox to say that similar language games may be embedded in different forms of life as it is to say, in respect of our previous discussion of remorse, that different language games may be implicated in similar forms of life. But it is not.

The Buddhist doctrine is absolutely clear that parricide is one of the five *ānantariya* sins, sins that must be played out in the long *karmic* round.[9] But *ānantariya* sinners do not suffer eternal damnation. The archetype sinner, Devadatta, will suffer for eons in the lowest hell, *avici,* but even he will be reborn on earth and become a minor Buddha (*pacceka Buddha*). And so the Buddha tells his monks, after Ajātasattu has departed, that if the king had not committed the sin of parricide he would even today have achieved *sotāpanna,* the first stage of *nirvāṇa,* such is the power of the joy that comes from listening to the Buddha-word. Instead of being born in the dreaded *avici,* he will spend a spell of thirty thousand years in the bottom of a lesser hell and from there ascend to the top of that same hell, where he will live for another thirty thousand years; and then by the virtue of the good he did today, he will live one hundred thousand eons (*kalpa*) enjoying the pleasures of heaven and earth and will then be redeemed from the cycle of existence (*saṃsāra*) when he will be born as a minor (*pacceka*) Buddha named Vijitasena. The suffering of Ajātasattu, in the Buddhist scheme of things, is small peanuts for a large crime.[10]

Parricide and Fratricide: The Story of King Asoka

If Ajātasattu, according to the myth, having received the cool compassion of the Buddha, directed the waters of love toward his own newly born son, he must surely have been disappointed by his son's lack of reciprocal love. For the *Mahāvaṃsa* records that Ajātasattu, a great patron of Buddhism, reigned for twenty-four years until he was slain by his son Udayabhaddhika.[11] Udayabhaddhika was not that lucky either, for after sixteen years he was slain by his son, Anuraddhaka, who in turn was killed by Munda, his son. "Traitors and fools, . . . in the reign of the two (last kings) eight years elapsed." But still no end to the parricide since "Munda's son Nāgadasaka slew his father and then did the evil doer reign twenty-four years."[12] But now the people were wrathful and said, "this is a dynasty of parricides" and elected the commander-in-chief, Sisunāga, as king. He reigned for eighteen years and was succeeded by Kālāsoka (the Black Asoka), whose tenth regnal year coincided with the hundredth year of the Buddha's death.[13] It was in Kālāsoka's reign that the Second Buddhist Council was held, according to Theravāda tradition. Kālāsoka had ten brothers who severally reigned for twenty-two years. With this the dynasty of the Nandas takes over, and nine Nanda kings reign for twenty-two years.

> Then did the brahman Canakka [Cānakya] anoint a glorious youth, known by the name Candagutta, as king all over Jambudipa, born of a noble clan, the Moriyas, when, filled with bitter hate, he had slain the ninth (Nanda) Dhanananda.[14]

This, needless to say, is Candragupta, the founder of the Maurya (Moriya) dynasty and grandfather of the great Buddhist king, Asoka. This new dynasty, according to one tradition at least, also commenced with a parricidal act of sorts. The *Mahāvaṃsa* simply says that Candragupta reigned for twenty-four years and his son Bindusāra for twenty-eight. Yet according to the *Mahāvaṃsa Tikā,* the commentary on the ancient text, when Candragupta died his body was taken over by a benevolent spirit named Devagabbha (divine womb). Bindusāra outwitted this spirit and killed him.[15] I think the tradition was strong that Candragupta was "killed" by his son Bindusāra, but it would not be quite proper for the dynasty that produced the exemplary Buddhist king, Asoka, to start with parricide. So the *Mahāvaṃsa* ignores it while its commentary says that Bindusāra only killed the deity that possessed his father's corpse. It is interesting to note that according to Jaina tradition, Candragupta renounced his throne in favor of his son and became an ascetic (culturally recognized as a kind of symbolic death). This move fits neatly with the extreme ascetic orientation of Jainism, whereas the (symbolic) killing of Candragupta by Bindusāra fits the Buddhist tradition of parricidal kings. Two religious traditions, two forms of history.

After Bindusāra's death the pious Asoka, the ideal Buddhist king, takes over. The life of this hero is described in great detail in many Sinhala and Pāli texts, but for convenience let me confine myself to the simple and straightforward account in the *Mahāvaṃsa.* Bindusāra had 101 sons from different wives, the most virtuous being Asoka, the future Buddhist emperor. But not yet; he slew ninety-nine of his brothers born of different mothers (but spared his own sibling) and assumed the kingship. Yet it is the killing of the oldest brother, Sumana, that all the texts, including the *Mahāvaṃsa,* focus on:

> When Bindusāra had fallen sick Asoka left the Government of Ujjenī conferred on him by his father . . . and when he made himself master of the city, after his father's death, he caused his eldest brother to be slain and took himself the sovereignty in the splendid city.[16]

Asoka's eldest brother's wife then fled through the east gate of the palace and went to a village of Caṇḍālas (untouchables). There she gave birth to a son under a *nigrōdha* (banyan) tree, and he was therefore named Nigrōdha. She lived for seven years as mistress of a Caṇḍāla chief. "Then as the thera Mahāvaruṇa saw that the boy bore the signs of his destiny, the arahant questioned his mother and ordained him, and even in the room where they shaved him he attained to the state of arahant."[17] These actions of the mother indicate her extreme fear of Asoka's wrath. First, by degrading herself as a mistress of the lowest of the low (a fate worse than death according to traditional South Asian beliefs), she herself becomes untouchable and therefore outside of Asoka's reach. A bleak sanctuary. Second, in order that her son might not suffer her caste fate, she has him ordained as a novice, ensuring once again protection from the king's wrath. It was Nigrōdha who, according to the chronicle, converted Asoka to Buddhism. But note that this is an extraordinary act for a young and not fully ordained monk. Thus the *Mahāvaṃsa* must employ a rationalization to justify this episode—it says that though Nigrōdha was a novice he attained *arahant* status when he was first shaved prior to his induction to the order!

Nigrōdha's conversion of Asoka is not mentioned in the king's inscriptions. There, in the famous Kālinga inscription, he says that though converted to Buddhism a few years back, the death of millions in his Kālinga war, the disruption of families, and hardships suffered by ascetics caused him to give up war and sound the drums of peace. Asoka then attributes his remorse of conscience to the killing of thousands; but it may well be that the Buddhist chronicles also tell us another side of the story, namely, the killing of his oldest brother (and perhaps other siblings also) who, after the death of the father, is not only the rightful heir but in Indian thought is generally regarded as a kind of father himself.[18] The *Mahāvaṃsa* tells us that the mere sight of the calm and detached Nigrōdha roused in Asoka feelings of kindness for him. The phrase "kindly feelings" is found three times in the text. He invited Nigrōdha to his palace and asked him to be seated. Asoka's kind reception of Nigrōdha was due to "a former life lived together," and the text goes on to recount a casuistic episode of a past life.[19] But I suspect the psychological reason is Asoka's remembrance of things past: his act of fratricide and symbolic former life from which there is no escape. The text continues:

> Since he saw no other bhikkhu he (Nigrōdha) approached the royal throne. Then as he stepped toward the throne the King thought: "Today this *sāmanera* (novice) will be lord in my house!" Leaning on the royal hand he (the monk) mounted the throne and took his seat on the royal throne under the white canopy, and seeing him seated there King Asoka rejoiced greatly that he had honored him according to his rank.[20]

A Buddhist exegesis of this text will of course insist that in Buddhist thought the monk is higher than the king, and this is prototypically recognized in the Asoka story. But remember that Nigrōdha is not even a fully ordained monk; he is a *sāmanera* or "novice." The deeper significance of this act is, I suspect, in relation to Asoka's act of killing his brother, the rightful heir to the throne. Nigrōdha symbolically appropriates the throne that should have been rightfully his; and Asoka assuages his conscience by a parallel symbolic act followed by his conversion to Buddhism. He makes his brother's son king for the day, to occupy the place that legitimately was Nigrōdha's father's and also justly Nigrōdha's. He then accepts the religion of the young novice, an act that makes psychological sense, but little logical or common sense in the way the events are presented in the Theravāda texts. In the *Mahāvaṃsa* the act of conversion is followed by a massive spate of feeding monks and nuns and giving them provisions. From Asoka's own inscriptions we can verify an initial conversion to Buddhism, which also might well have been his mother's religion (though this did not deter his bloody conquest of Kālinga). The Sinhala stories suggest that conversion was based on personal contrition. It is this act of mass killing and destruction that brought Asoka's contrition and the self-recognition of his troubled conscience to the surface (though its psychogenesis expectably could never be recognized). Asoka could now introduce a reign of justice after a spate of violence.

It is not necessary for our study of the Sinhala Oedipus to argue whether the chain of parricides among the Moriya (Maurya) clan and its predecessors were historical or mythic realities. The important thing is that even where the Sri Lankan chronicles write about the Indian past, they are not only scrupulous with the concern for chronology, but they recount, not always abashedly, a whole list of purported, historical parricidal kings, culminating in the great Asoka, the model of the ideal king for all Buddhists subsequently. The paradigmatic Oedipal myth of Sinhabāhu has its parallel in the Indian past as recreated by Sri Lankans as far as parricide is concerned at least, if not mother or sister marriage.

I think the difference between the Indian and Sri Lankan Oedipus in fact pertains to their respective religions, Hinduism (irrespective of the specific type) and Buddhism. Buddhism, very definitely in its doctrines, and to a great deal in the institutions it creates, eliminates all forms of familial sacramentalism (*saṃskaras*) from baptism and puberty to marriage and death. In Sri Lanka none of these except death receive religious (Buddhist) sanction; no monk officiates at them, and they are viewed basically as secular ceremonial. At death monks are present for part of the ritual to emphasize and give reality to the phrase that everyone utters at death—"impermanent are all conditioned things"—and to reassure the living that their dead kinsmen may be blessed with a happy rebirth and eventual *nirvāṇa*. There are no Hindu-type *saṃskaras* (sacraments) incumbent on the son to ensure the father's entry into heaven. On the institutional level Theravāda Buddhist societies, and some Mahāyāna ones (Tibet), are associated with the primacy of the nuclear family, as against the Hindu joint family, and, along with this, with the erosion of patripotestal authority and the religiously sanctioned role of the father.[21] I do not know whether Buddhism was a causal factor in transforming a previous joint family system into a more nuclear model; I am only stating the historical correlation which is all that is necessary for my argument. Finally on the kinship level Sri Lanka shares with much of South India the so-called Dravidian kinship terminology with its inbuilt norm of preferential cross-cousin marriage. The latter ensures that, ideally at least, the mother is the father's sister, in which case the in-marrying female is freed from the dread of the mother-in-law so characteristic of the Hindu family. I have not come across one Sinhala folk song directly indicating the woman's trauma of leaving the parental home for the alien home of the husband, a genre almost universal in Hindu India, especially in the north. These features of kinship make the mother less anxious, and the extreme symbiosis of the mother-child is loosened here. Furthermore, the mother's brother is viewed as a loving kinsman, and though not a member of the child's Oedipal circle as in Trobriand, he is relevant to any Oedipal crisis that might threaten relationships in the Sinhala nuclear family. In a confrontation with the father the child runs away to the mother's brother, or a surrogate avuncular figure. Cross-cousin marriage (and the terminology it enshrines) is so significant to Sri Lankan Buddhists that the *Mahāvaṃsa* attributes to the Sakya clan of the Buddha this form of preferential marriage.

The preceding discussion has relevance for the father-son relationship. The norms of filial piety and respect for the father are still strong, but no longer anchored on a religious foundation.[22] It is very common to see a child being cuddled by the father in Sri Lanka and not unusual for him to act as caretaker. The roles become more formal in later childhood and puberty when the mother becomes the object of love, tantamount to veneration. In the early nineteenth century a perceptive observer of Sinhala life, John Davy, lamented the existence of customs such as polyandry but then went on to say:

> As fathers and mothers, as sons and daughters, the Singalese appear in a more amiable light. Their families are generally small, one woman rarely bearing more than four or five children: a fact that does not at all agree with the assertion that has been made, that the women of Ceylon are remarkably prolific. The care of the children is almost equally divided between the parents; and an infant is more frequently seen with its father than mother. Mothers almost universally suckle their own children, and for the long period of four of five years, either in part or entirely. The only exception to this custom, when health permits, is in the instance of some fine ladies, who, even in the Interior of Ceylon, are occasionally more obedient to the voice of vanity than of nature; and, to preserve a little while a fine form of bosom, relinquish the first duty and most endearing office of a mother.[23]

The effect of the preceding discussion is that the Sinhala family situation produces different images of the father, some close to the

Hindu model and others quite removed from it. The latter, I think, is the more frequent. The extreme abnegation of the son in the type of myth where he renounces his sexuality for the father is simply nonexistent in the Sri Lankan repertoire as far as I know. If the Sinhala-Buddhist son is released from patripotestal authority and the obligations of the *saṃskaras* he is still governed by strong moral norms pertaining to filial piety. Yet in the Sri Lankan situation the son can displace the father. Myths of father killing as well as historical expressions of it are dominant in the culture.

What then is the crucial role of the mother for the Sri Lankan Oedipus? Here also I continue the general argument adopted in the previous lecture that the values of the culture affect the Oedipal circle of relations, since these relations are, at the very birth of the child (and indeed even before), fully value-governed. In the Sinhala case not only are incestuous relations with the mother unthinkable, but there is a parallel idealization of her to an unusual degree. The idealization is such that in puberty and adolescence a young boy will often consciously state that he would like to marry a woman like his mother, as Gaṇeśa does in the myth quoted in the previous chapter.

It is quite common for children who idealize the mother (or even the father, though this is less frequent) to wish the mother eventual Buddhahood—the Buddha being in Sinhala consciousness the embodiment of nonerotic idealization and benevolence. Yet in spite of the strong incest taboo and nonerotic idealization of the mother, the Sinhalas are obsessed with obscenities regarding incest. "Son of a prostitute" is a popular obscenity. Equally so are "son of a cunt" and "fuck your mother." The latter, in certain contexts, is the most hostile and humiliating obscenity one can imagine; in other contexts, it is used almost as an exclamation as when one says *ammaṭa* ("mother," "to your mother"). Nowadays I hear school children use the phrase *ammaṭa huḍu* as a normal and regular exclamation, as one might in English say "shit," "Jesus," "damn!" *Huḍu* is meaningless; it is simply a nonthreathening and euphemistic substitute for *hukanna,* "fuck." Even *ammaṭa* is ambiguous; it might mean "my mother" or "your mother"; the latter is often made explicit with a pronoun "your" if the context is one of insult and not innocuous swearing. (In my childhood it was *ammaṭa siri* or "blessings on mother," but I guess children are more worldly wise nowadays.) All this at least shows that idealization and degradation of the mother coexist in Sinhala culture. And yet it is the case that mythology shows no instance of the parricidal hero marrying his mother. It is the sister that is the mythologically desired sexual object and toward whom the incest taboo is weak.

The Sinhala situation is the very opposite of the Trobriand. Childhood sexual experimentation with the sister is not uncommon, and we also noted the sister's caretaking role as maternal surrogate. The sister then takes the place of the mother in the Sinhala myth of Oedipus. Insofar as the sexual degradation of the mother exists in the Sinhala consciousness one could indeed argue that the mother is a sexual object in unconscious ideation; but the Oedipal family romance is focussed on the sister. (It may well be that this is overdetermined by the son's awareness of the father's Oedipal feelings for his own daughter.) In her own right the sister is a sexual object in the Oedipal circle of the brother; but this is enhanced by possible displacements from the mother to the sister. This equivalence and displacement is seen in the myth of Sinhabāhu who carries the mother on the right shoulder and the sister on the left. He eventually marries his sister, after ensuring that his mother marries the culturally (and psychologically) appropriate partner, the mother's brother's son who is, in the ideal model, also the father's sister's son. The myth introduces a theme that is also significant in Sinhala familial life: the son usurps the father's role as the caretaker of his mother and sister.

The equivalence between mother and sister comes out clearly in the late Sinhala chronicle, the *Rājāvaliya* (seventeenth or eighteenth century). Here the origin of the Buddha's own clan is described. The relevant part says that four elder sons, rejected by their stepmother, retire into the forest accompanied by their sisters. Under the command of the sage Kapila they found the city of Kapilavastu, the Buddha's birthplace. Each of the four brothers marries a younger sister; they then place their eldest sister in the place of their mother and thus become the founders of the Buddha's own clan, the Sakyas.[24]

Vāsubandhu's Oedipus

In the previous chapter I made a case for viewing the Oedipus complex in Western psychoanalysis as a reification in a specific direction of select erotically desirable kin in the family. The Hindu and Sinhala Oedipus reify these kin in different ways. The ideal typical form of the complex in Sri Lanka is where the son kills the father and marries his sister. But then any reformulation of the Oedipus complex comes up against the example of Vāsubandhu, the great fourth-century Indian-Buddhist philosopher who formulated the complex in its almost Freudian form! It is Vāsubandhu's Oedipus that has been incorporated into present-day mortuary ritual in Tibetan Buddhism known as "the book of the dead."

Vāsubandhu's thesis is based on Mahāyāna cosmology of an intermediate state between death and the next rebirth. Both Vāsubandhu and Tibetan mortuary rites describe the journey of this intermediate-type being (which we will gloss for present purposes as "soul").[25] This "soul" has the five aggregates or the constituent elements that characterize all beings including humans, but it also possesses a pure divine eye and magical power. McDermott neatly summarizes Vāsubandhu's thesis regarding the entry of this "intermediate-type being" (*antarā bhava*) or "soul" into a human womb.

> Driven by karma, the intermediate-state being goes to the location where rebirth is to take place. Possessing the divine eye by virtue of its karma, it is able to see the place of its birth, no matter how distant. There it sees its father and its mother to be, united in intercourse. Finding the scene hospitable, its passions are stirred. If male, it is smitten with desire for its mother. If female, it is seized with desire for its father. And inversely, it hates either mother or father, which it comes to regard as a rival. Concupiscence and hatred thus arise in the *gandharva* as its driving passions. Stirred by these wrong thoughts, it attaches itself to the place where the sexual organs of the parents are united, imagining that it is there joined with the object of its passion. Taking pleasure in the impurity of the semen and blood in the womb, the *antarā bhava* establishes itself there. Thus do the *skandha*s arise in the womb. They harden; and the intermediate-state being perishes, to be replaced immediately by the birth existence (*pratisaṃdhi*).[26]

Vāsubandhu states his thesis with the utmost clarity, as if directly anticipating Freud: the witness of the primal scene, the love for the parent of the opposite sex, and the hatred for the parent of the same sex. He does not attempt to mythicize the complex as Freud did with Sophocles, but sees it as an entirely universal psychobiologically based phenomenon. Does this startling parallelism with the Freudian compel us to view the Oedipus complex as universal and the Hindu form discussed earlier as simply a variation of the positive Oedipus complex, as Goldman suggests?[27] Does the Vāsubandhu parallelism add fuel to the universalistic vision of the Oedipus complex? On the face of it, it is indeed impressive that two thinkers from radically different backgrounds and historical periods have come up with a near identical theory. In terms of my preceding argument, on the other hand, it would seem that *both* delineated identical sets of Oedipal relations from the larger circle; both independently invented the fiction of the Oedipus complex. I think the latter action is not unusual as it may seem at first blush. If culturally significant Oedipal myths of identical or near identical form can exist in different cultures, surely one could expect clinically significant Oedipal "fictions" also to be formulated in different cultural settings—with one difference, though. Myth is a form of representation common to the species; one would naturally expect to find mythic representations of culturally significant Oedipal relations rather than clinically significant Oedipus complexes since "clinical" investigation is a rare form of intellectual life in cross-cultural perspective. While I think this is true, I shall try to hypothetically reconstruct how Vāsubandhu's complex emerged in Indian Buddhist (not Hindu) culture.

Once Vāsubandhu's thesis is contextualized in terms of his cultural and historical background, one will see that the fiction he invented was in fact somewhat different from Freud's, though exhibiting a striking family resemblance. Vāsubandhu was a Mahāyāna Buddhist philosopher. Since Buddhism raises doubts about, and radically alters, the familial and sacramental structures of Hinduism, one can assume that he lived in a society that was close to contemporary Tibet or Sri Lanka, especially in relation to the absence of forms of patripotestal authority and the joint family. Moreover his version of the complex was "clinical," not in its medical sense, but metaphorically in its spiritual sense. Vāsubandhu's isolation of the Oedipus complex was rooted in the larger cosmological speculations of Mahāyānism, as Freud's was rooted in nineteenth-century European thought and clinical medicine. Vāsubandhu was primarily concerned with the journey of the "soul" after death. Mahāyāna Buddhism had some notion of a soullike substance, or "intermediate-state being," that survived the death of the body. Now, according to Buddhist ethics, the soul's transmigration and reincarnation into another form such as an animal, a demon, a divinity, or a human and to another place such as a hell or a heaven or back to earth is not foreordained but determined by the ethical quality of one's previous actions. This is what is meant by karma. Unlike in Trobriand, the reincarnated soul does not enter into the womb of a woman of its own matrilineal clan, since the compensatory ethics of karma render impossible any invariant predetermined destiny of the soul. Ethics, not fate or kinship, decides the shape and place of rebirth.

In this cosmology the "soul" at death has several ways of achieving rebirth, depending on its karma. Now in Buddhist thought the achievement of a human rebirth is much to be desired since it is only as a human being one can become a Buddha. The Oedipal references occur in relation to a "soul" achieving rebirth in a human womb—not, for example, an animal or divine reincarnation. In Mahāyāna Buddhist thought the soul has full consciousness and also magical power. Hence it is not created by biological processes but is only assisted by them to obtain its corporeal cover. If the soul is endowed with consciousness, it must of necessity observe and reflect on the primal scene, for intercourse is a necessary condition for conception. Vāsubandhu's speculations thus far are consonant with the framework of Mahāyāna cosmology. But the rest of his formulations, while they do not contradict Mahāyāna thought, are in all likelihood based on his own observations on childhood and adult sexuality among familial kin. Note, however, that his Oedipal theory fits nicely with Mahāyāna cosmology. If the soul at birth witnesses the primal scene it will inevitably be stimulated sexually and will also expectably experience human feelings like jealousy. The cosmology requires a focus on sexuality. But why this must result in love for the parent of the opposite sex and hatred for that of the same sex is not entailed or logically expectable in terms of the cosmology, though not contradicted by it. I assume that, like Freud, Vāsubandhu developed this idea on the basis of his observations and on his knowledge of Oedipal myths. The prior cosmological frame, however, introduced certain limits on speculation. Vāsubandhu (and also Freud, I think) had to focus on the *triangular and erotically* based relationships of the Oedipus complex unlike the expanded Oedipal *circle* that I dealt with. The reason is obvious. In the cosmological scheme, the "soul," invested with magical power, passion, and consciousness, has to observe the intercourse of the *parents*. This is the immediate context of the cosmological system as it deals with rebirth in a human womb. Siblings and other kin as well as nonerotic emotions are immaterial in this context, and are necessarily excluded in Vāsubandhu's Oedipus. So are they in Freud (for different reasons) except as displacements and transformations of a nuclear complex. Both universalized the Oedipus complex, and in both this universalization was based on the restrictive context of the thought or cosmology that framed their speculations. What I have done is to expand their argument a little further, but while I am building our knowledge of an important aspect of being human, I am also surely bound by the nature of my own theoretical prejudgments.

❷

Symbolic Parricide: The Conscience of Duṭṭhagāmaṇī Abhaya

King Duṭugämuṇu (or in formal parlance Duṭṭhagāmaṇī Abhaya) became the sovereign ruler of Sri Lanka in 161 B.C. after a fifteen-year war against Elāra, a Tamil king from Coḷa, who had conquered the northern part of the island known as the *rajaraṭa,* the traditional seat of the Sinhala monarchy. Duṭṭhagāmaṇī brought the whole island under his sway as a Sinhala-Buddhist nation. The *Dīpavaṃsa,* the Pāli chronicle written in the fourth or fifth century A.D., lists his accomplishments in one brief paragraph: it simply states that Duṭṭhagāmaṇī Abhaya defeated Elāra, a virtuous and just ruler, and goes on to record the king's construction of religious edifices.[28] However, in the *Mahāvaṃsa,* written perhaps two centuries later, the hero is Duṭugämuṇu, whose life and career occupy one-fifth of the chronicle. Though both chronicles, according to scholars, were based on earlier temple records, it seems very likely that the later work used popular versions of the life of the king. For unlike the older work, the *Mahāvaṃsa* relates the life of Duṭugämuṇu in the form of a story and recounts his battles with Elāra in "epic" terms.

The *Mahāvaṃsa* records that the king, having vanquished Elāra, the Tamil king, and having killed many Tamil soldiers, sat in the royal palace, but the victory did not bring him joy.

> Sitting then on the terrace of the royal palace, adorned, lighted with fragrant lamps and filled with many a perfume, magnificent with nymphs in the guise of dancing-girls, while he rested on his soft and fair couch, covered with costly draperies, he, looking back upon his glorious victory, great though it was, knew no joy, remembering that thereby was wrought the destruction of millions (of beings).[29]

A group of *arahants* (world renouncers) living in a sacred enclave, who because of their superior accomplishments could read the king's mind, sent eight representatives in the middle watch of the night to console him.[30] But the king says: "How shall there be any comfort for me, O venerable sirs, since by me was caused the slaughter of a great host numbering millions?" The monks respond to the troubled conscience of the king. They say:

> From this deed arises no hindrance in thy way to heaven. Only one and a half human beings have been slain here by thee, O lord of men. The one had come unto the (three) refuges, the other had taken unto himself the five precepts. Unbelievers and men of evil life were the rest, not more to be esteemed than beasts. But as for thee, thou wilt bring glory to the doctrine of the Buddha in manifold ways; therefore cast away care from thy heart, O ruler of men.[31]

The Sinhala *Saddharmālaṃkāra,* written eight centuries later, puts it even more graphically when it records that the *arahant*s asked the king not to be despondent (*domnas*), since those Tamils he killed were not only barbarians and heretics but their deaths were like that of cattle, dogs, and mice.[32]

There is not the slightest doubt that Duṭṭhagāmaṇī was a historical personage. His reign can be chronologically established from Sri Lankan records and confirmed by archaeological evidence. Nevertheless this king has not been exempt from the mythmaking propensity that frames the life of the hero in terms of existing myth models, or in terms of a story that better fits the genre of myth than of history. The broad outline of this story persists through time in practically all of the Sri Lankan chronicles and in more popular folk accounts. The only real difference in the various accounts pertains to the characterization of Elāra's righteousness and Duṭṭhagāmaṇī's conscience. In general one could say that where Elāra is viewed as evil, or is ignored, Duṭṭhagāmaṇī does not suffer from a troubled conscience. Thus it is not just the killing of a million Tamils that bothers Duṭṭhagāmaṇī, though this is what he, like Asoka, consciously proclaims. Earlier, in his battle with his brother, thousands of his own countrymen were killed, and yet he suffers no remorse.[33] There is a deeper unstated reason for Duṭṭhagāmaṇī's conscience that must be elucidated from a symbolic and psychoanalytic study of his life. It is really the killing of Elāra that causes remorse and troubles his conscience. To understand this, one must probe deeper into the story of Duṭṭhagāmaṇī.

The outline of the story is as follows: Duṭṭhagāmaṇī's father, Kāvantissa, the ruler of Ruhuṇa in southern Sri Lanka, and his queen,

Vihāra Mahā Devi, had no children. The queen persuaded a dying novice to be conceived in her womb. At the very death of the novice the queen felt the heaviness of conception. The nature of the hero to be born was indicated by her cravings, one of which was to drink the water from the sword used for decapitating a general of the Tamil king Elāra. One of the king's warriors, Velusumana, accomplished this task and satisfied her cravings.

On the day Duṭugämuṇu was born all sorts of auspicious events occurred. Also at that time was born the elephant Kanḍula, destined to become the war elephant of the king, and according to some accounts, the ten warriors of the king. The prince was given the name Gāmaṇī Abhaya. Nine days after this the father had intercourse with his queen who then gave birth to a second son, Tissa. Both were weaned at the same time, and on this occasion the king gave them milk rice and said, "If you my sons abandon the doctrine of the Sambuddha then shall this not be digested in your body." Both ate the food rejoicing as if it were ambrosia. Similarly when the two sons were ten and twelve years old respectively the father set before each three portions of rice. The father made the boys utter an oath before each portion was eaten by them. The first urged them not to turn away from the monks; the second not to fight between themselves. The boys ate the food as if it were ambrosia. But the third oath said: "Never will we fight with the Tamils." Tissa dashed away the food with his hand while Gāmaṇī, flinging away his morsel of food, went to bed and lay there in a curled-up position. The mother asked him why he did not stretch his limbs, and his famous reply was: "Over there beyond the river (Mahaväli) are the Tamils and on the other side is the ocean, how can I lie with out-stretched limbs?" And so the *Mahāvaṃsa* tells us that "growing duly Gamani came to sixteen years, vigorous, renowned, intelligent and a hero in majesty and might." The king, his father, found him ten warriors and mustered for him a large army. Gāmaṇī was stationed in the capital of Ruhuṇa at Māgama while his brother was sent to guard the open country in the eastern region.[34]

Prince Gāmaṇī, reviewing his army, wanted to make war on the Tamils, but his father urged him to desist, in order to protect him, and said, "The region, this side of the river, is enough." Three times the son urged, and three times the father refused permission. Then Gāmaṇī said, "If my father were a man, he would not speak thus; therefore he shall put this on," and sent his father female ornaments.[35] The Sinhala account in the *Saddharmālaṃkāra* is more detailed. Gāmaṇī informs his father that he is a woman and should not wear his crown and other male attire. He sends him women's clothes and ornaments instead. The father is angry and, in both accounts, decides to bind him in golden chains, since he also loves his son.[36] Gāmaṇī runs away from home and hides incognito in the hills of Malaya, identified in Sinhala texts as the region of Kotmalē, an area full of local myths of Gāmaṇī. After this event, he is named Duṭṭhagāmaṇī (Duṭugämuṇu), Gāmaṇī the angry, or disobedient, or cruel, because, says the *Saddharmālaṃkāra*, he ran away from home without telling his father.[37]

When Kāvantissa died the queen arranged for the funeral and the younger brother Tissa came from the east and carried out the funeral rites for the father, and soon, in fear of his brother, he went back taking his mother with him. Duṭugämuṇu (as he is henceforth called) came down from Kotmalē and was crowned king at Mahāgama. He sent a letter to his brother, demanding his mother and his elephant, but Tissa refused and said that he would take care of his mother himself. The texts describe the two battles between the brothers, but I shall omit this part of the story, except to say that Duṭugämuṇu was eventually victorious and got back his mother and his elephant. He sent his brother as regent to the eastern division and then proceeded to conquer the north, and eventually he vanquished the Tamil king Elāra.

What then is the ontogenesis of the conscience of Duṭṭhagāmaṇī Abhaya? Duṭṭhagāmaṇī's father is a vacillating person, on the one hand encouraging his son to build an army to defeat the Tamils and on the other refusing to do so. Yet he is also a loving father. The mother is strong: witness her craving to drink the water washed from the sword of the Tamil general. The sons are both devoted to the mother: they both want her, and eventually the elder gets her. Duṭṭhagāmaṇī, according to our texts, consults her often, even before the onset of battle. Both sons refuse to accede to the father's request, and Duṭṭhagāmaṇī tells his father that he is not fit to wear male clothes and sends him female attire. The implication is reasonably clear: the father is a woman, and it is the mother who is a man. He then avoids confrontation with an angry father and flees to Kotmalē. Running away from home is, on the one hand, a typical South and Southeast Asian reaction to Oedipal conflict with the father, as we noted in lecture two. On the other, it is a kind of moratorium (to use Erikson's term) to the adolescent identity crisis engendered by the surfacing of the Oedipal conflict.

Duṭṭhagāmaṇī's father dies, but it is the mother and the younger brother who perform the crucial funeral rites. The death of the father and the eldest son's inability to attend the funeral are the key events that would have roused Duṭugämuṇu's dormant guilt feelings. These guilt feelings must have always been there, for his very name—Gāmaṇī the disobedient—is a reminder of his breach of the norm of filial piety. The inability of the eldest son to attend the funeral of the father and perform the final rites is a grievous fault which aroused his guilty conscience, whether he was consciously aware of it or not. This troubled conscience could be held in check by the preparations for the war and the long campaign against the Tamil invaders.

The failure to attend the funeral of the father fits in nicely with the whole theme of the guilty conscience of the king. Yet this event is not found in later Sinhala versions, such as the *Rajāvaliya.* In that work, both brothers, after they wage battle among themselves, jointly attend the funeral of the father. "The next day having dressed [the corpse] in royal ornaments of gold, they cremated their father, and crying and crying they kissed each other, and [thereby] calmed the grief they felt for their father."[38] The *Rajāvaliya* version uses the funeral of the father to effect a reconciliation of the brothers. Since Duṭṭhagāmaṇī performed the customary funeral rites he does not suffer from his conscience: concomitantly Elāra also appears as unjust and the Tamils become evil marauders. The *Rajāvaliya* is therefore the expression of another debate on the conscience of the king precipitated by previous stories. The one is no more "historical" than the other. Though real life events are probably mythicized in the two accounts, one cannot infer from the narrative that some events are empirically real, unless confirmed by other (epigraphical and archaeological) evidence.

Other familial relationships of Duṭṭhagāmaṇī, though not immediately relevant to the theme of his conscience, are worth mentioning because of their psychological salience. The relation with the brother is a classic case of sibling rivalry, persisting from infancy to adulthood. The age difference between the two was slight, and they would inevitably have competed for the love of the mother, a competition they literally carried out later. When Duṭṭhagāmaṇī defeated his brother and sent him to the eastern district, the latter stayed there. There is no suggestion in extant texts that he in any way assisted his brother in the war against the Tamils.

The written texts have another lacuna. Duṭṭhagāmaṇī's relation to his mother is clearly highlighted, but there is no reference to his wife at all. Yet we know he had a son, Sāliya, who abdicated claims to the throne and paved the way for the ascension of Duṭṭhagāmaṇī's brother. If the classic texts make no reference to the wife the folk versions collected by Robinson from Kotmalē make it clear that he married a local woman during his sojourn there.[39] This wrong marriage probably is the reason for refusing to include the wife of the hero in chronicles extolling his glory. The wrong marriage also taints the offspring; the classic texts do mention that Sālirāja, the son, married an untouchable Candāla woman and renounced rights to the throne. Sālirāja was also repeating the rebellion against the father in his own terms by deliberately becoming an outcaste, rejecting family, dynasty, and wealth. The third son of the previous lecture has reappeared in princely guise in this one!

To come back to Duṭugämuṇu and continue the narrative—the war against the Tamils and the siege of the enemy fortress of Vijitapura is described in heroic style in the *Mahāvaṃsa.* Yet the face-to-face combat between Elāra and Duṭugämuṇu, which really should have had all the attention, receives scant reference. "Near the south gate of the city the two kings fought; Elāra hurled his dart, Gāmaṇī evaded it; he made his own elephant pierce (Elāra's) elephant with his tusks and he hurled his dart at Elāra; and this (person) fell there with his elephant."[40] *Saddharmālaṃkāra* is only slightly more detailed.[41] I suspect that this is because the combat between the protagonists presented a singularly inappropriate theme for heroic elaboration, since Elāra was an old man and Duṭugämuṇu a relatively young warrior! The *Mahāvaṃsa* tells us that Elāra reigned for forty-four years; assuming that he was at least twenty-five when he became king (a conservative estimate), he must have been near seventy when he was killed by Duṭugämuṇu (who could not be more than forty-five years old). Moreover, Elāra was the epitome of the righteous king who acted "with even justice toward friend and foe, on occasions of disputes at law" and "was a protector of tradition albeit he knew not the peerless virtues of the most precious of the three gems [Buddhism]".[42] Once when riding his chariot he accidentally injured a Buddhist *stupa*; he leaped out and said, "Sever my head also (from the trunk) with the wheel." But his ministers did not permit this, and so he spent a large fortune in repairing the *stupa.* The *Mahāvaṃsa* also attributes to this king acts of compassion and self-sacrifice that were conventionally associated with just kings of South India. One might therefore argue that Duṭugämuṇu unconsciously identified Elāra with his own father and ipso facto the killing of Elāra with his betrayal of Kāvantissa, his kindly father. The guilty conscience of the king that was kept at bay so long must surely have surfaced with his horrendous act of symbolic parricide.

The subsequent acts of Duṭugämuṇu bear out this interpretation. The *Mahāvaṃsa* says:

> "In the city he caused the drums to be beaten, and when he had summoned the people from a yojana around he celebrated the funeral rites for King Elāra. On the spot where his body had fallen he burned it with the catafalque, and there did he build a monument and ordain worship. And even to this day, the princes of Lanka when they draw near this place are wont to silence their music because of this worship."[43]

Geiger translates *cētiya* as "monument" because he felt it improbable that a layman could be given honor reserved for Buddhas and *arahant*s, but the Sinhala of the *Saddharmālaṃkāra* in its rendering of the event uses the word *dāgäba,* or "relic chamber," which is synonymous with *cētiya* or *stupa.* In the Buddha's time *cētiya* had the more general meaning of "cenotaph," but by Duṭugämuṇu's time in Sri Lanka a *cētiya, stupa,* or *dāgäba* was exclusively a place where Buddha or *arahant* relics were enshrined. When ordinary monks die, a miniature *stupa* is sometimes erected over their ashes, but it never becomes a place of worship. The commentary on the *Mahāvaṃsa,* written in the ninth century, mentions the existence of *elārapatimāghāra,* or "Elāra image-house," which most certainly implies that not only were Elāra's relics enshrined in a *stupa* but there was also a shrine housing his image, possibly based on the model of the Buddhist shrine often erected beside a *stupa.* This shrine must certainly have been built by Duṭugämuṇu himself. The exaggerated and unprecedented honor accorded a fallen enemy is, I believe, overdetermined by Duṭṭhagāmaṇī's unconscious identification of the noble Elāra with his own well-intentioned and loving father. I noted earlier that in Sri Lankan thought one customarily expresses reverence for one's mother, *gurus,* and other idealized figures by wishing them eventual Buddhahood. Duṭṭhagāmaṇī translates this into action by treating Elāra as a Buddha or *arahant*-like figure who must be honored in an extraordinary manner and worshiped by the people. Furthermore, if indeed he erected a statue of Elāra in an image-house, it meant that he saw him as a Bodhisattva or deity. The apotheosis of a hero who died by violence is well known in popular Sinhala (and South Asian) thought. I might even add that the compulsive religiosity of Duṭugämuṇu soon afterwards, impelling him to frantic construction of religious edifices and engaging in displays of conspicuous piety, expresses not only the actions of a good Buddhist devotee but also that of a man trying to assuage his conscience by unremitting and relentless merit making.

The conscience of Duṭṭhagāmaṇī Abhaya in turn produces an explosive political debate in history culminating in the violent polemic of the contemporary ethnic conflict between Sinhalas and Tamils in Sri Lanka. Since I have discussed in detail the history of this debate elsewhere, I shall highlight only its psychologically salient contours here.[44] Whenever Duṭṭhagāmaṇī appears as a conscience-stricken king, Elāra concomitantly appears as the righteous monarch; but when historical accounts present Duṭṭhagāmaṇī killing Tamils untroubled by his conscience, Elāra is transformed into a bad king and Tamils become marauders. Some versions, I noted, have the two brothers attending the funeral of the father: then also Duṭṭhagāmaṇī loses his conscience and Elāra becomes the evil king. Modern Sri Lankan scholars take one or the other position assuming that the preferred version was based on data or *evidence* that ancient writers possessed. I doubt whether these chronicles were concerned with evidence at all: they were carrying on a political argument against the idea of the king conscience-stricken at the killing of his enemies. Debate then is the contentious discourse that a narrative unleashes into history. It is the work of culture that appears in history, a key process in the transformation of one symbolic form into another. As such no history, not even modern historical writing with all its pretensions to objectivity and value of evidence, can escape its terrible embrace.

3

The True Parricide: Kāśyapa of Sigiriya, the "Lion Mountain"

Duṭugämuṇu, it should be noted, did not actually kill his father; yet his is clearly an Oedipal conflict that had two key components, namely, rebellion against the father and running away from home. Moreover the story of Duṭugämuṇu's agonistic relationship with his father was in all likelihood incorporated into the *Mahāvaṃsa* from popular (folk) legend, though this does not mean that the events described therein did not take place. Whether the narrative of Duṭugämuṇu's Oedipal conflict was true or false does not affect our argument. It was perceived by the compilers of the *Mahāvaṃsa* as a set of true historical events, as were the accounts of the monumental edifices he constructed (confirmed by archaeological evidence). The next parricidal king was also a historical figure in the same sense. The second book of the *Mahāvaṃsa* (dubbed the *Cūlavaṃsa* by Geiger) is almost a straightforward narrative of Sinhala kings. Unhappily, unlike Duṭugämuṇu, Kāśyapa is treated as an evil parricidal monarch and only the barest outlines of his reign are given. This reputation of the king is, I think, responsible for the total lack of interest in him in either Sinhala or Pāli literary works. The anthropologist is thus tempted to create an Oedipal history of this extraordinary monarch.

Book 2 of the *Mahāvaṃsa* deals at length with Dhātusena (mid-fifth century), the father of our parricide king.[45] His exemplary piety manifested in buildings and endowments to the Buddhist church and works of public welfare, such as asylums and homes for cripples, is described in detail. Among his many public works was the construction of the enormous irrigation reservoir, the Kalāväva, still extant as a monument to his greatness. But though the *Mahāvaṃsa* extols him as a pious monarch, Dhātusena was not all that nice.

> Dhātusena had two sons: Kassapa [Kāśyapa] by a mother of unequal birth and Moggallāna [Mugalan] by a mother of equal caste, and also a charming daughter who was dear to him as his life. On his sister's son he bestowed the dignity of *senāpati* (commander in chief) and gave him his daughter (to wife). Without blame on her part he struck her with his whip on the thigh. When the King saw the blood-stained garment of his daughter and heard (of the affair) he in his wrath had his nephew's mother burnt naked. From that time onwards (his nephew) nursed hatred (against the king), joined Kassapa, awoke in him the desire for the royal dignity, estranged him from his father, won over his subjects and took the ruler (Dhātusena) prisoner alive.[46]

Much of an Oedipal nature is hidden in this remarkable account. The king gives his beloved daughter to his sister's son, the ideal marriage in Sinhala custom. The sister's son whips his wife on the thigh, and the king burns his own sister naked! We are not told whether this was a branding or an execution, but in either case its sadistic and sexual component is clear. Let me construct a likely scenario that may help us understand this event. The *Mahāvaṃsa* says that the king's daughter was hit on the thigh "without blame on her part." The likelihood is that there *was* blame attributed to her and denied by the *Mahāvaṃsa* (and by her father). The blame must surely be adultery—hence the whipping on the thigh (perhaps even a recognized, if not standard, practice against an adulteress). But why burn the mother of the perpetrator of the act, who is after all the king's own sister? We only know that the king exacted a *lex talionis* type of revengeful act against her, perhaps overdetermined by his own Oedipal (and clearly sadistic) feelings for his own sister. This is a likely scenario only: the complex motivations of the actors in this story are impossible for us to unravel.[47]

To continue the story: Kāśyapa and his cross cousin (and sister's husband), Migāra, imprisoned the father and then on the latter's urging asked the king for his hidden treasures. The father took Kāśyapa's henchmen to the Kalāväva reservoir and after bathing there said: "This here, my friends, is my whole wealth."[48] Kāśyapa in his fury asked his cousin to slay his father; the latter bound him in chains and walled him alive in a niche in a wall. The *Mahāvaṃsa* ends this chapter with a *bon mot*: "Can a wise man when he sees the fleeting nature of the rich and of wealth crave for earthly joys?"[49]

In the next chapter (39) Dhātusena's son, now Kāśyapa I, assumed the throne while Mugalan, his brother, fled to India, biding his time. Through fear Kāśyapa built a fortress and palace in a huge rocky mountain rising six hundred feet from the plains of the dry zone south and east of the capital, Anurādhapura. The site was chosen because it was unscalable; the king "cleared (the land) round about, surrounded it with a wall and built a staircase in the form of a lion"—hence Sigiri or Sinhagiri, "lion rock."[50] The huge paws of the lion are extant today, and some of the greatest frescoes in Sinhala art still line the one outer gallery that remains. On the very top, recent archaeological excavations have revealed a site with a carefully laid out garden; extensive ones lie below, resembling later Mogul gardens, more elaborate than anything before in Sri Lankan history. One can appreciate the extraordinary nature of the conception and the achievement when we realize that it was probably completed in the early part of his reign. Since then it has remained unoccupied by any king, though a source of attraction to visitors through the ages.

The chronicle clearly says that later Kāśyapa "began to rue the deed he had done and with the thought: how can I be saved? he performed many meritorious works."[51] The later remorse of the king makes considerable psychological sense in terms of the information in the *Mahāvaṃsa.* His acts of merit making did not take the conspicuous character of his predecessors, but they are significant in relation to his wish for atonement. He gave his two daughters names crucial to Sri Lankan Buddhism, Bodhī and Uppallavannā. Bodhī is mentioned in the canonical text *Thēri Gāthā* (Psalms of the Sisters), but she is not as famous in Buddhist history as Uppallavannā. The Buddha considered the latter as the ideal female disciple, and her exemplary life and past births are recorded at great length in Buddhist texts. Especially significant is that she was once born in the dispensation of the Buddha Kāśyapa, the third Buddha of the present eon and namesake of our parricide king.[52] These names have other, even more powerful, connotations in Sinhala-Buddhist history. Bodhī is a feminization of the tree of Enlightenment (Bodhi) planted in the capital of Anurādhapura, and Uppallavannā is a feminization of Uppalavanna or Upulvan (Viṣṇu) who, according to Sinhala Buddhism, was given charge of the Island on a warrant from the Buddha himself. It was the god Uppalavanna who blessed Vijaya, the son of the parricide Sinhabāhu, when he first landed in Sri Lanka to found the Sinhala nation. Not only that, the *Mahāvaṃsa* says that Kāśyapa restored the great Isurumuniya temple in Anurādhapura and extended it and gave grants for its support. Further, he gave the names of his two daughters and his own to this temple. This is no invention of the *Mahāvaṃsa*; nearly four and a half centuries later an inscription by Mahinda IV states that the king had taken care that the Isuruamena-Bo-Upulvan-Kasubgiri Vihāra ("the temple known as Isurumuniya-Bo[dhi]-Uppulavan[na]-Sigiri Kāśyapa") be constantly supplied with water from the Tissaväva reservoir.[53] However, note that by this time the feminized names Bodhī and Uppallavannā have (significantly) reverted to their masculine forms, and if one had only the evidence of the inscriptions, one would have thought that this temple was named after the Bo tree and the God Uppalavanna, and of course after the king whose name here is a composite of Kāśyapa and Sigiriya, i.e., Kasubgiri.

The *Mahāvaṃsa* records the act of dedication of the temple as follows:

> When he handed it over to the *samanas* of the Thera school they were loth to take it, fearing the reproach of the people, because it was the work of a parricide. As, however, the King wished to give it to them, he presented it to the image of the Supreme Buddha. The bhikkhus agreed thinking: it belongs to the Master.[54]

I think one can be a bit skeptical of the account of the hesitancy of the monks. The crucial act is that the king dedicated the temple in honor of the Buddha himself, the exemplar of nonviolence and benevolence in Buddhist thought, and I think the embodiment of the good parental imago. Not satisfied with this, the king built a new temple near his mountain city, this time exclusively in the name of his two daughters.

Now our exegesis must unravel a hidden idea in the narrative—the strong belief among Sinhala people that the "sins" of the parents may be visited on their descendants. In Sinhala belief this is known as *divi dōsa* or *divula dōsa*. In myth the archetypal act of *divi dōsa* (leopard misfortune) relates to our paradigmatic myth—the betrayal of Kuvēni by Vijaya and narrated *in extenso* in the *Rajāvaliya*.[55] Kuvēni harbored her hatred and when King Panḍuvāsudēva (Paňḍuvas)—Vijaya's brother's son—became king, she took on a leopard guise and frightened the king to make him fall ill with *divi dōsa*. A famous ritual known as the *kohombā kankāriya* recounts this episode; the sin of *divi dōsa* is cured in that ritual and also in a low-country ritual of the *punā yāgaya*. I think the idea is an old one: Kāśyapa felt guilt and fear that, like Paňḍuvas, his ancestor, his daughters would be visited by the curse of parricide; this determined his actions, and in pity for them, he built a new temple entirely in their name.[56] In other words Kāśyapa did not, like Duṭugämuṇu and Asoka, construct a large number of religious edifices; he built only two and for very specific purposes. The later temple that he named for his daughters was given over to the Dharmaruci sect, a small religious group probably influenced by Mahāyāna, though sprung from the main Theravāda tradition and also supported by his own father, Dhātusena.[57]

The final act in the parricidal drama is the death of Kāśyapa, which again the *Mahāvaṃsa* and other historical sources have not (understandably) understood, or seem to have only partially understood. But with our knowledge of Kāśyapa's guilty conscience his death makes psychological sense. Before I examine the context of his death let me present some data that throws more light on Kāśyapa's conscience. His troubled conscience was internalized and involuted. The *Mahāvaṃsa* notes: "He kept the Uposatha festival and cultivated the *apamañña*, he took upon himself the pious duties [*dhutāngas*]. He made images, built alms halls and the like in great number: always he lived in fear of the other world and of Moggalāna."[58] The crucial references are to his observing the eight or ten precepts on *pōya* (holy) days; and *apamañña* are the cultivation of the four *Brahma vihāras*: *metta* (compassion), *karunā* (kindness, pity), *muditā* (empathy, tenderness), *upekkhā* (equanimity, serenity). Keeping the *uposatha* ("eight" or "ten precepts") was traditionally confined to old age; the deliberate cultivation of the *Brahma vihāras* was rare for ordinary laymen let alone kings involved in the world. One must assume that these acts were motivated by guilt and the need for expiation. What is quite extraordinary is Kāśyapa engaged in the practice of the *dhutāngas*, thirteen acts of extreme asceticism optional even for monks. These acts were rarely practiced by ordinary monks; only by some who lived in forest hermitages. I know of no king in Sri Lankan history who is said to have practiced them. It is not likely that Kāśyapa practiced *all* the *dhutāngas*, but the author of the *Mahāvaṃsa* was obviously impressed by his acts of extreme asceticism. It is almost certain one *is* dealing with a historical reality here or a well-known popular view of this king; otherwise the monks, who detested Kāśyapa, would not have recorded it. Consider some of these *dhutāngas*: living in the open without a roof (*abbhō kasika*); living in a cemetery (*sōsānika*); foregoing seats, as well as blankets and sheets (*yathāsantatika*); remaining seated without sleep (*nēsajjika*).[59] The conclusion is irresistible: Kāśyapa was practicing penances to expiate his guilt and punishing his body in acts of self-mortification. Like Ajātasattu, he too it seems, in killing his father, has also "murdered sleep." His death now begins to make sense in terms of the guilt-stricken, self-punitive parricide unable to sleep because of his troubled conscience.

According to the *Mahāvaṃsa,* Mugalan came from South India and gathered a large force and confronted his brother's army in the plains below. Kāśyapa on his royal elephant saw a marsh in front of him and turned around. His troops, thinking this a retreat, fled in disarray. "But the king with his dagger cut his throat, raised the knife on high and stuck it in the sheath."[60] The pragmatic interpretation of the chronicles must, I think, be supplemented with a psychological one, as Kāśyapa's final expiation for his act of parricide, a final act of self-punishment consonant with his acts of involuted asceticism. One can hardly blame the chroniclers for not having understood the full significance of this action.

Having considered Kāśyapa's parricide, we can now interpret the significance of his unique architectural achievement—the rock fortress of Sigiriya.

Kāśyapa's architectural feat was without parallel in the previous history of Sri Lanka. The importance of the city for the king is recognized in the Sinhala texts which prefixed the place name to his personal name, Sigiri Kasub (Kāśyapa of Sigiriya), which is how he is often popularly referred to even today. Like the composite name Kasubgiri of Vijaya IV's inscription, this too identifies the king with his monumental construction. The *Mahāvasā* says that he lived there because of his fear of the brother, but this fear, though reasonable, did not prevent Kāśyapa from coming down from his fortress to fight his brother openly in the plains below. Paranavitana in a more plausible hypothesis speculates that Kāśyapa was one of the first divine kings in Sri Lanka, and his fortress in the sky was in imitation of Kuvera (Vaiśravaṇa), and his argument is reinforced by the *Mahāvaṃsa* which says that his palace was "worthy to behold, like Ālakamandā, and [he] dwelt there like the God Kuvera."[61] But this is a simile used elsewhere in this text in respect of other kings. Though I think that his basic hypothesis that Kāśyapa was a divine king living in a cosmic city is correct, Paranavitana cannot explain why this fortified palace was called Sigiri or Sinhagiri, "lion rock." The huge paws of the lion at the entrance are still extant, and Geiger speculates that "there was a door between the two paws into the breast of the lion whence steps led through his body to the beginning of the stair case leading to the heights of the Sigiri rock."[62] Kāśyapa's was a unique and unusual conception, and without doubt his own vision. What then was his model? I suggest Sigiri is the lion city, for that is what it is. *Giri* in Sanskrit can mean "mountain"; in Sinhala it can also mean "city."[63] Kāśyapa identified himself with the archetypal parricide of Sinhala history, Sinhabāhu. Contrary to Geiger, Paranavitana, and other scholars who think that the entrance to the mountain was through a whole lion sculpture, I suggest that it was then as it is now—through the massive and imposing forelimbs of the lion.[64] Sinhabāhu means "lion limb," and this aspect of the ancestral hero's name is symbolized in the entrance to the fortress. In the myth the hero has the limbs and feet of his father, the lion; moreover the lion limb is the hand that did the dirty deed. The hero of myth, having killed his father, marries his sister Sinhasīvalī, and they build an entirely new city known as Sinhapura or "lion city." This is exactly what Kāśyapa did, and Sinhapura is equivalent to Sinhagiri, the "city of the lion." Kāśyapa identified himself with the primordial parricidal king of Sinhala myth, and insofar as this king is never blamed for his act of parricide, Kāśyapa also initially sought to absolve his conscience, not very successfully, for his own act of father killing. If I were to reinvent the Kāśyapa story I would see that he married his sister or half-sister, but that kind of true concordance between myth model and historical reality cannot occur because historical reality capitalizes on those Oedipal motives that are relevant to its own interests.

Who then can blame subsequent kings for abandoning the site, never to be occupied again as a royal capital?

What Happened Then? A Brief Afterword

After Kāśyapa's suicide, his brother Mugalan became king. The new king was no saint either, though the *Mahāvaṃsa* says that "he protected the world in justice."[65] He executed a thousand dignitaries who had supported his brother; he cut off their noses and ears and sent others into banishment. Consequently he was given the nickname the Rakkhasa (*rākṣasa*) or "demon." Yet he too built many religious and public works and was praised by the monks. One of his seemingly enigmatic acts that the *Mahāvaṃsa* does not explain is the installation of the statues of his maternal uncle and aunt in the temple that he built for housing the hair relic of the Buddha, an act that one must interpret as analogous to the installation of Elāra by Duṭugämuṇu. In the Sinhala kinship system the ideal marriage is where the mother's brother marries the father's sister, in which case Mugalan's act is one of recompense for those who suffered from his father's irrational rage and an unusual memorial for dead kinsmen.

Mugalan ruled for eighteen years, and he was one of the few in the dynasty of Dhātusena who died a natural death. His son, Kumāra Dhātusena, assumed the throne, but in his ninth regnal year he was killed by his mother's brother, Sīva. But Sīva had ruled only twenty-five days when he was killed by Kumāra Dhātusena's father's sister's husband. This man, Upatissa, now becomes king and he has a son, Kāśyapa. The second Kāśyapa commits suicide in the manner of his uncle and out of fear of an ex-monk, Silākāla, who was married to his mother's sister (his first wife) and his (Kāśyapa's) own sister (his co-wife). Upatissa dies of grief, and Silākāla usurps the throne. This man, the killer of his nephew cum brother-in-law and married to a woman who is a daughter to him in Sinhala kin classification, now becomes a pious king. Again tremendous acts of public welfare and the construction of religious edifices. Silākāla had three sons named Mugalan, Dāthāpabhuti, and Upatissa. Upatissa, the youngest, was favored by his father and stayed with him while the two elder brothers were made regents of provinces. Silākāla died in his thirteenth regnal year. Then Dāthāpabhuti killed his younger brother, Upatissa. Mugalan II, the oldest, confronted the fratricide in the field of battle. Dāthāpabhuti, realizing that the battle was going against him, cut his neck with his sword and committed suicide. He had reigned for only six months and six days. Now Mugalan II becomes king, a good king and perhaps the only decent person thus far. But not his wife. When Mugalan II died after a reign of twenty years, she had all his immediate kinsmen poisoned in order to install her own son, Kirti Siri Megha, as a puppet. But he only lasted nineteen days (nineteen years by other accounts), murdered by Mahānāga, a total outsider. A remarkable history: the murder of kings, fathers, uncles, brothers, nephews, and assorted patrilineal kinsmen. But never a single son. Not then, not before, not after.

Conscience and Culture: The Parricidal King in Buddhist History

We recorded three powerful parricidal kings in Buddhist history. What was their historical role? Following the lines of the preceding argument I suggest that the role of the parricide-king is overdetermined by two crucial "causal imputations"—by the existence or nonexistence of the king's remorse and by the values of the historical period in which he lived or, to put it differently, by a conjunction of deep motivation and culture. The parricide also poses a peculiar dilemma for the Buddhist monks who wrote these histories, a problem not unrelated to conscience and culture.

Two kings suffered great remorse: Asoka and Duṭugämuṇu. Both kings tried to assuage their conscience by acts of private and public piety. These typically are the feeding of monks, care for their welfare and solicitude, and the construction of extensive and gigantic religious edifices. Asoka is supposed to have built eighty-four thousand *stupa*s according to some accounts, and while the numbers are exaggerated there is no doubt that he did build many;[66] Duṭugämuṇu's works are amply confirmed by archaeologists. In addition to these both Buddhist kings instituted acts of public welfare—hospitals, reservoirs, alms halls, and so forth. Now these acts are expected of any good Buddhist king, and clearly there were nonparricidal kings who acted in similar fashion. However the ideal Buddhist king, self-consciously recognized by all Buddhists and reiterated in a variety of texts, is Asoka, the killer of his oldest brother; this act, if not literally parricidal, is symbolically so in Indian culture. It was this king then who initiated a type of historical regime that thereafter became the ideal for Buddhist kings. The parricidal king then overcompensates for his guilty conscience by acts of piety that make sense in terms of specifically Buddhist values.

The Asokan model is paralleled in Duṭugämuṇu's troubled conscience: he too is someone who symbolically killed his father, actually killed "millions of human beings," and killed an old man, Elāra, a just king and father figure. He recompenses in a similar fashion. These powerful kings then provide models for others who, even if they did not kill their actual fathers, killed the reigning monarch. If literal or symbolic parricide is exemplified in some of the best-known Buddhist kings, regicide is so common in Sri Lankan history as to be almost conventional if not predictable. The parricide provides a role model for the regicide, especially the kind of regicidal monarch who like the remorseful parricides performs acts of conspicuous merit making. Needless to say, while some regicides were committed as deliberate and calculated policy, some (especially those against older monarchs) might well have been overdetermined by Oedipal motives, since we know that the equation "king equals father" holds sway in fantasy life. This infantile equation is in a kind of feedback relation with the identical cultural equation of king as father (either as metaphor or symbol) in the polities of many nations, including Sri Lanka. Consequently even if the regicide's act was not initially instigated by Oedipal motives, it is likely to trigger guilt feelings based on the symbolic equation, king = father, that operates on the level of both childhood and culture.

The other parricidal king is Kāśyapa I. In his case he modelled himself on the Sinhabāhu myth, at least in the first part of his reign. The Sinhabāhu myth does not portray the troubled conscience of the killer in any explicit or implicit manner. The myth itself provides two techniques that help Sinhabāhu deny his remorse. First, insofar as his father is a lion and not a human being, it is possible to treat him as outside the human community and its ethical norms. The lion, on the final occasion, also lost *his* sense of paternal love, and this is why the arrow pierced him. It is interesting, though, that this rationalization is in fact made, something quite unlikely in paradigmatic Hindu Oedipal myths. In the dominant Sinhala Oedipus complex the father loves the son and does not demand his abnegation; the abdication of this love then makes the father vulnerable to the attacks of the son. There are, for example, a few Buddhist myths in the popular tradition in which the father kills the son, but, unlike the Hindu, these myths focus on the horrible nature of the crime, and the major point of the narrative is to condemn this lack of paternal love. In these stories, it is the Buddha, the very embodiment of goodness, who is the son.[67] Finally, in the modern stage drama, the son, as in the Greek *Oedipus,* does not know that it is the father that he is about to kill.

Kāśyapa then adopts this myth model in the symbolism of

Sigiriya. The king in this model thinks he can live without remorse. Initially he is not religious; he probably rejects the value system of his father. Sigiriya is an entirely secular city of the lion, as was Sinhapura built by his ancestor in the pre-Buddhist and preethical age. According to the *Mahāvaṃsa* account, the king was subsequently afflicted with remorse and then started building religious edifices and performing acts of personal piety on an unusual scale. The subsequent remorse of the king, I think, makes both psychological and historical sense. The suicide of the king in the field of battle with Mugalan, the legitimate heir, is the final atonement for parricide. The monks who composed the chronicle had no psychological understanding and interpreted the suicide in pragmatic terms.

The parricide in history was influenced by previous myth models, yet he himself can become a myth model operative in history, either of the long run or of the short run. Asoka and Duṭugämuṇu had a profound influence as models for emulation by later kings, but not Kāśyapa. Even in Kāśyapa's case, the manner of his death produced a model of the short run for the kings who followed him or for those who wrote about the kings who followed him. Prior to Kāśyapa the ideal death is through face-to-face combat between two kings. This important ideal is exemplified in the combat between Elāra and Duṭugämuṇu. With Kāśyapa a new model was created: suicide in the field of battle. This act was soon repeated by his sister's son, who also bore the name of Kāśyapa. He "cut his throat, wiped the blood from his dagger and stuck it in the sheath."[68] I noted that this was in fear of the rebel Silākāla, who was his mother's sister's husband and also incestuously married to his (Kāśyapa's) own sister. Empiricist historians might think this a piece of *Mahāvaṃsa* fakery, but, whether invented or not, the account makes psychological sense. Suicide, like other acts of violence, produces its own replicable fads.

The last suicidal king was Dāthāpabhuti, the son of the cruel and pious Silākāla. Dāthāpabhuti, as noted earlier, killed his younger brother and then had to face his older brother, Mugalan II, face to face in battle. But instead of fighting his brother as the classic model would have it, he cut his own neck. He probably did not have enough time to put his sword back in its sheath! This unfortunately produced a slight deviation from the ideal model, but, as I said earlier, a myth model can only in the rare case be exactly replicated in empirical reality or, for that matter, in imagined history.

The existence of parricidal kings not only poses problems for these kings in history, but insofar as such history is written by Buddhist monks, it also poses an ethical dilemma for these historians. Ever since Asoka the alliance between the king and the monk order was central to the social order of Buddhist nations. The king is the chief donor (*dāyaka*) and supporter of the order and defender of the faith; the order in turn gives legitimacy to his rule. The king's relation to the monk as donor is only an exaggerated form of that existing between ordinary layman and monk. When the layman gives alms or donations, the monk reciprocates by wishing him good karma (merit), a happy rebirth, and ultimate achievement of *nirvāṇa.* But parricides, regicides, and mass murderers in the field of battle violate the axiomatic basis of the faith as the religion of nonviolence. Yet, in a paradoxical way, it is the very guilt of the parricide-regicide that fuels the drive for supporting the religion and for ensuring the welfare of the people by beneficial public works. Therefore it should not surprise us too much if monks justify all sorts of violent acts such as regicides, mass killings, sexual violations by kings—all except the act of parricide. Thus Asoka and Duṭugämuṇu are forgiven and extolled in the texts. Asoka, murdering his eldest brother (and other siblings), cannot be *easily* forgiven since, in Indian thought, this comes close to parricide. Therefore the chronicles split him into two: Caṇḍāsoka (the cruel Asoka) and Dharmāsoka (the just Asoka). Once this distinction is made, idealization of Dharmāsoka can go on untrammelled by his dark past. History must absolve the killer-hero of his past sinful acts.

Duṭugämuṇu's case is somewhat different. Having insulted his father he ran away from home biding his time. Yet there isn't the slightest doubt that Sinhala people thought his actions horrendous, though not parricidal. Thus Gāmaṇī was renamed Duṭṭhagāmaṇī or Duṭugämuṇu, the "cruel" or "disobedient" son. He carries this taint with him in his very name (as indeed does Asoka, for those who know him as Dharmāsoka also know that he was once Caṇḍāsoka). However hard monks try to cover up the past, it cannot wholly be suppressed. According to the chronicle, Duṭugämuṇu is absolved for his sins, and he will end up in the heaven of the next Buddha, Maitreye, as his attendant. Yet *someone* was troubled by these monkish rationalizations and introduced a proviso, however pompous, into the *Mahāvaṃsa* account. The very chapter that deals with the monks absolving Duṭugāmuṇu for blame ends with the almost anomalous, yet ethically significant, observation that perhaps only through a recognition and awareness of past evil is "redemption" possible. "Should a man think on the hosts of human beings murdered for greed in countless myriads, and should he carefully keep in mind the evil (arising from that) and should he also very carefully keep in mind the mortality as being the murderer of all, then will he, in this way, shortly win freedom from suffering and a happy condition."[69]

The actual parricide by contrast gets short shrift in history. The reason is simple: parricide is viewed as one of the five *ānantariya* sins, those for which there is practically no forgiveness, except in the very long karmic run.[70] Thus Kāśyapa is roundly condemned, and the monks state clearly that there is no forgiveness for him. The great Sinhala king of the sixteenth century, Rājasinha I, another parricide whom I do not discuss here (see appendix 1) is, like Kāśyapa, still burning in the *avici* hell. Rājasinha receives solace in Saivism, and it is probably no accident that Kāśyapa supported the Dharmaruci sect, a Buddhist school influenced by Mahāyāna, possessing a more liberal soteriology and perhaps a path of atonement through penance. Modern historians by contrast adopt a different strategy: they either ignore the parricide of the king (Kāśyapa) or deny it (Rājasinha).

Not so, however, with ordinary people, who, untrammelled by priestly theology, were more forgiving of their kings and measured them in terms of other values. It is also likely that the parricidal king, like the hero of myth, permitted the people to express their own Oedipal feelings for the father by vicarious identification with him. Like Lévi-Strauss's sorcerer, the parricide in history abreacted for the people at large their own troubled fantasies. Be that as it may, ordinary people view the parricide differently. This comes out clearly in the case of Rājasinha I, who, in spite of parricide and apostasy, was a popular hero fighting the Portuguese, the first Western colonizers in Sri Lanka. He could muster enormous popular support for his military enterprises.[71] Regarding Kāśyapa I the evidence is scant, but it is clear that he was no mass killer like Asoka, or his own half-brother, Mugalan who, we noted, was nicknamed *rākṣasa* (demon). The internal evidence of the *Mahāvaṃsa* suggests that Kāśyapa was probably liked by some members of his family. His half-sister (Mugalan's own sister) married Upatissa, and they named their son Kāśyapa, an act quite unthinkable if he was not popular with at least some members of his family circle.[72]

The true parricide is tainted at birth. There is something wrong with his "blood," his descent. In the archetypal myth Sinhabāhu has the polluted blood that comes of bestiality, however noble the beast. A similar taint is reflected in the two actual parricides of history. The technique is simple: the parricide lacks legitimacy since he was the offspring of a woman of doubtful status. If the king had been a good guy, this would not cause the chroniclers much of a problem, but as a parricide they highlight (or invent) this feature. Thus Kāśyapa was the son of the king but born of "a mother of unequal birth."[73] Rājasinha's reign is only summarily dealt with in the chronicles, but the popular accounts depict him as the son of the king by a dancing woman. The symbolic parricide suffers from a milder taint, but it has nothing to do with his legitimacy, even if, as in the case of Asoka, that legitimacy could in fact be questioned. Both Asoka and Duṭugämuṇu carry the taint of their past actions in their names. Furthermore, Asoka, like Oedipus and Richard III, suffered a bodily defect: he was ugly from his very birth.[74] And Duṭugämuṇu's future bloody actions are anticipated by the unusual craving his mother had for the blood of the Tamil general, just as Ajātasattu's mother craved for blood from her husband's right shoulder. These cravings are not "normal." In Sinhala thought (and perhaps in South Asian thought in general) these bloody cravings are found in queens who will eventually give birth to bloodthirsty demons.[75] The unusual pregnancy craving is a sign of the nature of the being about to be born.

Within the framework of South Asian culture the long-term operation of Buddhism produces an unintended structure of the long run—an Oedipal complex, an Oedipal myth, and an Oedipal history that reverses the Hindu motivational structures. It does this, we noted, by undermining the sacraments of Hinduism and liberating the individual from the ties that bind him to the family and larger society and to sacramental religion and ritual. All of this meant that Buddhism released its own version of Oedipus that in turn produced two radical consequences. First, it introduced a profound moral paradox. Though killing of the parent is an *ānantariya* sin, the long-term operation of the religion gave the parricide a center stage in complex, myth, and history. Second, the parricidal monarch is a true innovator. The clear case is Asoka, who introduced a specifically Buddhist policy and conception of the state and public welfare, reversing the polity of his predecessors.[76] So was Duṭugämuṇu. Though Buddhism was introduced into Sri Lanka in the reign of Devānampiyatissa (250–210 B.C.) it was Duṭugämuṇu's reign that gave it a special stamp by identifying the religion with the dominant ethnic group. Kāśyapa was also a radical innovator—his monumental city was the first of its kind in South and Southeast Asia.[77] Insofar as there is some concordance between the Sinhala Oedipus complex, myth, and monarch, one can, I think, infer a third consequence for the people at large—a capacity to accept change, including radical change, a revolutionary potential in society. Radical social changes are not *caused* by the Sinhala Oedipus. This would be a naive formulation. Yet the Sinhala Oedipus complex, myth models, and historical examples, in conjunction with social institutions that have been introduced or erected, might effect radical changes in society. The Sinhala Oedipus can symbolically overthrow the father, and I think he has the potential, under favorable circumstances, to overthrow the political order legitimated by traditional paternal authority.

The Demonic Oedipus: Ethics, Conscience, and Culture

It seems clear that conscience is inextricably linked with ethics and ethics with culture. Buddhism is fundamentally an ethical religion but one with a universalist ethics. In Buddhist practice it has always been problematic to justify the ethical pluralism of caste. In this religion, there is no ethical arbiter like God; its ethics unfold in the operation of the impersonal law of karma. In popular practice Buddhists try to ward off bad karma and accumulate good by conspicuous "merit making." Undoubtedly there is a mechanical calculus to merit making as anthropologists have noted time and again, but it is a mistake to assume that merit making, owing to its compulsive nature, is cut off from inner morality and conscience. Western anthropologists, I believe, have not understood this phenomenon because they cannot understand how conscience can operate without personal responsibility and God. Personal responsibility is fundamental to karma theory, but it exists without God.

I am not suggesting that merit making is entirely fueled by conscience. This is to commit the reverse of the fallacy of mechanical merit making. Checkbook philanthropy can be as mechanical as merit making, but on the other hand it can also be provoked by felt inner morality and conscience.

Even the most mechanical type of philanthropy, American or Buddhist, is inextricably involved in morality, for it is a recognition of morality, however gross it may be, that instigates giving. One can question the *quality* of this morality by asking whether it is in fact fueled by inner conviction and conscience or not. The South Asian king, as Shulman has brilliantly shown, is a killer by the mere fact of his being king.[78] He has to cancel the bad effects of karma (*pāpa* or "sin") by the support of the religion and its specialists. The killer king by the very fact of playing the culturally prescribed role of donor recognizes the morality of karma, but he might not recognize it with conviction as a matter of conscience. What our Buddhist case studies suggest is that giving to monks and acts of public welfare such as the construction of hospitals and alms houses and irrigation reservoirs are related to such things that in the Western language game are labelled as guilt, remorse, and the wish for atonement—that is, the workings of the conscience. The ideal type of the king with a conscience is the actual or symbolic father killer; but others are not exempt. This does not mean that some (I cannot provide a numerical indicator) were not acting in a gross or mechanical manner. But a purely mechanical calculus of giving cannot function for long. The guilt-stricken kings are the ones that provide the unremitting drive toward atonement expressed in the ethic of works.

The myth of Sinhabāhu can be interpreted in this light. We noted earlier that these events occurred in a preethical, pre-Buddhist age. In this age the hero can act without conscience. He kills his father and marries his sister, but he is not troubled by either act. The father loves him, but he does not reciprocate this love. With Ajātasattu, the Buddhist age has dawned. Here is the killer of the father—the father who, like the lion, loves his son even though this love is not mutual. But something has changed: the hero is stricken by remorse, and he cannot sleep. When he hears of the birth of his own son he can empathize with how his own father might have felt when he, Ajātasattu, was born. The name Sinhabāhu ("lion limb") has heroic connotations, but with Buddhism, myth gives the hero a doubtful appellation: Ajātasattu, Caṇḍāsoka, Duṭugāmuṇu.[79] Arjuna, the true Hindu ruler, is worried about the killing of *kinsmen*; Asoka, the true Buddhist ruler, is worried about the killing of his *people*. Duṭugāmuṇu's example expresses the kind of paradox that emerges when a universalist religion is particularized as the ideology of the state. Ironically the very representatives of a universal religion have reneged on the universal ethics of that religion, as they have done in other religions. What then happens to the pre-Buddhist Oedipus in the age of Buddhism? Surely it would be naive to believe that the killer without conscience has suddenly vanished from history simply because of the introduction of an ethical religion? Sinhala thought clearly recognizes an age where ethics and conscience have surfaced, but unlike the Sinhabāhu myth which leaves open the powerful questions of responsibility, love, and ethics, the new remorseless killer is the subject of unequivocal criticism and moral judgment. He reappears not as a hero but as the *demon* of exorcistic ritual and myth. He is someone who must be banished from the mind and body of the patient and from the ethically grounded social and moral order.

Sinhala demon exorcism has been superbly analyzed by Kapferer, and I refer the reader to his account.[80] For my purpose, I shall describe the myths of two well-known demons from my previous research. One of the most important demons in the Sinhala pantheon is Sanni Yakā (the demon of fevers) who is propitiated in almost all low-country exorcistic rituals and especially in a ritual that bears his name (*sanni yäkuma*). Sanni Yakā is the parricide without conscience, as his myth of origin indicates. He is the son of the king of the Licchavis (an important republic in the time of the Buddha). According to myth, recorded in several ancient Buddhist texts and in contemporary ritual sources, the Licchavis also sprang from brother-sister incest. This was possible in a pre-Buddhist age, and people did not realize the bad karma of their origins.

> From them [siblings] were born the people of Licchavi
> Blessed with countless years of life
> They multiplied greatly, they were beautiful
> Such were the people (*gotra*) of Licchavi.
>
> O Licchavi people blooming with greatness
> They knew not death and decay
> They spent their days in love and happiness
> Till their old bad karma emerged.

This bad karma of course surfaced in the dispensation of the Buddha (by some accounts a previous Buddha, Dīpankara).

> Sankapala, a great king of the Licchavis,
> Married a beautiful princess.
> Constantly affectionate he lived with her
> —We shall recount how she conceived.
>
> The king did not know she was pregnant.
> He fought in a far country and returned victorious,
> To his palace he returned victorious
> But he saw the pregnant queen and was wroth.
>
> The king was angry at the foetus—which he had
> created—
> "If you do not inform me what happened here
> I shall torture you cruelly and put you to death,"
> Thus he told the maids whom he summoned.
>
> One maid invented a cruel lie,
> "The very day you left for the wars

She fell in love with the chief minister
And lay in the beautiful bed together."

The king's anger flared forth like fire:
"I don't want to see her ever again.
Take her to the cemetery and on a *käbälla* tree
Hang her and split her body in two."

The hangman [lit. torturer] heard the king's command.
He held the queen by her hands, dragged her along;
He tortured her continually and hung her on the tree,
Cut her in two with one part hanging on the tree.

The powerful prince lying in that womb
Fell down, but the parts united again.
Not the least bit weary he stood up.
Thus the powerful chiefly demon was born.

He grew up feeding on his mother's corpse.
He took various dreadful guises.
"I will destroy the cruel king my father.
All humans I see I'll tear apart."

He hoped to kill the king with poisons.
He collected poisons from the forest.
In the ancient manner he ground them into lumps.
Holding these lumps he charmed them.

The eighteen lumps that he had made
Changed into eighteen powerful demons.
The eighteen demons stood up in three lines
Waiting for warrant [*varan,* permission] for the demon dance.

"What warrant do you want? What warrant should I give you?
Capture humans and cause illness through wind, phlegm, and bile;
I'll give you warrant to enter the city of Visal and destroy the Licchavis."
"Let's us go," said the nineteen demons, and leapt into the city of Visal.

Shouting deathly cries they ran into Visal city.
Wearing the guise of death he [Sanni] entered the king's palace:
"You listened to falsehood and you slew my mother.
From today Death will stalk your citizens."

Thus he said and he broke the king's neck.
He ate the king's flesh and drank his blood,
He looked for all the humans hiding in the palace,
Having drunk their blood he went into the city.

Thousands daily they used to kill and eat;
The stench of dead bodies spread wide and far;
Hosts of *preta*s [evil spirits] invaded the city of Visal
Pestilence spread over the whole city.

The myth does not end here. The demon is ultimately tamed by the Buddha. He must desist from killing humans and accept the supremacy of the Buddha. Like all other demons, he is rendered ethically salient for Buddhists insofar as he represents the devalued Buddhist ideas of greed, hatred, and delusion. The father killer without conscience exists in the world, but he is now given a place in an ethically governed moral order. He is always out there in the demon world ready to strike. He is deliberately summoned by the exorcist and then banished from the body of the patient and his social world.

The dawn is about to break, alas!
The moon is about to leave, alas!
The demons have run helter-skelter, alas!
The Sanni demon departs, alas!

In all these rituals the demon is summonable from the demon world into the human world and the household of the patient; he enters the ritual arena and is brought under control by the exorcist; he is then sent back to the demon world. The reality of the world of violence and parricide is clearly recognized. It is out there and in the minds of patients. The demon who embodies it parades before the audience, expressing the demonomorphic reality he represents for those who are not yet afflicted, but well might be sometime or other, for all know that the demon that struck the patient can strike anyone.

What about incest and the wish to marry the sister? This is embodied in the myth of Garā, who appears at the conclusion of communal rituals for gods. Let me summarize below his myth of origins as reported by Paul Wirz.[81]

Garā was the son of a king. At his birth royal astrologers predicted that he would desire his own sister. To avoid this calamity the king sent his son to live away from home with the king's brother. As the prince grew up he was called Daḷa Kumāra, or Tusk Prince, because of his tusklike canines.

> The prince's mother gave birth to a beautiful girl named Giri Dēvi, but Daḷa Kumāra was never told about this. The girl grew up, and it was decided to give her in marriage. The king's brother was invited, but not Daḷa Kumāra. However, the prince heard about the wedding and went home to attend the nuptials. He demanded to see his sister, and in his rage he smashed everything around him and ate all the food. Ultimately he was shown the princess. Daḷa Kumāra was seized by a deep passion; he carried his sister away to the forest and lived with her there, subsisting on wild foods. One day, when her brother-husband was away, Giri Dēvi ran away and hanged herself from some forest vines.
>
> Daḷa Kumāra was in a rage; he caused great havoc. Even the gods were afraid of him, since he shook the wish-fulfilling tree (*parasatugaha*) under which the gods assembled. Ultimately he was shown his sister's corpse; but his rage, fever, and thirst grew worse. Finally the gods pleaded with him to desist from killing and destruction. He was given twelve attendants by the king of demons, Vessamuni.

Every single myth of origin of this demon refers to sibling incest or his marriage to his sister, Giri Dēvi. All accounts emphasize his ugliness: huge building phallic nose and eyes and protruding tusks. Saturn threw poison all over him to render him even more hideous. Sanni, Garā, and other demons are physically deformed because they, even more than the parricide of history, carry the taint of incest, parricide, an innate propensity to violence and with it the possible destruction of the social, moral, and cosmic order.

In most rituals Garā is presented in androgynous form as a combination of Garā and Giri. As an androgynous being Garā presents to the audience one of their deepest desires, forbidden yet tempting. In Garā rituals such as the ones I recorded in *Pattini,* his (her) sexual appetite and insatiable appetite for food are deliberately linked together, parodied, and subject to ribald humor—the typical Sinhala way of handling anxiety. Garā's ritual role is as the remover of impurity, the misfortune (*vas*) that might have arisen from error (however inadvertent) in the performance of ritual, and from such things as the evil eye, evil mouth, and evil tongue. He gobbles up these impurities since, as the embodiment of impurity (sibling incest), he cannot be polluted any further. Thus he appears in the conclusion of large-scale rituals. In the ones recorded by me he ends up by removing the misfortunes (*vas-dos*) from every portion of the house to the eaves, to the stile and the fence, and from there into the river that ultimately will take them to the mouth of Makara, the mythical dragon. The priest addresses him either in his male or female form or as an androgynous being. For example,

> Go away demoness, stay not in the doorway or within the house
> Go away demoness, not outside either, or on the roadway
> Not at streams, brooks, and places where we bathe, go away demoness
> Go away, we evoke the power [of the truth] of the many Buddhas.

Something more than physical pollution is being banished—from the minds of people. The fantasy of incest, as of parricide and other perverse desires of the unconscious, is brought from the world of demons into the social world, then paraded, laughed at, and once again sent back to the demonic world. In ethical terms such things as incest and parricide can exist without conscience, but not in humans. They have been pushed into the underground of the religious life, the world of demons, which is a symbolic transformation, at various levels of remove, of the *other* underground—the unconscious, the dark region where fantasy and forbidden desire prevail. In the ethical Buddhist age, a human being must become a demon—deformed, polluted, bloodthirsty—if he is to exist without ethics and conscience. As much as demons are born out of human wombs, so killers without conscience born of human wombs are not only demons of sorts, but can in fact be reborn as demons. Buddhism introduced an ethicization of life affecting every level of individual and communal living including the conscience. The priest, chasing Garā and Giri away from the house, recites:

> The blessings of the Buddha refuge for the doorway and inside the house
> The blessings of the Dharma refuge for the outside and wherever we go
> The blessings of the Sangha (Monk) refuge for this village and this land
> For me and those assembled here, the blessing of the Three Refuges.[82]

Cosmos and Psyche

When I first wrote on Kāśyapa, on the basis of the *Mahāvaṃsa* text, I said that unlike Duṭugämuṇu, who spawned a lot of stories, there were none on Kāśyapa. Then I caught myself short: Obeyesekere, you really don't believe this! It is certainly the case that there are no stories of Kāśyapa recorded in palm leaf manuscripts, since these were written by monks who had for the most part condemned Kāśyapa to the hell of *avici,* if not of oblivion. However, during a two-month period of intensive research, my assistant, Tissa Kumara, and I collected about forty texts about this king, of various degrees of interest, detail, complexity, and narrative skill, from contemporary villages in and around Sigiriya. One informant, M. Baiya (age sixty-two) of the drummer caste in the village of Nāgalaväva, startled us with the following example of the creativity of the folk tradition.

> According to our knowledge there were four entranceways to Sigiriya. One is the western gate at our village. There existed a road from there through the village of Nāgalaväva to Anurādhapura, we conjecture. We think that there was a road to Pollonaruva from the northern gate. For protection a moat was constructed right round. Because he could never enjoy the pleasures of heaven he built the Sigiriya fortress to be a heavenly world. He inquired from the *arahant*s and monks and found that the heavenly world was located in this way with the royal Mt. Meru surrounded by a "moat" (*äla*). In the great ocean on the top of the Mahāmeru Parvata Rāja ("the great king rock, great Meru") is the heaven world. Since I will surely go to hell, the king thought, I will create a heaven in this our human world. The moat is the Great Ocean. The royal mountain—Mahāmeru—is Sigiriya mountain. Here he painted divine damsels (*divya surangaṇā*) and *apsara*s and lived there enjoying heavenly pleasures, from what we have heard. Because of the sin of killing his father he knew he will not enjoy the pleasures of heaven. Thinking he would enjoy the pleasures of heaven on earth, he built a heaven on the Sigiriya fortress. He thought he will enjoy pleasure and got wall paintings done, and got architects to build a palace on top and resided there.

When I first heard this interpretation of Sigiriya, I was pissed off, my vanity wounded, since Baiya was practically giving me back in part my own interpretation of Sigiriya. But I immediately checked myself, and my momentary pique was replaced by the thrilling feeling that his tradition of thought had anticipated my own and that, insofar as interpretation is ontological and part of the human species condition, the informant might well come up with a sophisticated interpretation that the anthropologist foolishly thought was his special expertise or privilege. Close questioning of Baiya, a barely literate and dignified man with an impressive bearing, convinced me that this was not his unique interpretation, but one he had heard from his parental generation.

Will Heine-Geldern and Paul Mus rise from their graves, and what will they say to Baiya, I wonder? Let it pass. Yet let me remind the reader of the revolutionary significance of the scholarly interpretation of Southeast Asian cities in terms of cosmic kingship, with the capital as a replica of Mt. Meru and the king as an incarnation of a divinity.[83] It is this tradition of scholarship that led the early Paranavitana to interpret Sigiriya in similar terms, except that Paranavitana thought that Kāśyapa was an incarnation of Kuvera and the fortress itself a replica of Ālakamandā, Kuvera's kingdom. But the tradition represented by Baiya has anticipated—long before Heine-Geldern, Paul Mus, and Coedes—this theory of cosmic kingship. Is this so surprising? These three historians were trying to present to modern audiences an interpretation of Southeast Asian kingship they thought was consonant with the native point of view. They stated the unstated theory of the people. It therefore should not surprise us if in fact the indigenous traditions had explicit interpretations of cosmic kingship such as Mr. Baiya's. This has implications for our scholarly interpretations also. Local traditions, if used judiciously, might well help us solve problems pertaining to both history and myth. There is no technique or method to do this; only critical judgment and debate among us scholars. Therefore, let me now, tentatively, extend my symbolic interpretation of Kāśyapa's city of the lion based on indigenous sources that are consonant with my theory of culture and deep motivation.

The first part of Baiya's thesis—that of Sigiriya as the replication of the cosmic mountain (Meru)—was not related to us in any detail by other informants (except two who cursorily mentioned it). But the second—that Kāśyapa was engaged in heavenly pleasures—was widely cited. Most informants said that after he killed his father, he wanted to forget the terrible nature of what he had done by indulgence in sensual pleasures. One man said that an artist, a friend of the king, painted the beautiful women to distract the king from brooding. The frescoes were interpreted in this light, that is, as divine damsels (*apsaras*, *surangaṇā*) or as women of his harem, the *veśya* of Sanskrit literature.

The two interpretations are not contradictory. Shulman, dealing with a later period in South Indian literature, points out that the women of the harem or *veśya*s were the human counterpart of the *apsaras*.[84] In the cosmic model, the king is a divinity; as a divinity he is accompanied by divine damsels or *apsaras*. *Apsara* etymologically means "going in the water or between the water of clouds," and this is in fact how *apsaras* are represented in the frescoes, as Paranavitana has noted. Shulman correctly saw the fertility significance of the symbolism here. That this interpretation of contemporary villagers is an ancient one is clear from the poetry scribbled on the mirror wall, across from the extant frescoes, by educated tourists visiting Sigiriya between the eighth to tenth centuries. In a monumental study, Paranavitana has translated and annotated 685 of these poems.[85] These Sigiriya graffiti, as they are now called, are the fantasies of visitors provoked by the startling beauty of the women depicted there. One theme that emerges from these poems is that these women were divine damsels (this was not the only theme). The king lives with them enjoying sensual pleasure. The folk interpretations of today were the interpretations of educated visitors to the site about two centuries after the "actual" events.

The relation between the divine *apsaras* painted on the wall and the women of the harem can now be explicated. The *apsaras* are mythical beings who have a role in relation to the mythical persona of the king as divinity. As a divine being he lived in a palace at the very top of the peak, and much of this has been excavated by archaeologists. Yet note that the king is a live being, whereas the *apsaras* are not. The latter are therefore recreated in the women of the harem, the earthly incarnations of the mythic *apsaras*. The *apsaras* are painted among the clouds, for that is where the king as divinity himself resides. The king's human *veśya*s or courtesans live below on the lower levels where the king exists as a ruler among his subjects. Shulman says that the king's women came from different parts of his realm, binding him, as it were, to the larger body politic.[86] Modern excavations have revealed the most conspicuous feature of the lower levels: well-laid-out bathing pools. Overlooking several of these is a site of a pavilion which archaeologists have foolishly labelled "the summer palace."[87] Enclosed underground channels tap the rainwater coming down from the mountains, and these are ingeniously forced to erupt into fountains, some of which work even today. The women bathing in the pools and the fountains around them recreate symbolically the primordial meaning of *apsaras* as "going in the waters or between the waters of clouds." The women of the harem are *objects* of the king's pleasure, *subjects* of the realm, and *representations* of divine damsels. They are related to the multiple personae of the king.

The historicization of myth by the *Mahāvaṃsa,* the mythicization of events by the popular tradition—this is what the texts of Kāśyapa provide. The fact that we can question the *Mahāvaṃsa* historicity might be valuable in figuring out the historicity of the events of Kāśyapa's time, though this is outside our present task. The *Mahāvaṃsa* history constricted our interpretation by restricting the reign of Kāśyapa to eighteen years. We can easily prove this to be false, since eighteen is a popular category number in the literature of the time, and all kings who belonged to Dhātusena's patriline were honored with this number![88] It is therefore possible for Kāśyapa to have reigned much longer. This means that there could very well have been a considerable age gap between the early hedonistic Kāśyapa and the later ascetic. Kāśyapa acts out a special kind of myth model in Buddhism represented in the Buddha legend known to every Buddhist. In this myth the young Siddhārtha lived a life of unmitigated hedonism, ideal-typically represented in music, dancing, singing, and the pleasures of the harem. He is isolated in his palace, ignorant of the nature of the real world of suffering and impermanence. This isolation is shattered when he leaves the palace and sees "the four signs": illness, old age, death, and the transcendence of life's ills in the image of the composed monk. In this myth model the impetus to renunciation is satiation with hedonism. In Kāśyapa this is acted out in terms of his own life. He identifies with the parricide of myth and creates a city of the lion that is also a heavenly city. He tries to drown his guilt through hedonism! But this is no solution to the guilt of the parricide. He later seeks alleviation, penance, and forgiveness in his religion, Buddhism, not in the harsh orthodoxy of the main tradition, but in the Mahāyāna-influenced groups, the Dharmaruci and Sigāla sects, more forgiving of the king as the Buddha himself was of the other parricide, Ajātasattu. It is in this state that the brother arrives, the true legitimate heir, the shadow of his father, as the monk Nigrōdha was the shadow of his father, the brother that Asoka murdered. Remember that all the texts say that originally Kāśyapa fled to Sigiriya in fear of his brother. I believe this expresses the unconscious anxiety of the parricide—the irrational fear of punishment—and has nothing to do, in terms of the story, with objective reality at all. It embodies a psychological truth. When the brother returns, the older anxieties also return since the legitimate heir is the father himself, the son being the father of the man. This is beautifully expressed by one storyteller, P. Kiribanḍā, a physician of Kalundāva village.

> Mugalan came back and sent messengers to Kaśyapa to enter into battle. But that time Kaśyapa had had a dream during the day and tried to run away. His two queens restrained him. "Don't heed such things," they said. But he couldn't sleep owing to the sorrow he felt for the sin he committed. He used to get into a fright and run away.
>
> It was at this time that Mugalan sent his two emissaries. The emissaries told him that he must go fight his brother, but the queens told him not to go. Kāśyapa said: "I shall not let him be, I'll eat him up," and descended the rock. And with his army he is now going to confront Mugalan. Sigiri-Kaśyapa went in front on his elephant. Now he saw the vision of his father dead, with his head bent, broken, in front of him, like a shadow, or an illusion. This must have been an apparition (*avatāra*). But in order to avoid this he turned his elephant around, and his army thought: "Now he is lost and retreating," and they all ran away. This was between Sigiriya and Anurādhapura. Now Kaśyapa thought, "If he captures me he'll kill me or if not I'll be killed [by an assassin]." So it is said that he severed his head with his sword and fell down. The moment they heard it the two queens jumped to their deaths below, according to what we have heard.

The vision of the dead king, his father, expresses once again the guilt of the parricide. It is, like Ajātasattu's vision of the infant swathed in cobras, an image transformed into thought. This terrifying experience occurs just before he meets his brother returning from another land, the Rose-Apple continent (India) which in traditional cosmology was located south of Mt. Meru. The folk account, unlike the *Mahāvaṃsa* episode (quoted below) is psychologically closer to the truth. The parricide goes to confront the brother, the rightful heir. The return of the brother is, in the conscience of the parricide, the return of the father. He then has the terrifying experience of the returning father exactly as he appeared when he was killed on his (Kāśyapa's) orders (according to Kiribandā's story).

None of the folk accounts in my possession describe the battle between the brothers in any detail, though all of them refer to the turning back of the elephant. The *Mahāvaṃsa* (39:20–28) historicizes the folk tradition with a description of the battle scene and provides a rational explanation of Kāśyapa's defeat.

> Now in the eighteenth year the royal hero Moggallāna [Mugalan] came hither at the information of the Nigaṇṭhas [Jains] with twelve distinguished friends from Jambudipa and collected troops at the Kuṭhari-vihāra in the Ambaṭṭhakola district. When the King heard of it he thought: I will seize and devour him, and though the soothsayer declared it to be impossible, he went forth with an array of forces. Moggallāna likewise (set forth) with an army ready for battle, accompanied by the heroic friends, like the god Sujampati who fares forth to fight with the demons. When the two hosts fell on each other like two seas that have burst their bounds, they fought a mighty battle. Kassapa [Kāśyapa] espying a great stretch of swamp in front of him, turned his elephant to seek another road. When his troops seeing that, with the cry: Friends, our commander flees! broke up in disorder, the troops of Moggallāna cried: "We see their backs!" But the King with his dagger cut his throat, raised the knife on high and stuck it on his sheath.

This is a rationalization and an empirical rendering of a succinct folk version. In these folk versions, Kāśyapa's elephant gets stuck in the mud and retreats, or Kāśyapa in order to avoid the marsh turns his elephant around. The subjects interpret this as defeat. Why so? The simple commonsensical idea of the king's retreat is not sufficient. In Sinhala-Buddhist thought, when a kingdom has no heir (or no legitimate heir) the royal elephant is sent forth, and he roams around town and, picking the right person to be king, carries him back to the palace. The *retreat* of the royal elephant then is the reverse action and a cue for defeat, a symbolic event and not a simple literal one. It is a retreat occasioned by the return of the legitimate heir. Our oldest informant, a female, 115 years of age, put it thus: "Kāśyapa's elephant while going towards Hirivaduna came across a marsh and tried to avoid it. The king thought that the elephant was afraid of Mugalan and was therefore turning around. 'Better to die here than by my brother's hand,' he thought and cut his own throat." The elephant's retreat is also a cue to the guilt-ridden Kāśyapa to cut his throat and put the sword back in its sheath. Caput. End of anthropologist's fantasy.

❹

Psychic Structures of the Long Run: The Marriage of the Hero

The Oedipal circle of kin discussed in the previous lecture concerns a set of primordial motivations in the human family. According to Freud these motivations are manifest in representations, ideational and affective, such as those we know as dream or fantasy. An analyst might demarcate a subset of these as significant for the neuroses; they form what one might call an "Oedipus complex," forms of life that exhibit cross-cultural family resemblances. The work of culture may transform these ideational representatives into structures or relatively perduring clusters of meanings, values, or symbolic forms that often operate as "myth models." Oedipal *myths* are psychic structures of the long run in this sense; they are perduring symbolic forms that embody deep motivations. So is the parricide in Sri Lankan history, as is the filicide in the Hindu.

When one focuses on the *differences* among complex, myth, and history, one is faced with the importance of symbolic remove as a key process in the work of culture. If the complex is the analyst's delineation of a set of motives that are significant for the neuroses, the myths embody these motives at various levels of remove, some closer to the Oedipal motives and paradigmatic of them and others more distant, wearing many masks. The parricide in history is on an entirely different level of remove, for he must be constructed in the imagination of people out of their historical consciousness in a larger context of events and institutions. The parricide in history is reflective of neither the Sinhala Oedipus complex nor of their paradigmatic Oedipal myths, but without them he would not have emerged in history.

It might be argued that insofar as parricide (and regicide) concern the domain of politics, they have no bearing on the psyche. I have been told that succession to kingship was ill defined in Sri Lanka, and consequently parricide and regicide constitute a class of events that bear on the problem of succession, and consequently belong to the political domain.[89] This is in fact the case not only of the Sri Lankan Oedipus but also of the Greek, and of Shakespeare's Macbeth. But all these myths transcend their political dependence, as they do the societal, the psychic, and the cosmological domains. Thus even the fragmentary account in the *Mahāvaṃsa* that deals with the *story* of Kāśyapa transcends the issue of succession to embrace his inner anxieties, his fear of his brother's return, his concern for his daughters, his dread asceticism, and his dreadful suicide in the field of battle. I try to interpret these elements or details of the story. Moreover these elements occur in other discourses also. The folk versions I have collected hardly bother with the political issue. And as far as Sinhabāhu is concerned it has gone into so many areas of popular culture including ritual and theatre that the question of domain is meaningless. Wherever that myth surfaces it always deals with the fundamental problem of how the Sinhalas came into being.

A psychic structure of the long run exercises a hold on the imagination of people because it is *constitutive* of a variety of "domains" and straddles different, even contradictory, universes of meaning and experience such as those born of psyche, bios, cosmos, and polis. Interpretation unfolds these universes of meaning but is always incomplete, always tentative, since acts of interpretation, whether those of the anthropologist or the native, are themselves conditioned by time, place, and history.

Against this background let me now analyze the Sinhala manifestation of the marriage of the hero, a key element in the Freudian Oedipus. I noted earlier that the sister is the partner of fantasy and myth. But this is not the only type of marriage of the hero, for I also noted that the god Skanda's relationships to his wife and mistress are extolled in Sinhala myth and ritual life. I suggest that this theme, like the marriage of the sister, is also a psychic structure of the long run, a symbolic form that crystallizes a set of deep motivations. It also takes us back to the paradigmatic myth of Sinhabāhu.

Let me then get back to the later part of this myth of parricide and sister marriage where Sinhabāhu casts his son and rowdy followers in the ocean on a ship. Instead of the dry account in the *Mahāvaṃsa,* let us move into present-day life where the same events are sung by contemporary priests in an ancient ritual.[90]

> The teacher of the three worlds, our Muni,
> Was nearing his death hour
> He reached the cool shade of
> The sal-tree in Kusinārā.
>
> On the day of his death
> He summoned God Sakra
> He gave Sakra the charge
> Of preserving the kingdom of his teaching.

"To Vijaya who will land
In this blessed Lanka
Give him a *pirit huya* [sacred thread]
Sprinkle him with *pirit* water."

Thus he ordered and
Departed from life,
And God Sakra was given
In charge of this country.

The royal Prince Vijaya
Left his native land
With his band of soldiers,
Courtiers and great riches.

In his ship he sailed the seas,
Reached Tammännā forest.
When he got off his ship
A huge wilderness stared at him.

He was in a quandary
In the jungle he saw
A huge *nuga* [banyan] tree
And he lay under its shade.

Heeding the command of our Lord
The God Viṣṇu, together
With Sumana, his brother,
Accosted this mortal.

Disguised as hermits and,
As was the custom, with his hand
He sprinkled him with *pirit* water
And gave him the *pirit* thread.

Then Pulvan, the Sura [i.e., Uppalavanna or Viṣṇu]
Vanished from sight that day.
A *yakini* [demoness] named Kuvēni
Lived in this wilderness.

Serving this *yakini* was
Another hardhearted demoness.
She took the shape of a bitch
And appeared before the king.

Then the royal prince thought:
"There are humans in this forest."
In order to seek them
He dispatched his warriors.

As they arrived in groups
Kuvēni concealed them.
Not seeing them return, the tired king
Thought, "Demons live here."

"Many demons of all sorts
Live in this huge forest.
What use being a prince
When such misfortune has befallen me?"

Such the sorrow that visited him!
He drew his sword and swung it,
Rose up from his seat,
Walked, searching for signs [of his men].

He reached a vast pond
And when he looked around
Reclining, a slim creature
Her hair golden wires,

Her forehead like the sickle moon,
Her eyelashes like the rainbow,
Her nose curved like a goad,
Her twin eyes like blue lotuses.

Her two lips like tender *nā* leaves,
Her mouth like a petal,
Her teeth, dainty white flowers,
Freckles, shimmering on her breasts.

Her two hands like golden creepers,
Her breasts like golden pots,
A golden *pella* [distaff?] on her shoulders,
A gold spindle in her hand.

A damsel spinning cotton
Seeing the royal prince
Was fired by love's passion,
But concealed it in her heart.

"My warriors who arrived here
Did you hide them," he said,
"With your powerful spells?"
"I don't know about it," she said.

When she spoke thus
He drew his golden sword,

And clasped her flowing hair
With his other hand.

"If you don't release my men
I will chop off your head."
When he spoke thus sternly
The *yakini*'s heart quaked.

"If you make me your chief-queen
I shall release your warriors.
Keep me as your wife,
And rule over this country.

"The joy of being king
I'll see that you possess."
When she spoke thus to the prince
He was sorely tempted.

"It's marriage I ask you,
O my noble lord,
Never your affection to waver
Or leave me ever.

"With your hand on your golden sword
Swear to me and say,
'I will make you chief-queen.'"
Said the *yakini* then.

The royal prince was tempted,
His mind in a whirl,
Drunk with his passion,
Took her to him.

He took his golden sword,
Placed it on her bosom—
To live without betraying her,
With this adorable maiden.

He plighted his troth
To give her happiness and joy
And betray her never.
Thus he wedded the maiden.

She created a golden mansion
Hung with heavenly flowers,
Furnished for divine comfort,
For happiness immeasurable.

While he was with the maiden
Sleeping in her blissful bed
He heard a thunderous roar
As wide as many leagues.

Frightened the prince awoke,
"What noise is this," he cried,
"For a *yakā* [demon] in Laggala
A *yakini* [demoness] from Loggala.

"Would be taken away
To be married
On this day itself."
Then said the prince:

"Having listened to this nice chatter
Of Kuvēni, the *yakini,*
A royal prince like me
By a *yakini* like this

"Was given a kingdom.
What good has it done me?
I shall certainly leave you
And go back to my own country."

When the king spoke thus
Kuvēni who heard these words
Struck by a great sorrow
"What shall I do now?" she thought.

"I shall give you a joy
You will never regret of."
Without telling her husband
Early next morning,

She transformed herself into a mare,
Carried the king atop her.
They were ready to go,
And the prince was pleased.

The *yakini* made a chariot,
Took a sword in her hand
To slaughter the *yakā*s
Towards Tammännā forest

They rode, and slew the *yakā* hosts.
She thus banished the king's fear

And so they were happy
And lived for a time together.

Their palace was a heavenly city,
Divine ornaments they wore, and they
Lay together in heavenly bliss.
She was as beautiful as a goddess.

His prime minister zealously
Behind the *yakini*'s back
Tells the prince thus:
"Your happiness is unlucky,

"For the kingship of Sri Lanka
And wearing the crown thereof."
When it was spoken thus to the king,
"A chief-queen have I none,

"Hence to be king
It is not right," he said.
The ministers were overjoyed
And to South Madurāpura

They sent money of all kinds
And letters of friendship.
The Pāṇḍi king was pleased.
Her beauty shone like Sri Kānta's.

The royal princess
And all her various maidens
Gold, silver, pearls, and gems
He crowded the ship with.

And ordered that they sail
To Tammännā forest.
According to the king's orders
They sailed the high seas.

Beautifully, with unfurled sails
They swept the high waters
And landed at Mātoṭa.
When the king heard the news

He was greatly pleased.

[Vijaya now renounces his marital ties with Kuvēni and orders her to leave the kingdom with her children into the forest. Kuvēni makes a last and futile attempt to remind the king of his vow but to no avail. The king tells her that she is a *yakini* (demoness) and he cannot live with her.]

"O my loving lord,

"In the great Tammännā forest
Beside the vast pond
Under the shade of the *nuga* tree
Only yesterday, it seems, I spun cotton.

"With hearts so close together,
"I will not betray you," you said,
Placing your hand on your golden sword
You swore—how can you forget?

"When I was plucking cotton
Didn't you know I was a *yakini*?

"When I concealed your warriors
Didn't you know I was a *yakini*?
When I changed myself into a mare
Didn't you know I was a *yakini*?

"When I killed the advancing demons
Didn't you know I was a *yakini*?
What terrible sorrow are you giving me?
I even killed my kinsmen."

He wedded the princess
Sent by the Pāṇḍi king.
They came for the coronation
With a great following.

A cavernous hall was built
With doors seven.
They entered the great hall
And shut the doors.

The coronation over
They were pleasantly together,
But the *yakini* kept her old hatred
To drink the king's blood.

She created a diamond tongue
Seven leagues long,
Took a fearful leopard guise
To hack the king in two.

Then she stormed the seven doors
And stuck forth her tongue,
But God Sakra that day
Broke it by the root,

Broke it into fragments,
But one fell on the ground.
It gave a she-leopard roar.
The king beheld it in fear.

His heart began to quake,
Cough, phlegm, and such ailments.
He had got the *divi-dōsa* [leopard misfortune]
But was cured by the Thousand Eyes [i.e., Sakra-Indra].

When this *dōsa* was banished
He lived for thirty-eight years.

Both the *Mahāvaṃsa* and the ritual texts carry the story further. Vijaya's rightful consecrated queen from Madurai was barren, though the brother-sister union of his children by Kuvēni was fertile and produced the Väddas, the aboriginal hunters of Sri Lanka. In order to ensure the legitimacy of Sinhala kingship, ministers got down Pañḍuvas, Vijaya's brother's son, from Sinhapura to assume the throne. He did, but both the *Mahāvaṃsa* and popular accounts mention that the curse of Kuvēni now fell on Vijaya's patrilineal heir, Pañḍuvas, who fell ill with *divi dōsa,* or "leopard misfortune." We noted earlier that it was the fear of this kind of misfortune that prompted Kāśyapa to give his daughters Buddhist names and dedicate Buddhist temples in their honor. These ancient myths are recounted in modern-day rituals also to banish from present audiences the visitation of ancestral sins and the misfortune that comes from the utterance of false oaths.

The Vijaya myth is a continuation of the myth of Sinhabāhu, but paradigmatic for a different set of purposes. Sinhabāhu we noted is the myth of origin of the Sinhalas; it is also the paradigmatic myth of the Sri Lankan Oedipus. Vijaya is the oldest son of Sinhabāhu who establishes the Sinhala *nation* in Sri Lanka. The Buddha himself foretells that his religion will be established here and Upulvan ("the color of the blue lily," i.e., Krișṇa or Viṣṇu) becomes the guardian of the people and the nation. I noted that on the one hand Vijaya retains the blood of the lion through the sibling marriage of his parents. But on the other hand he is also tainted with the bestial and incestuous unions of his ancestors. So the myth requires that he must, while retaining his lion blood, be purified of the taint of bestiality and incest. This is achieved in the myth through several devices. Firstly, Vijaya is reborn in another land through the symbolism of the watery rebirth. Secondly he is blessed by Upulvan; the holy water washes the sins of the past and the holy thread protects him from the dangers that await him. He had been shaved (symbolically castrated) by his father; but now he is reborn and ready to people a new earth with a new nation.

Thus far the Vijaya myth is a sociological paradigm of the greatest significance for the Sinhalas, "the people of the lion." The history of their nation begins with Vijaya. But the Vijaya myth continues the Oedipal story, and on the level of unconscious signification it embodies a constellation of Oedipal motives different from those in the Sinhabāhu myth.

Vijaya, the myth emphasizes, is a rebel, though not an "admirable" character. His rowdiness in one sense is culturally expectable from someone born out of bestiality, incest, and parricide. Yet on another level of Oedipal motivation Vijaya rebels against his father, though it is not out of the love for the mother as with Gaṇeśa. The rebellion is not direct, but displaced on his father's subjects. The father shaves his head in half, an act of both humiliation and symbolic castration, and banishes him. A possible Oedipal confrontation is avoided by this. The myth therefore embodies the solution to Oedipal confrontation by avoidance—a version of the Skanda model. More significant for our present purposes is Vijaya's marriage, first to Kuvēni, the attractive demoness, and second to the unnamed princess from Madurai, his legitimate wife—again a continuation of the Skanda model but with a significant difference. According to early Sinhala custom a king cannot be consecrated unless he is married—and married, it is implied, to one of his own status. Though the *Mahāvaṃsa,* written by ascetic monks, gives a dry and wry account of Kuvēni, the popular versions are all in her favor. Her beauty and fidelity are extolled, and her sense of anguish at Vijaya's betrayal is expressed in beautiful verse. What then is the theme being expressed here? It is like the Sri Lankan Oedipus, a psychic structure of the long run, the first representation of the theme of Pattini and Mādēvi, and then of Dēvasēna and Valli Amma discussed in lectures one and two. Vijaya has two wives, as do Kōvalan-Pālanga and Skanda. Like Pālanga he betrays the seductive and attractive wild woman. His situation is the reverse of Skanda's, who leaves his legitimate spouse and enjoys bliss with the wild woman, Valli, the forest creeper. In spite of the substantive differences in the myth, there is a common core to all three. The sexually desirable woman whose beauty is extolled is the wild woman; the legitimate spouse is required by the necessities of conventional life, but she is not sexually desirable. In the Vijaya myth she appears simply as a figurehead or cipher. In both the Vijaya myth and the Pattini story, it is the sexually desirable woman who is fertile; the legitimate woman is barren or a virgin like Pattini. In the Skanda story it is true that Valli does not produce children, but this is because no Hindu deity produces children out of ordinary intercourse and conception, and this norm has to be maintained. Yet her *implicit* capacity for childbearing is clear in the customs at Kataragama. Women who are barren, or couples prior to marrying, make vows to Skanda and Valli for children (and needless to say to make their marriages erotically desirable). When a child is born the parents fulfill the vow by carrying the child on a pouch slung from a sugarcane branch—the sugarcane is the arrow of the Indian god of love, Ananga. So is it in the case of Vijaya; Kuvēni produces two children from him, the brother and a sister who then cohabit and produce the Pulindas or the Väddas, the aboriginal hunters and gatherers of Sri Lanka. But Vijaya's marriage with his legitimate spouse is barren. His line is continued by bringing in Pañḍuvas from India, Vijaya's brother's son, who can continue the inheritance of the lion.

The mythology of the two wives then, following the argument of the first lecture, is a later resolution of the Oedipal crisis—at least one type of resolution. In the Sinhabāhu myth model, the hero marries a sister; this fantasy can be objectified in myth but cannot be expressed in historical or ordinary reality. The second solution is of a different order: it is based on the erotic attraction to the mother. We noted that the incest taboo is so strong that the idea of marrying the mother can barely be countenanced. But paradoxically the mother becomes the object of sexual vilification and obscene abuse. One resolution to this paradox is at marriage; the "good mother" who is virginal and sexually unapproachable, and the sexually desirable "bad mother." The wish to split the maternal imago and possess both is a powerful fantasy that is expressed in the myth models that we have discussed. This basic psychic motive then can be incorporated into mythic structures that also incorporate other functions in Sri Lankan culture and consciousness. Thus Vijaya not only marries the desirable Kuvēni; her children produce the aboriginal hunters. Hence this part of the myth is a charter that recognizes and legitimates the Väddas, but also justifies their "anomalous status" with respect to the Sinhalas. The myth is not synonymous with unconscious motivation; it is an embodiment of it. Nor is the myth a replication of reality. This is naturally impossible, if we consider what happens in history.

In history the deep motivations of the double marriage get embodied in a different direction. The king, like Vijaya of the chronicle, must marry a legitimate princess who will provide heirs for the royal line. In addition to the *mahēsi,* "the chief queen," the king either marries a lesser queen (or queens) from among the nobility and ordinary folk, or he has sexually desirable women from his harem, or both.[91] Often the lesser queen is the exact symbolic substitute for the "wild woman." For example, Kāśyapa's mother, we noted, was a woman of "lower caste" according to the *Mahāvaṃsa,* while Mugalan, the rightful heir, is the product of a correct marriage. Popular texts I collected in the field clearly state that Kāśyapa's mother was a Tamil woman and extol her attractiveness, whereas Mugalan's was a Sinhala (and therefore legitimate). The *Mahāvaṃsa,* in the very chapter that deals with Kāśyapa's father, Dhātusena, states that an illustrious predecessor of Dhātusena, Mahānāma, had a son, Sotthisena (Sena, the cripple) "sprung from the womb of a Damila [Tamil] woman but his daughter Saṃghā was the daughter of the Mahēsi [the chief queen, legitimate woman]."[92] The low-caste or Tamil woman versus the legitimate or Sinhala wife is the implementation in the history of kingship of the dialectic of the harlot and the virgin, the wild woman and the tame wife. In the previous example, the illegitimate Sotthisena is made into a cripple and subsequently murdered by Saṃghā, the legitimate heir. In other words, the deep motivations are embodied at different levels of remove in the institution of the king's women.

Thus the deep motivations of parricide, Oedipal marriage to a sister, or the double marriage to the virgin and the harlot are conceptualized in a variety of psychic structures ranging from fantasy to myth and to history and back into everyday fantasy life. This fantasy emerges in adult consciousness which idealizes the mother; in adult language of abuse which degrades her. It appears very powerfully in the consciousness of adolescents who can unashamedly say that they would like to marry someone (idealized) like the mother. Yet the sexually desirable object in adolescent fantasy is the wild woman, represented traditionally in low-caste groups (like the untouchable Roḍiyas) and nowadays in the female servant in the domestic household. Contemporary society produces conditions that enhances the fantasy of the wild woman and the realistic desire to possess her. In bourgeois life, at least, the servant is the person who in fact performs the grosser aspects of maternal caretaking such as washing and cleaning the child. For the son, it is actually possible, as he grows up, to seduce this surrogate mother, the wild woman, and violate the incest taboo in fantasy while consciously adhering to it.

Appendix: Rājasinha I

Rājasinha I is one of the most fascinating of Sri Lankan kings, the first apostate in its history. The third book of the *Mahāvaṃsa* says that he killed his father, but Portuguese accounts do not corroborate this. Some Sri Lankan historians also do not accept the *Mahāvaṃsa* view. They are generally agreed, however, that Rājasinha's father, Māyādunne, and his (Māyādunne's) two brothers hired assassins to kill their father, Vijayabāhu. This event, though not recorded in the *Mahāvaṃsa,* is popularly known as the Vijēbākollaya (the despoiling of Vijayabāhu).

I also do not know whether it is simply an accident that when Rājasinha ascended the throne he took the name of *Rājasinha,* which means "royal lion," the first Sinhala king to adopt this name and the first king to have the name *sinha,* "lion," as part of his name. Since then the word *sinha* as part of one's name has become so popular both for kings and commoners that we fail to see its historical uniqueness. On the other hand it may well be that Rājasinha simply borrowed a name popular with South Indian Hindu kings (an act not unrelated to his parricidal motivation).

Rājasinha I was an extraordinarily resourceful monarch and military strategist. He began to expand into the territories subdivided in his father's reign. Some of these were now in Portuguese hands, and Rājasinha waged relentless war against the Portuguese and shrank their area of control to Colombo and its immediate environs. He also tried to subdue the new independent kingdom of Kandy but failed. From our point of view what is striking is his apostasy. He categorically rejected Buddhism and became the first and only royal convert to Shaivism. The *Mahāvaṃsa* speaks of him thus:

> His [Māyādunne's] son was the mighty Rājasīha [Rājasinha] by name. He went forth, fought here and there and won the victory. The victor, the great fool, even slew his own father and brought the royal dignity into his power, the

> deluded one. In the town of Sītavaka the king known by the name of Rājasīha, for a time did good, devoted in faith to the Order. But one day the king, after he had bought a gift of alms, asked the grand theras [monks] full of anxiety: "How can I undo the crime of my father's murder?" Then the wise theras expounded him the doctrine but could not win over the wicked mind of this fool. They spoke: "To end the committed crime is impossible." Full of fury like some terrible poisonous snake which has been struck by a stick, he asked the adherents of Siva. The answer they gave him that it was possible, he received like ambrosia, smeared his body with ashes and adopted the religion of Siva. He annihilated the Order of the Victor [Buddha], slew the community of bhikkus, burned the sacred books, destroyed the monasteries and thus barred his way to heaven. Become a (dead) tree-trunk in the cycle of births, he adopted a false faith.[93]

The historical reality was much more complicated than this simplistic account of the king suggests, yet it does express the parricide's rejection of the father's faith, his acceptance of an alien religion, which, if true, introduced a profound change in the history of Sri Lanka. Rājasinha was too involved in his war with the Portuguese and with the king of Kandy to institutionalize his adopted religion on a more general level, but the potential for doing so certainly existed. Rājasinha, like his great parricidal predecessors, was a radical innovator.

There are many popular stories about Rājasinha I, but unfortunately they have not been collected. Consequently I must postpone my analysis of the reign of this parricidal monarch.

LECTURE FOUR

Freud and Anthropology: The Place Where Three Roads Meet

❶

The First Intersubjectivity: The Anthropologist and the Native

Recent thought in the social sciences has attacked some of the fundamental assumptions anthropologists have entertained about the nature of intersubjective relations and consensual understandings in the cultures they study, including such fundamental notions as "community" and "culture." In this lecture I shall limit myself to the relevance of both anthropology and psychoanalysis in claiming to represent "the native's point of view," that is, an "emic" or a phenomenologically "correct" account of the other culture. This task cannot be accomplished, however, without facing squarely the prejudices many anthropologists share regarding the applicability of psychoanalysis to the study of other cultures.

One of the commonest criticisms directed against psychoanalysis by anthropologists, both at the coffee table and in more formal settings, is that it is a theory of the mind developed in the West and is only applicable to Western man. Some would even argue that it at best tells us about neurotic Victorian people, especially female hysterics. I have much to say about this criticism in my discussions of metatheory, but here I want to pin down the more flagrant and absurd parts of this argument, and some of the hidden ones.

Let me start with the latter—the hidden part of this point of view. In ordinary discourse among anthropologists one constantly hears about Western culture and non-Western culture, as if they were opposed entities. This discourse is especially deep-rooted in Anglo-American thought but extends to other Europeans also. There might be some broad unity in European cultures, but the attempt to subsume the rest of the world as non-Western is as bad as the "third world" label that is rapidly taking its place. I doubt that this is simply a manner of speaking through the use of a useful, if crude, binary distinction. It is certainly the case that anthropologists, more than anyone else, would be the first to defend relativism, but nevertheless this discourse is a reality and in my view contains implicit assumptions rooted in the Western anthropologists' cultural tradition. From the time of the earliest colonizations the Europeans felt themselves distinct, a superior race apart from the benighted savages who had neither civilization nor the true religion. This is only too well known as the attitude taken by missionaries and colonial administrators everywhere and often justified by intellectuals like Macaulay. It is unlikely that anyone was exempt from them, the anthropologists included. The nineteenth-century theories of evolution were not only theories; they were also ideologies that placed the Europeans on the top of the evolutionary scale. Hence the well-known statement by Tylor:

> The educated world of Europe and America practically settles a standard by simply placing its own nation at one end of the social scale and the savage tribes on the other, arranging the rest of mankind within these limits according as they correspond to savage or to cultured life.[1]

It is difficult to assume that these recent and deep prejudices have simply withered away. While the grosser forms of ethnocentrism rarely prevail among anthropologists, I do think that the distinction they make regarding the uniqueness of Western man in opposition to the rest of mankind is the continuation of the same tradition and, one might add, the same arrogance. Indeed one cannot undertake to study the other culture without such arrogance, for it defies ordinary common sense that a young person with imperfect language skills could go into the field and study another culture to present the native's point of view during the period of a year or, at most, two. This defiance of common sense and this arrogance, to which all of us nowadays subscribe, have paid high dividends in our discipline for it is indeed likely that ordinary common sense might simply be wrong in this regard and arrogance pays off—some of the time.

The Sinhalas have a proverb to describe people in their own society who think they are special. They say "Have you emerged from an elephant's arse hole?"—as against ordinary people born from human wombs. It is the fact that we are born from human wombs, they say, that gives us our common humanity underlying formal differences. I think psychoanalysis tells us a similar message: Victorian neurotics did not come from an elephant's arse hole, but share instead a common humanity with us all. As early as 1924, Ernest Jones in his address to the Royal Anthropological Institute claimed that the cross-cultural use of psychoanalytic theory would "humanize" the savage by showing the fundamental common nature that he shares with Western man.[2] I think this is what any theory (metatheory) should do: it should exhibit enough nomological rigor to show the rules or principles that govern our common humanity while at the same time possessing enough flexibility to illuminate the different forms of life that spring from this common base. The problem of universality versus relativism then becomes a largely empty one.

Now from the hidden discourse to the flagrantly absurd. It is of course true that psychoanalysis is a Western science, but I am puzzled as to how contemporary history, anthropology, and practically every intellectual discipline are not. One could perhaps argue that insofar as ethnography presents the native's point of view it is exempt from this criticism, but this surely cannot be the case since, for the most part, the native's point of view is reexpressed in the language of the ethnography, which is generally English or some other European language. One does not have to subscribe to a Whorfian position to know that language is not a culture-free tool and that the description of another culture in a language that is different from the one being described must render any attempt to mirror the original entirely dubious. Ethnographic translation is a mode of appropriation of the culture, but not through a fusion of horizons; it incorporates the description of the other into the familiar grammatical and semantic categories of one's own language. This is of course over and above the fact that it is simply impossible anyway to present a native point of view since such a viewpoint does not exist—as I shall show presently.

Both Giddens and Winch make the point that the informant is like the social scientist in several regards; he also has theories of his society and other conceptions, ideal and real, of how the world should be organized.[3] But what further complicates this picture is that he too has controversies (or "debates") with his own fellows regarding all of this. In this sense he shares our own contentious natures as scholars. In other words a native point of view perhaps exists only in the rare case, let us say, of key eschatological notions, such as, for example, the nature of the Buddha and the meanings of karma and salvation in Sri Lankan Buddhism. But even here, while there can be unanimity, there is no uniformity in the discourse that expresses that unanimity. One area of the sociocultural life might be more subject to controversy than other areas. Thus Buddhism, owing to its scriptural tradition and its educated monks who interpret the scriptures, may produce consensus on key eschatological meanings, but the spirit cults that have neither, permit greater leeway. And when it comes to things like politics, marriage, sexuality, and so forth, opinions begin to differ greatly. In other words internal controversy and hidden discourse or debate render any notion of a native point of view a complete impossibility, except in certain areas where specific historical and sociological parameters render it less amenable to controversy. But this cacophony of voices is never heard in the ethnography; that work presents that which does not exist in reality—the natives' point of view.

Many ethnographers give primacy to the natives' point of view by constructing an "emic" picture of the natives' society or culture. But an emic perspective is misleading for a variety of reasons. The very incorporation of the alien culture into the vocabulary and grammatical structure of the anthropologists' language makes nonsense of the emic claims of the investigation. Since, moreover, the natives' point of view is a misnomer, an emic presentation based on a misnomer must itself be a misnomer. The anthropologist never has a chance of sampling a range of native opinions, though ethnographies are peppered with pronouncements indicating that this is indeed the case—hence statements such as "villagers say that . . . ," "according to my informants . . .". In reality the anthropologist works with select or key informants who for the most part make themselves available to the investigator. An "emic" perspective in this situation? The classic monographs that claim to present the natives' point of view in fact have constructed ideal types of *X* or *Y* culture, based on a point of view taken, implicitly or explicitly, by the ethnographer. What Weber says of Christianity in the Middle Ages is as apposite to ethnography as it is to history and historical sociology:

> Those elements of the spiritual life of the individuals living in a certain epoch of the Middle Ages, for example, which we may designate as the "Christianity" of those individuals, would, if they could be completely portrayed, naturally constitute a chaos of infinitely differentiated and highly contradictory complexes of ideas and feelings. This is true despite the fact that the medieval church was certainly able to bring about a unity of belief and conduct to a particularly high degree. If we raise the question as to what in this chaos was the "Christianity" of the Middle Ages (which we must nonetheless use as a stable concept) and wherein lay those "Christian" elements which we find in the institutions of the Middle Ages, we see that here too in every individual case, we are applying a purely analytical construct created by ourselves. It is a combination of articles of faith, norms from church law and custom, maxims of conduct, and countless concrete interrelationships which we have fused into an "idea." It is a synthesis which we could not succeed in

> attaining with consistency without the application of ideal-type concepts.[4]

Weber recognized that an ideal type often requires analytical concepts, at the very least, of the sort Geertz calls "mega-concepts." And these concepts must be ordered logically and articulated systemically with the empirical data. This means they have to be "fused into an idea," to use Weber's phrase for characterizing the overall conceptual unity manifest in the ideal type. Thus even a seemingly phenomenological description of reality is impossible without ideal types. The "natives' point of view" is an arbitrary construction, an ideal type. Ideal types, mega-concepts: these very words imply a rational understanding of reality that is the investigator's. In other words, one cannot understand the world without the mediation of abstract concepts, ideal types, metalanguages, distantiating discourses; consequently all rational interpretation of the first intersubjectivity is "etic."

Informants, however, cannot be dispensed with, except by those anthropologists who deal with historical texts. But even here one can imaginatively reconstruct the voices of informants, though few ever do so! One might argue that even if the voices of informants are disparate one might be able to work with a few key informants whose opinions have greater force. Let me deal with this problem using religious texts as examples. Obviously, I might get similar texts from different informants, but it is their interpretation that is important, because I must incorporate this into my work as the native point of view.

1. Even the best informant may not know the meaning of the texts he presents. Often texts come from a long tradition, and during this period the meanings of the texts may have been lost or forgotten. *We* assume the existence of a continuous tradition, but this is our fiction and might have little reference to reality. Let me give examples of what I mean.

Meanings are sometimes inaccessible or unknown to the specialist. I have often interviewed priests and exorcists who were excellent *performers,* but I got no exegesis on the names of the deities, places, and so forth mentioned in some of their religious texts. I think this is a phenomenon of all ancient traditions: names of places, persons, and deities are mentioned, but they have ceased to have relevance for contemporary religion. They are mentioned in the text, and the text must be recited at religious rituals. But what is recited does not always make sense even to the specialist of the cult. In this situation the anthropologist is helpless except when he has independent historical evidence, in which case he is at an advantage: his very command of literary or historical material helps him to interpret the text that baffles the native specialist. A simple example: in a well-known Sinhala ritual for pregnant women known as *raṭa yäkuma,* there is an important collectivity of female deities known as Riddhi Bisavu (that can be glossed nowadays as "queens possessed with the power to fly"). I have not *yet* been able to get any informant to provide a gloss or exegesis or any reasonable account of these deities. Neither could I, until I found a reference to "Riddhi" in the *Mahābhāratha* as the consort of Kuvera, the overlord of demons. Now Kuvera appears in Sinhala ritual as Vessamuni (Vaiśravana), the god of the northern quarter and overlord of demons. It is his dread command that the exorcist uses to control demons. Thus it makes perfectly good sense that the Riddhi Bisavu are (or once were) consorts of Vessamuni-Kuvera in the Sinhala ritual also and incorporated into it from older sources traceable to as far back as the *Mahābhāratha.* From my superior historical knowledge and also from comparative material from other parts of the country, I can fill in the gaps that are left out or wrongly interpreted by the indigenous specialist.

The above is an example of a meaning hidden from the informant because it is buried in a tradition. To unravel a hidden meaning involves an archaeological thrust, a scholarly investigation into the past. But assume this tradition was inaccessible for scholarly investigation owing to the lack of historical or comparative data. The ethnographer must attempt an interpretation that is uniquely his. A great deal of ethnographic interpretation is of this quality. What then can mitigate the idiosyncratic nature of the ethnographer's interpretation in this situation? Comparison, search for family resemblances in other cultures, and above all theoretical understanding of the sort that psychoanalysis provides in its metapsychology.

Hidden meanings are only too common in ethnographic texts, but their existence is rarely conceded by us. *We* tend to assume that the meaning of a text is accessible to informants or that informants provide the only valid exegeses. I wonder whether this strategy would work if I were to consult informants of various sorts for interpretations of poetry, art, or music in the Western cultural tradition, not to mention its religious texts?

2. Among the range of informants available to me, to whom shall I turn for exegesis of texts? Ordinary persons who come to worship, religious specialists, the wise old man, combinations thereof, or

whatever? This difficulty forces us to reckon with the "open" nature of interpretation and exegeses (whether by natives or us); it also forces us to reckon with the arbitrary nature of what we make out of these levels of native interpretation in our descriptive presentation.

3. The puzzlement the anthropologist feels regarding whom to interview is compounded by the informants' puzzlement regarding whom the anthropologist *should* interview. Take a not too unusual scenario. The ethnographer asks an informant about the Christ, the Buddha, Śiva, God, or Whatever, and the informant tells him, "Go away, ask the priest." The priest tells him, "I don't know much about this but X priest in yonder village trained in the seminary knows, go see him." What do I make of this? My informant is telling me that ordinary people do not know much about scripture, and therefore I should go see the priest, and the priest tells me I should consult a knowledgeable specialist. True enough; but then will I miss the viewpoint of the ordinary person? But suppose I do manage to talk to ordinary people, and they present views that are different from the scriptures; do I say that the scriptural religion is not Christianity? This is patently absurd, but I can certainly say that there are different life-forms called Christianity, and these could be ideal-typically described on the basis of informant statements. But even this is not fully satisfactory, for some might say that the truth of the Truth cannot be articulated in words. They may be right, for the truth of the Truth exists in symbolic forms and rests on ambiguity, metaphor, overdetermination. It need not reside in a single place, but might be scattered in rites and myths, so scattered or so elusive that words cannot express its reality. Thus when one probes *nirvāṇa,* one encounters silence. In Christianity, words can only imperfectly capture the experience for the religiously musical of the *mysterium tremendum et fascinans,* the Eucharist. In this kind of situation the analyst must perforce move in with his (theoretical) interpretation to elucidate the hidden meaning.

4. Hidden meanings are different from unconscious meanings. For me unconscious processes are not problematic in the sense that I can believe in their existence, a belief supported by my personal experience, my literary and ethnographic experience, the texts of the Buddhist tradition, and my layman's knowledge of neurological structures. There are of course many intellectuals who deny this. But assume that unconscious processes do occur—the theory that explains them is irrelevant at this point—then it is likely that informant exegeses of cultural material that deal with deep motivation must be impaired, if not totally blocked, as Turner recognized.[5] With respect

to unconscious materials the anthropologist is in a peculiar dilemma. He must either deny that they exist; or he must adopt a comfortable sociologism that says that while they exist they do not manifest themselves in cultural form or social life; or he might ignore them and invoke his lack of training to handle them; or he must adopt a theory that helps him to understand them—whatever that theory might be. All but the last position would leave a large area of symbolic form and social life uninvestigated by the anthropologist and unexplained by his informant, or done badly on both levels, resulting in badly slanted descriptions of cultural life. This naturally would be particularly serious in societies that give premium to states that seem to tap unconscious motivation—for example, those altered states of consciousness that I have labelled "hypnomantic states." Here the ethnographer has one rational choice if he is to deal directly with these processes: he must make his interpretations on the basis of a theory, a set of abstract rules, or a philosophical grammar or some such nomological set of concepts that can help grasp those phenomena that are elusive by their very definition.

All of the foregoing implies that a good descriptive ethnography of symbolic forms must go beyond the natives' point of view and beyond the surface reality of everyday understandings. Consequently good ethnography must disturb, shock, or jolt us into an awareness that we did not have before. This sense of surprise is quite different from the *offense* that bad ethnography so often exudes. For this reason, the generality of native informants may not comprehend or even sympathize with the ethnographic representation of their life-forms. I disagree with Taussig on this issue.[6] Taussig takes his colleagues (Turner, Kapferer, Meyerhof, Moore) to task for their "unstated rites of academic text making" and their creation of "intellectual authority." But Taussig, it seems to me, while escaping from a bourgeois world perspective, is as much locked into academia as anyone else who writes for a professional audience. His inspirations are Walter Benjamin, Gramsci, Marx, and surrealism; his megaconcepts are "montage," "epistemic murk"; his audience consists of bourgeois academics; his emulators are graduate students who will try (hopelessly, I am sure) to do what he is doing. Santiago, Taussig's informant, wouldn't know what the hell all this is about. It is we who are jolted out of our complacency by Taussig's creation of a work of great power out of the mouths of shamans drunk on *yage*. Similarly, I feel that Rosaldo's recent paper is a good criticism of bad ethnography, or even ordinary ethnography, but a good ethnography need not necessarily be intelligible to the ordinary citizen in that society.[7] The reaction of the ordinary citizen cannot be a litmus test for ethnography as it cannot be for history, philosophy, or fiction.

Thus good ethnography is an ideal typical description that probes beneath the surface reality through the use of a nomological theory. Theory then takes us away from the particularities of X or Y culture and tells us something about culture or life in general. We are back to the problem discussed in lecture two. Theory has an ontological thrust in the human sciences, since it is about human beings and being human that we are talking about. One can *ignore* the ontological problem in the physical sciences, but not in the *Geisteswissenschaften.* This is where I part company with Wittgenstein and move closer to critical theory, hermeneutics, and phenomenology. Wittgenstein seems to think that such ontological inquiries are useless or impossible to ask. But surely this cannot be predetermined philosophically; it must be investigated empirically. This *is* the anthropological quest. This quest, it seems to me, involves a circular procedure. We cannot ask the empirical question without an ontological assumption; but when we start answering the empirical questions, we begin to revise the ontological assumptions. Indeed the ontological *assumption* ceases to be an assumption but becomes an open ontological question or a theoretical proposition as a result of the empirical investigation. And so we go back and forth in this circular fashion, but it is not a vicious or closed circle. Thus the hermeneutical circle is not only a technique of interpretation of cultural forms in terms of the meaning between part and whole but is also a technique of understanding man and culture through a circular logic of inquiry.

❷

The Second Intersubjectivity: Participation and Observation

Ethnography highlights, more than any other human science, the intersubjective relationship between the scholar and the subject of his study, by focussing on a single individual, or a couple at most, hopelessly trying to make do in an alienating field situation. According to hermeneutical thinkers the intersubjective nature of subject-object relationships lies at the root of all social inquiry, and it is one that anthropologists have at long last begun to accept. We are now willing to recognize that, contrary to traditional anthropological views of fieldwork, our informants are not simply giving us "facts"; they are involved with us in a crucial intersubjectve relationship and are engaged in a continuing dialogue with us.

One must not sentimentalize what goes on here. In the early development of fieldwork, the anthropologist carried with him a model of objectivity which caused him to take pains to deny dialogue. He stood outside of the dialogical situation: the anthropologist asked questions; the informant responded. Fieldwork was simply an extended form of the questionnaire; we used terms like "open ended" to distinguish *our* kind of questioning from *their* (sociologists') questionnaire. But the model was a false one, for there is no way to fully suppress dialogue. Even the most objectivist of us all must be able to relate to our informants as normal human beings when we are first "thrown" into the field situation and there taken over, or taken in, in one way or another by our informants. And as I close my notebook, or shut off my tape recorder, I am once again thrown into normal human interaction, from which I learn a great deal about the other culture. I begin to understand the other culture, not on the basis of accumulated data (that are by themselves empty of understanding) but when I can relate to my informants dialogically, such that their actions make reasonable sense to me, as mine do to them. I cease to be puzzled by their actions; they cease to laugh at my blunders. It is in this sense that one can say that anthropological fieldwork is participant-observation. Nowadays we are much more self-conscious about dialogue, and some (such as Marcel Griaule and Victor Turner) have opened themselves to engage in deep conversation with interesting informants, sometimes as fellow inquirers. Participation then is participation in dialogue, not identification with the other culture. Observation is not objectivism either; it is the disengaged identity at work alongside the participation.

If it is true that it is through dialogue that we understand the alien meanings of another culture, then no value-free, objective tool exists. Even the most innocuous-looking questionnaire that we administer is locked into an intersubjective situation and is loaded with value, for a nondialogical questionnaire is an impossibility. A questionnaire has cultural significance for those who read it, based on such things as their attitude to the government, their level of literacy and respect for the written word, their imagined expectations of what the investigator wants, and so forth.[8] It also possesses a value for the investigator, not its obvious methodological value as a tool, but as something that has cultural significance of methodological value as, for example, in American society where social facts to have significance must have a numerical value attached. The "fetishism of numbers" is a cultural value in American society, and the questionnaire is a methodological tool based on this cultural value and appropriate for studying a society governed by this, or a similar, cultural value.

Anthropologists who have long ignored this crucial intersubjective activity have recently awakened to its importance. The recognition of the dialogical relationships in fieldwork has undermined the objectivist stance in respect of the subject-object relationship. Though one must reject the *methodological* problem of objectivism, one must retain the *psychological* stance of disengagement in the arduous process of appropriating another culture into the framework of a descriptive ethnography. When I was an undergraduate, T. S. Eliot's lines on artistic creativity impressed me greatly: "the more perfect the artist," he says, "the more completely separate in him is the man who suffers and the mind which creates; and the more perfectly will the mind digest and transmute the passions which are its material."[9] Or E. K. Chambers, who said that Wyatt, like Donne, was capable of "watching his own emotions in detachment with his finger on the burning pulse."[10] I used both these quotations in the first paper I wrote in graduate school in anthropology. No doubt Eliot and Chambers exaggerate; but I think a case could be made that the "disengaged identity" is perhaps a *sine qua non* for all kinds of creative and intellectual activity.[11]

First let me state what disengagement or detachment is *not.* It is not a reversal to *methodological objectivism.* Anthropologists confuse the stance of detachment with "methodological objectivism" or the belief that the subject matter of investigation is unrelated, *except as object,* to the subject investigating. Methodological objectivism is a denial of the intersubjective or dialogical nature of fieldwork through which ethnographic understanding develops. Methodological objectivism produces a special form of detachment, quite different from intellectual, artistic, or ethnographic creativity. As method it carries with it an important ontological assumption: you treat the object investigated as if it were different in essence, or as species, from that of the investigator. It is this ontological issue that the "ethnographic thrownness" forces us to question. Thus investigator and subject (not object) are of the same essence, and as such they constitute an intersubjectivity governed by dialogue geared towards attempts at mutual understanding. This relation is often an unequal one, shifting ground in different times and places, and in different ways. Sometimes *I* am the dominant partner of the second intersubjectivity; sometime *he* is. It is only in this sense that an observer is a participant; otherwise it is only a pretense at participation, as, for example, when the fieldworker wants to participate by wielding an occasional hoe. There is no way the anthropologist can, in any significant sense, participate in the life of another culture. I doubt he can even when he is studying a segment of his own culture. Concern for the other, and empathy, must not be confused with attempts at identification with the other culture. Participation is participation in dialogue in the context of the intersubjectivity of the anthropologist and his informants. Only naive ethnographers identify with their subjects; but subjects rarely identify with ethnographers, unless it is a key informant or interpreter locked into a *personal* relationship with the investigator. You are always the other, the alien; and the most well-meaning investigator is a C.I.A. agent for some.

The stance of detachment coexisting with participation is not a reversal to methodological objectivism. Such a stance exists in the construction of a poem, as Eliot and Chambers recognize: the outpourings of the heart, if not always "recollected in tranquility," are at least mediated by detachment, the capacity to stand outside the experience, and to mould the experience into pregiven stanzaic forms.[12] The "disengaged identity" is not, as Taylor thinks, a heritage of the West; it exists wherever there is a quest for truth or knowledge or a search for some ontological or transcendental reality. Let me highlight a few of these contexts.

The meditator. Meditation is the ideal typical situation where I stand outside myself observing my own feelings in detachment with my finger on the burning pulse. Here also detachment does not mean seeing one's own body as an object; it is a subject to which I relate through my "detached awareness." Attachment is the ordinary condition of everyday being-in-the-world; detachment is the stance of the seeker of Buddhist truth. This detachment does not mean lack of empathy towards others. The ideal Buddhist meditator emphasizes the emotions of equanimity, kindness-empathy, tenderness, and compassion (love) towards others (but never erotic love, for that is inextricably tied to attachment).

The shaman. It is well known that some kinds of shamans and ecstatic priests experience initial spirit attack and despair. The shaman/priest later becomes a "controller of spirits"—those spirits that initially possessed him and now possess others. In the exorcism he adopts a stance of detachment that in no way impairs his capacity to empathize with the patient. Once our hypothetical shaman or priest has effective control over himself and the spirit world, he can switch his possession on and off very abruptly. Even experienced anthropologists misread this detached capacity as fakery or insincerity (though it is possible to fake this scenario). Conversely, a shaman may get into a deep trance; here also he distances himself from the immediate social situation of the ritual arena. Thus, detachment often requires *distantiation* whether in shamanism or in scholarship.

The diviner. I think the diviner is also close to the anthropologist examining an alien text. The diviner looks at cowrie shells, bones, or bowels: these are "texts" that can be interpreted. In his interpretation, he takes very often a kind of political stand or, I cannot resist saying, develops a "cultural critique." The anthropologist is also close to the diviner in respect of some kinds of fieldwork operations. Positivist anthropologists take pride in the tools and techniques of their trade. Few, however, will be willing to recognize that Rorschachs, TATs, and similar tests show a striking similarity to the outlook and operations of the diviner.

In many of these cases the specialist employs a metalanguage, or an esoteric (distantiating) form of discourse, ranging all the way from glossolalia to the use of specialized vocabularies to describe the experience or event. Thus a fundamentalist Christian possessed of the divine spirit may talk in tongues (glossolalia), while a Buddhist thinker may use a system of rational concepts as his metalanguage. I do not wish to be unfair to those who speak in tongues. Recent modern thinkers such as Heidegger, Wittgenstein, Derrida employ forms of speech that, though self-consciously derived from ordinary language, are virtually unintelligible to ordinary people. It seems that some forms of thought simply cannot escape the lure of distantiating language.

The disengaged identity in the context of the intersubjective relation between investigator and informant, complicated by the different values towards the same methodological tool, and further complicated by cultural presuppositions and psychological anxieties and transferences, renders dubious any simplistic distinction between the context of discovery and the context of validation. But still the nagging question—how does the anthropologist begin to understand another culture?

The end product is clear: the anthropologist begins to understand the other culture when the previously alien life-forms become intelligible to him, even though they do not possess the *immediate intelligibility* of the life-forms of his own society. It is certain that this does not come from language facility alone. There are people who are thoroughly fluent in an alien language but are quite incapable of understanding the alien culture. This is simply because culture is not coterminous with language. The variety of normative behavior governed by implicit meanings, nonverbal communication, and nonlingual symbolic forms shows that language provides at best access to the culture. Moreover most anthropologists have only imperfect command of the language, and they often require an interpreter to steer them through the mazes of the culture. Peter Winch employs a model of socialization; he believes that the anthropologist gets resocialized in another culture.[13] I doubt whether anything even remotely approximating socialization (that gives someone the capacity for immediate comprehension of action) ever occurs in the time period of under two years that the anthropologist spends in the field. I think our own socialization is relevant to understand the *processes* that occur in the field situation. Insofar as our own socialization gives us the capacity to understand symbolic forms, it also perhaps gives us the capacity to understand symbolic forms *not* our own. It is likely that the more alien the alien symbolic forms are to those in my own culture, the more difficult it is for me to empathize with them and grasp their surface significance. I use "surface" nonpejoratively, for depth analysis cannot occur unless we understand the surface significance of symbolic forms, since immediate intelligibility occurs on the surface level for the most part.

What in fact occurs in the field, I suspect, is a kind of bricolage in which the ethnographer puts together pieces of his skills and his accumulating experience to grasp what his informants tell him (dialogue) and what he sees before him (observation). In all of this the "disengaged identity" is I think indispensable, at least for good ethnography, as is the capacity to imaginatively and empathetically project oneself into an alien life world. This capacity for an "empathetic projection" is once again a gift of early childhood; not everyone can resurrect it for the adult business of empathetic understanding in fieldwork.

One thing that clearly affects fieldwork is the fact that the first field visit is by young persons preparing for a Ph.D. dissertation. Dissertation anxiety is compounded by other forces fostering alienation. The context is especially ripe for the anthropologist to be subtly, and sometimes not so subtly, inveigled into a variety of class, factional, and ideological positions and disputes. The anthropologist might not know it, but he might well come into the power of an interpreter or informant. This situation can be complicated if the informant/interpreter is more intelligent than the anthropologist, or if he is a better politician. What protects the anthropologist from all these seductions is his training. The worst scenario is the dead hand of competence that is happily seen for the most part in those ethnographies that remain forever Ph.D. dissertations.

The ethnographer who is "thrown" into the field situation is psychologically vulnerable. Psychoanalysis might provide some measure of understanding here since it is the only human science that systematically deals with the second intersubjectivity in the specific relationship of doctor and patient in the therapeutic session. By contrast anthropologists, to whom this intersubjectivity is central, whose work is often compounded by a third relationship with the interpreter-mediator, have either employed a naive laboratory model that ignored this intersubjectivity or a romantic model (e.g., the anthropologist as stranger) to describe it. In psychoanalysis the intersubjectivity of the doctor and the patient is central to both theory and therapy, not peripheral as in anthropology. The key notion in the psychoanalytic intersubjectivity is that of transference; the patient projects images of significant others and attitudes towards them on the therapist, and the therapist responds with his own "countertransference." Along with this is the "transference neurosis"; the patient repeats archaic material from his repressed past ("the repetition compulsion"), providing valuable information to the therapist regarding the patient's neurosis. Then there is *resistance,* the hostile stance taken by the patient to the analyst's attempt to penetrate the patient's defenses; and finally there is the difficult and complicated process whereby the analyst attempts to overcome resistance and ultimately bring to the patient's consciousness and to his self-conscious understanding that which had been hidden from consciousness.

I am not suggesting that this model could be transferred to anthropology; it is specific to the analytic situation. But the *analogy* may help us to focus on the issues that prevail in the ethnographic situation. I have no answers, but I can state some of the issues involved, with a plea that we open up this neglected area of research in order to formulate theoretically the rules that govern this key intersubjectivity.

1. In psychoanalytic parlance "transference" occurs on an unconscious level and has to do with the archaic motivations of infancy, especially the Oedipal relationships with parents. I have not the

slightest doubt that when the anthropologist enters into a long-term relationship with his informants, transference in this sense also occurs. I have had this experience in the case of Abdin: he had exaggerated respect for his father but hated him on another level and stood in abject terror of him. During the long relationship I had with him, I became the good father, and it is likely that it is not only the death of his father that helped him to give up his terrible penances but the existence of another father who could stand by him in this crisis. I have had extremely negative transferences in my initial interviews; but often the end product is positive, and the transference itself is expressed in a cultural idiom which in some instances masks the infantile transference. Many of my informants displaced some of the attitudes they had toward divine figures to me. For example, eroticism: some would express this nonverbally by kissing my hands when they saw me, while others simply called me "deiya," or "ape deiya," a variation on the term "deviyo," meaning "god" but having connotations of love and affection. While these latter attitudes may be rooted in deeper motivations, we are also dealing with a uniquely anthropological phenomenon which, for want of a better term, I shall tentatively formulate as *cultural transference*. This is simply a label I stick on to what are probably extremely complex phenomena.

2. There are sociocultural conditions that often affect "cultural transference." It is doubtful that the anthropologist is ever a stranger to the people he studies. The term *stranger* is the anthropologist's view of himself, a phenomenon that may affect counter-cultural transference: it is at best part of the phenomenology of Western culture, not a theoretical term. The people one studies, however, have models of the person who comes from the outside: in the case of white anthropologists, there are several models—that of the colonial administrator, the missionary, and so forth. It is almost certain that these models exercise powerful influences on fieldwork. The situation is different when one is working in one's own culture, I am sure. In Sri Lanka, two models seem to operate: the *guru* and the English-speaking high-status government administrator—or more idiosyncratic ones specific to a particular field situation. During my first village study in Laggala in Sri Lanka in 1958 suspicious villagers thought we were the agents of the absentee aristocrat who "owned" the village lands. There was resistance to our work which posed for us the task of overcoming this. But this cultural transference and resistance gave us many clues to the deeper relationships between the villagers and the aristocratic landlord: that is, beneath the facade of deference and re-

spect to him lay a deep resentment. Furthermore, owing to the nature of the world we live in and the nature of the communities we study, the relation between anthropologist and informant is almost never one of equality. The anthropologist is objectively dependent on the goodwill of his informants; yet the informant treats him most often as a status superior largely due to the operation of stereotypic models of the outsider. The latter affects what one might call the *flow of transference*: the initial attitudes, negative or positive, that the informants bring to bear on the outsider. Transference flow is also affected by the well-known phenomenon whereby the ethnographer is given a kinship term and incorporated into a family or larger kin group. This extension of kin terms is always a problem of structure, but it can also become a matter of sentiment affecting the flow of transference. It is transference flow that accounts for historical shifts in the perception of the anthropologist—for example, from colonial administrator to that of C.I.A. agent. Situations that affect transference flow are ubiquitous in every field situation and determine the character of transference and countertransference in its psychoanalytic sense.

3. The notion of social or cultural resistance poses a peculiar problem largely owing to our reluctance to face the issues of the second intersubjectivity. The anthropologist's view of potential social resistances is influenced by his own values in his own cultural countertransference. Western anthropologists often shy away from probing into the private and sexual lives of their informants but have no compunction in dealing with issues that may provoke considerable resistance on the part of the latter, as, for example, inter- and intracaste relations, land transfers and tenure, and even the study of secret societies. In my own work I found more resistance to probing on crucial land transactions than to inquiries on sexual life. In addition to resistance, needless to say, there are serious ethical problems involved here, for which there are no easy solutions.

4. What about the anthropologist's own transferences and countertransferences? I suspect that the anthropologist's transferences occur on two broad levels. First, there is the psychoanalytic type of countertransference which must occur in respect to selected informants with whom we have special long-term relationships and who are our key informants, and of course the interpreter. There are virtually no studies as far as I know of the complex interaction involved except for Crapanzano's *Tuhami* and his recent remarkable essay, and the sensitive study by Kracke.[14] Talking with, and gossip among, anthropologists show that there are some informants we just hate and

some we love, but we tend to gloss over or romanticize these relationships. The second kind of transference made by the anthropologist applies to the group as a whole, and I think some features of this are virtually universal. There is, for example, the universal feature of the anthropologist's intersubjective relationship with "his people" characterized by *ambivalence,* either as a permanent feature, or most often as a temporary one. Freud noted that any intense relationship entails ambivalence. In the field situation, the ethnographer "loves" the people he has appropriated. Yet there are those who frustrate him; thus ambivalence is inevitable in our relationship with informants. Informants might in addition serve as vehicles for the other personal frustrations the anthropologist faces in his sojourn in an alien world. This negative side of ambivalence surfaces when he talks to himself or to visiting friends about his people, expressed in half-affectionate, half-humorous, half-deprecating, and half-insulting references: those "sons of bitches," "bastards," "motherfuckers," and so on, to embrace whole texts of conversations that reflect ambivalence. Malinowski did just that. He foolishly spoke to his diary about his people—those "niggers" he was "fed up with," whose lives, on occasion seemed "as remote from me as the life of a dog."[15] I am sure he loved them also. I once remember attending a party where there were anthropologists and local intellectuals; the latter were totally baffled by the ambivalent talk of the anthropologists, and several asked me later how these people could work with those they hated so much! Anthropologists are almost always unaware of the underlying meaning of such talk and therefore do not guard against it in public situations, fostering, I would like to guess, negative images of anthropologists among indigenous intelligentsia. Hate of course is one component of ambivalence: there is also the love aspect of the relationship that exists and, most often, becomes predominant in the later stages of fieldwork, making disengagement from the field especially difficult for some of us. And once one removes oneself from the field the second intersubjectivity still operates in one's imagination: progressively the affective aspect of ambivalence increases, and one retrospectively sentimentalizes "our people." The frustrations of the field are over, and the time is right to nostalgically (if somewhat patronizingly) appropriate the other. It is, for the most part, after "the return" that the anthropologist refers to those left behind as "my people," "my village," "my group." With this appropriation there is a concomitant resistance to others studying "my people." As far as I know, anthropology is the only scientific discipline that discourages replication of scholarly work. No one wants others messing around with *my* people.

The sentimental appropriation of the other culture by the ethnographer is perhaps paralleled by a similar sentimental appropriation of the ethnographer by the people he has studied. However, this latter area is *terra incognita*: What are the effects on the informants when the anthropologist has left the field? And of course there is the further problem of what happens when the anthropologist comes home from the field. One scenario is clear though: the return produces critical self-reflections on his own culture.

5. The upshot of these comments is that we have neglected the emotional problems of the anthropologists and informants inasmuch as they affect the second intersubjectivity and the whole tenor and devolution of fieldwork. It must be remembered that it is the anthropologist, more than his informants, who is in an initially alienating situation where, as with Mr. Kurtz, the values of his own culture no longer seem to hold sway. While anthropologists do not take Kurtz's road to self-destruction, it is almost certain that the alienating nature of the field situation would trigger transferences and bring to the surface the anthropologist's own infantile motivations. Beyond this there are even more obvious questions we have ignored since they contradict our own image of the anthropologist as "scientist" constructed on the model of the physical scientist in his laboratory: How do anthropologists handle problems of sex, aggression, loneliness, and despair, especially when they are in the field as single individuals, and most importantly, how are these problems expressed (or denied expression) in respect of their relations with their informants?[16]

6. In *Medusa's Hair* I used the term "interpreter effect" to designate the influence of the interpreter in the progress of fieldwork. I stated there that this is one of the problems that we have refused to acknowledge. The relation between the anthropologist and his interpreter is not only a social and psychological one but also one that can affect the tenor of fieldwork and anthropological interpretation. The interpreter is the mediator *par excellence,* but he is not the neuter he is made to be. Virtually every anthropologist has had an interpreter at some point or another and must by the very nature of the situation have had a close relationship with him. But the interpreter almost always remains the faceless one receiving at best an acknowledgement in the preface. I think the refusal to acknowledge the presence of the

interpreter is due to the biases of the anthropologist's own ideology as scientist, having control over both the external situation and over himself in the activity of the investigation. Consequently it is not unusual to incorporate the interpreter into the anthropologist. Thus anthropological monographs do not hesitate to bring in the voices of informants; the voice of the interpreter is silenced. He is treated as the anthropologist's alter ego rather than a real presence as a human being whose own psychological propensities and social class position might well slant the investigation in one direction or another.[17]

The interpreter (or favorite informant) who establishes a long-term relationship with the investigator is unique to the anthropological field situation. The more the anthropologist is ignorant of the language the more dependent he is on this person. He is often a comfort or a cushion protecting the investigator from the alienating world outside. This relationship might well result in an extremely complex one governed by strong ambivalences. Other situations might produce a patron-client relationship, and sometimes guilt for having left the interpreter without alternative employment. It is not unusual for the anthropologist when he is speaking the native language to adopt the mannerisms of the interpreter. So is the reverse: I have known an interpreter who adopted the mannerisms of the anthropologist including the style and content of his discourse, becoming literally his alter ego. Whatever an interpreter may be he is certainly not the neuter, the faceless one, the anonymous being hiding behind the ethnography.

❸

The Third Intersubjectivity and the Idea of a Metatheory

In my usage, "the third intersubjectivity" refers to the relationship of the anthropologist with his reading public, most importantly his professional peers. The anthropologist establishes a dialogue with his colleagues through his work, and especially through the discussion of the theories he employs. These theories are not only nomological systems that help us understand other life worlds; they are also the metalanguages that help unite the practitioners of a discipline into a moral community. Before delving deeper into the nature of the theories that prevail in anthropology and psychoanalysis, let me pull together some of the methodological observations made in the course of these lectures in order to drive home what I think is a striking concordance between anthropology and psychoanalysis, beneath well-known differences in the goals of the two disciplines and their historical development.

Absolutely fundamental to psychoanalysis is the idea that "psychic reality," the subjective perception of the external world or event, is determinative of the neuroses. In the extreme case one can have a psychic reality that is truly delusional, as in paranoia, that flouts the ordinary reality of the average person. Psychic reality is for psychoanalysis what "cultural construction of reality" or "the definition of the situation" is for the anthropologist. Given this concordance, it seems to me that it is easy enough to assume that reality can be, and often is, both psychically *and* culturally constructed. Psychoanalysts might well find that the cultural constitution of the world will influence psychic reality, and consequently culture must be crucial to the understanding of mental events. Conversely anthropologists ought to be receptive to the idea that culturally constituted worlds may be psychically real for the individual and the group, so that, for example, evil spirits may be part of a complex culturally constituted cosmos and also, at the same time, demonomorphic representations of unconscious processes, existing at a different level of remove from their ideational parallels in the unconscious. The demonstration of the concordance between psychic reality and culturally constituted reality must be through a theoretical discussion of the work of culture. Both psychic and cultural reality imply that the social facts that we examine are not "things," but "meanings" interconnected with other meanings either systemically or chaotically. Hence context becomes especially significant, something more radical than the conventional term, context dependency, suggests.

Both disciplines deny methodological objectivism. The interrelation between subject and object is central to psychoanalysis. The ethnographic field situation exemplifies, even more than psychoanalysis, the vulnerability of the investigator in the field situation. It reverses the model of the scientist having control over the experimental subject or field. Now it is indeed the case that the Heisenberg principle indicates a similar situation in physics (and by extension in the other physical sciences), but the qualitative difference is striking. Moreover, in spite of the Heisenberg principle, physical scientists generally operate with a self-conscious model of the separatedness between subject and object and recognize in their philosophy and practice the dominance of the former over the latter. Finally, the lack of dialogue between subject and object is what is especially striking in the physical and natural sciences, including academic psychology.

In both psychoanalysis and anthropology, empathy, or the capacity to appreciate or empathize with the mind or life of the other, is essential. In both there are psychological blocks, such as countertransference, that might inhibit understanding. Empathy, however, can coexist with disengagement. The structure of the psychoanalytic therapeutic situation exemplifies this, so that Freud could even describe the technique of therapy as a kind of "differential calculus." In both psychoanalysis and anthropology the subject and object (or the two subjects) influence each other's judgments in a variety of ways.[18] Hence a major methodological problem: How does one construct a case history or an ethnography on the basis of such contamination? Neither psychoanalysis nor anthropology has even begun to address this issue, though both disciplines recognize that some of our insights in fact come from our subjects/informants—a situation naturally impossible in the natural sciences! Freud, for example, got his key notion, "the omnipotence of thoughts," from a patient.[19] What would have happened to "the forest of symbols" without Muchona, the hornet? In the natural science models it is quite impossible for the subject investigated to be a coparticipant in the production of the final scholarly work.

Both psychoanalysis and anthropology are empirical disciplines but of a peculiar sort. Random sampling is impossible by the intrinsic nature of psychoanalysis and ethnography in their different ways. A patient comes to the doctor seeking help; the anthropologist seeks those willing to talk to him. Yet both rely on observations that are "random" in a nonstatistical sense. Any generalization that one makes has a strong inductionist quality, often based on a single case. Observations in turn are continually being interpreted as they are in everyday life except that, as with all rational disciplines, observation is theory laden, even if "theory" here refers to unsystematized megaconcepts. But more of this later.

Given the nature of the subject-object relationship and the impossibility of random sampling, any statistical or experimental research design is simply impossible. Both disciplines highlight or represent in exaggerated form a problem that exists in *all* experiments with human subjects. No possible control for culture can exist, especially since for the most part both subject and object treat culture as if it were nature and a given. Take an early experimental study like Muzafer Sherif's "autokinetic experiment": here a beam of light is thrown in a dark room, and subjects are asked to measure the movement of the light (an illusion since the light does not really move). The upshot of the experiment is to show that while individual judgments may vary, this is not so when each individual in a group is asked to speak his judgment aloud. In the latter situation the whole group eventually comes to a common judgment (a norm or standard) regarding the movement of light.[20] The experiment in fact does not prove anything but merely illustrates what we know already: that people are socialized into recognizing the importance of standards and that in a group one must respect group norms. Even recent and more sophisticated experiments in the human sciences are in fact complex cases of self-fulfilling prophecies based on the acceptance of common cultural premises or a definition of the situation. Freud nicely expressed skepticism regarding research design and experimentation in psychoanalysis. In a letter to the American psychologist Saul Rosenzweig, who wanted to "test" some of his hypotheses, Freud wrote that he saw little value in it "because the wealth of dependable observations" on which psychoanalysis rests "makes them independent of experimental verification. Still, it can do no harm."[21]

Given the similarities mentioned above, it is not surprising that both disciplines eschew "prediction," and for that matter "retrodiction." This almost goes without saying in anthropology. For those to whom psychoanalysis is a natural science, this inability to predict poses embarrassing problems, though not for Freud. This is not to eschew causality or determination: events *are* caused; causes, however, cannot be isolated as variables subject to concomitant variations, but must be implicated in a case history. "Causal imputation" in Freud and Weber is similar: it is inextricably "historical causality." In anthropology this is not clear; some do accept the idea of cause embedded, or embodied, in a historical/ethnographic context; others see no room for cause and seek instead "patterns" in a narrative, or plain description that might end up as being thick, thin, or nondescript. However, till recently neither anthropologists nor psychoanalysts saw their disciplines as "historical." Freud certainly did not, though he recognized the centrality of interpretation.

Though unrecognized, both disciplines deal with historical-existential ("ontological") issues that defy encompassment into the framework of an "exact science." Freud noted perceptively in *Civilization and Its Discontents* (1930):

> It is not easy to deal scientifically with feelings. One can attempt to describe their physiological signs. Where this is not possible . . . nothing remains but to fall back on the ideational content which is most readily associated with the feeling.[22]

This is because psychoanalysis deals with human experience and existence; existence cannot be converted into variables; nor can it be quantified without losing its existential or experiential quality. Wittgenstein's general discussion of immediate experience is surely applicable here:

> The moment we try to apply exact concepts of measurement to immediate experience, we come up against a peculiar vagueness in this experience. But that only means a vagueness relative to these concepts of measurement. And, now, it seems to me that this vagueness isn't something provisional, to be eliminated later on by more precise knowledge, but that this is a characteristic logical peculiarity.[23]

Thus, while psychoanalysis deals with the causes of neuroses, these causes are qualitatively different from viruses or germs. The increasing demand nowadays to isolate physical causes for mental illness is perhaps the inevitable reaction against this patently nonpositivist aspect of psychoanalysis. Freud was himself a victim of the scientific imperative, for he sometimes advocated an eventual reduction of experiential issues (historical causes) to biogenetic variables. It should be emphasized that the case-historical mode eminently suits the genius of a discipline that deals with problems of human experience or existence, rather than with viruses or germs.

Now it is time to reflect on some crucial and radical differences between psychoanalysis and some descriptive ethnographies as well as conventional histories. Psychoanalysis broke the distinction between history and theory, between the well-known idiographic-nomothetic distinction formulated by Windelband. The idiographic does not exclude the nomothetic. I think Max Weber also recognized this, but he did not give a systematic rationale for nomothetic formulation of historical causality. Early British social anthropologists, without recognizing it as such, attempted, for example, to produce descriptive accounts of kinship through the use of a conceptual framework, but they mistook this kind of conceptual framework for a synchronic science, "a natural science of society." It was psychoanalysis that first broke the idiographic-nomothetic straightjacket by a metapsychology that introduced deductively interconnected "experience-distant" and "experience-near" concepts to understand problems of human existence, especially those pertaining to mental illness or neurosis, that defy isolation as specific pathogenic causes such as viruses or germs. What Freud was not aware of was the fact that psychoanalysis was *not* a natural science, but a historical and theoretical discipline, both idiographic and nomothetic at the same time. The metapsychology that he used as a theoretical framework was suited for a historical and human science, since a human science, by its very nature, must deal with problems of human existence and that makes it historical. What then is the nature of the Freudian metapsychology?

Before I address this question, let me reiterate a previous proposition: namely, that of disengagement, distantiation, and the uses of metalanguage for a specific form of rational understanding of the world. In rational systems of discourse such as philosophy and the human sciences where we aim at understanding human life-forms, we cannot employ a metalanguage that is totally removed from ordinary language. It is impossible to mathematize or convert into symbolic logic the essentially rational yet argumentative nature of these discourses. Consequently the metalanguages one employs share an affinity with ordinary language, and our concepts are embedded therein. I do not think that it is any longer reasonable to ask that our metalanguages be converted into artificial or purely denotative languages, as philosophers of science did in the first flush of logical positivism. When our metalanguages stray too far from the style of ordinary discourse, generally by a clutter of technical terminology, we are put off, and we rightly castigate such language as "jargon."

The language of rational discourse that probes things human, insofar as it is based on ordinary discourse, can be read and appreciated by nonspecialists. Hence there is a ready conduit from the professional discourse of the specialist into the world of modern culture, so that modern culture gets changed by the impact of these forms of knowledge. Indeed, as with economics, whole institutions like banking, commerce, and the stock exchange can be created out of the more specialized human sciences, rendering validation of the propositions of these sciences (economics, for example) both difficult and dubious—dubious because we are expecting validation of the theory/

hypotheses of economics from the workings of the very institutions it has helped to create. There is no escape from this dilemma of self-fulfilling prophecy in any of the human sciences—including psychoanalysis—except by the comparative method, whereby we *use* the propositions of the metatheories to understand other cultures which have not seen the impact of these theories in their own life-forms and institutions. Thus I do not share the opinion of those who think that theories created in the West should *not* be used in the nomothetic understanding of other cultures. Quite the contrary, I take the very opposite view, that we must self-consciously do so, with the proviso that it may also be useful to employ theories or philosophies developed in other cultures to Western society, for precisely the same reason. I also do not believe that ethnographers who claim not to use nomological theory can actually escape Western theories of culture in which they have been professionally socialized in their analysis of other life-forms. In other words, in order to get emancipated from its historical roots in one culture, a theory ought to be employed in another, and in this employment, it can be subject to critical review and reformulation in order to reflect its applicability to other life-forms.

While it is indeed true that the metatheories of the human sciences affect modern culture, more so than their philosophical counterparts did, it is also the case that theoretical disquisition is self-consciously addressed to professional colleagues, rarely to a larger public. This is the third intersubjectivity that I spoke of whereby the anthropologist uses the metatheory to have a dialogue with his colleagues, and it is in this dialogue or argument that consensual validation for the propositions of the theory is obtained. Thus while the metatheory is based on ordinary language it operates *primarily* in a different intersubjective field—that of the investigator and his public of professional scholars. One might ask whether the metalanguage of the scholar of the human sciences is in principle different from that of philosophy or of a natural science like biology or chemistry or physics. The answer is that the human sciences have closer affinity with philosophy; it does not use artificial or denotative languages; it eschews experimental methods and prediction-retrodiction; and it does not have a noncontestable set of terms of assumptions. There are no "genes" or "chromosomes" in anthropology; the term "culture" is contested and contestable, and it is "magnificent in its indefiniteness." What we try to achieve is not agreement on a set of assumptive terms but an agreement on the nature of human life that appears as complexes, patterns, forms of life, institutions, and so forth, exhibiting family resemblances within and across cultures, through the use of accepted and yet contested terms. We are not constructing so much a science of man but rather a knowledge of being human. Culture, charisma, rationalization, capitalism, alienation, and so forth are terms we all employ, but they are not terms that evoke consensus. They embody a history that is itself a product of debate. Unlike genes, chromosomes, phonemes, our terms contain an *unresolved* debate, an unresolved and an unresolvable history. Max Weber highlighted the endemic nature of that unresolved history in an almost lyrical sentence that managed to escape the straightjacket of the translation: ". . . there are sciences to which eternal youth is granted, and the historical disciplines are among them—all those to which the eternally flowing stream of culture perpetually brings new problems."[24]

From these thoughts on the uses of metalanguages in the human sciences let me get back to the specifically psychoanalytic metatheory that Freud labelled as his "metapsychology." I do not agree with recent revisionists like Klein, Gill, Holtzman, Schafer, and others who, in order to develop a new humanistic language for psychoanalysis, have made a distinction between the Freudian "clinical theory" of which they approve and the later metapsychology that they want to throw out.[25] I see the clinical theory as part of the metatheory (metapsychology), though it is the part more closely anchored into "observation" and clinical evidence. As Laplanche and Pontalis have shown, there is no clear discussion in Freud himself on exactly what he meant by the metapsychology;[26] this must be our task based on the Freudian practice. It is easy to show, however, that Klein, Schafer, et al. are wrong. In his "Papers on Metapsychology," Freud wrote the important theoretical papers "Repression" and "The Unconscious"; it would be naive to say that these topics are not part of the clinical theory! The real objection of Klein and Schafer is to the theory of the instincts which I shall consider later. The theoretical formulation in the papers on metapsychology were further developed eight years later in his path-breaking study *The Ego and the Id* (1923), which formulated the famous second topography. It makes sense to see the abstract and nomologically interrelated concepts in psychoanalysis as a metatheory (or a metapsychology) and then critically examine how they work.

The first major metatheoretical interpretation of the ideational products of the unconscious was *The Interpretation of Dreams*. I shall have more to say about this in a later part of this lecture; suffice here to note that the basic terms of the metapsychology—the systems conscious, unconscious, and preconscious—were clearly developed here and, along with other key theoretical terms, employed to explain the formation of dreams. In my view this is the model work; metatheory is close to the empirical data it purports to interpret. It is a *meta*theory, because Freud insisted that while his concepts help explain "facts," they are neither based on sense experience nor related to some specific part of the brain. The constructs are abstract, rational, and artificial, but they help us understand "facts" on the ground. *The Interpretation of Dreams* we now know was a radical reaction to his *Project of 1895* that employed a mechanistic neurological theory using such entities as "neurones," entities that were reflective of brain physiology and function. The theoretical terms in Freud's dream book by contrast were removed from this neurological anchorage and hence properly could be considered *meta*psychological, though Freud himself did not use that term at this time.

With *Papers on Metapsychology* (1915), Freud's metatheories took a huge speculative turn, culminating in *Beyond the Pleasure Principle* (1920) and the formulation of the second topography of the mind in *The Ego and the Id* (1923). It should be noted that all of Freud's great case studies were written prior to 1923 on the basis of the first topography of conscious, unconscious, and preconscious and other very basic and fundamental theoretical terms. In other words the earlier metatheoretical terms served Freud well enough to describe and interpret dreams, fantasies, and neurotic symptoms in relation to the history or life situation of a patient or dreamer. In the later work Freud developed a metapsychology of great ontological importance. Some of the latter metapsychological speculations, like those dealing with narcissism, repression, the unconscious and the ego and the id, were based on prior observational data and designed to illuminate them, but others, like his later theory of the instincts and his dualistic vision of life as a grand struggle between Eros and Thanatos, were profound ontological speculations but weakly tied to the data of clinical observation. Let me now consider briefly this later metapsychology to show how the metatheory was further complicated by two opposing yet coexisting analytical strategies, one dealing with the mechanical play of forces in the unconscious, and the other with motivations based on human relationships, the former exhibiting its ancestry in the *Project of 1895* and the latter in the dream book and the early case studies. Freud himself was unaware of this misalliance and did not see its problematic nature.

The two metapsychology papers, "Repression" and "The Unconscious," were theoretical elaborations of the first topography that in turn led to the construction of the second topography. These two papers were preceded by the very unsatisfactory work "Instincts and Their Vicissitudes," which I cannot discuss here. Both papers reveal the misalliance between the theory of the instincts (drives) and the more complex theory of motivation based on human relationships. For purposes of convenience I shall refer to the latter as the "motivational theory" and the former as the "drive theory"—admittedly an unsatisfactory distinction. The drive theory of the instincts produced such technical terms as libido (the reservoir of sexual energy) and the play of forces in cathexis, countercathexis, object cathexis, and so forth. It is also the drive theory that reduced the power of desire in human motivation to the drive reduction theory of pleasure; and to simplistic statements such as these: "A satisfaction of instinct spells happiness for us." "What decides the purpose of life is simply the programme of the pleasure principle."[27] Yet in fact in his actual detailed description of the paths of the different kinds of pleasure (from intoxicants to aesthetics) Freud could present a more complex picture of pleasure against a background of human finitude, suffering, and helplessness—the power of nature, the feebleness of one's own body (itself a part of nature), and the pain that comes from our relationships with others. Here lies the great Freudian paradox: the mechanical forces of the instincts are always in an ambiguous and paradoxical relation with the complexities of the human condition.

The two papers "Repression" and "The Unconscious" illuminate this paradox. In these papers Freud has a lot of trouble with the idea of drive or instinct (*Trieb*) and related words such as *impulse* and *instinctual impulse*. Let me give an example. Instincts and their derivatives are many, but in what sense can I say I repress them? Perhaps sex, maybe aggression, but what about the drive that Western man hardly bothered about—hunger. Can one legitimately speak of repressing a hunger drive? Not for very long surely, and not in the technical sense of "repression"! However, if I were to think I could satisfy my hunger drive by eating human flesh I might be able to repress the latter *idea* because it is an emotionally frightening one for me. Thus a theory that says drives, impulses, instincts can be repressed comes a cropper when it comes to obvious drives like hunger, unless we focus, as Freud also does, not so much on the drive per se but on its "instinctual representative," or the idea cum emotion that is the derivative of the hypothesized drive. This shift in focus does not necessarily entail a change in Freud's definition of repression: "*the es-*

sence of repression lies simply in turning something away, and keeping it at a distance, from the conscious."[28] We also can keep Freud's definition of primal repression and repression proper.[29] Thus it seems reasonable to say that it is an idea, and other ideas interconnected with it, most often concerning a human relationship, that are repressed, because they are associated with troubling or negative affects. Freud continues:

> [Psychoanalysis] shows us, for instance, that the instinctual representative develops with less interference and more profusely if it is withdrawn by repression from conscious influence. It proliferates in the dark, as it were, and takes on extreme forms of expression, which when they are translated and presented to the neurotic are not only bound to be seen alien to him, but frighten him by giving him the picture of an extraordinary and dangerous strength of instinct.[30]

Consider this statement. The first part deals with an affect-laden idea proliferating in the dark of the unconscious owing to repression. I have no problem with this. But to say that the patient is frightened by "instinct" is, I think completely untenable. For example, if I have a desire to have sex relations with my mother, is my reaction due to the "dangerous strength of instinct"? If so, is it the Oedipal instinct or impulse? But Freud notes elsewhere that the latter is not a simple matter of instinct but a *complex* or a system of affect-laden ideas about familial relationships. Freud's "dangerous strength of instinct" can be justified only if the patient subjectively feels the *idea* of a deadly force that threatens to overpower him. And drive/instinct is hardly the word to describe this sense of anxiety or dread. A drive satisfaction or need reduction theory may be suitable for infrahuman (or perhaps infraprimate) existence but not for human forms of life. Even more unsatisfactory is the mechanical ebb and flow of energy (cathexis and countercathexis) that gives strength or power to repressed ideas. What all forms of repression have in common, he argued, is "a *withdrawal of the cathexis of energy* (or of libido, where we are dealing with the sexual instincts)."[31] He gives an example from the famous Wolf Man case study.

> The instinctual impulse subjected to repression here is a libidinal attitude towards the father, coupled with fear of him. After repression, this impulse vanishes out of consciousness:

> the father does not appear in it as an object of libido. As a substitute for him we find in a corresponding place some animal which is more or less fitted to be an object of anxiety. The formation of the substitute for the ideational portion [of the instinctual representative] has come about by *displacement* along a chain of connections which is determined in a particular way. The quantitative portion has not vanished, but has been transformed into anxiety. The result is fear of a wolf, instead of a demand for love from the father.[32]

Let me examine this important statement in some detail.

What is repressed is an "instinctual impulse" coming from the libido, the energy reservoir of the sex drive. But even here the drive/instinct is not a simple phenomenon, but a "libidinal attitude to the father." Yet instead of saying that it is an *attitude* (ideas about a crucial relationship), Freud affirms that it is the "impulse" that vanishes out of consciousness. Concomitantly the earlier complex "attitude" is narrowed down and the father becomes "object libido."

Freud then discusses the fascinating process by which an animal figure (the wolf) is substituted for the father. I have no real objection if we simply say that there is a transformation of ideas here through displacement, rather than a mechanical transfer of energy.

But the mechanical model resurfaces at the end. The quantitative portion (instinctual energy, cathexis, libido) is converted into anxiety, so that instead of a demand for love from the father, there is fear of the wolf. The libido theory (itself based on the instincts) is a peculiar quantitative phenomenon since it isn't observable and consequently can never be quantified! Our question is, why have it? What useful purpose does it serve?

I suggest that the sufferer has a complex "attitude" to the father: ideas and affects that are based on a crucial and troubling relationship. These ideas and their transformations can be thickly described as Freud does in his famous Wolf Man case history. The ideas and the associated affects stem from a relationship, not from an instinct or derivatives of them. Affects are present in the relationship and in the ideas the sufferer has *about* that relationship ("libidinal attitude"). These ideas cannot be disaggregated into "units," variables, or the play of forces (cathexes), which is what the libido theory forces us to do. The relationship, and the frightening ideas emerging from it, can be described in context (understanding) and the determinative causes explicated by the metatheory (explanation, historical causality) and presented in a descriptive account or case study (interpretation). Freud himself realized that this latter strategy seemed to violate the canons of scientific method: "The case histories . . . read like short stories and . . . , as one might say, they lack the serious stamp of science. . . . [T]he nature of the subject is evidently responsible for this, rather than any preference of my own."[33]

This was in 1895, the year he completed the *Project* and was working on a paper on infantile cerebral paralysis (published in 1897). Consequently Freud had to continue the very type of mechanistic theory he had rejected in the *Project,* but converted from a positivist theory of neurones into a metapsychology of the instincts. This conflict persists right through the Freud corpus and is even enshrined in his great hermeneutical work, *The Interpretation of Dreams,* in chapter seven where he presents, in metapsychological language, the psychology of the dream processes. The mechanistic theory only gives the metapsychology an illusion of scientificity. Freud even seems to recognize this in his paper on repression: "The categories here employed are of course not enough to supply an adequate explanation of even the simplest case of psychoneurosis."[34] A similar doubt is expressed in his paper "The Unconscious" in the section dealing with "unconscious emotions" where he refers to the importance of the ideational representative: "The antithesis of conscious and unconscious is not applicable to instincts. An instinct can never become an object of consciousness—only the idea that represents the instincts can. Even in the unconscious, moreover, an instinct cannot be represented otherwise than by an idea."[35] Freud himself seems to realize, belatedly, that if it is the idea that is repressed, then the theory of the instincts isn't all that important: "When we nevertheless speak of an unconscious instinctual impulse or of a repressed instinctual impulse, the looseness of the phraseology is a harmless one."[36]

The whole libido theory with its mechanical play of forces expressed in terms like cathexis, countercathexis, object cathexis, hypercathexis, and all of the theoretical discussions of instincts I find quite unsatisfactory. I also think that Freud's clear and persuasive style of writing becomes tedious when he talks of the forces of the instincts. But this does not mean that we can do away entirely with some *assumptions* regarding drives and their nature. Freud himself wrote in 1933: "The instincts are mythical entities, magnificent in their indefiniteness. In our work we cannot for a moment disregard them, yet we are not sure that we are seeing them clearly."[37] Freud, I believe, was dead correct in this assessment. The instincts are a myth charter for psychoanalysis. They are reified entities, ultimately subsumable as "mythic entities" or "beings," Eros and Thanatos.

A good part of the Western philosophical tradition, at least from Hobbes onwards, assumed some form of intractable drives or needs that must be brought under social or political control. Modern social theories like Durkheim's (and also Weber's) made basic assumptions about drives or needs. The trouble with Freud is that he felt obliged to develop the traditional *assumption* about drives into a theory, and later into an ontology, without the proper biological foundation on which to erect such a metapsychological edifice. At the same time it is hard to reject the existence of drives. The theoretical edifice of psychoanalysis will collapse if it can be shown that human beings do not possess drives such as sexuality, elimination, dependency, aggression, and so forth, however they may be derived. The control of those drives by parents and other familial members is significant for both culture and the individual. And while I believe that the theory of *motivation* (which emphasizes ideas and emotions pertaining to human relationships) is more useful than a theory of drives, the former could not exist without the existence of the latter. Thus it seems to me that psychoanalysis, like much of post-Hobbesian sociology, must assume the existence of drives (primary and secondary), but one must bracket them for the time being, till we know more about them from biology, academic psychology, and other sciences that might want to study them.

This is not too difficult a task. Take a somewhat contested example as a drive for power. I can bracket its existence and then deal with its manifestation in human life minimally as (a) a set of ideas pertaining to domination and (b) a relationship governed by inequality. The notion of a drive that is manifest in ideas and connected to human relationships applies to others such as sexuality, hunger, nurture, dependency, and aggression.

The drives then constitute the mythological charter for psychoanalysis, the shaky foundation on which the metatheory is constructed. Some of the assumptions regarding drives will remain especially questionable. For example, consider the aggression drive, which Freud thought was as innate as sexuality. Freud did not derive this idea of a fundamental aggression drive, plausible as it is, from experimental work in biology; rather, he derived it from his observations on the human condition, as Shakespeare did in *King Lear*:

> Humanity must perforce prey on itself
> Like monsters of the deep.

Freud's pessimistic view of life as an interplay of Eros and Thanatos, with the ultimate triumph of the latter, may be a profound and penetrating insight into the human condition but, to me at least, it fails when it is anchored to his theory of the drives. To say that both life and death drives are "active in every particle of living substance" cannot be justified by our current scientific thought, though it may well prove to be so in the future.[38] Even less plausible are his speculations on the origin of these drives in unicellular organisms.[39] On the other hand, whether aggression is innate or not, its role in human life is surely important to both psychoanalysis and anthropology: its cultural control and canalization, its contribution to the formation of the neuroses, the conditions that inhibit or foster its development in early childhood and in adult life—to mention a few. I find it interesting that Hindu and Buddhist thinkers—some of whom also had a "pessimistic" view of life—believed in nonviolence as an ethical necessity because of the existence of violence and not because of an innate predisposition either way.

Though the formulations of the drive theory spelled out in *Instincts and Their Vicissitudes* and *Beyond the Pleasure Principle* must be rejected, it does not follow that the developments in his later metatheory must be accepted. As I said earlier, Freud himself wrote his great case histories before the second topography was finally formulated with the publication of *The Ego and the Id* (in 1923). While this work was a major metatheoretical reformulation of the structure of the mind, I believe it is not necessary to adopt it for the study of culture. The older topography can as easily serve us. My reservations about the second topography are precisely of the same order as the reservations of recent scholars regarding Freud's views on female sexuality—that they are (not surprisingly) influenced by his Judaic heritage and the larger European values of his time.[40] Take the case of the second topography of superego, ego, and id. This topography is not only based on the earlier primordial tripartite division in Indo-European culture, but more importantly its substantive content is vastly influenced by contemporary Judaic and Protestant values. It is true that Freud dethroned the primacy of consciousness; the ego, for him, is "a poor creature owing service to three masters and consequently menaced by three dangers: from the external world, from the libido of the id, and from the severity of the superego."[41] But the dethroning of the ego in this personology is paralleled with a discussion of the powerful id and superego. Though Freud recognizes that the ego and superego emerge from an undifferentiated id, he also strongly underscores the separateness of the three compartments by the barrier of repression. The id is the dark reservoir of primordial forces; it is predictably the underground; it is "chaos, a cauldron full of seething excitations," and it has negative moral connotations.[42] It is the reservoir of temptation where the "untamed passions" lie waiting and proliferating in the dark.[43]

In contrast to the dark underground is the "over-I" or superego, the "ego ideal" of the earlier Freud. "Psychoanalysis has been reproached time after time with ignoring the higher, moral, suprapersonal side of human nature," says Freud.[44] This accusation, though unjust, can now be met, for one can retort that the superego or ego-ideal is that "higher nature."[45] Though originating in the id, "what has belonged to the lowest part of the mental life of each of us is changed, through the formation of the ideal, into the highest in the human mind by our scale of values."[46]

Consider the language in which the superego is described. The ego must submit to "the categorical imperative" of the superego.[47] The superego is essentially negative and "manifests itself essentially as a sense of guilt."[48] Freud says that "it may be said of the id that it is totally non-moral, of the ego that it strives to be moral, and of the superego that it can be supermoral and then become as cruel as only the id can be."[49] One wonders whether this isn't a reification of the mind of a hyperconscientious person socialized in Western culture! While the superego can be excessively harsh in some individuals who turn their aggressions inward, even "ordinary normal morality has a harshly restraining, cruelly prohibiting quality. It is from this, indeed, that the conception arises of a higher being who deals punishment inexorably."[50]

Here is a clear indication that the characterization of the superego is based on the concepts of the deity and of the conscience in the Judaism and Protestantism of Freud's time. Furthermore, the cruel superego with its "higher nature" combined with the idea of an inexorable punitive Higher Being finds a parallel in the father, for it is through the identification with the father that the superego develops. It is consequently "the heir to the Oedipus complex." And since god himself is a refraction of the father, might one not infer that both superego and God must of necessity be heralded ontogenetically by a punitive father? Freud does not deal with the fact that the father of his time was a punitive figure, but this assumption is central to understanding the content of the Freudian superego. Once we recognize the genesis of the superego in the cultural and familial structures of

Freud's time, we can understand why the id itself is confined, as in a prison or a hell, to the dark underground. Repression operating in this cultural context will not permit unconscious forces access into consciousness and almost certainly will not permit their transformation into symbolic forms. Both superego and id have been structured in terms of what might be called "a Judaeo-Protestant conscience." It is this conscience that is both moral and punitive with guilt firmly established as an integral element. The ego, it would not surprise us, is in "dread of the superego." "The superior being, which turned into the ego-ideal, once threatened castration, and this dread of castration is probably the nucleus round which the subsequent fear of conscience has gathered; it is this dread that persists as the ear of conscience."[51] The extraordinary punitive nature of this conscience, both as internal and as externalized violence, has been described by Freud in *The Ego and the Id* and *Civilization and Its Discontents*.[52]

The second topography was a transformation of the first, but now articulated to a Judaeo-Protestant conscience. What is missing is any discussion in Freud of the "positive" aspects of this conscience; that it can be moved by compassion or kindness, irrespective of the negativity of guilt acting as a sanction. I suspect that this is due to Freud's neglect of the introjection of *maternal* values in the formation of the conscience (and possibly in the Oedipal resolution) in his cultural setting. In spite of this limitation the model could be usefully applied to Freud's own times and, perhaps with some modifications, to contemporary Euro-American cultures. But it needs drastic revision, or flexibility in application, in other cultural contexts, especially where the Judaeo-Protestant conscience does not operate and neither does capitalist individualism nor a predominant identification with the father. In South Asia where there is a greater back-and-forth movement among the three structural components of the mind, the contents of the id can be transformed, through the work of culture, into personal symbols or collective representations. In the case of personal symbols one can in fact reasonably reformulate Freud's famous statement "where id was, there shall ego be" into "where ego is, there shall id be." But it may well turn out to be that we do not need the second topography at all; the first is perhaps all that is necessary.

To address this important issue I must shift ground and deal with the structure, rather than the contents, of the second topography. Here also I have serious reservations regarding its usefulness in cross-cultural interpretations. Our great master of suspicion, in the initial burst of creativity that culminated in the dream book, deconstructed the Cartesian primacy of consciousness, by introducing the then radical view that motivation could be primarily unconscious. I think the terms of the first topography—consciousness, unconscious, preconscious—and those experience-distance concepts pertaining to the dream work (and later to the mechanisms of defense), combined with useful experience-near concepts like guilt, shame, anxiety, castration, narcissism, are more useful when they are not encompassed by the personology of the second topography. The idea of unconscious and preconscious motivation and "thought" is, in my view, consonant with forms of thought in many non-Western societies, whereas the personology of ego, superego, and id is far too rooted in Western language games and philosophical speculations. Both Buddhism and Hinduism clearly recognize unconscious motivation, and indeed delve more deeply into such processes than Freudianism, though they both lack the special theoretical slant that Freud gave it. It is indeed possible that a future psychoanalysis might well incorporate these Hindu-Buddhist insights. I also think that shamanism, spirit possession, and other kinds of hypnomantic states are widespread forms of life that recognize implicitly the centrality of unconscious motivation.

The second topography is of course the product of Freud's mature years. The ego ("I"), the superego ("over-I"), and id ("it") is a personology that is consonant with Western philosophical traditions because it fits neatly with the Western preoccupation with the self, the ego or the transcendental or reflective consciousness. Freud destroyed the primacy of consciousness, only to reassert in his later years the primacy of the ego. On the one hand he asserted that the ego is a helpless creature serving three masters, but he also took for granted, in almost Cartesian fashion, its indubitability. "Normally, there is nothing of what we are more certain than the feeling of our self, of our ego," he wrote in 1930.[53] How so, particularly if the ego has been described as a "helpless creature"? Yet it exists. In the second topography this hapless ego is partly unconscious, but beyond ego or "I" there is another still voice—that of the *super* ego or "over-I." Has the reflective Self returned disguised as the silent voice of the superego operating in a very un-Cartesian unconscious? The superego then is an extension of the ego, carrying with it the special force of the ego's reflectiveness—it has a punitive, self-critical nature. It is an ego that exists outside the realm of consciousness.

What about the id? Id is the neuter of the personology, for it must be remembered that Freud believed that primary processes possess this "impersonal" character. The id is, I believe, once again an inadequate metaphor to characterize the region of primary process that is often peopled with *beings*—distorted representations of significant others, archaic objects of fantasy, and in many cultures, at another level of symbolic remove, ghosts and demons. The id can never be associated with reflexivity; hence its domain, in psychoanalyzed persons at least, must to some extent be controlled by rational, reflexive ego processes. The goal of a successful psychoanalysis is precisely this: "where id was there shall ego be." The id's sway will be progressively diminished as will, paradoxically, the punitive sway of the superego. Thus ego reigns once again in the rational consciousness of the person successfully psychoanalyzed. If the later Freud affirmed the primary desideratum of the certitude of the self or ego, then it should not surprise us to see the ego's rethronement in the psychoanalytic cure. But this kind of cure is a far cry from the banishment of spirits and their replacement by benevolent guardians in the exorcisms discussed in lecture one and in *Medusa's Hair.* For cultural studies one needs to develop the first topography unencumbered by the personology of the second topography.

Irrespective of whether one prefers the first or the second topography, one must ask: how does one apply the metatheory? Here again Freud is most useful when he is off guard and not trying to justify psychoanalysis as a science on the model of physics. "We can now play about comfortably with our three terms, Cs., Pcs., and Ucs."[54] This is, I think, the heuristic value of the metatheory: the theory provides a nomological framework with enough flexibility for us to "play about" in order to understand unconscious processes in the life history of an individual. Contrary to Freud's assertions this is not exactly physics. But to reject the theory on those grounds is also absurd, since the metatheory is adapted to the intrinsic nature of the human sciences as it hovers somewhere between philosophy and physics! It must also be remembered that nowhere in Freud's work does he display any real interest in the philosophy of science. His well-known references to physics occur for the most part when he has to defend psychoanalysis against an imaginary opponent. While psychoanalysis is not a nomothetic science like physics, one can agree with Freud, that it did emerge in a scientific *Weltanschauung* and participates in it.[55] But participation in a scientific *Weltanschauung* does not make it into a natural science. Marxism and even hermeneutical theories like Dilthey's, not to mention much of history, religious studies, and literary criticism, share with modern culture a common participation in a scientific *Weltanschauung.*

Freud clearly states that his theory is a positivist science like physics, yet the *uses* of the metatheory bring it closer to a hermeneutical discipline. In the first encyclopedia article of 1922, he wrote of psychoanalysis as an empirical science:

> Psychoanalysis is not, like philosophies, a system starting out from a few sharply defined basic concepts, seeking to grasp the whole universe with the help of these and, once it is completed, having no room for fresh discoveries or better understanding. On the contrary, it keeps close to the facts in its field of study, seeks to solve the immediate problems of observation, gropes its way forward by the help of experience, is always incomplete and always ready to correct or modify its theories. There is no incongruity (any more than in the case of physics and chemistry) if its most general concepts lack clarity and if its postulates are provisional; it leaves their more precise definition to the results of future work.[56]

In the very same paper, however, he could speak of "the interpretative art of psychoanalysis" that has succeeded in showing that neurotic symptoms "had a meaning" and that in understanding them "the supposed gulf between normal and pathological events was narrowed."[57] This is what I see constantly in the Freudian corpus: physics as the reference model, interpretation as the practical reality.

Practice propelled Freud in the direction of interpretation, and the classic exemplar of this hermeneutical thrust is *The Interpretation of Dreams*. Freud was very clear that his science did not have "a ready made theoretical structure" as in philosophy, but it is doubtful whether he knew what kind of science it really was. It certainly was not a predictive science; it was not given to experimentation. Freud clearly recognized its clinical orientation: the responses of patients are the "facts" of psychoanalysis. To understand these difficult facts one must grope one's way forward, always ready to modify the always incomplete metatheory. This practice, this use of the metatheory to interpret the signs of desire, is stated with admirable modesty in his 1930 Goethe Prize address:

> My life's work has been directed to a single aim. I have observed the more subtle disturbances of mental function in healthy and sick people and have sought to infer—or, if you prefer it, to guess—from signs of this kind how the apparatus which serves these functions is constructed and what concurrent and mutually opposing forces are at work in it.[58]

This is practice: it isn't all that far removed from Geertz's view that cultural analysis is a guessing game, except that here the guessing game is directed by the metatheory as it also helps revise the metatheory.[59] A constant vision and revision of the metatheory is characteristic of Freud's work. Thus metatheory possesses no dogma; anthropologists are simply unaware of the development of the metatheory in historical terms when they speak of psychoanalysis as dogma. They have not read the Freudian texts and have instead relied on textbooks that freeze the second topography. The personal conflicts and excommunications in the ranks of psychoanalysis do not apply to the intellectual development of the metatheory, its essentially provisional and open character. In that very speculative work *Beyond the Pleasure Principle* (1920), Freud wrote:

> We have arrived at these speculative assumptions in an attempt to describe and to account for the facts of daily observation in our field of study. . . . This is the most obscure and inaccessible region of the mind, and, since we cannot avoid contact with it, the least rigid hypotheses it seems to me will be the best.[60]

This spirit is not confined to *Beyond the Pleasure Principle* but is intrinsic to the whole metatheory. A skeptical attitude towards the metatheory is paralleled by a sense of personal doubt regarding its value as theory. We now know that after practically every major piece he wrote in his later years he felt a deep sense of personal doubt and pessimism regarding its value.[61] This doubt, this pessimism extended to the whole corpus, as a letter to Ernest Jones states:

> As to the question of the value of my work and its influence on the future development of science I find myself very hard to form an opinion. Sometimes I believe in it; sometimes I doubt. I don't think there is any way of predicting it; perhaps God himself doesn't yet know.[62]

The Third Intersubjectivity Pursued: Metatheory and Thick Description

The question I now ask is absolutely imperative for any psychoethnography: Can metatheory be reconciled with a key objective of any ethnography, which is to describe and render intelligible an alien life world? Everyone is familiar with Clifford Geertz's essay on "thick description" in which he makes a case for the use of "megaconcepts," that is, "made in the academy" concepts such as "integration," "rationalization," "ideology," and so forth, "woven into a body of thick-description ethnography in the hope of rendering mere occurrences scientifically eloquent." He adds that one has to interpret at several degrees of remove from that of the actor's interpretations, and while one must "clarify what goes on . . . to reduce puzzlement," one must not practice a "disembodied schematicism."[63]

I do not think you can avoid the methodological issue of how you set about doing this. I agree that one of the major goals of ethnography is thick description, but a purely *ad hoc* approach is only going to compound the issue with each anthropologist discovering the "content of meaning" in his own terms, that is, his own view of the actor's point of view, his rootedness in his own intellectual tradition, and his consciousness of human culture. He cannot produce a viable dialogue with his colleagues: this is my profound dissatisfaction with recent works in hermeneutical and phenomenological anthropology in which one seems to lack a common language to carry on a debate and one is left with the puzzlement that purely ad hoc interpretation seems to have taken over.

For his part Geertz agrees that the anthropological task is case history very much like that of clinical medicine. But he ignores the fact that clinical medicine cannot operate with megaconcepts; it needs a more systemic nosological and nomological framework. Though Geertz talks of the usefulness of "systems of concepts" it is doubtful that the megaconcepts he lists can be systematically and deductively articulated into a meaningful set. Jung uses megaconcepts, and Ricoeur rightly says one cannot disagree with Jung and conduct a dialogue with him.[64] With Freud one can since he uses metatheories instead of megaconcepts. Metatheories, unlike megaconcepts, are systematically and deductively integrated; they not only facilitate interpretation but permit me to have a dialogue with my colleagues. But this dialogue is not simply about Bali or X culture which we "thickly describe." For good or ill anthropologists have dealt with a wide variety of human cultures, and we affirm that our field is the study of culture and society. If so, I must be able to talk about Bali, its relation to Hindu India, why it is different from the Manus or European industrial society—the dialogue I carry on with my colleagues is about X culture and Y culture and about cultures in the plural and about culture in general. This is what unites anthropologists in a kind of moral community bound together by a "cultural consciousness." You cannot do this purely phenomenologically, devoid of theoretical concepts. You need concepts that could effect a bridge across cultures; megaconcepts can do this, but metatheories can fulfill this task more effectively, I think. They can combine thick description with nomological adequacy and deductive order, and simultaneously facilitate communication with colleagues. They can be made to combine history with theory, determinism with contextual specificity. The methodological problem of metatheory is this: the refinement of the megaconcepts through the debate I carry on with my colleagues in my analysis of other cultures.

A metatheory enables one to practice what Habermas calls "general interpretation." This does not exclude thick description, but it does exclude "historical uniqueness." According to Habermas, "A general interpretation . . . must break this spell of the historical [sense of uniqueness] without departing from the level of narrative representation."[65] In the preceding lectures I have "thick descriptions" of histories and cases and simultaneously a general interpretation within the metatheoretical framework of psychoanalysis. But I am using a theory developed in the West in Victorian times; in my interpretations of Hindu-Buddhist culture I then carry out a kind of dialogue with my colleagues regarding the manner in which the metatheory can be applied to Sri Lanka or Hindu India; this facilitates the methodological problem of manipulating the theoretical terms in a different manner from their original Freudian sense. Then I can draw upon the metatheory to make limited general interpretations about types of symbol systems emerging from societies where the performance principle does not dominate and where, on the level of personality, fantasy is permitted to enter open consciousness and receive further objectification in symbol systems. What I have done is to practice a special type of language game in which I preform acts of interpretation (general interpretation) and acts of communication with my colleagues about cultures and culture.

This is where I agree with Habermas in seeing psychoanalytic theory as an ideal type of theory in the human sciences, a metatheory or a "metahermeneutics" as he calls it![66] Habermas has emphasized the nomological structure of the theory while I have, in addition, emphasized its usefulness in respect to the "third intersubjectivity" of the anthropologist's dialogical relation with his colleagues. By "ideal type" I do not mean that it is a perfect theory; it only suggests the *structure* or *form* that such a theory may take. If we move out of the area of psychoanalysis, there is Max Weber, who, I think, saw the problems of the human sciences in a similar way. Weber did not deal with mega-concepts but with metatheories, however imperfect.[67] When he uses terms such as charisma and routinization of charisma he employs them metatheoretically; these terms are conceptually integrated with other terms pertaining to leadership and authority and contrasted systematically with opposed sets of terms. Furthermore, these theoretical terms are rational concepts that operate within an ideal type, such as Weber's ideal type of prophecy. The ideal type in turn is constructed from a one-sided point of view: this permits one to disagree with Weber and enter into a debate with him. And finally his comparative analyses of religion in India, China, and ancient Judaism are a dialogue he carried out with us from the point of view of his own historical rootedness in European history and culture. This may not be our game as anthropologists but it is a related one. In Weber's case the metatheory embedded in an ideal type helps him to deal with case history, but as systematically generalized history. What Habermas said of Freud is equally applicable to Weber:

> It is *systematically generalized history,* because it provides a scheme for many histories with foreseeable alternative courses. Yet, as the same time, each of these histories must then be able to appear with the claim of being the autobiographical narrative of something individuated. How is this possible? In every history, no matter how contingent, there is something general, for someone else can find something exemplary in it. Histories are understood as examples in direct proportion to the typicality of their content. Here the concept of type designates a quality of translatability: a history or story is typical in a given situation and for a specific public, if the "action" can be easily taken out of its context and transferred to other life situations that are just as individuated. We can apply the "typical" case to our own. It is we ourselves who undertake the application, abstract the comparable from the differences, and concretise the desired model under the specific life circumstances of our own case.[68]

The question I pose now is this: Is the Freudian metatheory consonant with the ethnographer's goal of thick description? I shall answer this question by considering the Freudian theory of the dream work defined as "a set of rules for the interpretation of unconscious processes in dreams." These rules could not have been developed without the fundamental assumptions of the metatheory, that of the unconscious, preconscious and consciousness (Systems Ucs, Pcs, Cs).

Since the dream theory is well known I shall not go into its details, though some discussion of it is necessary. The thrust of my argument is to show the nature of metatheory through a well-developed and well-known example. I shall show the two basic orientations of a good metatheory: (1) it can deal with our common human nature through its deductively interrelated set of nomological terms, and (2) it can *at the same time* deal with the uniqueness of different life-forms. In the hands of a sensitive writer it can combine nomological analysis with thick description. I suggest that this is the type of theory that is appropriate to the human sciences and is the kind of theory that we in fact employ—but badly, since we do not recognize it for what it is.

There is a good reason for using *The Interpretation of Dreams* as our model since, as Ricoeur pointed out, it is a hermeneutical work *par excellence*.[69] There is an incomplete or mutilated text, the dream, and the idea is to replace this text with a more intelligible one. Freud himself recognized this; he viewed dream interpretation as translation, as decipherment, as replacement of one text by another.[70] As in classical hermeneutics, interpretation is never complete. Freud says that it is "never possible to be sure that a dream has been completely interpreted," largely owing to overdetermination and resistance.[71]

It is to the dream that the model of the text is mostly applicable. The dream Freud recognized is the dream as narrated, and not the dream as dreamt. It is thus a text. There is a real difference between the "dream" of recent dream research (the REM dream) and the "dream" of Freud (and of all peoples at all times). Dream researchers might say that the REM dream is *the* dream, but nowhere in human society has this definition been accepted. What is significant for human beings everywhere is the dream as related—as a text. This text can obviously be influenced by culture in a variety of ways including the predilection for narrative, and its style, in a particular culture. In addition, for most people, dreams *mean* something; this also affects the narration of the dream. Insofar as all of us as individuals have listened to stories in childhood it is inevitable that the dream gets affected by the style and content of the story as the story gets affected by the dream. Similarly, the situation of the human subject in an experimental situation will inevitably affect the narration of the dream. Furthermore the experimental procedures of interruption during REM periods might well produce disorganized thinking resulting in fragmented REM dreams. In fact, it is doubtful whether there are "dreams as dreamt"; REM dreams are badly narrated dreams occurring in the so-called experimental (i.e., interrupted) situation.

In Freudian thought dreams are the royal road to the unconscious; yet in Freudian praxis the unconscious was the royal road to the dream. The discovery of unconscious processes in hypnosis by Freud and Breuer led to Freud's initial and tentative formulation of the first topography. This topography is the metatheory that led to the investigation of dreams; and the investigation of dreams in turn led to additions to the topography (as, for example, the idea of the Censor) and to a more general appreciation of unconscious processes (primary process). Using the metatheory as a crutch Freud could now proceed to develop a theory of the dream, i.e., the mechanisms that lead to the formation of the dream out of infantile fantasies and wish fulfillments. These unconscious thoughts are elicited through the technique of free association. Thus the theory of the dream entails the following components: the idea of the wish (or desire); that of day residues and dream thoughts; the distortion of unconscious thoughts owing to the work of the Censor; and most importantly the specific mechanisms that transform unconscious thought into the dream, these being condensation, displacement, means of representation, and so forth. The special part of the metatheory that helps us understand the manner in which unconscious thoughts are transformed into images is the "dream work." Once dreams are interpreted through the theory it is possible for Freud to discuss "the logic of unconscious thought," or to put it differently, its very absence of ordinary logic. This "logic" is a kind of syntax or a "philosophical grammar" of the unconscious. No wonder Wittgenstein thought of himself as a disciple of Freud.[72]

I shall now consider three dreams—two of Freud's own and one reported by Abraham—to show how metatheoretical interpretation works by combining nomological analysis with thick description (or at the very least the possibility of thick description). The first is the short and simple, yet famous, dream of the "botanical monograph."

> I had written a monograph on a certain plant. The book lay before me and I was at the moment turning over a folded coloured plate. Bound up in each copy there was a dried specimen of the plant, as though it had been taken from a herbarium.[73]

Actually the dream deals mostly with "recent and indifferent material" rather than infantile fantasy. Note that one strategy of dream interpretation is to discover the day residues and antecedents of the dream elements through free association. I leave the reader to refer to Freud's analysis; here I want to emphasize that the interpretation takes about five pages as against the five lines of the dream text!

The second dream, "The Castle by the Sea," is almost Kafkaesque in its title and contents, though Freud doesn't quite see it this way.

> A castle by the sea; later it was no longer immediately on the sea, but on a narrow canal leading to the sea. The Governor was a Herr P. I was standing with him in a big reception room—with three windows in front of which there rose buttresses with what looked like crenellations. I had been attached to the garrison as something in the nature of a volunteer naval officer. We feared the arrival of enemy warships, since we were in a state of war. Herr P. intended to leave, and gave me instructions as to what was to be done if the event that we feared took place. His invalid wife was with their children in the threatened castle. If the bombardment began, the great hall was to be evacuated. He breathed heavily and turned to go; I held him back and asked him how I was to communicate with him in case of necessity. He added something in reply, but immediately fell down dead. No doubt, I had put an unnecessary strain upon him with my questions. After his death, which made no further impressions on me, I wondered whether his widow would remain in the castle, whether I should report his death to the Higher Command and whether I could take over command of the castle as being next in order of rank. I was standing at the window, and observing the ships as they went past. They were merchant vessels rushing past rapidly through the dark water, some of them with several funnels and others with bulging decks. Then my brother was standing beside me and we were both looking out of the window at the canal. At the sight of one ship we were frightened and cried out: "Here comes the warship!" But it turned out that it was only the same ships that I already knew returning. There now came a small ship, cut off short, in a comic fashion, in the middle. On the deck some curious cup-shaped or box-shaped objects were visible. We called out with one voice: "That's the breakfast-ship!"[74]

Freud notes: "The rapid movement of the ships, the deep dark blue of the water and the brown smoke from the funnels—all of this combined to create a tense and sinister impression."[75] Except for the "nonsensical conclusion," it is a well-constructed, rationally organized dream, and the "affects were distributed in such a way that any striking contradiction was avoided."[76] In his analysis Freud focuses solely on the manner in which affects are handled in the dream work, but even this limitation does not preclude a three-page analysis! Also striking is the fact that though condensation, displacement, substitution, and other mechanisms of the dream work operate to produce the dream, Freud does not have to use this technical terminology in the interpretation. Yet the interpretation could not have been made without at least an implicit knowledge of the theory and its technical terminology. The grammar of the unconscious is also used in interpretation—for example, the governor in the dream is Freud himself, the "I" appearing as a third person. Yet no reference to this grammar is made in the analysis, since it is assumed that the reader is familiar with these features of the primary process. It is of course possible at any point to introduce technical terminology, but there is no need to, as long as the reader is aware of the dream theory.

Once again I refer the reader to Freud's analysis of this dream. Here I want to focus on a peculiar feature of the metatheory: *the interpretation is not only longer but it is also more complicated than the dream text.* In other words a more detailed and more complex text is substituted for the dream text. If simplicity and parsimony are characteristic of many natural-science explanations, the opposite is true of metatheoretical interpretation. It is impossible to understand the dream in terms of a mathematical formula; and it simply does not make sense even to say that this dream can be explained in terms of condensation, displacement, and the technical vocabulary of the dream work. The operation of the dream work has to be *demonstrated in context* i.e., in terms of the life situation of the dreamer. And, of course, it would be totally bizarre to even attempt to predict the dream, or even the dream types, through any kind of theoretical knowledge of the mind of the dreamer. It is true that Freud thought that typical dreams exist, but they cannot be predicted theoretically. Moreover typical dreams are difficult to interpret owing to the lack of free associations. "The dreamer fails as a rule to produce the associations that would have led us in other cases to understand it, or else his associations become obscure and insufficient so that we cannot solve our problem with this help."[77] Consider finally what has happened here. A dream or a set of unconscious thoughts transformed into images is now *re-represented* as a narrative or story by Freud. The images of the dream are translated into words. If in the dream thoughts are transformed into images, in the narrative images are transformed into thought on the logocentric model.

Now let us examine a third dream, from Karl Abraham's female patient (also referred to by Freud).

> I am alone in a long room. Suddenly I hear a subterranean noise, which does not astonish me, however, as I immediately remember, that from a place below a subterranean canal runs out to the water. I lift up a trap-door in the floor, and immediately a creature appears clothed in a brownish fur that resembled very nearly a seal. It threw off the fur and appeared clearly as my brother, who prayed of me, exhausted and breathless, to give him shelter, as he had run away without permission and swum under water the whole way. I induced him to stretch himself out on a couch in the room, and he fell asleep. A few moments later I heard renewed a much louder noise at the door. My brother sprang up with a cry of terror: they will take me, they will think I have deserted: He slipped on his furs and tried to escape through the subterranean canal, turned about immediately, however, and said: Nothing can be done, they have occupied the passage from here to the water! At this moment the door sprung open and several men rushed in and seized my brother. I cried to them despairingly: he has done nothing. I will plead for him!—At this moment I awoke.[78]

In this case I quote in full Abraham's interpretation.

> The dreamer had been married for some time and was in the early period of pregnancy. She looks forward to her confinement, not without anxiety. In the evening she had had various things about the development and physiology of the fetus explained to her by her physician. She had already pretty well oriented herself in relation to the whole subject from books but still had some erroneous ideas. She had, for example, not correctly grasped the significance of the waters. Further, she represented to herself the fine fetal hair (lanugo) as thick like that on a young animal.
>
> The canal that leads directly into the water = the birth canal. Water = amniotic fluid. Out of this canal comes a hairy animal like a seal. The seal is a hairy animal that lives in water quite as the fetus lives in the amniotic fluid. This creature, the

expected child, appears immediately: quick, easy confinement. It appears as the brother of the dreamer. The brother is, as a matter of fact, considerably younger than the dreamer. After the early death of the mother she had to care for him and stood in a relationship to him that had much of motherliness in it. She still preferably called him the "little one" and both younger children together "the children." The younger brother represented the expected child. She wished for a visit from him (she lived at a considerable distance from her family), so she awaited first the brother, second the child. Here is the second analogy between brother and child. She wished, because of reasons that have no particular interest here, that her brother leave his place of residence. Therefore he has "deserted" his residence in the dream. The place lies on the water; he swims there very often (the third analogy with the fetus!). Also her residence lies on the water. The small room, in which she had the dream, has an outlook upon the water. In the room stands a lounge that can be used as a bed; it serves as a bed when there is a guest who remains over night. She awaited her brother, as such a guest, in this room. A fourth analogy: the room will later become a nursery, the baby will sleep there!

The brother is breathless when he arrives. He has swum under the water. Also the fetus, when it has left the canal, must struggle for breath. The brother falls to sleep at once like a child soon after its birth.

Now follows a scene in which the brother exhibits a lively anxiety in a situation out of which there is no escape. One such imminent to the dreamer herself is the confinement. This prepares anxiety for her already in advance. In the dream she displaces the anxiety to the fetus by way of the brother representing it. She induces him to lie down because he is so exhausted. After the confinement she will be exhausted and lie down—in the dream she is active and lets the brother lie down. She extends the affair in still another way: The brother is a jurist and must act as an advocate, "plead." This role she takes from him, she will plead for him. Therefore she displaces her anxiety on him.

This dream contains symbols which may serve as typical examples. Between a child and a seal, between a subterranean canal and the birth canal there exist only vague analogies.

> Notwithstanding one is used for the other in the dream. The brother of the dreamer appears in place of the child, although he has been grown up for a long time. For her he is just the little one (der Kleine). The dream makes use by preference of such words which can be understood in different senses.[79]

Abraham also focuses on a limited theme, what Freud called "representation by symbols." But what renders the analysis plausible is that the symbols can be related to the life situation of the dreamer. Here also, in spite of the limited theme, the text that replaces the dream text is longer and more complex. Again the interpretation is rendered possible by the rules of the dream work that can be imaginatively manipulated to interpret the dream. I reiterate: there cannot be a mechanical application of the metatheory; nor can there be a formulation of a calculus of the dream work.

Let me now develop the special strategy that underlies dream interpretation, and suggest its possible extension to ethnography. The dream text is the descriptive account of the dream; insofar as this is the case it can be "thickly described." The botanical monograph dream is too simple and scarcely warrants thick description. But not so with the two Kafkaesque dreams. Here there is thick description or, if you do not agree with this judgment, the possibility of thick description. The description is followed by an interpretation that renders the text intelligible in terms of the dreamer's deep motivation. Now this model can easily be applied to ethnography (and not just to psychoethnography). One could have a thick description of, let us say, a festival, a ritual, a myth, or whatever. This description—the ethnography—can be followed by an interpretation based on a set of metatheoretical rules, if one also recognizes that the description itself is influenced by these rules. In fact much of ethnographic work is of this order, except that the rules of interpretation are rarely clearly formulated. Instead there is ad hoc theory or interpretation through megaconcepts.

The preceding view of the dream work as "rules of interpretation" does not mean that I accept them. Quite the contrary: the rules must be validated in a variety of ways and then revised or extended. In Freud's own case the crack in the dream theory came with the key work, *Beyond the Pleasure Principle,* where it was shown that those dreams associated with traumatic neuroses defied the wish-fulfillment theory of the dream. With this, as Devereux disapprovingly notes (but I applaud), Freud becomes much more sympathetic to such things as occult phenomena and telepathic dreams.[80] The *possibility* existed to extend the dream theory to telepathic dreams, though Freud himself did not introduce any extensions of the dream work to cover this interesting phenomenon.

Let me now reflect back on the dream theory from the perspective of the *fort-da* game in *Beyond the Pleasure Principle* (1920) where the young child, as yet unable to express himself in language, creatively invents a game that helps him to express his sense of loss and to triumph over it. Here Freud saw the creative side of repetition as against its neurotic manifestations in the obsessive-compulsive neuroses of adults. Yet in his earlier *Interpretation of Dreams* he denied any real intellection or creativity in the dream work except as a weak by-product of waking (the secondary process).[81] But in a later analysis, "Some Dreams of Descartes," he sees this extremely complex set of dreams as creative and intellectually significant, but qualifies this by stating that it is not a true dream.[82] The dream set is related to preconscious processes and as such deals directly with the waking thoughts of the dreamer. This explanation is not satisfactory since the dream set had a terrifying—indeed nightmarish—quality that frightened Descartes. In terms of psychoanalytic theory it has surely to be admitted that the fearsome features of the dream must send tentacles into the depths of the psyche. If so, it seems that Descartes' dreams were like the game of *fort-da*; a terrifying infantile reality has been creatively converted into a dream that is both cognitively organized into a narrative and intellectually satisfying. So is it with Freud's dream of "the castle" and the dream of "the seal-like creature coming up through the trap door." I cannot agree with Freud that his dream had a ludicrous ending; it has the bizarre quality of a surrealistic setting or of a Kafka short story. In both dreams, the dream thoughts are converted into a story with a *plot.* In an earlier discussion I said that the principles of the dream work appear in the work of culture. Now it appears as if the work of culture appears as part of the dream work. I suggest one could use the well-known term "enplotment" to describe part of the dream work in complex dreams. This term enables us to designate the process whereby the dream thoughts are creatively organized into a narrative that can, in some instances at least, stand on its own as story. To miss this is not simply to miss something significant about dreams; it is to miss understanding an aspect of cultural creativity that can transform deep motivation into narrative.

An alternative model of metatheoretical interpretation is one in which description and interpretation intermesh in a narrative. This is the model of the great case histories in psychoanalysis—Little Hans, the Rat Man, the Wolf Man, and so forth. In some of these case histories there is a section that illustrates the metatheory—a discussion of theoretical concepts in relation to the case history—but in others the metatheory is integrated into the case study. In all, interpretation goes hand in hand with thick description. Needless to say this type of approach is also typical of some of the finest anthropological interpretations such as Geertz's "Balinese Cockfight"—if we make the proviso that Geertz employs megaconcepts instead of metatheory. In the Freudian case histories the metatheory is imaginatively and selectively employed in the construction of the case history. Consequently prediction and generalization rarely appear. It is the case that when Freud discusses metatheory in the abstract he might well deal with stages of development (the genetic theory, the Oedipus complex), but when applied to the concrete case there is only a guarded and limited generalization and prediction. This relation between the theory and the specific case history has been forcefully expressed in his 1920 essay on a case of homosexuality in a woman.

> So long as we trace the development from its final outcome backwards, the chain of events appears continuous, and we feel we have gained an insight which is completely satisfactory or even exhaustive. But if we proceed the reverse way, if we start from the premises inferred from the analysis and try to follow these up to the final result, then we no longer get the impression of an inevitable sequence of events which could not have been otherwise determined. We notice at once that there might have been another result, and that we might have been just as well able to understand and explain the latter. The synthesis is thus not so satisfactory as the analysis; in other words, from a knowledge of the premises we could not have foretold the nature of the result. . . . But we never know beforehand which of the determining factors will prove the weaker or the stronger. We only say at the end that those which succeeded must have been stronger. Hence the chain of causation can always be reorganized with certainty if we follow the line of analysis, whereas to predict it along the line of synthesis is impossible.[83]

In plain language Freud is telling us that prediction and the testing of causal hypotheses through techniques of concomitant variation are not possible when it comes to case history. Since the kind of complications that we find in case history is that found in all human life histories, any form of experimental proof of psychoanalytic hypotheses, except the most limited kind, is also problematic. Once again the Freudian case history employs a strategy of analysis that is closer to Weber's historical sociology than to Durkheim's *Suicide*.

Validation in Psychoethnographic Interpretation

The previous statement that techniques of formal proof or falsification of hypotheses on the model of a scientific experiment are problematic in psychoanalytic case history and in ethnography does not mean that the scholar is exempt from the responsibility of validating his interpretations. In lecture two I gave an example of a validation of a specific psychoethnographic hypothesis by means of "myth associations." Here I shall address the issue of validation in disciplines such as psychoanalysis and anthropology that are essentially historical-nomological.

A single case study, however persuasive, be it an ethnography or a case history, can never satisfy the demand for validation. Let me take up once again the two kinds of symbolic forms discussed in lecture one and in *Medusa's Hair* and *The Cult of the Goddess Pattini,* namely, personal symbols and collective representations. *Medusa's Hair* contains thick descriptions of ascetics with matted hair; but the multiple case histories presented there simultaneously provide validation for the psychoanalytic interpretations formulated in that work. Case historical validation, however, becomes much more problematic when it comes to collective representations.

Collective representations are by definition symbolic forms in which the group rather than the individual is involved and must of necessity deal with group motivations or what Durkheim called the "collective consciousness." We noted that if personal symbols are those symbolic forms invented by the culture to objectify the intrapsychic conflicts of the individual, collective representations deal with the more recurring demands faced by a plurality of individuals. But this assumption, though necessary, cannot as easily be demonstrated, since case history, so effective in the realm of personal symbols, does not work as easily in the realm of collective representations. Consider the cathartic rituals discussed in the first lecture. What I did was to infer certain motivations common to the group on the basis of these representations, and then relate these motivations to the representations once again, albeit enriched by a discussion of the genesis and spread of these motivations in the group. But this circular reasoning does not employ the proper use of the hermeneutical circle, since the process of circular inference does not tell us much that is new. It only expands the ideas contained in the premise of the argument. The conventional solution to this problem is the one adopted in psychoanalytic anthropology in general from the early "national character" studies of culture at a distance to the theoretically sophisticated work of Abram Kardiner, Erik Erikson, George Devereux, and Melford E. Spiro. All of these studies are premised on the shared experiences of a plurality of individuals (the group) that are projected and objectified in collectively shared symbolic forms. However there is nothing to say, outside of my own a priori prejudice, that collective representations in which a plurality of individuals participate indicate intrapsychic problems common to that same plurality. The fact that I participate in the ritual might simply indicate my presence there with others; it need not indicate the presence of an anxiety that I share with them. These cathartic rituals are part of a larger cycle that has to do with the common weal, and my participation might well be related to that larger communal goal, instead of the more specific one of resolving my castration and impotence anxieties. The *quantitative* assumption is only an assumption; one might argue that it is always a minority of individuals who share a *qualitatively* high level of these anxieties. The latter then receive symbolic objectification in special types of collective representations.

These kinds of awesome methodological problems are not unique to psychoanalytic anthropology but are endemic to the human sciences. There is no perfect solution, and I can only state my own strategy and then suggest means by which their limitations may be overcome in a piecemeal manner through ethnographic research.

I start off with the assumption that the strength of the Freudian approach lies in its case history method, and I treat, as Freud did, the case of a group on the analogy of the case history of the individual—an ideal type of the "case history" of the group. Thus I ask questions about the *values* held by the group, about maternal and family relations, sexuality, and so forth, and then show that these values, if implemented in the consciousness of the ideal typical person, might well result in the kind of anxieties that are externalized in the collective representations. Weber's notion of the ideal type can be used to deliberately reify the individual case history method to that of the group level.

In *The Cult of the Goddess Pattini,* I constructed hesitantly (since I was trying to escape from the Kardiner paradigm) an ideal type of this sort. In that work, however, analysis stopped with the construction of the ideal type. But this won't do. Once one sketches the ideal type of a collective case history (the collectivity as an individual), one must begin to use the ideal type as a methodological tool—to show how actual cases deviate or conform in whatever degrees to the ideal type. Thus the second step in the strategy is one of "validation." One must deal with actual case studies of individuals and demonstrate the existence of the ideational representations of castration and impotence anxieties in fantasy life and in symptoms (such as sexual inadequacy) and also in symbolic actions at various levels of remove from these specified deep motivations. For example, tying of talismans to ensure a successful insertion on the wedding night; or on a more complex level of symbolic remove an astrological obsession with the proper matching of vaginal and penile size. If these can be demonstrated from individual case studies, then one can make the plausible argument that these problems occur with "enough frequency" to be further objectified, on another level of symbolic remove, as comic ritual dramas (collective representations). Humor then has a variety of functions including the reflexive, letting one to stand back and laugh at one's own anxieties. The fact that these anxieties are unconscious does not negate the reflexive and ludic function of the performance.

It therefore seems that in psychoethnography also case histories must provide validation for the interpretation. Case history belongs to the same genre as the ethnography: it combines description and analysis; it is historical; it shuns operationalism for contextualization; it fuses the multifarious stimuli floating in the empirical world into an ideal-type conception; consequently, it expresses reality but can never replicate it. One cannot be satisfied with a descriptive psychoethnography of a group; one must move towards a case-historical validation of psychoethnographic hypotheses. This strategy also brings into psychoethnography the power of the psychoanalytic case history method, a power demonstrated in the case studies in *Medusa's Hair* in respect of personal symbols.

This mode of validation fits the genius of our discipline. Validation does not constitute proof in the sense of an intersubjective test of a hypothesis that is falsifiable. This kind of proof simply eludes us. Case histories also do not meet with criteria for random sampling; and the phrase "enough frequency" that I employed earlier is remote from the statistical criterion of "frequency distribution." As far as the collective representations of my study are concerned, it is possible for the statistically minded to take a further step in the analysis and record, for example, the frequency (in a statistical sense) of actual cases of sexual inadequacy in the population or the wearing of talismans (or their substitutes) on the wedding night or whatever behavioral index seems appropriate to test a hypothesis of impotence anxiety. This, however, at best can tell us that such anxiety exists in the population; it is not a test of the psychoethnographic hypothesis that these anxieties are projected, at various degrees of remove, into symbolic forms. The latter has to be *demonstrated*; and the demonstration of the hypothesis must be in terms of case studies. If we have enough case studies that demonstrate the psychoethnographic hypothesis we can speak of its validation—but not proof. Others can then use similar data to produce a counterdemonstration that "invalidates" the previous thesis. This strategy is true of ethnography in general: it contains a procedure of *disagreement* through an act of *counterdemonstration* that takes the place of falsification in the experimental sciences. It is impossible to falsify an ethnographic or historical description or hypothesis except through a detailed presentation of counterevidence. Consequently it is not a question of rejecting Popper out of hand but of adapting his insights to tackle problems of validation intrinsic to the human sciences.

How does this procedure of demonstration-validation-disagreement-counterdemonstration-invalidation, and so forth, differ from philosophical speculation? Take the case of any philosophical ontology like Hegel's or Heidegger's; it remains on the level of ideology or thought and lacks empirical validation. There is no dialectical back-and-forth movement such as the demonstration-validation circuit produces. Sometimes social science theories come close to philosophical visions of the world, as does Freud's view of the conflict over man's soul between Life and Death, Eros and Thanatos; this is exactly of the same ontological order as Heidegger's view of man as a "being towards death." One can construct metatheories on the basis of these kinds of ontologies; or one can construct ontological views about man on the basis of the analysis of data by metatheories. In this sense ontological speculations or conclusions enrich the discourse and the potential for debate in the human sciences. Our ontological vision, however, does not exist by itself; it is formed out of the backdrop of the theories we employ or as further inferences from our theories-hypotheses. Extreme deconstructionists might protest that the dialectical form of validation sketched above still grounds us in the objectivist tradition. I will accept this criticism but will not bow my head in shame. I agree with Taylor that we are all too deeply imbued with the "disengaged identity" to dismiss it lightly. Rather we have to free it of its illusory pretensions "without attempting the futile and ultimately self-destructive task of rejecting it altogether."[84]

The Expansion of the Third Intersubjectivity: The Idea of a "Cultural Consciousness"

Every intellectual discipline has a body of ideas that overflow the bounds of the third intersubjectivity into a variety of areas of modern life. Anthropology too has contributed to modern life in bringing out into the open the hidden life-forms of ordinary people debarred from history. The accumulating knowledge of other cultures and life-forms has lead to a long-term and continuing process of intercultural understanding. I think one can look forward to a developing "cultural consciousness" that helps place one's own culture in a larger human scheme of things. Cultural consciousness in my usage is not an attempt to embrace a shallow relativism or a shallower cultural universalism. Instead cultural consciousness deriving from our ethnographic knowledge could lead to a deep reflection on the nature of one's own culture and Culture: hence, the enduring moral value of ethnographic description. This is what will stay with us after our theories have been blown out by other theories.

Let me spell out in more detail what I mean by "cultural consciousness." As anthropologists, at least in our self-conscious practice, we hesitate to fuse our horizon with the other. We see the other culture not only in relation to our own culture but also in relation to other cultures outside our own and the group we study. This awareness of other cultures is part of the training of anthropologists and is also what we wish to inculcate into beginning students in our classes. I am hesitantly introducing this notion for I confess that I have not fully ingested it myself. I believe that over the years one of the real intellectual revolutions of our time has been the description of societies and forms of life that have not yet emerged into formal history. Thus anthropologists have been conscious—whatever our backgrounds—of the rich plenitude of human culture. This for some of us is a liberalizing and humanizing experience. It is a cumulative one, and it is not merely learned but experienced in fieldwork. It makes anthropologists constitute a special kind of moral community—

sometimes alienated from the other social sciences, but I think in a good alienation. Cultural consciousness for most of us involves a twofold *critical* attitude. Often when we write about another culture there is an implied critique of it—sometimes we cannot handle this well. There is also another critique: a critique of one's own culture and traditions. This is, I believe, a very important part of our discipline—or should be—and must supplement the conservative notion of Gadamer's view of one's historical consciousness—the importance of one's own traditions and the notion of the text as the merging of the past with the present. In studying another society it is the idea of "cultural consciousness" that must supplement Gadamer's notion of effective history, historical consciousness, and the "fusion of horizons."[85]

When I study a peasant village in Sri Lanka, I might do several things. I might make a personal self-discovery into my past; I might also make a critique of my own culture; I might see Sri Lanka not in isolation but in relation to the larger Indic or Hindu culture; I might see its parallels with Buddhist Burma and Thailand, and I might ask myself why is it different from Kenya or Highlands New Guinea or lowland New Jersey. What I do as an anthropologist is to understand culture, or a culture; and such understanding must surely be through the prism of my own cultural subjectivity. Yet the dialogue I carry on is not with the culture: it is an understanding about culture that I carry out in dialogical form with my colleagues from where it spills over into modern life and thought, influencing that life in a variety of ways. This spill, this overflow has affected the discourse of the intelligentsia in probably every modern city in the world today. While it cannot provide the energy, the blindness, and the passion that religious and political fundamentalism give to their adherents, it has at least the potential to influence a vision of a more humane world order.

❹

Language and Symbolic Form in Psychoanalysis and Anthropology

In line with the prejudice of this lecture that social science can have no methodological foundations, that in it epistemology is subsumed under ontology, I sketch a view of language that is appropriate to symbolic anthropology and psychoanalysis. To do this I engage in an argument with Charles Taylor and Paul Ricoeur, both of whom have a philosophy of language that has helped to formulate my own. Taylor's essay "Language and Human Nature" in its very title suggests a view of language that is ontological. Following Heidegger, and more recently Gadamer and Habermas, he views man as a "self-interpreting animal."[86] In this ontology it is not society that is the primordial reality, but rather self-understanding and history. Language is crucial to this scheme, not simply in relation to our self-understanding, but also to the way that desires and needs have their bearing on human emotional life. Taylor rejects a view of language that some anthropologists share, namely that, insofar as emotions are expressed in words, one can construct a vocabulary of the emotions (or of madness or anger or whatever) by considering the vocabulary of emotional language as the primary desideratum. By contrast, taking a cue from Searle, he says that in relation to our "subject referring emotions" language is "constitutive." Language is constitutive because the meanings of words or sentences neither *designate* things nor are explained by reference to a state of affairs in the world. Instead the meaning of the expression cannot be separated from the medium, because it is only manifest in it. He says this expressive view of language comes from the three H's—Herder, Humboldt, and Heidegger.[87]

This view of language releases us from the tyranny of the word and the sentence and takes us to larger chunks of speech or discourse and to the importance of what might be called "indirect representations." This is Freud's term, and while Taylor does not use it, it can be sympathetically extended to cover similar ground and, further, to embrace the metaphoric and symbolic language characteristic of poetry. Thus even when a particular culture possesses a specific vocabulary of emotion, it is not always used. Instead, emotions are often expressed indirectly in metaphor, symbol, or poetic language. Hotspur's speech

> I better brook the loss of brittle life
> Than those proud titles thou has won of me
> They wound my thoughts more than thy sword my
> flesh . . .

is one about shame and honor, but its power comes from its use of indirect metaphoric language and not from a "vocabulary of the emotions."

For the purposes of this lecture, I suggest that one must look at the problem from the other side also. A particular culture may lack a vocabulary of the emotions—it may not have words for what in English we call guilt or remorse—yet it might be able to formulate emotions that have family resemblances to these ideas *indirectly* (that is, without conceptual language) in those larger chunks of discourse that one calls narrative. For example, there may be no word for incest in a language, but there are whole narratives (myths, legends, stories, proverbs) that deal with the horrors or temptations of incest, the fears and penalties for violation, without any recourse to that word at all, or even to direct speech. It thus becomes a moot point whether in fact such narratives (at least in their finer forms) are not better vehicles for expressing complex emotions that often elude conceptual thought and direct verbal formulation. It is true that the *anthropologist* can and must express these indirect formations in the language of rational discourse in order to communicate with *his* colleagues; but this is quite different from his often unstated assumption that the informants' world into which he is locked must possess a parallel language of the emotions. It is the Western *analysis* of the emotions that has produced its own vocabulary of the emotions. Where there are terms for emotions in a particular culture we can reasonably assume that ideas about these emotions exist; but an absence of terms does not warrant an inference regarding the absence of the emotions.[88]

The moment we begin to look at language in this special way, we must also begin to question the primacy of language that hermeneutical thought enshrines. One must question the extreme position taken by Heidegger, for whom language is "the house of Being."

> Man behaves as if he were the creator and maker of language, whereas on the contrary, it is language which is and remains his sovereign. . . . For in the proper sense of these terms it is language which speaks. Man speaks in so far as he replies to language by listening to what it says to him. Language makes us a sign and it is language which first and last conducts us in this way towards the being of a thing.[89]

Juxtapose this with the following statement by George Steiner, who formulates a view of language that is close to mine.

> It is appropriate that [Western man] should have used the Greek language to express the Hellenistic conception of the *Logos*, for it is to the fact of its Greek-Judaic inheritance that Western civilization owes its essentially verbal character. We take this character for granted. It is the root and bark of our

experience and we cannot readily transpose our imaginings outside it. We live inside the act of discourse. But we should not assume that a verbal matrix is the only one in which the articulations and conduct of the mind are conceivable. There are modes of intellectual and sensuous reality founded not on language, but on other communicative energies such as the icon or the musical note. And there are actions of the spirit rooted in silence. It is difficult to *speak* of these, for how should speech justly convey the shape and vitality of silence?[90]

What Steiner is saying is that the Western tradition gives primacy to the word and to speech whereas another tradition, like the Buddhist, may give primacy to silence. One might add that even the Western literary tradition follows other traditions of narrative in rendering into verbal form an essentially indirect, imagistic, and pictorial form of thought and experience—a form of thought and experience consonant with unconscious ideation.

To take the view that language is constitutive of the emotions is, as I said, to bring "indirect representation" in narrative, metaphor, and symbol as crystallizations of complex emotions and feelings into center stage. But the logical result of such centering is the *decentering of language.* For the moment I talk of symbol and indirect representations, I must of necessity extend my argument to embrace *other* symbolic forms that parallel expressive language. Taylor was well aware of this, though he did not see it as a problem. "The range of activity is not confined to language in the narrow sense, but rather encompasses the whole gamut of symbolic expressive capacities in which language, narrowly construed, is seen to take its place."[91] Thus, says Taylor, it is not language in its narrow sense but, following Heidegger, it is *logos* or "rational discourse-thought" that defines us as human, an animal possessing *logos.* "If this has something to do with what distinguishes us from other animals, then the effect of the expressive doctrine is to make us see the locus of our humanity in the power of expression by which we constitute language in the broadest sense, that is, the range of symbolic forms. It is this range of expressions which constitute what we know as logos."[92]

One can justly use the term *logocentric* to characterize the subsumption of symbolic forms under the rubric of language.[93] A logocentric encompassment of symbolic forms is almost inevitable in Western thought given the primacy of logos in the constitution of our being in the world. However, anthropologists work in other cultures where this primacy rarely obtains, and while the appropriation of symbolic forms into the logocentric model may be unexceptionable for many purposes, it would not do for those whose task is to render intelligible another culture, however difficult this may be, thereby enriching our notion of human culture in general.[94]

In *Freud and Philosophy,* Ricoeur is also tied to the logocentric model, as is Charles Taylor. In several places Ricoeur explicitly sees symbolic forms as essentially linguistic, and only hesitantly recognizes the power of nonlingual symbols. He does not deal with such nonlingual symbols as the cross, or the tree of Enlightenment in Buddhism, or the milk tree of the Ndembu, or the matted hair of the Sri Lankan Medusa. What is more important is that Ricoeur grasps the essentially nonlingual nature of the unconscious and its representations, yet he seems unable to give up seeing the Freudian unconscious either on the model of, or on the analogue of, language. In an extremely important discussion Ricoeur says he has used the term "linguistic" to describe relations of meaning among symptom, fantasies, dreams, ideals, and unconscious themes. But this term makes sense only if used in its widest application. Questioning Lacan he rightly notes that the contents of the unconscious do not coincide with Saussure's *langue.* The absence of logic in dreams, the ignorance of negation and of the laws of contradiction, and so forth that Freud spelled out in detail do not accord with the state of real language; so is it with distortion and pictorial representation. Nor does Freud himself take language into consideration when he deals with the unconscious; language enters in preconscious and conscious thought alone. "The signifying factor (i.e., significant) which he finds in the unconscious and which he calls the 'instinctual representative' (ideational or affective) is of the order of images as is evidenced moreover by the regression of the dream thoughts to the fantasy stage."[95] The idea of "representative" is crucial; an instinct (drive) reaches the psychism in this form, but this signifying factor is not yet linguistic. Again, the dream thoughts dissolve dream regression to "pictorial representation," which is also not language. When Freud talks of distortion, the key element in the dream work, he always relates it to images or fantasy, not language. "In these three different circumstances Freud focuses on a signifying power that is operative prior to language. The primary process encounters the facts of language only when words are treated in it as things."[96] Thus Ricoeur can conclude: "If we take the concept of linguistics in the strict sense of the science of language phenomena embodied in a given and therefore organized language, the symbolism of the unconscious is not *stricto sensu* a linguistic phenomenon. It is a symbolism common to various cultures regardless of their language."[97] Though not strictly linguistic, nevertheless "we are in the presence of phenomena structured like a language; but the problem is to assign an appropriate meaning to the word 'like'."[98] The discussion concludes with the encompassment of the Freudian unconscious into the logocentric model. "In conclusion, the linguistic interpretation has the merit of raising all the phenomena of the primary process and of repression to the rank of language; the very fact that the analytic cure itself is language attests to the mixture of the quasi language of the unconscious and ordinary language."[99]

Fortunately Ricoeur rids himself of his logocentric bias as far as the symbol is concerned in his short and superb work *Interpretation Theory*.[100] Here he develops a theory of the symbol that is useful for both psychoanalysis and anthropology. I refer the reader to the details of the theory in Ricoeur's book but shall select those aspects relevant to the present argument. Ricoeur is too much influenced by Heidegger and contemporary hermeneutics to fully abandon logocentrism, but he does escape the logocentric trap in his theory of the symbol. He says that metaphor occurs in the universe of discourse and is essentially a linguistic phenomenon, whereas "symbolic activity lacks autonomy. It is a bound activity, and it is the task of many disciplines to reveal the lines that attach the symbolic function to this or that non-symbolic or pre-linguistic activity."[101] Thus, for example, in psychoanalysis, symbolic activity is linked to the "boundary between desire and culture, which is itself a boundary between impulses and their delegated or affective representatives."[102] The symbol in psychoanalysis interconnects bios and logos whereas metaphor remains within the rarefied universe of the logos. The symbol then is rooted in areas of experience that cannot be confined to a single domain, such as the sociological. Furthermore insofar as symbolism occurs across boundaries, it is open to different methods of investigation. The symbol's transcendence of the semantic level applies also to poetry and the history of religion. Thus Rudolf Otto's idea of the numinous is not primarily a question of language and need not even be expressed in language. "It is true that the notion of hierophany, which Eliade substituted for the too massive notion of the numinous, does imply that the manifestations of the Sacred have a form or structure, but even then no special privilege is bestowed upon speech. The Sacred may equally well manifest itself in stones or trees as bearers of efficacity."[103] Needless to say that though many symbols are not verbal at all, they must invariably possess that character if they are enshrined in discourse.

It is clear that Ricoeur has moved away from the restriction that bound the symbol, more or less completely, to logos in *Freud and Philosophy*. In his later view the symbol draws its strength by plunging its roots "into the durable constellations of life, feeling and the universe."[104] Thus in psychoanalysis symbols send taproots into the unconscious, the libidinal sphere of archaic and primordial motivations. It is from the vast encompassing sphere of symbol that metaphor derives its own resources. Let me give an example: God, the father, could be a symbol interconnecting psyche, bios, and cosmos in Ricoeur's terms; but this symbol can also be introduced into discourse as a metaphor that interlinks it with other metaphors from the Hebraic tradition as King, Husband, Lord, Shepherd, Judge, and further as Rock, Fortress, Redeemer, Suffering, and Servant.[105] "The symbol is bound in a way that the metaphor is not. Symbols have roots. Symbols plunge us into the shadowy experience of power. Metaphors are just the linguistic surface of symbols, and they owe their power to relate the semantic surface to the presemantic surface in the depths of human experience to the two-dimensional structure of the symbol."[106]

If indeed the symbol plunges us into life and experience, we can rephrase the narrow schematic representation of the symbol in Ricoeur's earlier book, which identified symbol with logos and logos with life, as a broader scheme consonant with the expanded theory of the symbol in *Interpretation Theory* and with anthropological theories of symbolism such as Victor Turner's, thus:

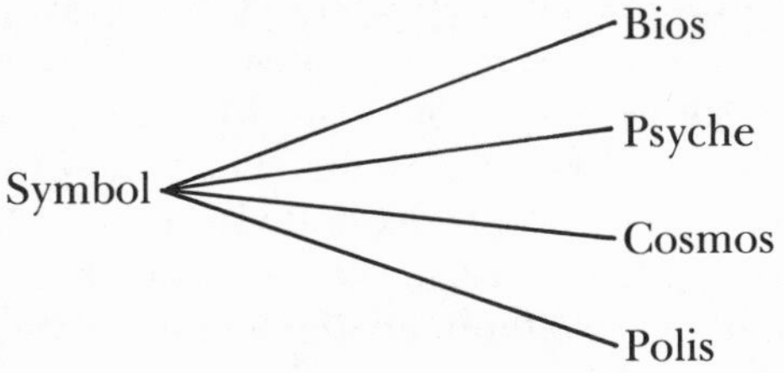

It is the rootedness of the symbol in diverse areas of life that produces paradoxical, ambiguous, overdetermined, and often contradictory meanings that must be incorporated into the theory of the symbol.

Let me push the lines of argument so promisingly started by Taylor and Ricoeur to their irresistible conclusion. It is necessary, I think, to make a clear distinction between the description of the nature of the unconscious and the mechanisms of the primary process from the analytic therapy. The therapy that Freud uses is based on a demystified *rational* discourse ("the talking cure"); it must of necessity be logocentric since the therapist is no priestly or shamanic healer, but a modern substitute for one and an heir to an intellectual tradition that has already demystified magic and demythologized religion. Freud, for example, could not possibly substitute a religious discourse for the discourse of the patient.

Freud's patients also expectably used ordinary discourse when they talked about their symptoms. But though the modern patient speaks ordinary language, it is a distorted one that is ultimately traceable to unconscious processes that are *not* structured as language. The analyst for his part, according to Benveniste, will take this discourse "as a stand in for another 'language' which has its own rules, symbols and syntax and which refers back to the underlying structures of the psychism."[107] Ignoring the term "language" for the moment, the successful cure must result in the patient himself recognizing the nature of his text and substituting for it a "rational" text which, while not conforming to the nomological structure of the analyst's own theory, nevertheless corresponds with its rational explanation of the patient's emotional conflict. The rational discourse of the therapist is guided by psychoanalytic theory; eventually the patient must understand the irrational nature of his illness in terms of a rational discourse.[108] The result would be quite different if the patient went to a priest or a shaman; but then he would be another type of patient. The psychoanalytic *therapy* is a rational logocentric technique and bears no resemblance to the contents of the unconscious understood in terms of psychoanalytic *theory*. The latter is essentially pictorial, imagistic, nonrational.

The unconscious is never seen; it is inferred from its manifestations. These manifestations are the ideational representatives—dreams, symptoms, fantasies—that are related to the unconscious in *indirect* ways, since direct expression is blocked by threats of censorship (superego) and distortion (*entstellung*). Dreams are the royal road to the unconscious, and they are essentially *images* or "thoughts transformed into images." People in most cultures do not say "I had a dream," but "I saw a dream." These ideational representatives are the elementary forms of the objectifications of unconscious processes. Their nonlingual nature is due to two important reasons. First, they are prelinguistic and originate at a time before the child has learnt language. Freud characterized the unconscious as "thinking in pictures."[109] Some people, he said, have the capacity to retain the "visual imagery which is so vivid in the early years" longer than others.[110] Second, as Victor Turner has argued, the images of the unconscious might well be rooted in the primordial structures of the brain.[111] The anthropologist cannot solve this latter problem, but he has to recognize its reality. The crucial nature of unconscious structure and process (not the contents) is that once formed they are, more or less, stably constituted by the end of infancy, around age five or six. The psychological reasons are elaborated by Freud; the neurological reasons must await the results of research in that field.

If the language of the analyst is similar to that of the patient in psychoanalysis, the techniques of shamanic cure, also, parallel that of the patient and belong to the same symbolic order. With one difference, though: the *radical* hiatus between the mode of signification of the unconscious and the discourse of the analyst-analysand does not exist in personal symbols. In the Sri Lankan case, expression of illness-conflict and the cure both belong to the same order of "representation through images," though the cognitive integration of these images must surely be of a higher order when the oneiric images of the unconscious are transformed, at various levels of symbolic remove, to the status of cultural symbols articulated to a cosmology. Hence, insofar as these cultural symbols are removed at various levels from the sources of motivation, one needs the notion of the *work of culture,* over and above the mechanisms of the dream work, to depict the processes of transformation of unconscious motives into cultural symbols that have significance to the individual in respect of both person and culture at the same time. To put it differently, if ideational representatives are the primary objectifications of unconscious processes, we need to describe or identify the mechanisms that are involved in the more complicated *higher* objectifications entailed in the relationship between unconscious processes and culturally constituted symbolic forms.

In this work I have discussed at length two kinds of symbolic formations—personal symbols and collective representations—that can be meaningfully related to deep motivation. Since these symbolic forms are primarily constituted of images, they share an *ontological affinity* with the products of the unconscious, preeminently dreams.[112] However, they are not themselves unconscious phenomena; they exist in consciousness, yet they connect with unconscious processes. This interconnection can be demonstrated best in respect to personal symbols as I do in the first lecture where, in Abdin's case for example, the mother goddess is simultaneously the informant's own mother with whom he identifies in the abreactive context of the ritual.

Both personal symbols and collective representations are, however, cultural products, and consequently they are embodied in language, in which one talks about them, and in myth, which contains stories about them. Yet personal symbols such as the visions experienced by the priestesses in *Medusa's Hair* are so much rooted in the inner experience of the individual that they are primarily nonlingual symbols, whereas collective representations, owing to their public character, achieve greater embodiment in language. Thus the drama of *Shooting the Mango* in the first lecture is also a psychic drama; the power of the latter (its communicative efficacy) is also dependent on the aesthetic and ludic elements. In the *Gun* ritual the language is coarse, vulgar, without complexity, and directly related to the underground experiences it exemplifies—the smelly world of the fox is the world of primary processes. In the ritual of *Shaving* there are no words; we are directly in the archaisms of childhood and the terror of castration. People want to laugh, but they cannot. The dialogue is cut, and the viewer directly sees the power of nonverbal communication and the paramountcy of images. The first ritual is articulated into a larger cosmological scheme even though its significance is temporarily suspended; as we proceed into the more imagistic mode the connections with a larger cosmic and mythic order are progressively elided. Informant exegesis of the *Gun* ritual is minimal; in *Shaving* there is none. It is as if the terror of castration has turned the drama and its audience into stone.

In the preceding analysis I have looked at the manner in which symbols are articulated with discourse in the three ritual dramas discussed in lecture one. Let me now shift perspective and consider each drama as a total integrated symbolic performance. When considered a symbolic totality—as a collective representation—one can pinpoint the fundamental similarity of the three dramas in terms of the interconnectedness of the symbolic representation with life and experience. Thus while they are aesthetically satisfying performances, it is not as art or as play that they take their bearing. Both art and play are obviously there, but as a genre whereby a deeper drama, a deep play tapping deep motivations, is being enacted. In all three language and imagery send taproots into bios and psyche, recapturing and transforming the archaic terrors of childhood into a symbolic performance that we inappositely designate as "ritual drama," "collective representation," and so forth. In this sense each performance as a totality shows a larger unity in which the symbol, to use Ricoeur's language, plunges us into life, in this case the life of the psyche. It is this psychic drama that holds primacy in all three performances, thereby showing an affinity with personal symbols discussed earlier. Those social and cultural anthropologists who assume that rituals, insofar as they are held in a collective arena, must necessarily be sociological are victims of the very constructs they have reified. Participants are much more sophisticated; they perform a variety of rituals that defy encompassment within the analytic category favored by social anthropologists.

Wittgenstein, like Heidegger, believed that there was no access to life and experience outside of language. As far back as the *Tractatus* he could say: "the limits of my language mean the limits of my world."[113] Similarly, language in Taylor's usage is *constitutive* of experience. But this logocentric view must be abandoned; the logical implications of Taylor's argument must, as he himself recognized, lead us to consider *symbolic forms* as the vehicles that crystallize experience.

"Symbolic forms" in this usage is narrower than Cassirer's, which would include all signs in this class, including the signs of mathematics and symbolic logic. "Symbolic forms" in my restricted usage refers to those signs that are constitutive of the experiences they embody, such that it is through the analysis of these forms that one gets at the experience, to which we then give a conceptual label, either borrowed from ordinary language or invented by us for analytical purposes. Art, music, poetic language are all symbolic forms in this sense, and so are the Freudian ideational representatives such as dreams, symptoms, and fantasy. The difference between Freud and Wittgenstein is that for the latter an experience could not exist outside of the symbolic form (i.e., language for Wittgenstein) whereas Freud believed that the symbolic form, in embodying the experience, also *represents* it indirectly. Thus to rephrase the Freudian position in terms of the preceding argument: symbolic forms are both constitutive *and* representative. Once one adopts this position one can talk about the experience in metatheoretical terms. This discourse is for the most part, as Habermas recognizes for social science terminology in general, a carryover of ordinary language, since such discourse is part of our human language use.[114] Thus it is possible, though not necessary, for us to speak of Macbeth's or Oedipus' "remorse" even though that term is almost never used in either drama to describe the mind of the protagonist. And some of us may even develop this speech about guilt into a theoretical language. From here we can make a move towards our goal—the further development of this theoretical language to understand other cultures and then attempt to communicate this understanding to our colleagues.[115]

EPILOGUE

The problems of life are insoluble on the surface and can only be solved in depth. They are insoluble in surface dimensions.

Ludwig Wittgenstein,
Culture and Value

Concluding Inconclusive Afterthought: The Operations of the Spider

A striking feature of contemporary cultural anthropology is its failure to bring in the idea of human agency, intentionality, or motivation to the study of culture. As much as Cartesian thought made a radical distinction between mind and body, contemporary anthropologists make a parallel distinction between mind and culture, motivation and symbolic forms, even though many are willing to recognize that culture is generated out of the minds of people. Agency, motivation, and the idea of man making himself within the context of a preexistent tradition have been nearly eliminated in British social anthropology, in structuralist thought including the structural Marxism of Althusser, and even in the work of scholars such as Schneider and Geertz who, in their own ways, have developed the Weberian notion of culture. This is one of the striking differences between modern and fin-de-siècle social thought. I think it is a regressive change, for what is required is not to reject theories of motivation, deep or surface, individual or collective, but to bring them in line with contemporary theoretical thinking and empirical investigation.

Geertz, in a well-known essay, speaks of culture thus: "Believing with Max Weber, that man is an animal suspended in webs of significance he himself has spun, I take culture to be those webs, and the analysis of it to be therefore not an experimental science in search of a law but an interpretive one in search of meaning."[1] This seems an unexceptionable statement, yet in reading Geertz I see webs everywhere but never the spider at work. But move beyond Geertz; let me react to the three recent ethnographies that I admire. Taussig's brilliant book *Shamanism, Colonialism and the Wild Man*[2] brings the creator of culture into center stage. We see the spider at work: the spider-people out there in the steamy forests of the Amazon creating webs of significance that the spider-anthropologist transforms into culture. This is also true of Fernandez's book on a new African religion in which people create new holistic symbolic forms to overcome a fragmented identity.[3] By contrast Jean Comaroff's *Body of Power, Spirit of Resistance,* undoubtedly an important work, silences the voices of the spider people of the Church of Zion—she records only a few myths or stories; there are no lives and little spirit in the resistance.[4] It is Comaroff's form of structuralism that orients the ethnography away from life. Structuralist thought is radical in its rejection of motivation and the importance of the subject even though it postulates a kind of collective unconscious that underlies the formation and transformation of structures. God, according to an early Upanishad, is the spider creating the world out of nothing, or out of himself. But the anthropologist is not god; he must create the world out of the world and not from his own navel. Instead of the voices of people, the anthropologist's own voice is heard loud and clear spinning webs of significance—but out of what?

Much of modern social thought might, paradoxically, admit that a thinker can be a creator of culture, in the sense that his ideas have moved into the culture at large (as, for example, Marx's or Freud's). Yet while there are plenty of studies of Western thinkers as makers of modern culture, there is among anthropologists a refusal to recognize non-Western thinkers as culture creators. It is therefore not surprising that anthropologists rarely take the further step in the analysis of culture—to examine the relation between motivation and symbolic forms in any ongoing human society. If I may be permitted to parody the poet once again, it seems that for most contemporary culture theorists, the spider appears to have suspended its operations.

Yet this was not the case with the classical social theorists—Marx, Durkheim, Freud, Weber—for whom life-forms in the making were of central concern. While there was a big difference between Durkheimian and Freudian theories of motivation, both focussed on the spider at work. *The Elementary Forms of Religious Life* can be seen as a work that deals with the creation of collective representations.

> [Every religious force] comes to be outside of the object in which it resides. It is because the idea of it is in no way made up of the impressions directly produced by this thing upon our senses or minds. Religious force is only the sentiment inspired by the group in its members, but projected outside of the consciousnesses that experience them, and objectified. To

> be objectified, they are fixed upon some object which thus becomes sacred; but any object might fulfill this function. In principle, there are none whose nature predestines them to it to the exclusion of all others; but also there are none that are necessarily impossible. Everything depends upon the circumstances which lead the sentiment creating religious ideas to establish itself here or there, upon this point or upon that one.[5]

In this work Durkheim is dealing with symbolic forms in the making. So is it with Weber for whom culture as a system of meanings was intimately related to its creation via human consciousness. Consider his discussion of the prophets whose work introduced continuing changes in the tradition of ethical prophecy. The prophet, he tells us, is a "purely individual bearer of charisma, who by virtue of his mission proclaims a religious doctrine or divine commandment." He is a "tool of the divine will" who presents to his followers "a unified view of the world, derived from a consciously integrated and meaningful attitude towards life". For his own part his prophetic message is an attempt "to systematize all the manifestations of life . . . regardless of the form it may assume in any individual case."[6] His work of prophecy advances the preexisting tradition of biblical prophecy and a development of an ethically meaningful attitude to the world—a spider if ever there was one!

The classical social theorists were in a sense pre-Freudian. Durkheim and Weber were Freud's contemporaries, but Freud's thought arrived too late for it to have an impact on them. With Freud one is in the realm of deep motivation, not only in the genesis of culture, but in its production and reproduction. Though much of modern thought has been deeply influenced by Freud, social and cultural anthropologists have assiduously rejected his insights. It seems to me that to ignore deep motivation in the formation and transformation of culture is to miss an important dimension in our species condition. Deep motivation throws light into the dark side of life, something that recent Western capitalism, with its incredible optimism, has brushed aside. Indian cultures by contrast have faced this dark side squarely and openly in their philosophic thought and the symbolic forms they have created. But not just the Indic: this dark side of life is manifest in the symbolic forms and thought of many African cultures, those of Highland New Guinea, and the dream-time of the Australians. It erupts disruptively into modern political movements, in ethnic conflicts where they have taken root. To ignore this dark side is bad enough, but worse to misread its meaning and significance for human culture. It is easy enough to do this. The painful yet creative activities of modern-day ecstatic priests and shamans and their culture-creating propensities can easily be glossed as "performance" or as "theatre." It is easy to adopt this model and indeed to boldly extend it to describe even certain polities, as Geertz does for the Balinese "theatre state."[7] But the trouble is that *any* model or analogy works—but up to a point only. Thus Schumpeter used the model of the machine to describe ancient (and modern) armies. "*Created by wars that required it, the machine now creates the wars it required.* A will for broad conquest without tangible limits, for the capture of positions that were manifestly untenable—this was typical imperialism."[8] And of course the model works, but Schumpeter's is only a fringe understanding of the army, as a kind of mechanical institution which, like a machine, cannot stay idle but must do what it is meant to do, that is, fight wars. So with the analogy of the theatre. The theatre *is* an analogy or a fringe model; it is not a theoretical model. It breaks down soon: there is a sufferer or patient, not an actor; there is a priest, not a director; there is a congregation, not an audience; there are sacred words, not a secular script; there is a willingness to believe, not a willing suspension of disbelief. When anthropologists take over the model of the theatre, they focus on the performative and expressive elements for the most part; not on the themes embodied in it as, for example, a tragic vision. Pain and human suffering are easy enough to eliminate from the model, but not from life. The great social theorists, like great philosophers and poets, were centrally concerned with human suffering, impermanence, and death. Current anthropology, however, is like the modern funeral parlor or, better still, like a bourgeois bathroom: everything is tidy, everything smells clean, and the shit is flushed into the dark, rat-infested sewers that line the belly of the city. Like the id, it is the lower part separated by a barrier from the clean life in middle-class households. What is hidden is dung and death. And like dung and death, pain and human suffering are also confined to sanitized environments. There are, however, the few who will be attracted to such forms of experience and thought, in spite of the physical and social environment in which they live, because they have searched, as Freud did, the dark recesses of their own lives and from there have had a vision of the dark side of life in general. The moment you label this vision as pessimistic and oppose it to "optimism," you miss the point of it all. Neither Freud nor the Buddha gave way to gloom or nihilism by his recognition that the purpose of all life is death.

Psychoanalysis provides a much-needed corrective to a complacent worldview fostered by the increasing *enbourgeoisement* of our lives by focussing on human suffering and pain and the root of suffering in desire (*Wunsch*). There is something Buddhist about this, but psychoanalysis lacks a soteriology. This is as it should be in the human sciences. Instead of soteriology we must in our empirical operations be guided by the metatheory—to build up a view of man that will, in the long run, be ontological or existential. Not a religious ontology on the basis of truth; not a philosophical ontology on the basis of logic; but a back-and-forth groping towards understanding man in culture.

Freudianism per se is no solution. The trouble with the Freudian analysis of culture is precisely its inability to see man within the context of a cultural tradition and encompassed by the institutions of a society in which he is placed. The whole thrust of this work has been to partially redress the balance by introducing the idea of the work of culture, that discontinuous movement from the ideational representatives of deep motivations to their transformations into culturally constituted symbolic forms. That process of transformation is the work of culture; it deals with symbolic transformation, but it is one that refuses to put life and death, Eros and Thanatos, into plus and minus signs; or into a web of signs alone of the sort that cost the Aztecs their empire, or James Cook his life.[9] In it "symbolic remove" is the fundamental movement. Once this is recognized it might be possible to formulate rules that bring about transformations in special areas of cultural life; sometimes this might not be possible, and only an "archaeological" or historical account or a simple description of the processes of transformation might make sense. I, a modern-day Ajātasattu, standing nervously outside the mansion of my intellectual forebears, with my ballpoint pen tied to my thigh, have hesitantly outlined the form of such a project. It might, perhaps, have a future.

NOTES

PREFACE

1. The titles of the original Morgan lectures are as follows. General title: *Psychoanalytic Anthropology and Some Problems of Interpretation*; Lecture 1: "After *Medusa's Hair*: Progression and Regression in Personal Symbols"; Lecture 2: "Dromena and Cathartic Rituals: Regression and Progression in Collective Representations"; Lecture 3: "The Positivist Tradition in Psychoanalytic Anthropology: A Critique"; Lecture 4: "Impact of Psychoanalysis on Anthropology: Prospect and Retrospect."

2. Part of this lecture appeared as "Culturally Constituted Defenses and the Theory of Collective Motivation," in *Personality and the Cultural Construction of Society: Papers in Honor of Melford E. Spiro,* edited by David Jordan and Marc Swartz (Tuscaloosa: University of Alabama Press, 1990).

3. Sigmund Freud, *Civilization and Its Discontents* (1930), Standard Edition (S.E.), vol. 21 (London: Hogarth Press, 1981), 144.

4. Ibid., 114.

5. Paul Ricoeur, *Freud and Philosophy: An Essay on Interpretation* (New Haven and London: Yale University Press, 1977).

6. Ibid., 496–97, 521–22.

7. I use the terms "first topography" and "second topography" following Paul Ricoeur and French fashion in general.

8. Johnson notes that there are 415 self-referential terms in Webster's dictionary. By contrast there are only a very few in Sinhala and, I suspect, in other Indic languages also. See Frank Johnson, "The Western Concept of Self," in *Culture and Self: Asian and Western Perspectives,* edited by Anthony J. Marsella, George de Vos, and Francis L. K. Hsu (New York and London: Tavistock, 1985), 91–138. See also my paper "The Illusory Pursuit of the Self," in *Philosophy: East and West* (forthcoming).

9. See Pontalis's important essay, "The Birth and Recognition of the 'Self'," in *Frontiers in Psychoanalysis: Between the Dream and the Psychic Pain* (London: Hogarth Press, 1981), 126–47. For an American criticism of ego psychology and self-theory see Roy Schafer, *A New Language for Psychoanalysis* (New Haven: Yale University Press, 1976), 187–93. For a general overview of the French critique of self and ego psychology see the recent book by Marion Michel Oliver, *Cultivating Freud's Garden in France*

(Northvale, New Jersey, and London: Jason Aronson Inc., 1988), 12–15. Oliver also discusses the French rejection of psychoanalysis as "science" and a great deal of Anglo-American and German "ego psychology."

10. Max Weber, "Social Psychology of the World Religions," in *From Max Weber,* ed. Hans Gerth and C. Wright Mills (New York: Oxford University Press, 1976), 293.

11. Adolf Grünbaum, *The Foundations of Psychoanalysis* (Berkeley: University of California Press, 1984).

12. Ibid., 51.

13. Ibid., 47.

14. This well-known text is from the *Anguttara Nikāya.* I have used the translation in Ven. Nārada, *The Buddha and His Teachings* (Colombo: The Colombo Apothecaries, 1973), 284.

LECTURE ONE

1. Gananath Obeyesekere, *Medusa's Hair: An Essay on Personal Symbols and Religious Experience* (Chicago: University of Chicago Press, 1981), 10.

2. Paul Ricoeur, *Freud and Philosophy: An Essay on Interpretation* (New Haven and London: Yale University Press, 1977).

3. G. Morris Carstairs, *The Twice Born* (Bloomington and London: Indiana University Press, 1973), 158–62.

4. Lewis L. Langness, "Hysterical Psychosis in the New Guinea Highlands: A Bena-Bena Example," *Psychiatry* 28 (1965): 258–77.

5. For a discussion of this common fallacy of epidemiology, see Gananath Obeyesekere, "Buddhism, Depression and the Work of Culture in Sri Lanka," in *Culture and Depression,* ed. Arthur Kleinman and Byron Good (Berkeley and Los Angeles: University of California Press, 1985), 134–52.

6. Max Weber, "Objectivity in Social Science," in *The Methodology of the Social Sciences,* ed. and trans. Edward A. Shils and Henry A. Finch (New York: Free Press, 1969), 75. For a related discussion of understanding, consider the following statement by Hans Georg Gadamer (*Truth and Method* [New York: Continuum, 1975], 6):

> Whatever "science" may mean here and even if all historical knowledge includes the application of general experience to the particular object of investigation, historical research does not endeavour to grasp the concrete phenomenon as an instance of a general rule. The individual case does not serve only to corroborate a regularity from which predictions can in turn be made. Its ideal is rather to understand the phenomenon itself in its unique and historical concreteness. However much general experience is

> involved, the aim is not to confirm and expand these general experiences in order to attain knowledge of law, e.g., how men, peoples, and states evolve, but to understand how this man, this people, or this state is what it has become—more generally, how has it happened that it is so.

7. Sigmund Freud, *Beyond the Pleasure Principle* (1920), Standard Edition (S.E.), vol. 18 (London: Hogarth Press, 1981), 15. The child in this case study was Freud's own grandson.

8. Ricoeur, *Freud and Philosophy,* 314.

9. Ibid., 286.

10. Ibid., 314.

11. Sigmund Freud, *The Interpretation of Dreams* (1900–1901), S.E., vol. 5, 547, where he speaks of "progressive current" opposed to the dominant regressive movement.

12. Ricoeur, *Freud and Philosophy,* 175–76, 491–93, 522–24.

13. Emile Durkheim, *The Elementary Forms of the Religious Life* (1912), trans. J. W. Swain (London: George Allen and Unwin, 1954), 25–26.

14. Sigmund Freud, *Civilization and Its Discontents* (1930), S.E., vol. 21, 81.

15. Sigmund Freud, *Moses and Monotheism* (1938), S.E., vol. 23, 80.

16. Ibid., 58.

17. See Abram Kardiner, *The Psychological Frontiers of Society* (New York: Columbia University Press, 1946); W. H. M. Whiting, "Socialization Process and Personality," in *Psychological Anthropology,* ed. Francis L. K. Hsu (Homewood, Illinois: Dorsey Press, 1961), 355–80; Melford E. Spiro, "Religious Systems as Culturally Constituted Defense Mechanisms," in *Context and Meaning in Cultural Anthropology,* ed. M. E. Spiro (New York: Free Press, 1965), 100–13; A. L. Epstein, "Tambu: The Shell-Money of the Tolai," in *Fantasy and Symbol,* ed. R. H. Hook (New York: Academic Press, 1979), 188–90.

18. See, for example, the account in Christopher Isherwood, *Ramakrishna and His Disciples* (New York: Simon and Schuster, 1965), especially the section "The Vision of Kali," 58–68. See also the comparable study of Vivekananda in Sudhir Kakar, *The Inner World: A Psychoanalytic Study of Childhood and Society in India* (New Delhi: Oxford University Press, 1981), 160–81.

19. George Devereux, "Normal and Abnormal," in *Basic Problems in Ethnopsychiatry,* trans. B. M. Gulati and George Devereux (Chicago: University of Chicago Press, 1980), 17–18.

20. Jurgen Habermas, *Knowledge and Human Interests* (Boston: Beacon Press [paperback], 1971), 227–28.

21. Ibid., 227.

22. Ricoeur, *Freud and Philosophy,* 389.

23. T. S. Eliot, "A Dialogue on Dramatic Poetry," in *Selected Essays 1917–1932* (New York: Harcourt Brace, 1938), 35–36.

24. The discussion that follows is based on my book *The Cult of the Goddess Pattini* (Chicago: University of Chicago Press, 1984). I refer the reader to this book for a fuller description and discussion of the texts described in this section.

25. Sigmund Freud, "A Special Type of Object Choice Made by Men" (1910), and "The Most Prevalent Form of Degradation in Erotic Life" (1912), in *Collected Papers,* vol. 4, trans. Joan Riviere (London: Hogarth Press, 1956), 192–202 and 203–16. For a more recent translation of the latter by Alan Tyson, see "On the Universal Tendency to Debasement in the Sphere of Love" (1912), S.E., vol. 11, 177–90.

26. Freud, "The Most Prevalent Form of Degradation," 207; my italics.

27. Ibid., 208.

28. Ibid.

29. Kakar, *The Inner World,* 95.

30. Quite unlike in Burma or parts of Italy. See Melford E. Spiro, *Buddhism and Society: A Great Tradition and Its Burmese Vicissitudes* (New York: Harper and Row [paperback], 1970); Anne Parsons, "Is the Oedipus Complex Universal?" in *The Psychoanalytic Study of Society* 3 (1964): 278–328.

31. Kakar, *The Inner World,* 95.

32. Sigmund Freud, "On Narcissism: An Introduction" (1914), S.E., vol. 24, 94.

33. For details, see Obeyesekere, *Pattini,* 451–82.

34. David Shulman, *Tamil Temple Myths: Sacrifice and Divine Marriage in the South Indian Śaiva Tradition* (Princeton: Princeton University Press, 1980), 298–99.

35. J. C. Flugel, "Polyphallic Symbolism and the Castration Complex," *International Journal of Psychoanalysis* 5 (1924): 176.

36. August Starcke, "The Castration Complex," *International Journal of Psychoanalysis* 2 (1921): 179–201; Nolan D. C. Lewis, "The Psychology of the Castration Reaction," *Psychoanalytic Review* 15 (1928): 174–77.

37. Starcke, "The Castration Complex," 183; Lewis, "The Psychology of the Castration Reaction," 177.

38. Henry Whitehead, *Village Gods of South India* (Calcutta: Oxford University Press, 1921), 85.

39. Shulman, *Tamil Temple Myths,* 202–9, 294.

40. Obeyesekere, *Pattini,* cover page and frontispiece.

41. Nur Yalman, "Dual Organization in Ceylon," in *Anthropological Studies*

of Theravada Buddhism, ed. Manning Nash (New Haven, Connecticut: Yale University Press, 1966), 214.

42. Victor Turner, *The Forest of Symbols* (Ithaca, New York: Cornell University Press, 1967), 24, 38.

43. For a related analysis, see Dan Handleman, "The Ritual Clown: Attributes and Affinities," *Anthropos* 76 (1961): 321–70.

44. For a discussion of this problem, see Friedhelm Hardy, *Viraha-Bhakti: The Early History of Kṛṣṇa Devotion in South India* (New Delhi: Oxford University Press, 1983).

45. Shulman, *Tamil Temple Myths,* 282.

46. Ricoeur, *Freud and Philosophy,* 32–36.

47. Habermas, *Knowledge and Human Interests,* 259–64.

48. Richard A. Shweder, "Menstrual Pollution, Soul Loss and the Comparative Study of 'Emotions'," in *Culture and Depression* 182–215.

49. *The Interpretation of Dreams* first appeared in 1900. The section "Representations by Symbols," S.E., vol. 5, 350–404, was added and developed in the 1909 and 1911 editions.

50. Ricoeur, *Freud and Philosophy,* 89; Freud, *The Interpretation of Dreams* (1900), S.E., vol. 4, 96, for dream as "hidden meaning"; 277–78, as "a picture puzzle, a rebus"; 207–8, as "text"; vol. 5, 353, as a kind of "Chinese script."

51. In *Civilization and Its Discontents,* 103., Freud used the term "work of civilization," but he also stated in this work that he scorns to make the distinction between "civilization" and "culture." The term "work of culture" is used in passing by Ricoeur in *Freud and Philosophy* and by Peter Gay in *Freud for Historians* (New York: Oxford University Press, 1985).

52. Obeyesekere, *Medusa's Hair,* 77–78, 122–23.

53. Sigmund Freud, "Obsessive Actions and Religious Practices" (1907), S.E., vol. 9, 115–27.

54. Devereux, "Normal and Abnormal."

55. I use the term "isomorphic replacement" advisedly, since I do not have a better word to express the similarity and difference among the various symbolic expressions of a common motive.

56. Freud, *The Interpretation of Dreams,* 330, 339, 507. "What I have called dream-displacement might equally be described [in Nietzsche's phrase] as a transvaluation of psychical values. I shall not have given an exhaustive estimate of this phenomenon, however, unless I add that this work of displacement or transvaluation is performed to a very varying degree in different dreams." "On Dreams" (1901), S.E., vol. 5, 654–55. Freud's notion of psychical transvaluation is broader than "symbolic remove," though it operates in that sphere also.

57. Freud, *New Introductory Lectures* (1933), S.E., vol. 22, 24, where he discusses the symbolism of the bridge. Here is the relevant quotation:

> The other symbol I want to talk to you about is that of the *bridge,* which has been explained by Ferenczi (1921 and 1922). First it means the male organ, which united the two parents in sexual intercourse; but afterwards it develops further meanings which are derived from this first one. In so far as it is thanks to the male organ that we are able to come into the world at all, out of the amniotic fluid, a bridge becomes the crossing from the other world (the unborn state, the womb) to this world (life); and, since men also picture death as a return to the womb (to the water), a bridge also acquires the meaning of something that leads to death, and finally, *at a further remove from its original sense,* it stands for transitions or changes in condition generally. It tallies with this, accordingly, if a woman who has not overcome her wish to be a man has frequent dreams of bridges that are too short to reach the further shore. [My italics]

58. Charles Brenner, *An Elementary Textbook of Psychoanalysis* (New York: Doubleday paperback edition, 1958), 162–63.

59. Ibid., 163.

60. See Wendy Doniger O'Flaherty, *Hindu Myths* (New York: Penguin Books, 1978), 141–54.

61. Gilbert Herdt, *Guardians of the Flutes* (New York: McGraw-Hill, 1981), especially chapter 7, "Masculinity," 203–54.

62. The Baining have been studied extensively by Jane Fajans of the University of Chicago. This is a society that has poorly developed symbolic systems. For a preliminary statement on these extraordinary people read Jane Fajans, "The Person in Social Context: The Social Character of Baining 'Psychology'," in *Person, Self and Experience,* ed. Geoffrey M. White and John Kirkpatrick (Berkeley and Los Angeles: University of California Press, 1985), 367–97. More relevant is her paper "Where the Action Is: An Anthropological Perspective on 'Activity Theory' with Ethnographic Applications," delivered in Princeton, 29 November 1988.

63. I am not suggesting that reflexivity never occurs in cathartic rituals, but that most often they are not of a philosophical and speculative nature. The exception is perhaps some kinds of clowning as in the case of the Fool in Shakespeare. For the reflexive aspect of clowning, see Handleman, "The Ritual Clown." For Sri Lanka, see Bruce Kapferer, *The Celebration of Demons* (Bloomington, Indiana: Indiana University Press, 1983).

64. My criticism of Whiting's work is precisely this.

65. Freud, *New Introductory Lectures,* 79–80.

66. Herbert Marcuse, *Eros and Civilization* (Boston: Beacon Press, 1955); for a critical discussion of Marcuse's thesis, see Obeyesekere, *Medusa's Hair,* 165–67.

67. Kakar, *The Inner World*; see especially the chapter "Mothers and Infants," 52–112.

68. Ibid., 105.

69. Ibid., 20.

70. A. I. Hallowell, "The Self and Its Behavioral Environment," in *Culture and Experience* (Philadelphia: University of Philadelphia Press, 1974), 75–110.

71. For some of these arguments, read George Devereux, *Mohave Ethnopsychiatry and Suicide* (Washington, D.C.: Smithsonian, 1961); idem., "Shamans as Neurotics," *American Anthropologist* 63 (1961): 1088–90; Julian Silverman, "Shamans and Acute Schizophrenia," *American Anthropologist* 69 (1967): 21–31; Boyce L. Boyer, "Shaman: To Get the Record Straight," *American Anthropologist* 71 (1969): 307–9; Edwin A. Ackerknecht, "Psychopathology, Primitive Medicine and Primitive Culture," *Bulletin of the History of Medicine* 14 (1943): 30–67; Alice B. Kehoe and Dody H. Giletti, "Women's Preponderance in Possession Cults: The Calcium-Deficiency Hypothesis Extended," *American Anthropologist* 83 (1981): 549–61. For a sober assessment of the effect of vitamin A excess on *pibloktok* read David Landy's excellent article "Pibloktoq (Hysteria) and Inuit Nutrition: Possible Implication of Hypervitaminosis A," *Social Science and Medicine* 21, no. 2 (1985): 173–85.

72. Kakar, *The Inner World,* 20.

LECTURE TWO

1. Melford E. Spiro, *Oedipus in the Trobriands* (Chicago: University of Chicago Press, 1982).

2. Sigmund Freud, *Civilization and its Discontents* (1930), Standard Edition (S.E.), vol. 21 (London: Hogarth Press, 1981), 119.

3. Sigmund Freud, *Group Psychology and the Analysis of the Ego* (1921), S.E., vol. 8, 1.

4. This fantasy was neatly echoed by W. H. Auden (excerpted from "Heavy Date," in W. H. Auden, *Collected Poems* [New York: Random House, 1945]):

> Malinowski, Rivers,
> Benedict and others
> Show how common culture
> Shapes the separate lives:

Matrilineal races,
Kill their mother's brothers
In their dreams, and turn
Their sisters into wives.

5. A. K. Ramanujan, "The Indian Oedipus," in *Oedipus, A Folklore Casebook,* ed. Lowell Edmunds and Alan Dundes (New York: Garland Publishing Company, 1983), 234–61.

6. Ramanujan, "Indian Oedipus," 237.

7. Ibid., 238.

8. See also Sudhir Kakar, *The Inner World: A Psychoanalytic Study of Childhood and Society in India* (New Delhi: Oxford University Press, 1981), 104–8.

9. Ramanujan, "Indian Oedipus," p. 243.

10. Ibid., pp. 246–48.

11. Claude Lévi-Strauss, "The Structural Study of Myth," in *Structural Anthropology,* translated by Claire Jacobson and Brooke Grundfest Schoepf (New York: Basic Books), 215.

12. R. P. Goldman, "Fathers, Sons and Gurus: Oedipal Conflict in the Sanskrit Epics," *Journal of Indian Philosophy* 6 (1978): 325–92.

13. Ibid., 360–61.

14. Ibid., 363.

15. Ibid., 333.

16. Ibid., 363.

17. Ibid., 364.

18. Ibid., 329.

19. Ibid., 330–31.

20. Ibid., 332.

21. Ibid., 350.

22. Talcott Parsons, "Social Structure and the Development of Personality: Freud's Contribution to the Integration of Psychology and Sociology," *Psychiatry* 21 (1958): 321–46. See also the collection of his important papers on this subject in *Social Structure and Personality* (New York: Free Press, 1965).

23. Kakar, *The Inner World,* 135.

24. Sigmund Freud, *The Ego and the Id* (1923), S.E., vol. 19, 12–59.

25. Ibid., 31–32, my italics.

26. Ibid., 33.

27. Ibid.

28. Ibid.

29. Sigmund Freud, "Some Neurotic Mechanisms in Jealousy, Paranoia and Homosexuality (1922)," S.E., vol. 28, 223–32.

30. The best example is the study of Schreber. See "Psychoanalytic Notes on an Autobiographical Account of a Case of Paranoia" (1911), S.E., vol. 12, 3–88. See also "Little Hans" (1909), S.E., vol. 10, 20.

31. Sigmund Freud, "Female Sexuality" (1931), S.E., vol. 21, 223–43.

32. Ibid.

33. Ibid., 235.

34. Freud, *The Ego and the Id,* 32. Freud discusses the parallelism between the male and female Oedipus complex in many other places, for example, in *Group Psychology and the Analysis of the Ego,* 106.

35. Freud, "Female Sexuality," 225.

36. Ibid.

37. Ibid.

38. Ibid.

39. Ibid., 226. In fact Freud was not consistent in regard to the roots of neurosis in the Oedipus complex. See J. Laplanche and J. B. Pontalis, *The Language of Psychoanalysis,* trans. D. Nicholson-Smith (New York: Norton, 1973), 284–85.

40. Ibid.

41. Ibid.

42. Ibid., 233.

43. "Erotically desirable" does not exclude nurture, domination, etc., but implies that whatever motivation one isolates for consideration entails others.

44. This is Richard Rorty's term in *Philosophy and the Mirror of Nature* (Princeton: Princeton University Press, 1980).

45. Ludwig Wittgenstein, *Philosophical Investigations,* 3rd edition, trans. G. E. M. Anscombe (New York: Macmillan, 1968), 223, italics in original.

46. Ludwig Wittgenstein, *Zettel,* trans. G. E. M. Anscombe (Berkeley: University of California Press, 1970), 69e.

47. Nicholas F. Gier, *Wittgenstein and Phenomenology* (Albany, New York: SUNY Press, 1981), 130.

48. Wittgenstein, *Philosoophical Investigations,* 223.

49. Ludwig Wittgenstein, *Remarks on Frazer's "Golden Bough,"* ed. Rush Rhees, trans. A. C. Miles (Atlantic Highlands, New Jersey: Humanities Press, 1979).

50. Wittgenstein, *Frazer,* 1e.

51. Ibid., 3e.

52. Ibid., 7e.

53. Ibid., 1e.

54. Ibid.

55. Ibid., 6e.

56. Ibid.

57. Ibid., 16e–17e, my italics.

58. Wittgenstein, *Philosophical Investigations,* 11. D. C. Grayling has an excellent summary of this key idea in *Wittgenstein* (Oxford: Oxford University Press, 1988), 67–89. For the idea of "family resemblances," see the discussion by Renford Bambrough, "Universals and Family Resemblances," in *Wittgenstein, the Philosophical Investigations,* ed. George Pitcher (Notre Dame: University of Notre Dame Press, 1968), 186–204. Wittgenstein himself says in *Philosophical Investigations* (5), "I shall call one whole, consisting of language and the action into which it is woven the 'language game'."

59. This is a reference to an unpublished work quoted in Gier, *Wittgenstein,* 130.

60. Wittgenstein, *Philosophical Investigations,* 82, section 206: "The common behavior of mankind is the system of references by means of which we interpret an unknown language."

61. Gier, *Wittgenstein,* 24–26; Grayling, *Wittgenstein,* 87.

62. Anthony Kenny, *Wittgenstein* (Cambridge: Harvard University Press, 1973), 224.

63. Ludwig Wittgenstein, *Culture and Value,* trans. Peter Winch (Chicago: University of Chicago Press, 1984), 37e–38e.

64. Ludwig Wittgenstein, *Lectures and Conversations on Aesthetics, Psychology and Religious Belief,* ed. Cyril Barrett (Berkeley: University of California Press, n.d.), 24. Regarding Wittgenstein's naivete, remember his predictions about science and the impossibility of sending a man to the moon. Also his love affair with the bomb (*Culture and Value*, 248e–249e):

> The hysterical fear over the atom bomb now being experienced, or at any rate expressed, by the public suggests that at last something really salutary has been invented. The fright at least gives the impression of a really effective bitter medicine. I can't help thinking: if this didn't have something good about it the *philistines* wouldn't be making an outcry. But perhaps this too is a childish idea. Because really all I can mean is that the bomb offers prospect of the end, the destruction, of an evil—one disgusting soapy water science. . . . The people now making speeches against producing the bomb are undoubtedly the *scum* of the intellectuals.

65. John B. Thompson, *Critical Hermeneutics: A Study in the Thought of Paul Ricoeur and Jurgen Habermas* (Cambridge: Cambridge University Press, 1981), 34.

66. Wittgenstein, *Frazer,* 5e.

67. Peter Winch, *Idea of a Social Science and Its Relation to Philosophy*

(London: Routledge and Kegan Paul, 1958); "Understanding a Primitive Society," in *Rationality,* ed. Bryan Wilson (Oxford: Blackwell, 1974), 78–111.

68. For an important analysis of the development of Freud's notion of the Oedipus complex and its cultural background, see Peter Rudnytsky, *Freud and Oedipus* (New York: Columbia University Press, 1987). For a succinct summary see Laplanche and Pontalis, *The Language of Psychoanalysis,* 282–87. Regarding his own self-analysis Freud says in a letter to Fliess dated October 15, 1897: "I have found, in my own case too [the phenomenon of] being in love with my mother and jealous of my father, and I now consider it a universal event in early childhood. . . . [T]he Greek legend seizes upon a compulsion which everyone recognizes because he senses its existence within himself." *The Complete Letters of Sigmund Freud to Wilhelm Fliess, 1887–1904,* trans. and ed. Jeffrey Moussaieff Masson (Cambridge: Harvard University Press, 1985), 272. A recent monumental study of Freud's self-analysis is Didier Anzieu, *Freud's Self-Analysis,* trans. Peter Graham (London: Hogarth Press, 1986).

69. For a similar use of the term "fiction" see Paul Ricoeur, *Freud and Philosophy: An Essay on Interpretation* (New Haven and London: Yale University Press, 1977), 265: "The pleasure principle, taken absolutely, is a fiction that has never been the actual condition of man."

70. Spiro in *Oedipus in the Trobriands* has a nice summary of the evidence. A word of caution, though. In a recent paper Robert A. Hinde tells us: "Since there are about two hundred different species of nonhuman primates, and an even larger number of recognizably distinct societies, it is not difficult to find parallels to prove whatever one wishes. . . . [C]onclusions about the human condition drawn from simple parallels with monkeys or apes should be treated with great caution." See Robert A. Hinde, "Can Nonhuman Primates Help us Understand Human Behavior," in *Primate Societies,* ed. Barbara B. Smuts et al. (Chicago: University of Chicago Press, 1987), 413.

71. Bob Scholte, "The Structural Anthropology of Claude Lévi-Strauss," *Handbook of Social and Cultural Anthropology,* ed. John J. Honigmann (Chicago: Rand McNally, 1973), 639.

72. Wittgenstein, *Zettel,* 69e. He adds (70e): "These men would have nothing human about them. Why?—We could not possibly make ourselves understood to them. Not even as we can to a dog. We could not find our feet with them.

"And yet surely there could be such beings, who in other respects were human."

73. George Devereux, "Why Oedipus Killed Laius: A Note on the

Complementary Oedipus Complex in Greek Drama," in *Oedipus, A Folklore Case Book,* 215–33.

74. Devereux, "Why Oedipus Killed Laius," 216.

75. Ibid., 216.

76. Ibid., 218.

77. Ibid., 219.

78. Ibid., 220.

79. Ibid.

80. Ibid., 221.

81. Ibid., 230.

82. Wittgenstein, *Lectures and Conversations,* 48.

83. Anne Parsons, "Is the Oedipus Complex Universal?" *The Psychoanalytic Study of Society,* 3 (1964): 278–328.

84. Valerio Valeri, *Kingship and Sacrifice: Ritual and Society in Ancient Hawaii* (Chicago: University of Chicago Press, 1985); Clifford Geertz, *Negara, The Theatre State in Nineteenth-Century Bali* (Princeton: Princeton University Press, 1980).

85. E. R. Leach, "Pulleyar and the Lord Buddha: An Aspect of Religious Syncretism in Ceylon," *Psychoanalysis and the Psychoanalytic Review* 49, no. 2 (1962): 80–102.

86. E. R. Leach, "Pulleyar and the Lord Buddha" (slightly abridged), in *Reader in Comparative Religion*, ed. William A. Lessa and Evon Z. Vogt (New York: Harper and Row, 1972), 303–13.

87. Ibid., 302.

88. Leach, "Pulleyar," 1962, 82.

89. Ibid., 82.

90. Ibid., 83.

91. Ibid.

92. Leach, "Pulleyar," 1972, 305.

93. Leach, "Pulleyar," 1962, 87.

94. Ibid., 88. Christ's asexuality, however, is not all that clear. Leo Steinberg in *The Sexuality of Christ in Renaissance Art and in Modern Oblivion* (New York: Pantheon, 1983) has documented a tradition that emphasized his sexuality, especially his infantile sexuality. Unfortunately Steinberg is completely apsychological and cannot interpret the psychodynamic significance of the materials he presents.

95. Ibid., 89.

96. Ibid., 89, 92.

97. Ibid., 92.

98. Ibid., 89.

99. Ibid., 92.

100. Ibid., 91. Though this analysis purports to deal with the prototype *Hindu* versions of Ganeśa, this myth, according to Leach's presentation, was communicated to him by Yalman from among the Sinhala *Buddhists* of the central hill country of Sri Lanka.

101. Ibid., 93.

102. Ibid.

103. Ibid., 84.

104. Paul Ricoeur, *Interpretation Theory: Discourse and the Surplus of Meaning* (Fort Worth, Texas: Texas Christian University Press, 1976), 87. See also Paul Ricoeur, *Hermeneutics and the Human Sciences,* ed. John B. Thompson (Cambridge: Cambridge University Press, 1981), 153–57.

105. Leach, "Pulleyar," 1962, 96.

106. Ibid., 95.

107. Ibid.

108. Ibid.

109. Ibid.

110. Ibid., p. 96.

111. Richard F. Gombrich, *Precept and Practice: Traditional Buddhism in the Rural Highlands of Ceylon* (Oxford: Clarendon Press, 1971), 153, 205, 230.

112. Leach, "Pulleyar," 1962, 97.

113. Ibid., 98.

114. Ibid.

115. Ibid., 99.

116. Ibid.

117. Ibid., 99n.

118. Ibid., 99.

119. Gananath Obeyesekere, *The Cult of the Goddess Pattini* (Chicago: University of Chicago Press, 1984), 470–74; Yalman, "Communication," in Leach, "Pulleyar," 1962, 91.

120. Gananath Obeyesekere, *Medusa's Hair: An Essay on Personal Symbols and Religious Experience* (Chicago: University of Chicago Press, 1981), 11.

121. Paul B. Courtright, *Gaṇeśa, Lord of Obstacles, Lord of Beginnings* (New York: Oxford University Press, 1985), p. 44.

122. Henry Parker, *Ancient Ceylon* (London: Luzac and Company, 1909), 156.

123. Courtright, *Gaṇeśa,* 70–71.

124. Leach, "Pulleyar," 1962, 89.

125. Courtright, *Gaṇeśa,* 65, 77.

126. Obeyesekere, *Pattini,* 471.

127. K. K. Pillay, *The Sucindram Temple* (Madras, 1953), 77. I am indebted to David Shulman for this reference.

128. Obeyesekere, *Pattini,* 427–50.

129. Ramanujan, "The Indian Oedipus," 451–83; see also the third lecture in this book.

130. Present-day ecstatic priests in the urban areas of Sri Lanka have told me that they can get possessed by Gaṇeśa, but I have not witnessed any.

131. I am indebted to John MacAloon for the notion of "flow." See his paper "Deep Play and the Flow Experience in Rock Climbing," coauthored with M. Czikszentmihalyi, in *Play, Games and Sports in Cultural Contexts,* ed. Janet C. Harris and Roberta J. Park (Champaign, Illinois: Human Kinetics Publishers, 1983). See also Mihaly Czikszentmihalyi, *Beyond Boredom and Anxiety* (San Francisco: Jossey Bass, 1975). Mac Aloon uses "flow" in the experiential sense of an individual merging with an activity or being in harmony with it. I have adapted the idea of "flow" to designate a deliberate fuzziness in a concept, so as to question or obliterate paired distinctions or oppositions.

132. B. Malinowski, "Myth in Primitive Psychology," in *Magic, Science and Religion* (New York: Doubleday Anchor, 1955), 112.

133. Ibid., 117.

134. Courtright, *Gaṇeśa,* 70–71.

135. Ibid., 51.

136. Ibid., 49.

137. David Dean Shulman, *Tamil Temple Myths: Sacrifice and Divine Marriage in the South Indian Śaiva Tradition* (Princeton: Princeton University Press, 1980), 84; Courtright, *Gaṇeśa,* 111–12.

138. Courtright, *Gaṇeśa,* 112.

139. Leach, "Pulleyar," 1962, 91.

140. These social changes are discussed in Richard Gombrich and Gananath Obeyesekere, *Buddhism Transformed* (Princeton: Princeton University Press, 1988).

LECTURE THREE

1. *Mahāvaṃsa* 1, 1:2–3. The first book of the *Mahāvaṃsa* was written in the sixth century, the second in the thirteenth, and the third in the eighteenth. Wilhelm Geiger, the great Indologist, has translated all three volumes. Unfortunately Geiger has reserved the title *Mahāvaṃsa* for the first book only; he uses the title *Cūlavaṃsa* (the little dynasty) for the second and third books. Following Buddhist tradition I refer to them as *Mahāvaṃsa* 1, 2, and 3 and cite chapter and verse instead of page references. I refer to Geiger's titles only when I have to cite his own comments found in footnotes

and introductions. I employ the following editions: *The Mahāvaṃsa, or the Great Chronicle of Ceylon,* trans. Wilhelm Geiger (London: The Pali Text Society, 1980); *Cūlavaṃsa,* being the more recent part of the *Mahāvaṃsa,* Parts 1 and 2, trans. W. Geiger (Colombo: Government Information Department, 1953).

2. R. A. L. H. Gunawardana, "The People of the Lion," *Sri Lanka Journal of the Humanities* 5 (1979): 1–51.

3. Gananath Obeyesekere, *The Cult of the Goddess Pattini* (Chicago: University of Chicago Press, 1984), describes these processes in chapters 6, 7, and 8, 283–552.

4. *Mahāvaṃsa* 1, 6:1–38.

5. *Rājāvaliya, The Rājāvaliya* (a historical narrative of Sinhalese kings from Vijaya to Vimaladharma Sūriya II), ed. and trans. B. Gunasekara (Colombo: Government Press, 1900), p. 13.

6. There is veiled reference here to a homosexual bond between Ajātasattu and Devadatta.

7. See *Pūjāvaliya,* ed. Pandit Kiriällē Ñānavimala. Colombo: M. D. Gunasena and Co., 1965, pp. 617–75.

8. Sigmund Freud, *Civilization and Its Discontents* (1930), Standard Edition (S.E.), vol. 21 (London: Hogarth Press, 1981), 137.

9. *Ānantariya* sins. From Sanskrit *ānantarya,* "coming immediately." *Ānantarika kamma* (Pāli), the five heinous actions which carry immediate effect: parricide, matricide, killing an *arahant,* wounding a Buddha, creating a schism in the order.

10. Buddhist texts give us further information regarding Ajātasattu's conscience. At the death of the Buddha, Ajātasattu's excessive grief was overdetermined by his guilty conscience and his relation to the Buddha as a father figure. Malalasekera summarizes the texts that deal with this event:

> When the Buddha died, in the eighth year of Ajātasattu's reign, the latter's ministers decided not to break the news at once, in case he should die of a broken heart. On the pretext of warding off the evil effects of a dream, they placed him in a vat filled with the four kinds of sweet (*catumadhura*) and broke the sad news gently to him. He immediately fainted, and it was not till they put him into two other vats and repeated the tidings that he realized their implication. He forthwith gave himself up to a great lamentation and despair, "like a madman" calling to mind the Buddha's various virtues and visiting various places associated in his mind with the Buddha. (G. P. Malalasekera, *Dictionary of Pali Proper Names,* vol. 1 [New Delhi: Orient Reprint, 1983], 32.)

11. Buddhist sources say that Ajātasattu was afraid that his son might kill him and hoped secretly that Udayabhaddhika would become a monk. What is interesting is that Ajātasattu, a violent man, did not even countenance imprisoning his son as, for example, the Hindu text on political strategy, the *Arthaśaṣtra,* advocates. See Malalasekera, *Dictionary,* 34.

12. *Mahāvaṃsa* 1, 4:1–4.

13. Ibid., 4:5–8.

14. Ibid., 4:16–18.

15. Wilhelm Geiger, *The Dīpavaṃsa and Mahāvaṃsa and Their Historical Development in Ceylon,* trans. Ethel M. Coomaraswamy (Colombo: Government Printer, 1908), 40.

16. *Mahāvaṃsa* 1, 5:39–41.

17. Ibid., 5:45–56.

18. This identification of the older brother with the father is also fairly widespread in Sri Lanka.

19. *Mahāvaṃsa* 1, 5:49–61.

20. *Mahāvaṃsa* 1, 5:64–67.

21. Barbara Aziz in *Tibetan Frontier Families* (Durham, North Carolina: Carolina Academy Press, 1979), 122, says: "There is no ancestor cult, no clan land, no hereditary leadership and no lineage gatherings; all examples of social behavior which would manifest itself where patriliny continued as an organizing principle are absent." For a superb psychoanalytic study of Tibetan religion that complements and contrasts with mine, see Robert A. Paul, *The Tibetan Symbolic World* (Chicago: University of Chicago Press, 1982).

22. Leach says that the relation between father and son in the Sinhala family is tantamount to avoidance. However, one must qualify this with two observations. First, we are concerned with pre-Oedipal and Oedipal relationships that Leach does not mention. Second, Leach's example is from the Nuvarakalāviya District which borders the Hindu areas of Sri Lanka and has been influenced by them. See E. R. Leach, *Pul Eliya: A Village in Ceylon* (Cambridge: Cambridge University Press, 1960), 126.

23. John Davy, *An Account of the Interior of Ceylon* (London: Longman, Hurst, Rees, Orme and Brown, 1921), 215.

24. *Rājāvaliya,* 7–9. The *Rājāvaliya* account is based on popular Buddhist texts that antedate it.

25. It should be remembered that all forms of Buddhism deny a transcendental ontology like that of the soul.

26. James P. McDermott, "Karma and Rebirth in Early Buddhism," in *Karma and Rebirth in Classical Indian Traditions,* ed. Wendy Doniger O'Flaherty (Berkeley: University of California Press, 1980), 171–72.

27. R. P. Goldman, "Fathers, Sons and Gurus: Oedipal Conflict in the Sanskrit Epics," *Journal of Indian Philosophy* 6 (1978): 325–92.

28. *Dīpavaṃsa. The Dīpavaṃsa, An Ancient Buddhist Historical Record,* ed. and trans. Hermann Oldenberg (New Delhi: Asian Educational Services, 1986), 207–8.

29. *Mahāvaṃsa* 1, 25:101–3.

30. *Arahant* or *arahat* refers to Buddhist renouncers who have achieved final release or *nirvāṇa.*

31. *Mahāvaṃsa* 1, 25:109–11.

32. *Saddharmālaṃkāra,* ed. Kiriälle Ñānavimale (Colombo: Gunasena and Company, 1954), 550.

33. *Mahāvaṃsa* 1, 24:19–20.

34. Ibid., 22:32–88.

35. Ibid., 24:5.

36. *Saddharmālaṃkāra,* 528.

37. Ibid.

38. My translation from *Rājāvaliya* [Sinhala edition], edited by A. V. Suraweera (Colombo: Lake House Publishers, 1976), 177.

39. Marguerite Robinson, "The House of the Mighty Hero or the House of Enough Paddy," in *Dialectic in Practical Religion,* ed. E. R. Leach (Cambridge: Cambridge University Press, 1968).

40. *Mahāvaṃsa* 1, 25:69–71.

41. *Saddharmālaṃkāra,* 546–47.

42. *Mahāvaṃsa* 1, 21:14–15, 21–23.

43. Ibid., 25:72–75.

44. *A Meditation on Conscience,* Social Scientists Association of Sri Lanka, Occasional Papers 1, 1988. For contemporary myth making on Duṭṭhagāmaṇī see R. F. Gombrich and Gananath Obeyesekere, *Buddhism Transformed* (Princeton: Princeton University Press, 1988).

45. *Mahāvaṃsa* 2, chapter 38.

46. Ibid., 38:80–85.

47. I later collected stories from informants which in fact state that Migāra's wife was punished for adultery.

48. *Mahāvaṃsa* 2, 38:103.

49. Ibid., 38:115.

50. Ibid., 39:3–4.

51. Ibid., 39:9.

52. For Bodhī, see *The Elders' Verses: Therīgāthā,* trans. K. R. Norman (London: Luzac and Company for the Pali Text Society, 1971), 41; and for Uppallavannā, see an excellent summary of her life in Malalasekera, *Dictionary,* pp. 418–20.

53. Geiger, *Cūlavaṃsa,* 43, n. 7.

54. *Mahāvaṃsa* 2, 39:12–14.

55. *Rājāvaliya*; there are also many ritual texts dealing with this myth.

56. This temple is nowadays identified as Pidurāngala.

57. *Mahāvaṃsa* 2, 38:75.

58. Ibid., 39:18–19.

59. Buddhaghosa, the great Buddhist commentator, has a fine account of *dhutāngas*. See Buddhaghosa, *The Path of Purification,* ed. and trans. Bhikkhu Ñānamoli (Kandy: Buddhist Publication Society, 1975), 59–83.

60. *Mahāvaṃsa* 2, 39:27.

61. Senarat Paranavitana, "Sigiri, the Abode of the God King," *Journal of the Royal Asiatic Society* (Ceylon branch), n.s., vol. 1, 129–62; *Mahāvaṃsa* 2, 39:5–6.

62. Geiger, *Cūlavaṃsa,* 42, n. 2.

63. Several Sinhala names of cities located on flat land have the suffix *giri* (or *giriya*) attached to them, for example, Mädirigiriya, Aturugiriya, Rājagiriya.

64. The dimensions of the lion's paws are approximately as follows: length, 5.5 m.; height, 3.5 m.

65. *Mahāvaṃsa* 2, 39:33.

66. The number eighty-four thousand is a categorical one. According to popular Buddhist tradition there are eighty-four thousand *dharmaskandha*s, "the constituents of existence." Hence it is highly appropriate that the *stupa*s containing Buddha relics should have that number.

67. The most famous of these stories is the *Culladhammapāla Jataka.* In it the Buddha in a former birth was born as Dhammapāla while his arch enemy Devadatta was his father, the king. The evil king had Dhammapāla cruelly mutilated and killed when he was only seven months old.

68. *Mahāvaṃsa* 2, 41:24–25.

69. *Mahāvaṃsa* I, 25: 116

70. For *ānantariya* sins, see no. 9.

71. This is not to say that Rājasinha I was uniformly popular. According to the Dutch writer Baldeus people complained that Rājasinha forced them to carry earth on their heads (in baskets) to build the fortifications of Sītāvaka, his capital. See Philip Baldeus, *A True and Exact Description of the Great Island of Ceylon* (1672), trans. by Peter Brohier (Colombo: Ceylon Historical Journal, 1958–59), 7.

72. The name Kāśyapa (Kasub) was also a popular personal name. Several *laymen* with this name scribbled poems on the Sigiriya, "mirror wall," during the eighth to tenth centuries. Since Kāśyapa was the first king by that name, it is likely that the popularity of that name was due to him. There was

a former Buddha named Kāśyapa, but it is unlikely that laymen would have borrowed his name. See S. Paranavitana, *Sīgiri Grafitti,* 2 vols. (London: Oxford University Press, 1956).

73. *Mahāvaṃsa* 2, 38:80.

74. Asoka's ugliness is described in great detail in the Mahāyāna text, *Asokāvadāna.* See John S. Strong, *The Legend of King Asoka* (Princeton: Princeton University Press, 1983), 17.

75. See Gananath Obeyesekere, "Symbolic Foods: Pregnancy Cravings and the Envious Female," *International Journal of Psychology* 20 (1985): 637–62.

76. For a discussion of this problem, see S. J. Tambiah, *World Conqueror and World Renouncer* (Cambridge: Cambridge University Press, 1976), 54–72.

77. This is a speculation on my part. However, it is clear that Kāśyapa's city was built long before the classic Southeast Asian cities such as Angkor Wat, Borobadur, etc.

78. David Dean Shulman, *The King and the Clown in South Indian Myth and Poetry* (Princeton: Princeton University Press, 1985), 15–33.

79. The idea of the king as a possessor of a strong limb is carried out in the names of Sinhala kings such as Gajabāhu (elephant limb), Jayabāhu (triumphant limb), Vijayabāhu (victorious limb), Vīrabāhu (heroic limb). The prototype model for this is of course Sinhabāhu.

80. Bruce Kapferer, *The Celebration of Demons* (Bloomington, Indiana: Indiana University Press, 1983); see also Gananath Obeyesekere, "The Ritual Drama of the Sanni Demons: Collective Representations of Disease in Ceylon," *Comparative Studies in Society and History* 2, no. 2 (1969): 174–216.

81. This summary of Wirz is from Obeyesekere, *Pattini,* 183.

82. This verse and the previous one are from Obeyesekere, *Pattini,* 182, with minor changes.

83. The better-known studies are Paul Mus, *Barabadur* (Hanoi: Impr. d'Extreme Orient, 1935); R. Heine-Geldern, "Conceptions of State and Kingship in Southeast Asia," *Far Eastern Quarterly* 2 (1942): 15–30; G. Coedes, *The Indianized States of Southeast Asia* (Honolulu: East-West Center Press, 1968).

84. Shulman, *The King and the Clown,* 303–12.

85. S. Paranavitana, *Sīgiri Grafitti.* 2 vols. London: Oxford University Press, 1956.

86. Shulman, *The King and the Clown,* 303–12.

87. Why one should have a summer palace at the lower levels of Sigiriya in the driest and hottest part of Sri Lanka is quite inexplicable.

88. I plan to deal with this chronology in later papers. The *Mahāvaṃsa*

gives the following information naively accepted by modern scholars: Dhātusena, eighteen years and built eighteen irrigation reservoirs and eighteen temples; his son, Kāśyapa, also eighteen years; his brother, Mugalan, eighteen; Mugalan's son, Kumāra Dhātusena, broke the hoodoo and reigned for nine years, but since his son, Kirti Sena, ruled for nine months, we are still stuck with the number eighteen! In fact the *Pujāvaliya* refines the *Mahāvaṃsa* chronology by adding nine years to Kumāra Dhātusena and making it eighteen.

89. Formally inheritance is patrilineal with kingship descending to the brother or the king's eldest son. But this itself provided considerable ambiguity. Usurpation through regicide was also fairly common.

90. The following text is discussed at length in Gananath Obeyesekere, "The Ritual of the Leopard's Pot," in *Honoring E. F. C. Ludowyk,* ed. Percy Colin-Thome and Ashley Halpe (Dehiwela: Tisara Press, 1984).

91. Shulman, *The King and the Clown,* 303 ff.

92. *Mahāvaṃsa* 2, 38:1–2. *Mahāvaṃsa* 2 also states that King Dhātusena had a mother of "the same caste" as his father, implying clearly that his father was also married to another woman of *lower* caste (38:15–16).

93. *Mahāvaṃsa* 3, 93:3–12.

LECTURE FOUR

1. E. B. Tylor, *The Origins of Culture* (1871), part 1 of *Primitive Cultures* (New York: Harper Torchback, 1958), 26.

2. Ernest Jones, "Psychoanalysis and Anthropology," *Journal of the Royal Anthropological Institute* 54 (1924): 49.

3. Anthony Giddens, *New Rules of Sociological Method* (New York: Basic Books, 1976), 15–18, 79; also Peter Winch, "Understanding Primitive Society," in *Rationality,* ed. Bryan Wilson (Oxford: Blackwell, 1974) and *Idea of a Social Science and Its Relation to Philosophy* (London: Routledge and Kegan Paul, 1958). The idea of the subject as a self-reflective individual is, however, not Giddens's but is central to phenomenology and hermeneutics.

4. Max Weber, "Objectivity in Social Science," in *The Methodology of the Social Sciences,* ed. and trans. Edward A. Shils and Henry A. Finch (New York: Free Press, 1969), 96.

5. Victor Turner, *The Forest of Symbols* (Ithaca, New York: Cornell University Press, 1967), 24, 38.

6. Michael Taussig, *Shamanism, Colonialism and the Wild Man: A Study in Terror and Healing* (Chicago: University of Chicago Press, 1987), 440–45.

7. See the important paper by Renato Rosaldo, "Where Objectivity Lies: The Rhetoric of Anthropology," in *The Rhetoric of the Human Sciences,* ed.

John S. Nelson, Allan Megill, and Donald N. McCloskey (Madison: University of Wisconsin Press, 1987), 87–110. Rosaldo insightfully notes how a cultural encounter or argument between the anthropologist and the informant can lead to important insights: ". . . we ethnographers should be open to asking not only how our descriptions of others would read if applied to ourselves, but also how we can learn from other peoples' descriptions of ourselves" (91). His general point that objectivist anthropology has represented people as if they were emotionless robots is, I think, only too true.

Validation of the scholar's descriptions of his subjects' culture has evoked considerable methodological objectivization in sociology. For example, see M. Bloor, "On the Analysis of Observational Data: A discussion of the Worth and Uses of Inductive Technique and Respondent Validation," *Sociology* 12 (1978): 545–52; R. Emerson and M. Pollner, "On the Uses of Members' Responses to Researchers' Accounts," *Human Organization* 47, no. 3, (1988) 189–98. For similar "emic" views in anthropology see C. Frake, "How to Ask for a Drink in Subanum," *American Anthropologist* 66 (1964): 127–32; and C. Frake, "A Structural Description of Subanum Religious Behavior," in *Explorations in Cultural Anthropology,* ed. Ward Goodenough (New York: McGraw Hill, 1964), 111–29.

8. For a neat (and lucid) discussion of the naive anthropologist attempting to administer a questionnaire among worldly-wise informants see Paul Stoller and Cheryl Olkes, *In Sorcery's Shadow* (Chicago: University of Chicago Press, 1987), 9–10. See also Manda Cesara, *Reflections of a Woman Anthropologist: No Hiding Place* (New York: Academic Press, 1982), 103–5.

9. T. S. Eliot, "Tradition and the Individual Talent," in *Selected Essays* (New York: Harcourt Brace, 1938), 7–8.

10. E. K. Chambers, *Sir Thomas Wyatt and Some Collected Studies* (London: Sidgwick and Jackson, 1933), 130.

11. "Disengaged identity" is Charles Taylor's term in "Introduction," *Philosophy and the Human Sciences: Philosophical Papers,* vol. 2 (Cambridge: Cambridge University Press, 1985) 7.

12. "Recollected in tranquility"—Wordsworth's words that Eliot criticizes in "Tradition and Individual Talent," 10.

13. Winch, "Understanding a Primitive Society,"; see also his *The Idea of a Social Science.*

14. Vincent Crapanzano, *Tuhami, Portrait of a Moroccan* (Chicago: University of Chicago Press, 1980); "Text, Transference and Indexicality," *Ethos* 9, no. 2 (1981): 122–48; Waud Kracke, "Encounter with Other Cultures: Psychological and Epistemological Aspects," *Ethos* 15 (1987): 58–81.

15. Bronislaw Malinowski, *A Diary in the Strict Sense of the Term* (New York:

Harcourt, Brace, 1967), 167, 175. It should be remembered that his phrase "exterminate the brutes" is much more ironic and not to be taken literally, even though it expresses his ambivalence. The phrase itself comes from Conrad as Leach has recently shown in "Writing Anthropology," *American Ethnologist* 16, no. 1 (February 1989): 140. For an early view of Malinowski's diary as a "safety valve" see George Stocking, "Empathy and Antipathy in the Heart of Darkness," *Journal of the History of the Behavioral Sciences* 4 (1968): 189–94. See also the negative response by Francis L. K. Hsu, "The Cultural Problem of the Cultural Anthropologist," *American Anthropologist* 81, no. 3 (1979): 517–32, and E. R. Leach's response, "On Reading *A Diary in the Strict Sense of the Term: Or the Self-Mutilation of Professor Hsu*," in *RAIN* 36 (1980): 2–3. Both Leach and Hsu, I believe, have misunderstood the psychological significance of Malinowski's diary. For an important historical review and assessment of Malinowski's interest in psychoanalysis see George W. Stocking, "Anthropology and the Science of the Irrational," in *Malinowski, Rivers, Benedict and Others: Essays on Culture and Personality,* ed. George W. Stocking (Madison: University of Wisconsin Press, 1986), 13–46.

16. Over the last fifteen or twenty years there have been an increasing number of accounts of the ethnographer's relationship to his informants and on his own personal reflections on fieldwork, for example, the sensitive studies by Paul Rabinow, *Reflections on Field Work in Morocco* (Berkeley: University of California Press, 1977); Jane Briggs, *Never in Anger* (Cambridge: Harvard University Press, 1972); Paul Riesman, *Freedom in Fulani Life* (Chicago: University of Chicago Press, 1977), and of course Stoller and Olkes, *In Sorcery's Shadow.* What is lacking in these studies, however, is a theoretical formulation of what goes on in the second intersubjectivity.

17. The role of the interpreter in slanting the tenor and direction of fieldwork is nicely discussed by Gerald Berreman in his early fieldwork among the Pahari. Berreman's first interpreter was a Brahmin; it was only when this person left the field and he found a Muslim substitute that Berreman realized how much information people withheld from him. Informants had been reticent to talk about their everyday violation of Brahmin values which were the ideal values of the society. Berreman's case illustrates a deeper problem of the second intersubjectivity, namely, as much as the ethnographer tries to empathize with, or imagine, what the informant thinks and wants, so does the informant vis-à-vis the ethnographer. This is a general phenomenon of close intersubjective relationships. Thus for some informants the interpreter's values represent the values of the ethnographer (or at least are perceived as sanctioned by the latter); while others (informants and interpreter) try to ferret out the ethnographer's own

intentions and values and slant their "volunteered" information accordingly. This is one of the perils of fieldwork (including questionnaire administration); it is not easy to guard against getting what one wants to get. Gerald D. Berreman, *Behind Many Masks* (New York: Society for Applied Anthropology, 1962) See also Michael K. Gallagher, *Beating Around the Bush; Fieldwork and the Inter-Subjective Nature of Ethnography* (Princeton, B.A. Honors dissertation, 1985).

18. In psychoanalysis Ferenczi was the first to translate empathy into a kind of mystical harmony with the patient. Freud rightly objected to this, since empathy must coexist with detachment. See Peter Gay, *Freud, A Life for Our Time* (New York: W. W. Norton and Company, 1988), 580.

19. The patient is the famous "Rat Man" whose case study appears as "Notes upon a Case of Obsessional Neurosis" (1909), Standard Edition (S.E.), vol. 10 (London: Hogarth Press, 1981), 153–318. Freud recorded his debt to this man in *Totem and Taboo* (1913), S.E., vol. 13, 85–86: "I have adopted the term 'omnipotence of thoughts' from a highly intelligent man who suffered from obsessional ideas. . . . He had coined the phrase as an explanation of all the strange and uncanny events by which he, like others afflicted with the same illness, seemed to be pursued." Freud also recognized that his own interpretation of the case history of a psychotic patient might well possess a delusional component, while the patient's delusions might have a truth component. In his study of Judge Schreber Freud says: "It remains for the future to decide whether there is more delusion in my theory than I should like to admit, or whether there is more truth in Schreber's delusion than other people are as yet prepared to believe." Freud, "Psychoanalytic Notes on an Autobiographical Account of a Case of Paranoia" (1911), S.E., vol. 12, 79. He also referred to Schreber as "this gifted paranoic" (ibid., 80).

20. M. Sherif, *The Psychology of Social Norms* (New York: Harper, 1936).

21. Quoted in Peter Gay, *Freud,* 523 n. See also Freud, *Beyond the Pleasure Principle* (1920), S.E., vol. 28, 8.

22. Freud, *Civilization and Its Discontents* (1930), S.E., vol. 21, 65.

23. Ludwig Wittgenstein, *Philosophical Remarks,* trans. R. Hargreaves and R. White (Oxford: Blackwell, 1975), 263. Wittgenstein was not of course talking about experience in the Freudian sense.

24. Max Weber, "Objectivity in Social Science," in *The Methodology of the Social Sciences,* ed. and trans. Edward A. Shils and Henry A. Finch (New York: Free Press, 1969), 104.

25. For an overview of these theories see Merton M. Gill and Philip S. Holzman, *Psychology Versus Metapsychology: Psychoanalytic Essays in Memory of George S. Klein* (New York: International Universities Press, 1976); Roy

Schafer, *A New Language for Psychoanalysis* (New Haven: Yale University Press, 1976); George S. Klein, *Psychoanalytic Theory* (New York: International Universities Press, 1976). See also Donald P. Spence, *Narrative Truth and Historical Truth: Meaning and Interpretation in Psychoanalysis* (New York: Norton and Company, 1982). My primary objection to these theories is that they have watered down the intellectual content and conceptual thinking that went into Freud's metapsychology.

26. J. Laplanche and J. B. Pontalis, *The Language of Psychoanalysis*, trans. Donald Nicholson-Smith (New York: W. W. Norton, 1973), 249–50.

27. Freud, *Civilization and Its Discontents*, 76, 78.

28. Sigmund Freud, "Repression" (1915), S.E., vol. 24, 147. Italics in original.

29. Ibid., 148.

30. Ibid., 149.

31. Ibid., 154–55.

32. Ibid.

33. Joseph Breuer and Sigmund Freud, "Fräulein Elizabeth von R.," in *Studies in Hysteria* (1883–85), S.E., vol. 2, 160.

34. Freud, "Repression," 155.

35. Sigmund Freud, "The Unconscious" (1915), S.E., vol. 14, 177.

36. Ibid.

37. Sigmund Freud, *New Introductory Lectures* (1933), S.E., vol. 22, 95.

38. Freud, *The Ego and the Id* (1923), S.E., vol. 19, 41.

39. Ibid., 40–50.

40. For the most recent, and penetrating, diagnosis of Freud's Jewish prejudices that affected his analysis of female psychology, see Estelle Roith, *The Riddle of Freud: Jewish Influences on His Theory of Female Sexuality* (London: Tavistock, 1987). I do think, however, that Roith, and others who wrote on Freud's Jewishness, exaggerated this influence by minimizing his Europeanness. This Europeanness (German or French) was true of other Jewish social theorists like Durkheim and Lévi-Strauss. Moreover, some of the so-called Jewish attitudes towards sexuality and authority are also those of Victorian Protestant culture.

41. Freud, *The Ego and the Id*, 56.

42. Freud, *New Introductory Lectures*, 73.

43. Ibid., 76.

44. Freud, *The Ego and the Id*, 35.

45. Ibid., 36.

46. Ibid.

47. Ibid., 48.

48. Ibid., 53.

49. Ibid., 54.

50. Ibid.

51. Ibid., 57.

52. See especially *Civilization and Its Discontents,* 123–38. Here he explicitly brings the father in as the source of the "bad conscience."

53. Freud, *Civilization and Its Discontents,* 65.

54. Freud, *The Ego and the Id,* 15.

55. Freud discusses the scientific *Weltanschauung* of psychoanalysis in *New Introductory Lectures,* 158–82.

56. Sigmund Freud, "Two Encyclopaedia Articles: (A) Psychoanalysis" (1922), S.E., vol. 18, 253–54.

57. Freud, "Two Encyclopedia Articles," 239–40.

58. Sigmund Freud, "Address Delivered at the Goethe House at Frankfurt" (1930), S.E., vol. 21, 208.

59. Clifford Geertz, "Thick Description: Towards an Interpretive Theory of Culture," in *The Interpretation of Cultures* (New York: Basic Books, 1973), 20.

60. Freud, *Beyond the Pleasure Principle,* 7.

61. For example, he says of *Group Psychology and the Analysis of the Ego* (1921), S.E., vol. 18: "Not that I consider this work particularly successful, but it points a way for the analysis of the individual to the understanding of society." About *The Ego and the Id* (1923) he said that it was "unclear, artificially put together, and nasty in diction." He castigated *The Future of an Illusion* (1927) as "childish," "feeble analytically," and "his worst book." See the details in Gay, *Freud,* 404, 411, 524–25.

62. Ernest Jones, *Sigmund Freud,* vol. 11 (London: Hogarth Press, 1955), 446.

63. Geertz, "Thick Description," 16, 17.

64. Paul Ricoeur, *Freud and Philosophy* (New Haven: Yale University Press, 1977), 176.

65. Jurgen Habermas, *Knowledge and Human Interests* (Boston: Beacon Books, 1971), 263.

66. Ibid., 254.

67. For Weber's discussion of authority and charisma, see the section, "Types of Legitimate Domination," in *Economy and Society,* vol. 1, 212–99; for his brilliant ideal type of prophecy, see vol. 2, 439–50.

68. Jurgen Habermas, *Knowledge and Human Interests,* 263.

69. Paul Ricoeur, *Freud and Philosophy,* 87–102.

70. Sigmund Freud, *The Interpretation of Dreams* (1900), S.E., vol. 4, 276–77, 307–8; vol. 5 (1900–1901), 353.

71. Ibid., 279.

72. Wittgenstein, *Lectures and Conversations on Aesthetics, Psychology and Religious Belief*, ed. Cyril Barrett (Berkeley: University of California Press, n.d.), 41. I believe that Wittgenstein's attitude to Freud must be seen in the context of his guilt regarding homosexuality, his preoccupation with the suicide of his brothers, his own temptations with suicide, and his fears of enveloping madness.

73. Sigmund Freud, *The Interpretation of Dreams*, 169.

74. Ibid., 463–64.

75. Ibid., 464.

76. Ibid.,

77. Ibid., 241.

78. Karl Abraham, *Myths and Dreams: A Study in Race Psychology*, trans. William A. White, *Journal of Nervous and Mental Disease*, monograph no. 15, 1909, 22–23.

79. Ibid., 23–25.

80. George Devereux, "Cultural Thought Models," in *Ethnopsychoanalysis* (Berkeley: University of California Press, 1978), 291.

81. Freud often hints at the *possible* creativity of dreams, but does not actually put it in those terms. Take his discussion of the creation of composite structures in dreams. "The possibility of creating composite structures stands foremost among the characteristics which so often lend dreams a fantastic appearance, for it introduces into the content of dreams elements which could never have been elements of actual perception." Freud, *The Interpretation of Dreams*, vol. 4, 324.

82. Sigmund Freud, "Some Dreams of Descartes" (1929), S.E., vol. 21, 200–201. I reproduce this fascinating dream set below:

> Then, during the night, when all was fever, thunderstorms, panic, phantoms rose before the dreamer. He tried to get up in order to drive them away. But he fell back, ashamed of himself, feeling troubled by a great weakness in his right side. All at once, a window in the room opened. Terrified, he felt himself carried away by the gusts of a violent wind, which made him whirl round several times on his left foot.
>
> Dragging himself staggering along, he reached the building of the college in which he had been educated. He tried desperately to enter the chapel, to make his devotions. At that moment some people passed by. He wanted to stop in order to speak to them; he noticed that one of them was carrying a melon. But a violent wind drove him back towards the chapel.
>
> He then woke up, with twinges of sharp pain in his left side. He

did not know whether he was dreaming or awake. Half-awake, he told himself that an evil genius was trying to seduce him, and he murmured a prayer to exorcise it.

He went to sleep again. A clap of thunder woke him again and filled his room with flashes. Once more he asked himself whether he was asleep or awake, whether it was a dream or a day-dream, opening and shutting his eyes so as to reach a certainty. Then, reassured, he dozed off, swept away by exhaustion.

With his brain on fire, excited by these rumours and vague sufferings, Descartes opened a dictionary and then a collection of poems. The intrepid traveller dreamt of this line: "*Quod vitae sectabor iter*?" Another journey in the land of dreams? Then suddenly there appeared a man he did not know, intending to make him read a passage from Ausonius beginning with the words "*Est et non.*" But the man disappeared and another took his place. The book vanished in its turn, then re-appeared decorated with portraits in copperplate. Finally, the night grew quiet.

83. Sigmund Freud, "The Psychogenesis of a Case of Homosexuality in a Woman" (1920), S.E., vol. 18, 167–68.

84. Charles Taylor, "Introduction," in *Philosophy and the Human Sciences: Philosophical Papers,* vol. 2 (Cambridge: Cambridge University Press, 1985), 7.

85. In an earlier version of this manuscript I had an extended discussion and critique of Gadamer's "philosophical hermeneutics" and its appropriateness for ethnography. A crucial notion in Gadamer is the "fusion of horizons," a special dialectical process whereby a text belonging to the past is fused with the scholar's own horizon, itself a product of his tradition and his historical placement and consciousness. Fusion of horizons in this sense is appropriate when the text belongs to one's own tradition, but this model of the text is inadequate for studying an alien culture. Here, I believe, one must *resist* the fusion of horizons and try as best one can to restore in one's work the integrity of alien life-forms. See Hans-Georg Gadamer, *Truth and Method* (New York: Continuum, 1975), especially the section entitled "The Elevation of the Historicity of Understanding," 235–74. For an excellent sampling of Gadamer see the book edited by David E. Linge, *Philosophical Hermeneutics* (Berkeley and Los Angeles: University of California Press, 1977).

86. Charles Taylor, "Self Interpreting Animals," in *Human Agency and Language: Philosophical Papers,* vol. 1 (Cambridge: Cambridge University Press, 1985), 45–76.

87. Ibid., 255–56.

88. Since this book was written I have had a chance to look briefly at a sophisticated treatment of "the vocabulary of the emotions" by Catherine A. Lutz in *Unnatural Emotions: Everyday Sentiments on a Micronesian Atoll and Their Challenge to Western Theory* (Chicago: University of Chicago Press, 1988). Lutz's general goal is well taken: it is not to deny "the biological basis of human experience, including that termed emotional" but rather "to critique essentialism in the understanding of emotion and to explore the relatively neglected ways in which social and cultural forces help to give emotions their observed character" (210). The result is a powerful ideal typical construction of the vocabulary of the emotions among Ifaluk. Unfortunately Lutz misunderstands her own project, seduced as she is by a naive "emic" perspective. She thinks that on the basis of Ifaluk verbal statements occurring naturally or in their talks with the ethnographer, she can construct an ethnopsychology of Ifaluk emotions. In the first place it is doubtful whether long conversations with Ifaluk do not orient the discourse in a "one-sided" direction, with the Ifaluk "cooperating" (itself an Ifaluk value) with the guest-ethnographer in furthering her own theoretical project, that is, by not providing statements that contradict the theories produced by the collaboration of informants and ethnographer. Second, related to the above, the ethnopsychology constructed by her is not an Ifaluk one at all, but Lutz's own ideal typical construction of Ifaluk ethnopsychology based on construct criteria that are inescapably Eurocentric. Indeed the very assumption that any particular group will have an ethnopsychology is probably false. Moreover the terms "psychology" and "mental processes" that she plans to investigate are already loaded with Western assumptions of psyche and mind (83). Again, she says that "the importance of ethnopsychological theory is also indexed in Hallowell's argument that self-awareness and concepts of the person are universal and at the same time cultural phenomena" (84). Here ethnopsychology is, rightly, presented as the author's own theory, and one constructed on the universal existence of "self," a thoroughgoing Western assumption that must itself be questioned (for example, see Ernest Tugendhat, *Self-Consciousness and Self-Determination* [Cambridge: M.I.T. Press, 1986]). Lutz also assumes that there is a "lexicon of the self" and that "words descriptive of self and other constitute the primary elements from which ethnopsychological statements are built" (85). One also wonders what kind of "ethnopsychology" emerges when the ethnographer elicits stories "prompted by two versions of the Thematic Apperception Test (TAT) cards (one with island scenes, the other with the often vaguely 'Western' figures of the Murray TAT cards)" (45). Finally Lutz simply ignores the fact that the whole quest for a "vocabulary of emotions" is predicated on Western

logocentrism. There is little evidence whether Lutz pushed the Ifaluk to question this assumption. None of my criticisms render Lutz's work invalid; they only render invalid the epistemological assumption of an *Ifaluk* "ethnopsychology." Her assumptions are not in principle different from those underlying the very theories she criticizes.

89. Quoted in Taylor, *Human Agency,* 239.

90. George Steiner, "The Retreat from the Word," in *Language and Silence* (New York: Atheneum, 1967), 12.

91. Charles Taylor, *Human Agency,* 234.

92. Ibid., 235.

93. My rather obvious use of this term to embrace the Western preoccupation with the word (both writing and speech) should not be confused with the more technical meaning given to "logocentric" by Jacques Derrida.

94. This means that it is the "expansion of our horizon" of understanding rather than a "fusion of horizons" that occurs, or ought to occur, in ethnography. The idea of "fusion of horizons" is spelled out in Hans-Georg Gadamer, *Truth and Method,* especially 267–78; see also n. 85 above.

95. Paul Ricoeur, *Freud and Philosophy,* 398.

96. Ibid.

97. Ibid., 399.

98. Ibid., 402.

99. Ibid., 405.

100. Paul Ricoeur, *Interpretation Theory: Discourse and the Surplus of Meaning* (Fort Worth, Texas: Texas Christian University Press, 1976).

101. Ibid., 58.

102. Ibid.

103. Ibid., 61.

104. Ibid., 64.

105. Ibid.

106. Ibid., 68.

107. Cited in Ricoeur, *Freud and Philosophy,* 396.

108. Freud noted the complex relationship between the patient's language and psychoanalytic discourse. "Therapeutic success is, however, our primary aim; we endeavour rather to enable the patient to obtain a conscious grasp of his unconscious wishes. And this we can achieve by working upon the basis of the hints that he throws out, and so, with the help of our interpretative technique, presenting the unconscious complex to his consciousness *in our own words.* There will be a degree of similarity between that which he hears from us and that which he is looking for, and which, in spite of all resistances, is trying to force its way through to consciousness;

and it is this similarity that will enable him to discover the unconscious material." Freud, "Analysis of a Phobia in a Five Year Old Boy" (1909) ("Little Hans"), S.E., vol. 10, 120–21. Again, in the famous Rat Man case, he says: "I took the opportunity of giving him a first glance at the underlying principles of psychoanalytic therapy." "Notes upon a Case of Obsessional Neurosis" (1909), S.E., vol. 10, 175. The case of the Rat Man is particularly fascinating since Freud clearly enjoyed the interaction, and the intellectual exchange, with him. For example, he respected the Rat Man's insights and said that "he had incidentally hit upon one of the chief characteristics of the unconscious, namely, its relation to the *infantile*" (177). Freud also offers reassurance to the Rat Man. "In this connection I said a word or two upon the good opinion that I had formed of him, and this gave him visible pleasure" (178). The relation between doctor and patient is dialogical (179); Freud constantly brings in the theory to explain symptoms to his patient ("I thought it advisable to bring a fresh bit of theory to his notice" [180]). He brings in admonitions (184) and moralizings (185).

109. Freud, *The Ego and the Id,* 21.

110. Freud, *Interpretation of Dreams,* 552. See also 339, where he talks of the "abstract expression in the dream-thought being exchanged for a pictorial and concrete one." Or 340: "A dream thought is unusable so long as it is expressed in an abstract form."

111. Victor Turner, "Body, Brain and Culture" and "The New Neurosociology," in *On the Edge of the Bush,* ed. Edith L. B. Turner (Tucson, Arizona: University of Arizona Press, 1985), 249–73 and 275–89.

112. "Ontological affinity" is my replacement for Weber's "elective affinity." The two ideas are close, except my phrase does not imply the "voluntarism" that Weber's "elective" implies. For a discussion of Weber's notion see Hans Gerth and C. Wright Mills, eds., *From Max Weber: Essays in Sociology* (New York: Oxford University Press, 1976), 62–63.

113. Ludwig Wittgenstein, *Tractatus Logico Philosophicus,* (London and New York: Routledge and Kegan Paul, 1981, proposition 5.6), 149.

114. Jurgen Habermas, *Knowledge and Human Interests,* trans. Jeremy J. Shapiro (Boston: Beacon Press, 1971), 262–64.

115. For an excellent study that contains a view of language different from the one sketched here see John Forrester, *Language and the Origins of Psychoanalysis* (New York: Columbia University Press, 1980). Forrester says that he uses language in a broad sense to include what might be called "word" and "thought" (4). I am not sure that this does not undermine the very thesis that he is making.

EPILOGUE

1. Clifford Geertz, "Thick Description: Towards an Interpretive Theory of Culture," in *The Interpretation of Cultures* (New York: Basic Books, 1973), 5.

2. Michael Taussig, *Shamanism, Colonialism and the Wild Man: A Study in Terror and Healing* (Chicago: University of Chicago Press, 1987).

3. James Fernandez, *Bwiti, An Ethnography of the Religions Imagination in Africa,* (Princeton: Princeton University Press, 1982).

4. Jean Comaroff, *Body of Power, Spirit of Resistance* (Chicago: University of Chicago Press, 1985).

5. Emile Durkheim, *The Elementary Forms of the Religious Life* (1912), trans. J. W. Swain (London: George Allen and Unwin, 1954), 229.

6. Max Weber, *Economy and Society,* ed. Guenther Roth and Claus Wittich (New York: Bedminster Press, 1968), 439, 450, 451.

7. Clifford Geertz, *Negara: The Theatre State in Nineteenth-Century Bali* (Princeton: Princeton University Press, 1980).

8. Joseph Schumpeter, *Imperialism and Social Classes* (New York: Meridian Books, 1961), 25. Italics in the original.

9. I refer to Tzvetan Todorov, *The Conquest of America* (New York: Harper and Row, 1984); and Marshall Sahlins, *Historical Metaphors and Mythical Realities* (Ann Arbor, Michigan: University of Michigan Press, 1981).

BIBLIOGRAPHY

Abraham, Karl. *Myths and Dreams: A Study in Race Psychology*. Translated by William A. White. *Journal of Nervous and Mental Disease*, Monograph no. 15, 1909.

Ackerknecht, Edwin A. "Psychopathology, Primitive Medicine and Primitive Culture." *Bulletin of the History of Medicine* 14 (1943): 30–67.

Anzieu, Didier. *Freud's Self-Analysis*. Translated by Peter Graham. London: Hogarth Press, 1986.

Asokāvadāna. John S. Strong, trans. and ed. *The Legend of King Asoka*. Princeton: Princeton University Press, 1983.

Aziz, Barbara. *Tibetan Frontier Families*. Durham, North Carolina: Carolina Academy Press, 1979.

Baldeus, Philip. *A True and Exact Description of the Great Island of Ceylon* (1672). Translated by Peter Brohier. Colombo: Ceylon Historical Journal, 1958–59.

Bambrough, Renford. "Universals and Family Resemblances." Pp. 186–204 in *Wittgenstein, the Philosophical Investigations*, edited by George Pitcher. Notre Dame: University of Notre Dame Press, 1968.

Berreman, Gerald D. *Behind Many Masks*. New York: Society for Applied Anthropology, 1962.

Bloor, M. "On the Analysis of Observational Data: A Discussion of the Worth and Uses of Inductive Technique and Respondent Validation." *Sociology* 12 (1978): 545–52.

Boyer, Boyce L. "Shaman: To Get the Record Straight." *American Anthropologist* 71 (1969): 307–9.

Brenner, Charles. *An Elementary Textbook of Psychoanalysis*. New York: Doubleday paperback edition, 1958.

Breuer, Joseph, and Sigmund Freud. "Fräulein Elizabeth von R." In *Studies in Hysteria*, (1883–85), Standard Edition, vol. 1. London: Hogarth Press, 1981.

Briggs, Jane. *Never in Anger*. Cambridge: Harvard University Press, 1972.

Buddhaghosa. *The Path of Purification*. Edited and translated by Bhikkhu Ñānamoli. Kandy: Buddhist Publication Society, 1975.

Carstairs, G. Morris. *The Twice Born*. Bloomington and London: Indiana University Press, 1973.

Cesara, Manda. *Reflections of a Woman Anthropologist: No Hiding Place.* New York: Academic Press, 1982.

Chambers, E. K. *Sir Thomas Wyatt and Some Collected Studies.* London: Sidgwick and Jackson, 1933.

Coedes, G. *The Indianized States of Southeast Asia.* Honolulu: East-West Center Press, 1968.

Comaroff, Jean. *Body of Power, Spirit of Resistance.* Chicago: University of Chicago Press, 1985.

Courtright, Paul B. *Gaṇeśa, Lord of Obstacles, Lord of Beginnings.* New York: Oxford University Press, 1985.

Crapanzano, Vincent. *Tuhami, Portrait of a Moroccan.* Chicago: University of Chicago Press, 1980.

———. "Text, Transference and Indexicality," *Ethos* 9 (2):122–48.

Czikszentmihalyi, Mihaly. *Beyond Boredom and Anxiety.* San Francisco: Jossey Bass, 1975.

Davy, John. *An Account of the Interior of Ceylon.* London: Longman, Hurst, Rees, Orme and Brown, 1921.

Devereux, George. "Why Oedipus Killed Laius: A Note on the Complementary Oedipus Complex in Greek Drama." Pp. 215–33 in *Oedipus, A Folklore Case Book,* edited by Lowell Edmunds and Alan Dundes. New York: Garland, 1984.

———. *Mohave Ethnopsychiatry and Suicide.* Washington, D.C.: Smithsonian, 1961.

———. "Shamans as Neurotics." *American Anthropologist* 63 (1961): 1088–90.

———. "Cultural Thought Models." In *Ethnopsychoanalysis.* Berkeley: University of California Press, 1978.

———. "Normal and Abnormal." In *Basic Problems in Ethnopsychiatry,* translated by B. M. Gulati and George Devereux. Chicago: University of Chicago Press, 1980.

Dīpavaṃsa. The Dīpavaṃsa, An Ancient Buddhist Historical Record. Edited and translated by Hermann Oldenberg. New Delhi: Asian Educational Services, 1986.

Durkheim, Emile. *The Elementary Forms of the Religious Life* (1912). Translated by J. W. Swain. London: George Allen and Unwin, 1954.

The Elders' Verses: Therīgāthā. P. 41. Translated by K. R. Norman. London: Luzac and Company for Pali Text Society, 1971.

Eliot, T. S. "A Dialogue on Dramatic Poetry." In *Selected Essays 1917–1932.* New York: Harcourt Brace, 1938.

———. "Tradition and the Individual Talent." In *Selected Essays 1917–1932.* New York: Harcourt Brace, 1938.

Emerson, R., and M. Pollner. "On the Uses of Members' Responses to Researchers' Accounts." *Human Organization* 47, no. 3 (1988): 189–98.

Epstein, A. L. "Tambu: The Shell-Money of the Tolai." In *Fantasy and Symbol,* edited by R. H. Hook. New York: Academic Press, 1979.

Fajans, Jane. "The Person in Social Context: The Social Character of Baining 'Psychology'." In *Person, Self and Experience,* edited by Geoffrey M. White and John Kirkpatrick. Berkeley and Los Angeles: University of California Press, 1985.

———. "Where the Action Is: An Anthropological Perspective on 'Activity Theory' with Ethnographic Applications." Paper delivered in Princeton, 29 November 1988.

Fernandez, James. *Bwiti, An Ethnography of the Religious Imagination in Africa.* Princeton: Princeton University Press, 1982.

Flugel, J. C. "Polyphallic Symbolism and the Castration Complex." *International Journal of Psychoanalysis* 5 (1924), 155–96.

Forrester, John. *Language and the Origins of Psychoanalysis.* New York: Columbia University Press, 1980.

Frake, C. "A Structural Description of Subanum Religious Behavior." Pp. 111–29. in *Explorations in Cultural Anthropology,* edited by Ward Goodenough. New York: McGraw Hill, 1964.

———. "How to Ask for a Drink in Subanum." *American Anthropologist* 66 (1964): 127–32.

Freud, Sigmund. *The Complete Letters of Sigmund Freud to Wilhelm Fliess, 1887–1904.* Translated and edited by Jeffrey Moussaieff Masson. Cambridge: Harvard University Press, 1985.

———. *The Interpretation of Dreams* (1900), Standard Edition (S.E.), vol. 4. London: The Hogarth Press, 1981.

———. *The Interpretation of Dreams* (1900–1901), S.E., vol. 5.

———. "On Dreams" (1901), S.E., vol. 5.

———. "Obsessive Actions and Religious Practices" (1907), S.E., vol. 9, 115–27.

———. "Analysis of a Phobia in a Five Year Old Boy" (1909) ("Little Hans"), S.E., vol. 10, 5–149.

———. "Notes upon a Case of Obsessional Neurosis" (1909), S.E., vol. 10, 153–318.

———. "A Special Type of Object Choice Made by Men" (1910). Pp. 192–202 in *Collected Papers,* vol. 4. Translated by Joan Riviere. London: The Hogarth Press, 1956.

———. "Psychoanalytic Notes on an Autobiographical Account of a Case of Paranoia" (1911), S.E., vol. 12, 3–88.

———. "The Most Prevalent Form of Degradation in Erotic Life" (1912). Pp. 203–16 in *Collected Papers,* vol. 4. Translated by Joan Riviere. London: The Hogarth Press, 1956.
———. "On the Universal Tendency to Debasement in the Sphere of Love" (1912), S.E., vol. 11, 177–90.
———. *Totem and Taboo* (1913), S.E., vol. 13, 1–162.
———. "On Narcissism: An Introduction" (1914), S.E., vol. 14, 69–116.
———. "Repression" (1915), S.E., vol. 14, 143–58.
———. "The Unconscious" (1915), S.E., vol. 14, 161–204.
———. *Beyond the Pleasure Principle* (1920), S.E., vol. 18, 7–64.
———. "The Psychogenesis of a Case of Homosexuality in a Woman" (1920), S.E., vol. 18, 147–72.
———. *Group Psychology and the Analysis of the Ego* (1921), S.E., vol. 18, 67–143.
———. "Some Neurotic Mechanisms in Jealousy, Paranoia and Homosexuality" (1922), S.E., vol. 18, 223–32.
———. "Two Encyclopaedia Articles: (A) Psychoanalysis" (1922), S.E., vol. 18, 235–54.
———. "The Ego and the Id (1923), S.E., vol. 19, 12–59.
———. "Some Dreams of Descartes" (1929), S.E., vol. 21, 199–204.
———. *Civilization and Its Discontents* (1930), S.E., vol. 21, 64–145.
———. "Address Delivered at the Goethe House at Frankfurt" (1930), S.E., vol. 21, 208–12.
———. "Female Sexuality" (1931), S.E., vol. 21, 223–43.
———. *New Introductory Lectures* (1933), S.E., vol. 22, 3–182.
———. *Moses and Monotheism* (1938), S.E., vol. 23, 7–137.
Gadamer, Hans Georg. *Truth and Method.* New York: Continuum, 1975.
Gallagher, Michael K. *Beating around the Bush: Fieldwork and the Inter-Subjective Nature of Ethnography.* Princeton, B.A. Honors dissertation, 1985.
Gay, Peter. *Freud for Historians.* New York: Oxford University Press, 1985.
———. *Freud, A Life for Our Time.* New York: W. W. Norton and Company, 1988.
Geertz, Clifford, "Thick Description: Towards an Interpretive Theory of Culture." Pp. 3–30 in *The Interpretation of Cultures.* New York: Basic Books, 1973.
———. *Negara, The Theatre State in Nineteenth-Century Bali.* Princeton: Princeton University Press, 1980.
Geiger, Wilhelm. *The Dīpavaṃsa and Mahāvaṃsa and Their Historical Development in Ceylon.* Translated by Ethel M. Coomaraswamy. Colombo: Government Printer, 1908.

Geiger, Wilhelm, trans. *Cūlavaṃsa,* Parts 1 and 2. Colombo: Government Press, 1953.

Gerth, Hans, and C. Wright Mills, eds. *From Max Weber: Essays in Sociology.* New York: Oxford University Press, 1976.

Giddens, Anthony. *New Rules of Sociological Method.* New York: Basic Books, 1976.

Gier, Nicholas F. *Wittgenstein and Phenomenology.* Albany, New York: SUNY Press, 1981.

Gill, Merton M., and Philip S. Holzman. *Psychology Versus Metapsychology: Psychoanalytic Essays in Memory of George S. Klein.* New York: International Universities Press, 1976.

Goldman, R. P. "Fathers, Sons and Gurus: Oedipal Conflict in the Sanskrit Epics." *Journal of Indian Philosophy* 6 (1978): 325–92.

Gombrich, Richard F. *Precept and Practice: Traditional Buddhism in the Rural Highlands of Ceylon.* Oxford: Clarendon Press, 1971.

Gombrich, Richard, and Gananath Obeyesekere. *Buddhism Transformed.* Princeton: Princeton University Press, 1988.

Grayling, D. C. *Wittgenstein.* Oxford: Oxford University Press, 1988.

Grünbaum, Adolf. *The Foundations of Psychoanalysis.* Berkeley: University of California Press, 1984.

Gunawardana, R. A. L. H. "The People of the Lion." *Sri Lanka Journal of the Humanities* 5 (1979): 1–51.

Habermas, Jurgen. *Knowledge and Human Interests.* Translated by Jeremy J. Shapiro. Boston: The Beacon Press (paperback), 1971.

Hallowell, A. I. "The Self and Its Behavioral Environment." In *Culture and Experience.* Philadelphia: University of Philadelphia Press, 1974.

Handleman, Dan. "The Ritual Clown: Attributes and Affinities." *Anthropos* 76 (1961): 321–70.

Hardy, Friedhelm. *Viraha-Bhakti: The Early History of Kṛṣṇa Devotion in South India.* New Delhi: Oxford University Press, 1983.

Heine-Geldern, R. "Conceptions of State and Kingship in Southeast Asia." *Far Eastern Quarterly* 2 (1942): 15–30.

Herdt, Gilbert. *Guardians of the Flutes.* New York: McGraw-Hill, 1981.

Hinde, Robert A. "Can Nonhuman Primates Help us Understand Human Behavior?" In *Primate Societies,* edited by Barbara B. Smuts et al. Chicago: University of Chicago Press, 1987.

Hsu, Francis L. K. "The Cultural Problem of the Cultural Anthropologist." *American Anthropologist* 81, no. 3 (1979): 517–32.

Isherwood, Christopher. *Ramakrishna and His Disciples.* New York: Simon and Schuster, 1965.

Johnson, Frank. "The Western Concept of Self." Pp. 91–138 in *Culture and*

Self: Asian and Western Perspectives. New York and London: Tavistock, 1985. 91–138.

Jones, Ernest. "Psychoanalysis and Anthropology." *Journal of the Royal Anthropological Institute* 54 (1924).

———. *Sigmund Freud,* vol. 11. London: Hogarth Press, 1955.

Kakar, Sudhir. *The Inner World: A Psychoanalytic Study of Childhood and Society in India.* New Delhi: Oxford University Press, 1981.

Kapferer, Bruce. *The Celebration of Demons.* Bloomington, Indiana: Indiana University Press, 1983.

Kardiner, Abram. *The Psychological Frontiers of Society.* New York: Columbia University Press, 1946.

Kehoe, Alice B., and Dody H. Giletti. "Women's Preponderance in Possession Cults: The Calcium-Deficiency Hypothesis Extended." *American Anthropologist* 83 (1981): 549–61.

Kenny, Anthony. *Wittgenstein.* Cambridge: Harvard University Press, 1973.

Klein, George S. *Psychoanalytic Theory.* New York: International Universities Press, 1976.

Kracke, Waud. "Encounter with Other Cultures: Psychological and Epistemological Aspects." *Ethos* 15 (1987): 58–81.

Landy, David. "Pibloktoq (Hysteria) and Inuit Nutrition: Possible Implication of Hypervitaminosis A." *Social Science and Medicine* 21, no. 2 (1985): 173–85.

Langness, Lewis L. "Hysterical Psychosis in the New Guinea Highlands: A Bena-Bena Example." *Psychiatry* 28 (1965): 259–277.

Laplanche, J., and J. B. Pontalis. *The Language of Psychoanalysis.* Translated by Donald Nicholson-Smith. New York: W. W. Norton, 1973.

Leach, E. R. *Pul Eliya: A Village in Ceylon.* Cambridge: Cambridge University Press, 1960.

———. "Pulleyar and the Lord Buddha: An Aspect of Religious Syncretism in Ceylon." *Psychoanalysis and the Psychoanalytic Review.* 49, no. 2 (1962): 80–102.

———. "Pulleyar and the Lord Buddha" (slightly abridged). Pp. 302–13 in *Reader in Comparative Religion,* edited by William A. Lessa and Evon Z. Vogt. New York: Harper and Row, 1972.

———. "On Reading *A Diary in the Strict Sense of the Term*: Or the Self-Mutilation of Professor Hsu." In *RAIN* 36 (1980): 2–3.

———. "Writing Anthropology." *American Ethnologist* 16, no. 1 (1989): 137–41.

Lewis, Nolan D. C. "The Psychology of the Castration Reaction." *Psychoanalytic Review* 15 (1928): 174–77.

Lévi-Strauss, Claude. "The Structural Study of Myth." In *Structural Anthropology*. New York: Basic Books, 1963.

Linge, David E., ed. *Philosophical Hermeneutics*. Berkeley and Los Angeles: University of California Press, 1977.

Lutz, Catherine A. *Unnatural Emotions: Everyday Sentiments on a Micronesian Atoll and Their Challenge to Western Theory*. Chicago: University of Chicago Press, 1988.

MacAloon, John, and M. Czikszentmihalyi. "Deep Play and the Flow Experience in Rock Climbing." In *Play, Games and Sports in Cultural Contexts,* edited by Janet C. Harris and Roberta J. Park. Champaign, Illinois: Human Kinetics Publishers, 1983.

Malalasekera, G. P. *Dictionary of Pāli Proper Names,* vol. 1. New Delhi: Oriental Books Reprint Corporation, 1983.

Malinowski, Bronislaw. "Myth in Primitive Psychology." In *Magic, Science and Religion*. New York: Doubleday Anchor, 1955.

———. *A Diary in the Strict Sense of the Term*. New York: Harcourt, Brace, 1967.

Marcuse, Herbert. *Eros and Civilization*. Boston: Beacon Press, 1955.

McDermott, James P. "Karma and Rebirth in Early Buddhism." In *Karma and Rebirth in Classical Indian Traditions,* edited by Wendy Doniger O'Flaherty. Berkeley: University of California Press, 1980.

Mus, Paul. *Barabadur*. Hanoi: Impr. d'Extreme Orient, 1935.

Nārada, Venerable. *The Buddha and His Teachings*. Colombo: The Colombo Apothecaries, 1973.

Norman, K. R., ed. *Therīgāthā*. London: Luzac and Company for Pāli Text Society, 1971.

O'Flaherty, Wendy Doniger. *Hindu Myths*. New York: Penguin Books, 1978.

Obeyesekere, Gananath. "The Ritual Drama of the Sanni Demons: Collective Representations of Disease in Ceylon." *Comparative Studies in Society and History* 2, no. 2 (1969): 174–216.

———. *Medusa's Hair: An Essay on Personal Symbols and Religious Experience*. Chicago: University of Chicago Press, 1981.

———. *The Cult of the Goddess Pattini*. Chicago: University of Chicago Press, 1984.

———. "The Ritual of the Leopard's Pot." In *Honoring E. F. C. Ludowyk,* edited by Percy Colin-Thome and Ashley Halpe. Dehiwela: Tisara Press, 1984.

———. "Buddhism, Depression and the Work of Culture in Sri Lanka." In *Culture and Depression,* edited by Arthur Kleinman and Byron Good. Berkeley and Los Angeles: University of California Press, 1985.

———. "Symbolic Foods: Pregnancy Cravings and the Envious Female." *International Journal of Psychology* 20 (1985): 637–62.

———. *A Meditation on Conscience,* Social Scientists Association of Sri Lanka, Occasional Papers 1, 1988.

———. "The Illusory Pursuit of the Self." In *Philosophy: East and West.* Forthcoming.

Oliver, Marion Michel. *Cultivating Freud's Garden in France.* Northvale, New Jersey, and London: Jason Aronson Inc., 1988.

Paranavitana, S. *Sīgiri Grafitti,* 2 vols. London: Oxford University Press, 1956.

———. "Sigiri, the Abode of the God King." *Journal of the Royal Asiatic Society* (Ceylon branch), n.s., 1: 129–62.

Parker, Henry. *Ancient Ceylon.* London: Luzac and Company, 1909.

Parsons, Anne. "Is the Oedipus Complex Universal?" *The Psychoanalytic Study of Society,* 3 (1964), 278–328.

Parsons, Talcott. "Social Structure and the Development of Personality: Freud's Contribution to the Integration of Psychology and Sociology." *Psychiatry* 21 (1958): 321–46.

———. *Social Structure and Personality.* New York Free Press, 1965.

Paul, Robert A. *The Tibetan Symbolic World.* Chicago: University of Chicago Press, 1982.

Pillay, K. K. *The Sucindram Temple.* Madras, 1953.

Pontalis, J. B. *Frontiers in Psychoanalysis: Between the Dream and the Psychic Pain.* London: Hogarth Press, 1981.

Pūjāvaliya. Edited by Pandit Kiriällē Ñānavimala. Colombo: M. D. Gunasena and Co., 1965.

Rabinow, Paul. *Reflections on Field Work in Morocco.* Berkeley: University of California Press, 1977.

Ramanujan, A. K. "The Indian Oedipus." In *Oedipus, A Folklore Casebook,* edited by Lowell Edmunds and Alan Dundes. New York and London: Garland Publishing Company, 1983.

Rājāvaliya [Sinhala edition]. Edited by A. V. Suraweera. Colombo: Lake House Publishers, 1976.

Rājāvaliya, The Rājāvaliya (a historical narrative of Sinhalese kings from Vijaya to Vimaladharma Sūriya II). Edited and translated by B. Gunasekara. Colombo: Government Press, 1900.

Ricoeur, Paul. *Interpretation Theory: Discourse and the Surplus of Meaning.* Fort Worth, Texas: Texas Christian University Press, 1976.

———. *Hermeneutics and the Human Sciences.* Edited by John B. Thompson. Cambridge: Cambridge University Press, 1981.

———. *Freud and Philosophy: An Essay on Interpretation.* New Haven and London: Yale University Press, 1977.

Riesman, Paul. *Freedom in Fulani Life.* Chicago: University of Chicago Press, 1977.

Robinson, Marguerite. "The House of the Mighty Hero or the House of Enough Paddy." In *Dialectic in Practical Religion,* edited by E. R. Leach. Cambridge: Cambridge University Press, 1968.

Roith, Estelle. *The Riddle of Freud: Jewish Influences on His Theory of Female Sexuality.* London: Tavistock, 1987.

Rorty, Richard. *Philosophy and the Mirror of Nature.* Princeton: Princeton University Press, 1980.

Rosaldo, Renato. "Where Objectivity Lies: The Rhetoric of Anthropology." Pp. 87–110 in *The Rhetoric of the Human Sciences,* edited by John S. Nelson, Allan Megill, and Donald N. McCloskey. Madison: University of Wisconsin Press, 1987.

Rudnytsky, Peter. *Freud and Oedipus.* New York: Columbia University Press, 1987.

Saddharmālaṃkāra. Edited by Kiriälle Ñānavimala. Colombo: Gunasena and Company, 1954.

Sahlins, Marshall. *Historical Metaphors and Mythical Realities.* Ann Arbor: University of Michigan Press, 1981.

Schafer, Roy. *A New Language for Psychoanalysis.* New Haven: Yale University Press, 1976.

Scholte, Bob. "The Structural Anthropology of Claude Lévi-Strauss." In *Handbook of Social and Cultural Anthropology,* edited by John J. Honigmann. Chicago: Rand McNally, 1973.

Schumpeter, Joseph. *Imperialism and Social Classes.* New York: Meridian Books, 1961.

Sherif, M. *The Psychology of Social Norms.* New York: Harper, 1936.

Shulman, David. *Tamil Temple Myths: Sacrifice and Divine Marriage in the South Indian Śaiva Tradition.* Princeton: Princeton University Press, 1980.

———. *The King and the Clown in South Indian Myth and Poetry.* Princeton: Princeton University Press, 1985.

Shweder, Richard A. "Menstrual Pollution, Soul Loss and the Comparative Study of 'Emotions'." In *Culture and Depression,* edited by Arthur Kleinman and Byron Good. Berkeley and Los Angeles: University of California Press, 1985.

Silverman, Julian. "Shamans and Acute Schizophrenia." *American Anthropologist* 69 (1967): 21–31.

Spence, Donald P. *Narrative Truth and Historical Truth: Meaning and*

Interpretation in Psychoanalysis. New York: Norton and Company, 1982.

Spiro, Melford E. "Religious Systems as Culturally Constituted Defense Mechanisms." In *Context and Meaning in Cultural Anthropology.* New York: Free Press, 1965.

———. *Buddhism and Society: A Great Tradition and Its Burmese Vicissitudes.* New York: Harper and Row paperback edition, 1970.

———. *Oedipus in the Trobriands.* Chicago: University of Chicago Press, 1982.

Starcke, August. "The Castration Complex." *International Journal of Psychoanalysis* 2 (1921): 179–201.

Steinberg, Leo. *The Sexuality of Christ in Renaissance Art and in Modern Oblivion.* New York: Pantheon, 1983.

Steiner, George. "The Retreat from the Word." In *Language and Silence.* New York: Atheneum, 1967.

Stocking, George. "Empathy and Antipathy in the Heart of Darkness." *Journal of the History of the Behavioral Sciences* 4 (1968): 189–94.

———, ed. *Malinowski, Rivers, Benedict and Others: Essays on Culture and Personality.* Madison: University of Wisconsin Press, 1986.

Stoller, Paul, and Cheryl Olkes. *In Sorcery's Shadow.* Chicago: University of Chicago Press, 1987.

Strong, John S. *The Legend of King Asoka.* Princeton: Princeton University Press, 1983.

Tambiah, S. J. *World Conqueror and World Renouncer.* Cambridge: Cambridge University Press, 1976.

Taussig, Michael. *Shamanism, Colonialism and the Wild Man: A Study in Terror and Healing.* Chicago: University of Chicago Press, 1987.

Taylor, Charles. "Introduction." In *Philosophy and the Human Sciences: Philosophical Papers,* vol. 2. Cambridge: Cambridge University Press, 1985.

Thompson, John B. *Critical Hermeneutics: A Study in the Thought of Paul Ricoeur and Jurgen Habermas.* Cambridge: Cambridge University Press, 1981.

Todorov, Tzvetan. *The Conquest of America.* New York: Harper and Row, 1984.

Tugendhat, Ernest. *Self-Consciousness and Self-Determination.* Cambridge: MIT Press, 1986.

Turner, Victor. *The Forest of Symbols.* Ithaca, New York: Cornell University Press, 1967.

———. "Body, Brain and Culture." Pp. 249–73 in *On the Edge of the Bush,* edited by Edith L. B. Turner. Tucson: University of Arizona Press, 1985.

———. "The New Neurosociology." Pp. 275–89 in *On the Edge of the Bush,* edited by Edith L. B. Turner. Tucson: University of Arizona Press, 1985.

Tylor, E. B. *The Origins of Culture* (1871), Part 2 of *Primitive Cultures.* New York: Harper Torchback, 1958.

Valeri, Valerio. *Kingship and Sacrifice: Ritual and Society in Ancient Hawaii.* Chicago: University of Chicago Press, 1985.

Weber, Max. *Economy and Society,* vols. 1 and 2. Edited by Guenther Roth and Claus Wittich. New York: Bedminster Press, 1968.

———. "Objectivity in Social Science." In *The Methodology of the Social Sciences,* edited and translated by Edward A. Shils and Henry A. Finch. New York: Free Press, 1969.

———. "Social Psychology of the World Religions." In *From Max Weber,* edited by Hans Gerth and C. Wright Mills. New York: Oxford University Press, 1976.

Whitehead, Henry. *Village Gods of South India.* Calcutta: Oxford University Press, 1921.

Whiting, W. H. M. "Socialization Process and Personality." In *Psychological Anthropology,* edited by Francis L. K. Hsu. Homewood, Illinois: Dorsey Press, 1961.

Winch, Peter. *The Idea of a Social Science and Its Relation to Philosophy.* London: Routledge and Kegan Paul, 1958.

———. "Understanding a Primitive Society." Pp. 78–111 in *Rationality,* edited by Bryan Wilson. Oxford: Blackwell, 1974.

Wittgenstein, Ludwig. *Philosophical Investigations.* 3d ed. Translated by G. E. M. Anscombe. New York: Macmillan, 1968.

———. *Zettel.* Translated by G. E. M. Anscombe. Berkeley: University of California Press, 1970.

———. *Philosophical Remarks.* Translated by R. Hargreaves and R. White. Oxford: Blackwell, 1975.

———. *Remarks on Frazer's "Golden Bough."* Edited by Rush Rhees. Translated by A. C. Miles. Atlantic Highlands, New Jersey: Humanities Press, 1979.

Wittgenstein, Ludwig. *Tractatus Logico Philosophicus.* London and New York: Routledge and Kegan Paul, 1981.

———. *Culture and Value.* Translated by Peter Winch. Chicago: University of Chicago Press, 1984.

———. *Lectures and Conversations on Aesthetics, Psychology and Religious Belief.* Edited by Cyril Barrett. Berkeley: University of California Press, n.d.

Yalman, Nur. "Dual Organization in Ceylon." In *Anthropological Studies of Theravada Buddhism,* edited by Manning Nash. New Haven: Yale University Press, 1966.

AUTHOR INDEX

SUBJECT INDEX

Abdin, Tuan Sahid, 3–11, 14, 15, 19, 20–21, 23, 68, 232
Aggression, 249–50
Aiyanar, 107, 110, 112, 117, 118, 123, 127, 138
Ajātasattu, 189, 289, 305 n. 6, 306 n. 11; Buddha as father figure for, 305 n. 10; as Oedipal figure, 148; story of, narrated, 148–54, 156–57; remorse felt by, 155–56, 179, 305 n. 10
Ālakamandā, 180, 196
Alphabet songbook, 124, 128–29
Ānantariya sins, 156, 186, 187, 305 n. 9
Androgyny of Garā, 193–94
Anthropologists: arrogance of, 217–19; criticism of psychoanalysis by, 217; cultural models for, as outsiders, 232–33; dialogue among, 236, 242, 257–58, 274, 276, 284; as "diviners," 229; informants' relationship with, 219, 220, 221–36, 310 n. 7, 312 n. 16; as moral community, 273; understanding of other cultures by, 229–30, 284. *See also* Fieldwork; Informants; Interpreter effect
Anthropology: contemporary orientation of, 285–89; contrasted with natural science, 237–40; language and symbol in, 274–84; and psychoanalysis, xx–xxiii, 217–19, 222, 237–40, 250, 252, 259–69, 289; validation in, 121–26, 269–74; validation in, through demonstration, 263, 272–73
Apsaras, 195, 197–98
Arahants. *See* Monks, *arahant*
Arena culture, 10
arjuna, 78–79, 80, 189
Art, xviii, 16, 92
Asoka, 147, 148, 182, 186, 187, 309 n. 74; as Caṇḍāsoka/Dharmāsoka, 185, 189; conversion to Buddhism of, 158–59; as fratricide, 158–59, 182, 185; as model king, 157, 160, 182, 184, 189
Atonement. *See* Merit making
Attis, 108, 123
Avici. *See* Hell
Avidya, 65

Babhruvāhana, 78, 80
Baining society, 296 n. 62
Bali, 102, 257, 288
Baṁbura (deity), 43
Baṁbura rituals: analyzed, 42–45,